The New Accounts Payable Toolkit

The New Accounts Payable Toolkit

Christine H. Doxey

WILEY

Published by John Wiley & Sons, Inc., Hoboken, New Jersey.
Published simultaneously in Canada.

For general information on our other products and services or for technical support, please contact our Customer Care Department within the United States at (800) 762-2974, outside the United States at (317) 572-3993, or fax (317) 572-4002.

Wiley publishes in a variety of print and electronic formats and by print-on-demand. Some material included with standard print versions of this book may not be included in e-books or in print-on-demand. If this book refers to media such as a CD or DVD that is not included in the version you purchased, you may download this material at http://booksupport.wiley.com. For more information about Wiley products, visit www.wiley.com.

Library of Congress Cataloging-in-Publication Data

Names: Doxey, Christine H., 1955- author. | John Wiley & Sons, Inc.,
  publisher.
Title: The new accounts payable toolkit / Christine H. Doxey.
Description: Hoboken, New Jersey : Wiley, [2021]
Identifiers: LCCN 2020055859 (print) | LCCN 2020055860 (ebook) | ISBN
  9781119700500 (hardback) | ISBN 9781119700531 (adobe pdf) | ISBN
  9781119700524 (epub)
Subjects: LCSH: Accounts payable. | Invoices.
Classification: LCC HF5681.A27 D69 2021 (print) | LCC HF5681.A27 (ebook)
  | DDC 658.15/26—dc23
LC record available at https://lccn.loc.gov/2020055859
LC ebook record available at https://lccn.loc.gov/2020055860

Cover Design: Wiley
Cover Image: yewkeo/Getty Images

Printed in the United States of America.

SKY10025350_030421

Contents

1

Introduction

Welcome to *The New Accounts Payable Toolkit!* This toolkit is a guide for "everything AP." As we look at all the processes that impact AP and procure to pay (P2P), the author will present best practices and current trends. As we drill down into the pertinent process details, an overview will be provided, followed by a process flow diagram with additional insights. Standards of internal controls are also presented for the AP and P2P processes explored in this toolkit.

CHAPTER ONE

About This Toolkit

The New AP Toolkit is an excellent reference book for anyone new to the AP or P2P space. It can be used to evaluate current processes and identify improvements. This book also serves as a reference for AP managers and directors, P2P managers and directors, shared services managers and directors, external and internal auditors, internal control professionals, CPOs, controllers, and CFOs. Here's how the book is organized.

How This Toolkit Is Organized

Section Number	Title	Chapter Number	Chapters
1	**Introduction**	1	About This Toolkit
2	**The New AP Department**	2	The New AP Department
		3	Automating the AP Process
3	**Dissecting the P2P Process**	4	What is the P2P Process?
		5	Transforming the P2P Process
		6	Structuring the AP Process

(Continued)

	How This Toolkit Is Organized		
Section Number	**Title**	**Chapter Number**	**Chapters**
4	How Procurement and Receiving Impact AP	7	Supplier Selection and Management
		8	Contract Management
		9	Purchasing and Ordering
		10	Receiving
5	A Laser Focus on AP	11	The Supplier Master File
		12	Invoice Processing
		13	P-Cards
		14	Travel and Entertainment
		15	The Payment Process
		16	Accounting, Reconciliation Processes, Self-Audit Tools, and Internal Controls
		17	Customer Service
		18	Reporting, Analytics, and Benchmarking
6	Other AP Business Processes	19	Supply Chain Financing (SCF)
		20	Escheatment
		21	Sales and Use Tax
		22	Independent Contracts and the 1099 Process
		23	Business Continuity Planning
7	Addendum		Accounts Payable: Quarterly Controls Self-Assessment Questionnaire
			Glossary

INDEX OF AP TOOLS

As an additional bonus, AP Tools are provided within each applicable section. Each AP Tool is numbered for your reference and cross-referenced to a chapter. Every AP Tool includes an introduction titled "About This Tool" which serves as an overview of the tool. Each type of tool is classified as a checklist, template, or best practice.

This index provides the listing of all the tools for controllers that are included in this book and provides a quick glance of an inventory of all the helpful tools provided. The index is organized by: (1) Section Number, (2) Section Title, (3) Chapter Number, (4) Chapter Title, and (5) AP Tool Title and Number.

			Index of AP Tools	
(1) Section Number	**(2) Section Title**	**(3) Chapter Number**	**(4) Chapter Title**	**(5) AP Tool Title and Number**
1	Introduction	1	About This Toolkit	
2	The New AP Department	2	The New AP Department	1. AP Process Improvement and Automation Checklist
				2. Procurement Spend Analysis
				3. Types of Internal Controls
				4. The Benefits of Segregation of Duties (SoD) Controls
				5. Mitigating Risk with Internal Controls
				6. Compensating Controls to Mitigate Risk
				7. Your Roadmap for Implementing an Internal Controls Program
				8. The Top Twenty Controls for the AP Process
				9. Internal Controls Checklist
				10. Sample Internal Controls Program for Accounts Payable for Companies Using the SAP ERP
				11. Metrics to Drive Process Improvements
			3	Automating the AP Process	

(*Continued*)

Index of AP Tools				
(1) Section Number	(2) Section Title	(3) Chapter Number	(4) Chapter Title	(5) AP Tool Title and Number
3	Dissecting the P2P Process	4	What Is the P2P Process?	12. Dependencies and Interdependencies within the P2P Process
		5	Transforming the P2P Process	13. Current State Analysis 14. P2P Transformation Roadmap 15. Other Recommendations for P2P Transformation 16. Managing Change 17. P2P Transformation Metrics 18. Streamlining Your P2P Process Without Automation 19. How to Begin Your P2P Automation Journey
		6	Structuring the AP Process	
4	How Procurement and Receiving Impact AP	7	Supplier Selection and Management	20. The Top Ten Best Practices in the Supplier Management Lifecycle 21. Five Steps to Use When "Fine Tuning" Your Supplier Master File 22. Supplier Diversity 23. Eight Critical Supplier Master Practices 24. Managing the Supplier Master File
		8	Contract Management	25. Defining the Types of Contracts 26. Ten Recommendations for Establishing Contracts
		9	Purchasing and Ordering	27. Five Steps in an Electronic Procurement Process 28. Four Best Practices to Consider for the Purchase Requisition Process
		10	Receiving	

Index of AP Tools

(1) Section Number	(2) Section Title	(3) Chapter Number	(4) Chapter Title	(5) AP Tool Title and Number
5	A Laser Focus on AP	11	The Supplier Master File	29. Supplier Master File Process Best Practices
				30. Supplier Master File Coding Standards
		12	Invoice Processing	31. Establishing Tolerances
				32. Five Factors Driving the Automation of Invoice Processing
				33. The Most Common Forms of Invoice Automation
				34. Six Best Practices for Invoice Processing
				35. Three Components of Imaging and Workflow
				36. Nine Performance Indicators for Invoice Processing
				37. The Twenty-Five Top Reasons for Problem Invoices
		13	P-Cards	38. P-Card Program Best Practices
				39. P-Card Program Implementation Best Practices
				40. The P-Card Holder Agreement
				41. The P-Card Scorecard
		14	Travel and Entertainment	42. Red Flags for the T&E Process
		15	The Payment Process	43. Effectively Managing Your Payment Process
				44. Five ACH Controls
				45. Preventing Duplicate Payments
				46. Eight Best Payment Practices
				47. Tackling Payments Fraud

(Continued)

2

The New AP Department

The accounts payable (AP) department plays a critical role within an organization as it is a last point of control before a payment is made and sent to a supplier. The function of accounts payable provides several benefits: performing due diligence related to supplier setup and timely invoice processing; assuring that payments are processed based on terms; and providing a high level of customer service.

AP are "an entity's short-term obligation to pay suppliers for products and services, which the entity purchased on credit." If accounts payable are not paid within the payment terms agreed to with the supplier, the payables are considered to be in default, which may trigger a penalty or interest.

The integrity of AP results is directly influenced by the functions of securing and qualifying sources of supply; initiating requests for materials, equipment, merchandise, supplies, or services; obtaining information as to availability and pricing from approved suppliers; placing orders for goods or services; receiving and inspecting or otherwise accepting the material or merchandise; accounting for the proper amounts due to suppliers; and processing payments in a controlled and efficient manner.

AP departments are responsible for the traditional tasks of setting up suppliers, invoice processing, creating manual checks, and expense reporting. In about half of the larger organizations, they are also involved in sales and use tax, electronic funds transfers (EFT), foreign currency payments, and petty cash management. They also occasionally perform bank reconciliation and P-Card issuance and management. However, in larger organizations, they are less likely to print checks, make tax payments, or issue travel advances.

CHAPTER TWO

The New AP Department

 INTRODUCTION

Improving the financial transaction processes has been the focus of most organizations since the 1980s. Financial transaction processing includes those traditional "back office" processes such as procure to pay (P2P), payroll, travel and entertainment (T&E), fixed asset accounting, and accounts receivable. There has been an evolution of transitioning financial transaction processes to financial management centers, then to shared service centers, and finally to an outsourced model. In today's economy, organizations are now focused on process improvements and automation initiatives to garner additional efficiencies and cost reduction opportunities. It's not just about transitioning processes to shared service centers any more.

 CASE STUDY: JOURNEY TO EXCELLENCE

In 1987, Digital Equipment Corporation took a futuristic approach to improving the productivity of their financial transaction processes. Prior to 1987, Digital established several manufacturing plants across the United States. Each plant was supported by a separate general ledger and stand-alone accounts payable, and T&E processes. Some plants even had their own payroll processes.

The inefficiencies and cost of these disparate ledgers and processes was recognized. As a result, a project was initiated to consolidate twenty-eight general ledgers and financial transaction processes into four financial management centers. The financial management centers were eventually transited to a single US shared service center in the mid 1990s before Digital was acquired by Compaq Computer Corporation in 1998. Compaq was then acquired by Hewlett Packard (HP) in 2002.

HP's journey to excellence can be attributed to the company's drive for value and innovation. "HP was an early adopter of the shared services model when it began this journey over 15 years ago. In the early 1990s, the company set a strategic goal to reduce operating costs by 30% within three years. At that time, the outsourcing market had not yet come into being for F&A. The only viable means of achieving the type of savings HP had targeted was to build captive shared services operations. As part of that effort HP wanted to integrate the back-end work of individual business units and countries, and reap the benefits of consistency in process, operating efficiency, and first time quality."[1]

 ## FOCUS ON CORPORATE PRODUCTIVITY

Many organizations have not had the opportunity to realize the tremendous cost savings that HP did with the acquisition of Compaq and the transition to a shared service center organization. So they continue to focus on productivity improvements in financial transaction processing and are spotlighting the P2P cycle.

Additionally, many organizations have found the hidden value that the accounts payable process, as a key component of the P2P cycle, can bring to an organization in cost saving opportunities and process improvements. These cost saving opportunities and improvements can be recognized by process efficiencies and automation. This continues to be a critical focus in today's difficult economy. Recommendations and best practices for improving the P2P process are included in the following section.

The New AP Professional

The new AP professional understands the importance of eliminating the silos within the process and has a good understanding of all the components that impact the cost, accuracy, and controls of the accounts payable process. The AP process flow provides an overview of the end-to-end accounts payable process.

---

[1]Dian Schaffhauser, "HP's Journey to Shared Services Finance & Accounting Success," *Sourcing-Mag*, September 24, 2007, accessed on September 9, 2020, https://sourcingmag.com/2007/09/hps-journey-to-shared-services-finance-accounting-success/.

The new AP professional is not just focused on transaction process, but on automation and process improvements that can reduce cost and improve internal controls. The new AP professional has moved from a clerical role to financial and business analyst role that looks into new metrics, analysts, and automation solutions. With a continued focus on internal controls and risk management, the new AP professional will look into self-audit tools, payment audit processes, and implementing automated controls solutions. Today's savvy AP professional is able to link all AP processes together and understands the linkage with their company's P2P process. The new professional is able to break down the silos and make recommendations that will benefit the entire organization.

ACCOUNTS PAYABLE AND PROCURE-TO-PAY (P2P) PROCESS IMPROVEMENTS

AP represents an organization's obligation to pay off a short-term debt to its creditors. AP also refers to short-term debt payments to suppliers and banks.

Many organizations no longer look at accounts payable as a stand-alone entity. The integrity of AP results are directly influenced by the functions of securing and qualifying sources of supply; initiating requests for materials, equipment, merchandise, supplies, or services; obtaining information as to availability and pricing from approved suppliers; placing orders for goods or services; receiving and inspecting or otherwise accepting the material or merchandise; accounting for the proper amounts due to suppliers; and processing payments in a controlled and efficient manner.

"Shared services" is a term defining an operational philosophy that involves centralizing those administrative functions of a company that were once performed in separate divisions or locations as noted in the Case Study: Journey to Excellence section. The focus of shared service organizations is not only on financial transaction processing, but on procurement, inventory accounting, payroll, human resources, and information technology.

Moving the AP process to a shared service center can generate significant cost savings, but all its processes should be understood. Any process weaknesses, control issues, and risk should be defined and mitigated. To ensure the success of any AP transition, all process improvements should be realized before centralizing or moving accounts payable to a shared service organization.

AP TOOL 1: AP PROCESS IMPROVEMENT AND AUTOMATION CHECKLIST

About This Tool: The "touchless" AP process isn't too difficult to achieve. A savvy AP leader should have the strategy in place to move to a paperless environment. It all starts with implementing some best practices including electronic payments, the automated clearing house (ACH) remittance, and the automated workflow process. Best practices establish the foundation for accounts automation and the achievement of your "touchless" process. The success of your new "touchless" process can be measured not only by improvements in metrics, but by the results of your automated self-assessment process. Lastly, dynamic discounting is a "win-win" option for both buyers and suppliers in the "touchless" accounts payable process.

Examples of AP best practices include delegation of authority via workflow. Many leading practice companies are already paying their suppliers electronically, but are now utilizing the ACH remittance process to reduce paper. And to ensure that your "touchless" environment is working properly, I suggest using an automated self-assessment process that validates the accuracy of your payment process. Lastly, leading practice accounts payable companies also consider dynamic discounting solutions. We'll now explore the components of the "touchless" accounts payable process in detail as listed in the following table.

1. **Automated PO Requisition Process:** Upon approval, POs can be electronically invoiced from suppliers directly for a paperless process in which automated matching occurs between the PO and the invoice when it arrives to validate price, quantity, line amount, and items ordered. All invoices matched can be tracked against the PO until the PO is closed to account for blanket POs or partial payment against an open PO.

2. **eInvoicing:** eInvoicing is the exchange of the invoice document between a supplier and a buyer in an integrated and agreed-upon electronic format with the goal of reducing paper and cost. Imagine no more paper invoices!

3. **Automated Approval Process:** In an automated approval process, the invoice approval process is linked to your company's delegation of authority (DoA) policy. The invoice approval process is completely automated based on defined rules via workflow. The workflow determines if an invoice needs approval; who the appropriate approvers are; and in what order approvers should approve payment of the invoice. The workflow then sequentially asks each approver in the approval list to approve invoices online. For example, you can define a rule so invoices over $100,000 (or a specific amount designated in your DoA policy) require CFO approval and then CEO approval.

4. **Link Approvals to Job Levels:** Most leading practice companies link the DoA policy to the job levels within the employee master file. A DoA table is then established as the driver of the approval workflow. If an approver moves to a different position or department, or leaves the company, the approval tables are automatically updated.

5. **Automated ACH Remittance:** As companies increase their electronic payments to suppliers, many are moving toward sending the automated remittance advice as confirmation indicating that the invoice has been paid. This best practice helps reduce paper and moves closer to a "touchless" process.

6. **Supplier Portal:** As supplier portals move beyond invoice status tools, many solutions are now delivered as a shared buyer service which accommodate eInvoicing and provide many additional benefits. Supplier portals provide:
   - Reduction in paper invoices as suppliers send their invoices electronically;
   - Faster transactions with integration to ERP software;
   - Stronger supplier relationships with a well-defined onboarding process and real-time invoice status;
   - Digital signatures to guarantee authenticity and security;
   - Flip purchase orders for easy invoicing;
   - The ability to correct errors on the spot to prevent payment delays further down the line;
   - The ability to begin using sales catalogs for greater accuracy.

7. **Accounts Payable Self-Assessment Process:** The goal of any accounts payable department is to pay a supplier "once and only once." Rather than have a third party or external audit firm identify a control weakness, many companies have worked with a solution provider to implement a self-assessment process that identifies a possible duplicate payment before the payment is initiated. This software considers "fuzzy" logic algorithms that flag a potential duplicate or erroneous payment. This self-assessment process can often be included in a company's internal control program.

8. **Dynamic Payables Discounting:** Dynamic discounting is a solution that gives buyers more flexibility to choose how and when to pay their suppliers in exchange for a lower price or discount for the goods and services purchased. The "dynamic" component refers to the option to provide discounts based on the dates of payment to suppliers. Solution providers help both buyers and suppliers optimize their working capital positions by: providing a collaborative platform where buyers, suppliers, and third-party financing providers can negotiate and execute early payment offers.

 ## P2P REPORTING, UNDERSTANDING, AND PERSPECTIVE

Purchasing Insight notes that, "P2P is all about helping to optimize the processes associated with purchasing and recognizing that the process does not end at the purchase order but extends to include accounts payable and payment processes."[2]

---

[2]Pete Loughlin, "Definition of Procure to Pay," Purchasing Insight, accessed on September 8, 2020, http://purchasinginsight.com/definition-of-purchase-to-pay/.

Purchasing Insight noted that the P2P process extends even into the future. The process includes the strategies and technologies that are drivers of the procurement process. These strategies and technologies apply to the procurement spend analysis process as defined in the next section.

 ## AP TOOL 2: PROCUREMENT SPEND ANALYSIS

About This Tool: This tool provides insight on how to achieve accurate and timely spend analysis that is often driven by the procurement process.

1. **Identify Leverage with Existing Suppliers:** Determine the "parent-child relationships" within the supplier master file and determine if multiple contracts can be consolidated or leveraged.

2. **Supplier Rationalization:** This is a straightforward analysis commonly using the Pareto principle (80/20) that highlights how many suppliers comprise 80% of the spend for each category. Using this type of analysis we can quickly identify the categories where there are too many suppliers comprising the bulk of the spending.

3. **Perform a Spending Stratification Analysis:** This analysis will highlight the volume of low dollar invoices processed by accounts payable. The results will indicate if these transactions can be moved to a P-Card or to an automated process.

4. **Preferred Supplier Spend:** Many organizations have a preferred supplier list. Including this information in the spend analysis application will provide visibility into two areas: (1) categories where preferred suppliers are in place but not used, and (2) categories where no preferred supplier exists.

5. **Spend by Buying Channel:** One of the benefits of spend analysis is that it helps to identify process inefficiencies. Companies with procurement systems in place can quickly identify business units and individuals that are circumventing existing processes. Driving spends toward approved buying channels will improve overall controls, yield better compliance, improve data quality, lead to faster sourcing cycles, and provide term discount opportunities. This will also reduce accounts payable costs associated with check requests.

6. **Purchase Price Variance:** This step in the process highlights that different prices may be paid for the same good or service.

7. **Sourcing Compliance:** The final step includes a review of key contracts to determine if there are significant variances from the contract's terms and conditions.

8. **Quarterly Spend Analysis:** Implement a process to track supplier spending on a quarterly basis. This process can be used to track the results of the implementation of a strategic sourcing initiative.

STRATEGIC SOURCING

Strategic sourcing was first established by General Motors in the 1980s and is now a common tool in the procurement toolkit. Strategic sourcing is dependent upon the results of the spend analysis process described in the previous section.

Strategic sourcing is often used as a procurement best practice to source high-value goods and services used in the production process along with large volume, and low-value non-production goods and service. The steps in the strategic sourcing process include:

- Review the results of the spend analysis and determine the suppliers to focus on.
- Review the pricing differences offered for the same goods and services. Also, review the terms and conditions of the contracts currently in place.
- Determine the cost benefit analysis of moving to a single supplier.
- Schedule discussions with targeted suppliers.
- As noted in the previous section, review the results on a quarterly basis and update the strategic sourcing plans.

 ## OTHER PROCURE-TO-PAY BEST PRACTICES

Here are some additional best practices that should be considered to improve efficiencies within the P2P process that include:

- Perform an annual "clean-up" of the supplier master file which includes either purging or blocking suppliers that have not had any activity for eighteen months.
- Establish a process to designate P-Card suppliers within your organization's supplier master.
- Review the supplier master file on a quarterly basis to combine multiple suppliers and multiple remit to addresses.
- Implement a company-wide procurement policy which specifies that purchase orders are required for all purchases over a specified dollar limit which is depending on the size of the organization. The procurement policy supports the requirement that a purchase order is needed for every obligation. The procurement policy also stipulates a P-Card will be used for any purchases below the specified dollar amount. An example of recommended best practices for implementing and expanding a P-Card program are included in the next section.

AP PROCESS IMPROVEMENT IMPACTS ON WORKING CAPITAL

Working capital is an important measure of an organization's efficiency, its short-term financial health and operating liquidity. Positive working capital means that the organization is able to pay off its short-term liabilities without increasing debt. Negative working capital means that an organization currently is unable to meet its short-term liabilities with its current assets (cash, accounts receivable, and inventory).

AVERAGE PAYABLE PERIOD

Each time a purchase is made from a supplier without paying for it at the time of the purchase, an account payable is created (a payable) for the business. Accounts payable are amounts owed to suppliers that are payable sometime within the near future – "near" meaning 30 to 90 days.

- The average payable period is the best indicator of success in managing cash outflows.
- Using the payable period to slow down outflows can significantly improve cash flow.
- The accounts payable aging schedule is an important tool for keeping track of payables on a monthly or weekly basis.

MEASURING AVERAGE PAYABLE PERIOD

The average payable period measures the average amount of time each dollar of trade credit is used. That is, it measures how long a company uses their trade credit before paying the obligations to those businesses or individuals who extended credit to the company. This measurement gauges the relationship between trade credit and cash flow. A longer average payable period allows trade credit to be maximized. Maximizing trade credit means delaying cash outflows and taking full advantage of each dollar in the company's own cash flow.

The average payable period is calculated by dividing accounts payable by the average daily purchases on account:

$$\text{Average Payable Period} = \frac{\text{Accounts Payable Balance}}{\text{Average Daily Purchases on Account}}$$

The average daily purchases on account are computed by dividing total purchases on account by 360:

$$\text{Average Daily Purchases on Account} = \frac{\text{Annual Purchases on Account}}{360}$$

The accounts payable balance and the total purchases on account from the prior year are usually accurate enough for analyzing and managing cash flow. However, if more recent information is available, such as the previous month's accounts payable information, then use that instead. Be sure to compute the average daily purchases on account correctly using the number of days actually reflected in the purchases on account figure. For example, use 30 if one month's accounts payable information is used.

WHEN TO TAKE A TRADE DISCOUNT

How do you know if it's worth taking the discount? First the general rule on trade discounts: a company should always take advantage of trade discounts of 1% or more if the supplier requires full payment within 30 days. If suppliers offer payment terms beyond 30 days, it may be more advantageous to skip the trade discount and delay paying the supplier until the full payment is due.

For situations outside the scope of the general rule, or to test the general rule, a company can determine if taking a trade discount is advantageous. The following will help the company make that determination:

In order to determine if a trade discount is advantageous, consider the annualized interest rate you earn by taking the trade discount. If this annualized interest rate is greater than the interest rate charged to borrow the money from a bank, for example, then the discount is definitely worth taking. On the other hand, if the interest rate charged to borrow the money from a bank is greater than the annualized interest rate earned by taking the discount, then you shouldn't take the trade discount.

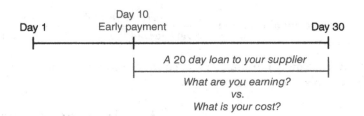

When taking a trade discount, consider the early payment a loan to the supplier.

Take, for example, a supplier that offers a discount if their invoice is paid within 10 days, or accepts full payment within 30 days. When a company pays this supplier in 10 days, instead of waiting the full 30 days, this supplier is actually borrowing money from the company for 20 days. The amount of the discount is the interest the company earns on the loan to the supplier. If the company views the early payment as a loan to suppliers, a company can then determine the annualized interest rate they are actually earning. Once the company knows the annualized interest rate, they can then compare it to the cost of borrowing money and determine if taking the discount is worthwhile.

The annualized interest rate is calculated as follows:

$$\text{Annualized Interest from the Trade Discount}$$
$$= \frac{\text{Discount Percent}}{100\,\text{Percent} - \text{Discount Percent}}$$
$$\times \frac{360}{\text{Credit Days} - \text{Discount Days}\,(\text{Number of Loan Days})}$$

 ## NEGOTIATING PAYMENT TERMS

Negotiating payment terms with suppliers and suppliers, or deferring expenses, are two more methods of delaying cash outflows. Negotiating extended payment terms with suppliers is a technique that can be used to delay cash outflows and improve overall cash flow. Most suppliers will require payment within 20 or 30 days after a company receives their bill. Some suppliers may be willing to negotiate longer credit terms. Their willingness to offer better credit terms may be based on one of the following factors included in the following list:

- The company's past and present business relationship with them
- The company's past payment history and perceived credit worthiness
- The option to secure a large order or a company's continued business

This is one of those situations where it can't hurt to ask. But be prepared to justify the request. Suppliers will likely extend payment terms if presented with a strong case.

Dynamic Discounting

So why is dynamic discounting so compelling? Just consider what a 2% discount means for early payment in terms of return on capital. If, instead of earning interest on your cash you invest cash for 20 days to get a 2% return – that's over 36% return on capita

Dynamic discounting solutions provide suppliers the flexibility to discount their approved invoices at any point up to the maturity date and pass on a portion of the finance charges to buyers. This functionality has gained acceptance and popularity as it offers financing to suppliers at attractive rates while delivering an additional income stream to buyers. Solution providers and banks facilitate the transactions through a simple, intuitive Web interface that provides visibility to all parties, including the ability to change rates and terms in real time, thus the term dynamic.

Many buyer companies are not nimble enough to take advantage of valuable discounts, while others do not have the required spend that will allow for discounts. Some have investment alternatives so attractive that they outweigh the opportunity cost of missing a discount. And for most buyers, extending payment terms is generally more beneficial for working capital management than capturing a few discounts from participating suppliers. On the other side, suppliers too often find themselves financing sales by factoring their accounts receivables or through asset-based lending, both expensive sources of capital. Some suppliers, particularly smaller companies, do not have access to either option and are frequently strapped for cash.

Dynamic discounting serves the cash management needs of buyers and suppliers alike. Solution providers create the technological framework to facilitate this process. The transaction can be self-funded by the buyer or a bank can stand in as a short-term lender. Through Web-based buyer-supplier networks, buyers are able to project compressed settlement terms through supplier discounts. Suppliers are able to pick and choose among an array of payment options for each outstanding invoice. Banks pay the bill and collect from the buyer the full original price minus a percentage of the discount savings; an arrangement often referred to as "revenue sharing."

There are a number of good reasons why dynamic discounting is gaining popularity as a best practice. Two related developments are the advent of the Internet and solution providers' willingness to harness its capabilities and apply them to cash management. Two other related developments are the attention being paid to what's now called the financial supply chain and the willingness of banks to look at the disparity between the cash management needs of buyers and suppliers in a new, innovative light.

However you characterize the reason these changes have come about, the results are the same. Buyers are enjoying improved working capital requirements and suppliers have more control over their cash-flow prospects. These results foster improved relations between buyers and suppliers, all made possible by visionary technologists and treasurers who are interested in tapping into new sources of income.

Dynamic discounting is an arrangement between a buyer and supplier whereby payment for goods or services is made early in return for a reduced price or discount. The arrangement includes the ability to vary the discount according to the date of early payment – the earlier the payment, the greater the discount. The supplier offers a discount for early payment. It's not always been easy to achieve arrangements that work for both supplier and buyer and, because of practical problems, it hasn't always been easy for buyers to actually pay early.

But with the increased use of P2P technologies and methods there is now no reason why a supplier cannot pay promptly – or late, for that matter – depending on how the collaborative arrangements with the supplier have been agreed.

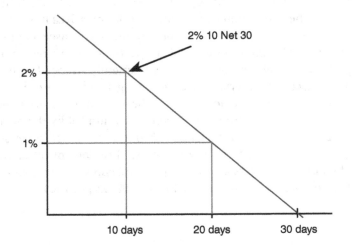

OVERVIEW OF THE REQUIREMENTS OF THE SARBANES-OXLEY ACT OF 2002

Impact to the Overall Company

The primary objectives of the Sarbanes-Oxley Act of 2002 were to: prevent accounting and reporting problems from recurring; rebuild public trust in corporate practices and reporting; define a higher level of responsibility, accountability, and financial reporting transparency; and provide new or enhanced standards for corporate accountability and penalties for wrongdoings.

The Sarbanes-Oxley Act of 2002, specifically Section 404, had a significant impact on all publicly traded companies. As part of the certification related to periodic reporting requirements, the CEO and CFO are certifying that: they are responsible for establishing and maintaining disclosure controls and procedures ("DC&P"), have designed DC&P to ensure specified information is made known to them, as well as evaluated and reported on the effectiveness of those controls and procedures as of a date within 90 days of the report filing. Additionally, on an annual basis, to be included with the annual report, management must state their responsibility for establishing and maintaining an adequate internal control structure and procedures over financial reporting and their assessment as of the end of the fiscal year of the effectiveness of such internal control structure and procedures. In addition, the Company's external auditor is to attest to and report on management's assessment of internal controls.

Sarbanes-Oxley Section 302

- The requirements of Section 302 focus on management's responsibilities.
- CEOs and CFOs must personally certify that they are responsible for disclosure controls and procedures.
- Each quarterly filing must contain an evaluation of the design and effectiveness of these controls.
- The certifying executives must state that they have disclosed to their audit committee and independent auditor any significant control deficiencies, material weaknesses, and acts of fraud.
- An expanded certification requirement that includes internal controls and procedures for financial reporting may also be included when the SEC issues its final rules.

Sarbanes-Oxley Section 404

- Section 404 mandates an annual evaluation of internal controls and procedures for financial reporting.
- It also requires the company's independent auditor to issue a separate report that attests to management's assertion on the effectiveness of internal controls and procedures for financial reporting.

In order to properly represent an assessment of internal controls, management accepts responsibility (written assertion) for the effectiveness of control. It is important that controls are suitably designed to achieve the objective (reliability of financial reporting) using established criteria and control objectives, and related controls need to be appropriately documented. Finally, management assesses the effectiveness of internal control over financial reporting and reports thereon (both design and operating effectiveness).

Section 404 is focused on a 100% controls-based approach. The company must evaluate and test controls across business and functional areas to opine on effectiveness (broad and deep); and the lack of errors, historically, in financial statements is not de-facto evidence unto itself, of an appropriate internal control structure.

Preparing for Section 404 is very different than a financial statement audit. The overall objective is the rendering of an opinion on the financial statements, not to opine on internal controls. Internal control reports have been very rare in practice and are the subject of different auditing standards.

Summary of Section 404 vs. Section 302

Section 404:
- Annual assertion by management
- Responsible for effectiveness of controls over reliable financial reporting – e.g. a deep view of internal control procedures and practices
- Focus on both design and operational effectiveness of financial reporting controls
- External auditor to render opinion ("attestation") on management's internal control assertion

Section 302:

- Quarterly certification by CEO and CO
- Responsible for "Disclosure Control Procedures" (DCP) – a broad range of information (financial and non-financial)
- Certify to effectiveness of DCPs based on evaluation within 90 days
- Disclose to audit committee and external auditor any significant deficiencies/material weakness or fraud (material or not)

ACCOUNTS PAYABLE, RISK, AND FRAUD

According to Accenture, the corporate payments market is at a critical juncture in today's banking landscape. Improved customer experience in the retail payments segment – driven by mobility, cashless transactions, easy accessibility, and cost-effectiveness – has increased expectations in the corporate payments system considerably. For example, it takes a few minutes to browse, select, and purchase grocery items through an online app, whereas it takes days, or even weeks, and loads of paperwork to procure stationery items for the office through the traditional corporate payments system. In such a scenario, there is a growing demand to usher in substantial change in the corporate payments landscape on both sides of the bank-client relationship.

Additionally, unlike consumer payments where the consumer is usually protected by the bank or company against fraudulent activity, companies and banks share responsibilities for fraud prevention. In situations of conflict regarding which party bears responsibility for an act of fraud, many times legal action is required. Court cases generally determine that the responsible party is the one that had the best chance of preventing the fraud. Therefore, companies must ensure that their internal policies, practices, and controls are adequate, updated based on new market experiences, documented, and enforced.

To achieve these objectives, the corporate payments sector has to first overcome several challenges, such as fragmented banking products and relationships, rigid and paper-based processes, lack of transparency in payments, costs of complying with new regulations, and problems related to cross-border transactions.

FRAUD STATISTICS

Payment and Business Process Fraud Statistics			
Organization	Report	Key Findings	Source of Information
Association of Certified Fraud Examiners (ACFE)	2020 Report to the Nations	Consistent with the findings in prior years, it is estimated that organizations lose 5% of revenue to fraud each year. A lack of internal controls contributed to nearly one-third of the frauds reported. Median losses per case were $125,000, while the average loss per case was $1,509,000. Fraud schemes were detected by a tip 43% of the time, and half of those tips came from employees. A lack of internal controls contributed to nearly one-third of the frauds reported. Based on information in the report, small businesses are more likely to experience billing fraud, payroll fraud, and check and payment tampering fraud than large organizations. The report notes, the typical fraud lasts 14 months before detection and causes $8,300 per month in losses, and there is correlation between the length of the fraud and the median loss. Asset misappropriation is the most common form of occupational fraud, in terms of frequency, representing 86% of cases in the ACFE's study. However, the median loss related to asset misappropriation cases was only $100,000, which is significantly less than the other two types. Corruption schemes fell in the middle, representing 38% of cases and a median loss of $250,000. However, corruption was identified as the most common scheme in every global region. Financial statement fraud was seen in only 10% of the cases investigated; however, it was certainly the most expensive type of fraud with a reported median loss of $945,000.	https://www.acfeinsights.com/acfe-insights/announcing-the-2020-report-to-the-nations

Payment and Business Process Fraud Statistics

| Association of Finance Professional (AFP) | 2020 AFP Payments Fraud and Control Survey Report | According to the survey, 81% of companies were targets of payments fraud last year, once again proving that no industry is immune.

75% of organizations experienced Business E-mail Compromise (BEC).

54% of organizations reported financial losses as a result of BEC.

42% of BEC scams targeted wires, followed by ACH credits at 37%.

74% of organizations experienced check fraud in 2019 – up from 70% in 2018.

Nearly one-third of organizations indicated that they have not received advice from their banking partners about mitigating potential risks associated with same-day ACH credit and debit transactions. | https://www.afponline.org/docs/default-source/registered/2020paymentsfraudandcontrolreport-highlights-final.pdf |
| Kroll | Global Fraud & Risk Report 11th Annual Edition 2019–2020 | Only 58% of respondents deemed both their anti–money laundering controls and their whistleblowing functions effective in detecting incidents compared to global averages of 69% and 66% for anti–money laundering and whistleblowing functions, respectively.

The digital threat is compounded by emerging technologies such as cryptocurrency. Nearly all (91%) of the global business leaders surveyed are investigating or have already adopted distributed ledger technology, while 81% are considering or already using cryptocurrencies.

More than one in three (35%) global businesses cited risk of fraud or theft as the primary concern when considering investing in such areas, followed by lack of clear regulatory oversight (29%), untested technology (19%), and potential involvement with bad actors (16%).

Data theft and reputational damage caused by third-party relationships was next on the list of significant incidents reported by global business leaders, with 29% of respondents affected. | https://kroll.com/en-ca/about-us/news/global-fraud-and-risk-report-2019 |

(Continued)

Payment and Business Process Fraud Statistics			
Experian	The 2020 Global Fraud and Identity Report	57% of businesses are reporting higher losses associated with account opening and account takeover fraud in the past 12 months, compared to 55% in 2018 and 51% in 2017. Experian's research found that 86% of businesses claim advanced analytics is a strategic priority. Surprisingly, only 67% of businesses consider the use of advanced analytics, like artificial intelligence, to be important for fraud prevention and only 57% for identifying customers. 84% of businesses believe if they can better identify customers, then they will more easily spot a fraud instance.	http://images. go.experian. com/lb/ Experian Information SolutionsInc/ Percent7B4c 9cc02b-353a-4f07-9abe-2449234853dd Percent7D_ global-identity-and-fraud-report-2020. pdf

INTRODUCTION TO INTERNAL CONTROLS

The Committee of Sponsoring Organizations (COSO) of the Treadway Commission issued a report in 1992 entitled "Internal Control – Integrated Framework." This brought together widely differing views about internal control into what has now become generally recognized as a best practice approach to internal control.

Within an internal controls program, controls are defined within a process area. As an example, within the accounts payable function, examples of process areas are supplier maintenance and invoice processing. More information will be provided for these specific process areas throughout this book.

As controls are defined, the first step is to define the control objective. A control objective is aimed at ensuring the accuracy, completeness, and timeliness of reporting of financial statements.

STANDARDS OF INTERNAL CONTROL

The standards define a series of internal controls that address the risks associated with key business processes, sub-processes and entity level processes.

The standards are the product resulting from over 30 years of experience in the finance, accounting, and internal controls field.

The standards are a body of work that leverages experience at large technology companies. The standards for each sub-process within the P2P process are included in this toolkit for your reference. The standards include the internal control for each specific process, the type of control using the definitions provided in the following tool, and the risks mitigated. The standards are numbered by applicable chapter and are included in Chapters 7–18 of the toolkit.

 ## AP TOOL 3: TYPES OF INTERNAL CONTROLS

About This Tool: After the control objective is defined, a specific control activity is established to support the control objective. A control activity is a task or action reflected in a policy or procedure with the intent to mitigate identified risks allowing the achievement of control objectives. A control should be evaluated based on its effectiveness to mitigate risk. Control activities are the policies and procedures that help ensure that the necessary actions are taken to address risks related to the achievement of the organization's objectives. There are specific types of control activities as depicted in the following table.

Control Type	Examples
Compensating	Effective compensating controls can improve the design of a process that has inadequate segregations of duties and ultimately provide reasonable assurance to managers that the anticipated objective(s) of a process or a department will be achieved.
	However, compensating controls are less desirable than the segregation of duties internal control because compensating controls generally occur after the transaction is complete. Also, it takes more resources to investigate and correct errors and to recover losses than it does to prevent an error.
Corrective	Designed to correct errors or irregularities that have been detected.
Detective	Designed to detect errors or irregularities that may have occurred. Examples are reconciliations, authorized signatures, credit checks and approvals.
Manual	Manual reconciliations, authorized signatures, credit checks and approvals that are not executed systematically.

(Continued)

Control Type	Examples
Management Review	Requirements from the Public Company Accounting Oversight Board are causing auditors to require a level of precision and specificity for management review controls beyond prior years. Auditors are also reviewing far more documentation than they used to. At the same time, there is a lack of clarity on what exactly is sufficient in management review controls and how precise they need to be. This is troubling, since MRCs are crucial to the financial reporting process.
	Management review controls (MRCs) are the reviews conducted by management of estimates and other kinds of financial information for reasonableness. They require significant judgment, knowledge, and experience. These reviews typically involve comparing recorded amounts with expectations of the reviewers based on their knowledge and experience. The reviewer's knowledge is, in part, based on history and, in part, may depend upon examining reports and underlying documents. MRCs are an essential aspect of effective internal control.
	Examples of MRCs include:
	■ Any review of analyses involving an estimate or judgment (examples: estimating a litigation reserve or estimating the percentage of completion for long-term construction projects); ■ Reviews of financial results for components of a group; ■ Comparisons of budget to actual; and ■ Reviews of impairment analyses.
Organizational	Organizational controls should cover all aspects of the company's business processes without overlap, and be clearly assigned and communicated.
	■ Responsibility should be delegated down to the level at which the necessary expertise and time exists. ■ No single employee should have exclusive knowledge, authority, or control over any significant transaction or group of transactions. ■ Agreeing on realistic qualitative and quantitative targets strengthens responsibility. ■ The structure of accountability spends upon continuing levels of competence of employees in different positions and the development of competence so that responsibility and reporting relationships can be regrouped in more efficient ways.
Policy	Policy controls are the general principles and guides for action that influence decisions. They indicate the limits to choices and the parameters or rules to be followed by the company and its employees. Major policies should be reviewed, approved, and communicated by senior management. Policies are derived by:
	■ Considering the business environment and process objectives. ■ Identifying the potential categories of risks that the environment poses toward achievement of the objectives.

Control Type	Examples
Preventive	Control mechanism that prevents problems from occurring and business rules supported by systems. **Note:** There is no difference between preventive and preventative controls. They are both adjectives that mean "used to stop something bad from happening." Both words are commonly used in contexts concerning internal controls as in "preventive/preventative controls." Preventive, however, is used much more frequently than preventative.
Procedure	Procedure controls prescribe how actions are to be performed consistent with policies. Procedures should be developed by those who understand the day-to-day actions that will be subject to the procedures.
Supervisory	Supervisory Controls are situations in which managers ensure that all employees understand their responsibilities and authorities, and the assurance that procedures are being followed within the operating unit. They can also be considered as a compensating control in which a supervisory review is necessary to augment segregation of duties controls.
System	These are system-generated controls which include the three-way match of invoices for payment, batch control totals, field level edits/validations, duplicate payment validation, and the identification of segregation of duties conflicts.

 ## DEFINING CONTROL ACTIVITIES

Control activities should be defined to address inherent risk and control risk. Inherent risk is the susceptibility of an account balance or a class of transactions to material misstatements, without consideration of internal control. A control risk is the risk that an entity's internal control system will not prevent material misstatements or detect on a timely basis any that do reach the financial statements.

Additionally, control activities can include the following list of items:

- **Completeness:** Documents grouped and a numerical total is calculated, i.e. number of documents, total dollar amount, hash total. Batch total is entered into the system and total is calculated and compared to total entered.
- **Sequence checking:** Set range of tracking numbers on documents, system will not accept duplicate numbers or numbers out of the range, missing numbers are addressed.
- **Matching:** Match number on document to listing of acceptable numbers, unmatched numbers are addressed.

- **One-for-one checking:** Comparing each individual document with a report of accepted records, all originating documents must be on hand.
- **Accuracy:** Information (including standing data) is input and processed correctly.
- **Programmed edit checks:** Tests to make sure that data falls within reasonable limits, tests to make sure that the relationship between data is reasonable, tests to make sure data matches possible data for that field.
- **Pre-recorded input:** Used to update master file data. New data is entered along with the old data. Old data is matched to a master file. If matched, new data overwrites old data. If not matched, reported as an exception.
- **Validity:** Transactions and updates are authorized by appropriate personnel. Transactions are supported by valid source documents.
- **One-for-one checking:** Selected manual authorization. Only high-risk or unusual transactions would be individually authorized.
- **Restricted access:** The ability to modify information is restricted to appropriate personnel. Company assets are protected from theft and misuse.
- **Systems access restrictions:** Periodic review of users on the system to ensure that users only have access to functions and data relevant to their responsibilities/roles. IT personnel are only granted temporary access to production data as needed. Security over physical assets.
- **Segregation of Duties (SoD):** Segregation of employee duties and systems access to prevent incompatible functions. The SoD control is considered to be one of the three critical corporate controls that are foundational to any internal controls program. This control will be explained in more detail in the next section.

THE THREE CRITICAL CORPORATE CONTROLS

The three most critical internal controls for any company can be established by corporate policies that should be "operationalized" into your company's business processes and monitored by the applicable internal control programs. The implementation of these controls set the foundation for good payment controls and risk mitigation. These controls are: (1) segregation of duties, (2) systems access, and (3) delegation of authority. Many companies have implemented these controls as "core controls" but need to keep them updated by following some of the best practices that are recommended here.

1. **The Segregation of Duties (SoD)** control is one of the most important controls that your company can have. Adequate segregation of duties reduces the likelihood that errors (intentional or unintentional) will remain undetected by providing for separate processing by different individuals at various stages of a transaction and for independent reviews of the work performed.

   The SoD control provides four primary benefits: (1) the risk of a deliberate fraud is mitigated as the collusion of two or more persons would be required in order to circumvent controls; (2) the risk of legitimate errors is mitigated as the likelihood of detection is increased; (3) the cost of corrective actions is mitigated as errors are generally detected earlier in their lifecycle; and (4) the organization's reputation for integrity and quality is enhanced through a system of checks and balances.

   Although SoD is a basic, key internal control, it is one of the most difficult to accomplish often due to limited headcount, broadly defined responsibilities, and constantly changing responsibilities. Basically, the general duties to be segregated are: planning/initiation, authorization, custody of assets, and recording or reporting of transactions. Additionally, control tasks such as review, audit, and reconcile should not be performed by the same individual responsible for recording or reporting the transaction.

   Best Practice: One of the most common "root causes" of fraud is the lack of SoD controls, weak SoD controls, inappropriate compensating controls, or failure to update SoD controls when responsibilities change. As a best practice, many organizations review their SoD controls on a quarterly basis, and whenever staff turnover occurs, as part of their control self-assessment (CSA) process. As a result of this review, the applicable SoD controls are updated appropriately.

2. **System Access:** The principle of SoD in an information system environment is also critical as it ensures the separation of different functions such as transaction entry, online approval of the transactions, master file initiation, master file maintenance, system access rights, and the review of transactions.

   In the context of application level controls, this means that one individual should only have access rights which permit them to enter, approve. or review transactions, but no combination of two for the same transaction. Therefore, assigning different security profiles to various individuals supports the principle of SoD. As an example, operational or process SoD within an AP department will determine the system access rights that should be granted for each associate based on roles and responsibilities.

Best Practice: System access rights are reviewed on a periodic basis (usually monthly or quarterly) to ensure that system access capabilities are appropriate for current staff members and reflect any changes in responsibilities or movements to other departments.

3. **Delegation of Authority (DoA):** The last critical control for your company is the DoA policy and control. The purpose of the DoA is to ensure the efficient operation of the company while maintaining fiscal integrity and adherence to policy. Accountability for the overall management of the property, assets, financial, and human resources of the company rests with the chief executive officer (CEO). In many cases the "governance" of the DoA policy is the responsibility of the controller. Individuals that have been assigned authority under the terms of the DoA must safeguard company resources by establishing and maintaining internal controls that deter and detect any potential misuse of resources.

Best Practice: Many companies assign levels of authority to the job grades or levels within the organization and apply workflow to streamline the approval process. If an individual is promoted or moves to another department, his or her level of authority is automatically updated in the employee master file.

AP TOOL 4: THE BENEFITS OF SEGREGATION OF DUTIES (SOD) CONTROLS

About This Tool: Segregation of duties controls provides four primary benefits: (1) the risk of a deliberate fraud is mitigated as the collusion of two or more persons would be required in order to circumvent controls; (2) the risk of legitimate errors is mitigated as the likelihood of detection is increased; (3) the cost of corrective actions is mitigated as errors are generally detected relatively earlier in their lifecycle; and (4) the organization's reputation for integrity and quality is enhanced through a system of checks and balances. (Refer to the previous section, The Three Critical Corporate Controls.)

Applying SoD Controls to Systems Access

The principle of segregation of duties in a cloud environment is also critical as it ensures the separation of different functions such as transaction entry, online approval of the transactions, master file initiation, master file maintenance, user access rights, and the review of transactions. This means that one individual should not have access rights which permit them to enter, approve, and review transactions. Therefore, assigning different security profiles or roles to various individuals would support the principle of segregation of duties. This principle is reinforced in a systems access policy and by the ongoing review of system access controls as part of your internal controls program.

Categories of SoD Controls to Consider

The following general categories of duties or responsibilities are considered when implementing segregation of duties controls and should be considered when validating system access roles by asking the question, "Who can perform a specific transaction that may be in conflict with another task?" An example is accessing master file data and issuing a payment to a supplier. These controls can be used to develop your internal controls checklist and when considering compensating controls for a specific business process.

1. Formulating policy, plans, and goals
2. Approving policy, plans, and goals
3. Developing/analyzing business case justification
4. Initiating a transaction
5. Authorizing the transaction
6. Recording the transaction
7. Monitoring or having custody of physical assets
8. Monitoring and/or reporting on performance results
9. Reconciling accounts and transactions
10. Authorizing master file transactions
11. Processing master file transactions
12. Providing information systems development, security administration, and other related support
13. Following up and resolving issues or discrepancies

AP TOOL 5: MITIGATING RISK WITH INTERNAL CONTROLS

About This Tool: Many companies have ineffective internal controls programs due to an overwhelming amount of controls that don't adequately consider risk. These organizations are only focused on testing the controls and not properly evaluating the effectiveness of the control when conducting a self-assessment or preparing for the annual SOX 404 internal controls assessment process. A risk-based controls approach properly leverages resources and can reduce the cost of an overall internal controls program and, more importantly, this approach ensures that the control properly mitigates the risk. Risk-based controls focus on the key controls that will mitigate risk within the business process. Failing to take a true risk-based approach may result in identifying more controls that the operation needs. The operation may erroneously focus on perceived "key controls" that do not properly address the risk for a specific business process.

All companies, regardless of size, structure, nature, or industry, encounter risks at all levels within their organization. Risks affect each company's ability to survive, successfully compete within its industry, maintain financial strength and positive public image, and maintain the overall quality of its products, services, and people. Since there is no practical way to reduce risk to zero, management should determine how much risk should be prudently accepted, and strive to maintain risk within acceptable levels by considering the implementation of risk-based controls.

Risk is exposure to a potential loss as a consequence of uncertainty. There are global risks and risks in every phase and stage of a business process, with certain risks of greater importance during each stage. Understanding the types of risk faced within each process sets the foundation for the development of risk-based controls. Refer to the following section to get more information on the implementation process.

Ten Tips for Implementing Risk-Based Controls

1. The focus should be on the business process and any sub-processes rather than just the audit process.
2. The control should be focused on the end-to-end process and its dependencies rather than just on transactions. Although the control should address the accuracy of a transaction, a risk-based control addresses the total business process – not just a single transaction.
3. The expected outcome is to identify and mitigate risk as well as determine opportunities for process improvements within the operation.
4. There should be a focus on risk management rather than solely on current policies and procedures. Current policies and procedures may be outdated or incorrect.

5. The goal should be on continual risk assessment coverage through a continuous controls monitoring (CCM) process.
6. Risk-based internal controls facilitate change since they should be updated when there is a significant change to the business process or if the control is found to inadequately mitigate a potential risk.
7. This approach should set the foundation for implementing operational metrics and analytics.
8. Risk-based controls can identify risks and business process gaps across financial operations.
9. Risk-based controls can help prevent and detect fraud since they should represent the end-to-end business process.
10. Risk-based controls should always be developed by the business process owners, but approved by management with well-defined implementation and remediation plans.

Lastly, to assist with validating your internal controls process, here are five questions to ask when developing a series of risk-based controls along with the five key metrics to consider when measuring results.

Five Questions to Ask

1. Does the control consider a failure that may rise to the level of a material weakness?
2. Can the control be relied upon to either prevent or detect (in a timely manner) a material misstatement of the filed financial statements?
3. Has the control been updated recently to reflect the current business process?
4. Has your organization considered remediation actions resulting from a fraudulent activity, findings from external and internal audits, and other control self-assessment processes?
5. Is the control a key component of your continuous controls monitoring (CCM) initiative?

Five Metrics to Consider

1. Number of incidences per period
2. Average value of incidences identified per period
3. Estimate of total value of incidences identified per period

4. Average hourly rate of person remediating incidents per period
5. Percent of transactions tested per period

AP TOOL 6: COMPENSATING CONTROLS TO MITIGATE RISK

About This Tool: As we continue our discussions on how risk can be managed by the standards of internal control, we know that segregation of duties is an important internal control element.

Segregation of duties promotes the use of sound business practices and supports the achievement of a business process objective. When designing segregation of duties controls for a business or financial process, most business process owners start with identifying incompatible functions and then define the segregation of duties and systems access controls. However, the segregation of duties control cannot always be achieved in certain situations due to staffing limitations.

In some cases, an employee will perform all activities within a process. In this scenario, segregation of duties does not exist and risk cannot be identified nor mitigated in a timely manner. As a result, the implementation of additional compensating controls should be considered.

Definition of Compensating Controls

A compensating control reduces the vulnerabilities in ineffectively segregated functions. A compensating control can reduce the risk of errors, omissions, irregularities, and deficiencies, which can improve the overall business process.

Compensating Controls, CSA, and CCM

However, it should be noted that many companies include compensating controls in their internal controls programs as additional measures to reduce risk. These controls can be embedded in continuous controls monitoring (CCM) and controls self-assessment (CSA) processes. Continuous controls monitoring (CCM) refers to the use of automated tools and various technologies to ensure the continuous monitoring of financial transactions and other types of transactional applications to reduce and mitigate risk. A CCM process includes the validation of authorizations, systems access, system configurations, and business process settings.

Examples of Compensating Controls

1. **Skim through detailed transactions report:** A manager should consider performing a high-level review of detailed report of transactions completed by an employee that performs incompatible duties. As an example, a manager may simply skim through the report sections that contain high-risk transactions or account and may review specific payment types or amounts before the payment is made.

2. **Review sample of transactions:** Using a CSA or CCM process, a manager may select a few sample of transactions, request for the supporting documents, and review the documents to ensure that they are complete, appropriate, and accurately processed. In addition to detecting errors, the knowledge of a periodic review could create a disincentive (that is, reduce the opportunity) for the person performing the incompatible duties to process unauthorized or fraudulent transactions. This review identifies transactional anomalies which can be used as a flag to indicate collusion. As an example, unchanged pricing and using the same suppliers for several years can indicate possible collusion between buyers and suppliers.

3. **Review system reports:** Applications that support business or office operations have embedded reporting capabilities that enable the generation of reports based on pre-determined or user-defined criteria. A review of relevant system exception reports can provide good compensating controls for an environment that lacks adequate segregation of duties. As an example, I suggest a review of report of deleted or duplicated transactions, report of changes to data sets, and report of transactions exceeding a specific dollar amount on a quarterly basis.

4. **Perform analytical reviews:** Another example of compensating control is the comparison of different records with predictable relationships and the analysis of identified unusual trends. For example, a budget vs. actual expenditure comparison, or current year vs. prior year subscription fees analysis, or comparison of selected asset records to actual physical count of asset might indicate unusual variances or discrepancies that may need to be investigated. In this review, an analytical review should occur on a monthly basis.

5. **Reassign reconciliation:** If there is an opportunity to reassign one activity from the person performing the incompatible function to another employee, a manager may consider reassigning the reconciliation activity. As an example, reassigning the bank account reconciliation function to someone other than the person receiving cash and depositing it to the bank could improve the quality of internal controls in the cash receipt process.

Reconciliations should occur monthly as a standard of internal control.

6. **Increase supervisory oversight:** Other forms of activities a manager may perform as compensating control are observation and inquiry. Where appropriate, increasing supervisory reviews through the observation of processes performed in certain functions and making inquiries of employees are good administrative controls that may help to identify and address areas of concerns before a transaction is finalized.

7. **Rotate jobs:** Many companies rotate jobs in the finance and accounting department every one to two years. This creates an environment of control and can prevent collusion. As an example, accounts payable processors should be rotated on a regular basis so that they don't become too involved with specific suppliers. And as noted earlier, a buyer's responsibility should be rotated within the purchasing organization.

Effective compensating controls can reduce the risk for a process that has limited or inadequate segregations of duties and ultimately can provide reasonable assurance to management that the anticipated objective(s) of a process or a department will be achieved. As a detective risk management technique, compensating controls tend to look at the accuracy of a transaction after it has occurred but can be used as preventive controls within CSA and CCM processes.

 ## AP TOOL 7: YOUR ROADMAP FOR IMPLEMENTING AN INTERNAL CONTROLS PROGRAM

About This Tool: We've defined internal controls as a critical component throughout business strategies, operations, and processes. The correct controls that are operationally effective are the linchpin to assure that the organization can reliably achieve objectives while addressing uncertainty and acting with integrity. Where do we start the internal controls journey?

Many organizations take an approach to internal control management that has defined intersections with risk, compliance, and audit processes and use a set of standards. But typically, all organizations face the following challenges with building and maintaining an internal controls program.

- **Providing** an integrated strategy and view of financial and operational controls across the organization.
- **Defining** a common language for risk and control.

- **Increasing** confidence in ongoing risk coverage throughout all business processes.
- **Establishing Overall Responsibility** for a company's internal controls program to ensure consistency and to avoid duplication of effort.
- **Capturing** business changes with updated and changing controls.
- **Combining** finance and operational control teams and revamping processes to address a controls weakness.
- **Prioritizing** the key controls for a business process that can truly mitigate risk.
- **Managing** the human element in controls management.
- **Expanding** and reacting to the ongoing regulatory requirements for internal controls management.
- **Addressing** a lack of resources while being tasked with more internal control responsibilities across controls.
- **Keeping** controls aligned with business processes and a changing environment.
- **Implementing** a system and technology to manage all controls across the organization.
- **Developing Transparency**, reporting, and monitoring.
- **Integrating** controls into daily workflow particularly when staff transitions occur.

So how does a company establish an internal controls program to address these challenges? Here is what to consider when establishing or enhancing your internal controls program.

1. **Define the Organization and Process Context:** For most organizations, inefficiencies from an internal controls program fragmentation are so great that huge savings are possible by taking the simple step of eliminating silos and operating on a common context and structure with well-defined responsibilities. What business process is your focus that may have a control weakness, an audit finding, or has had a fraudulent activity? The outcome of these efforts will enable an organization to:
   - Coordinate planning across all business units.
   - Eliminate gaps and duplication in coverage.
   - Decrease time spent by business process owners.
   - Increase ability to spot control issues and trends as they develop.

- Utilize a single strategy and methodology for risk mitigation.
2. **Establish a Common Language for Risks and Controls:** Without a standard naming convention or common methodology for determining or classifying risks and controls, business process owners are unable to share information. The benefits of utilizing a common language for risks and controls include:
   - Improved reporting throughout the organization.
   - Audit and control issues are embedded in your program and are promptly assigned and remediated.
   - Consistent coverage – all risks are considered and there is a focus on materiality and the risk of material misstatement is considered.
   - Improved business performance – risks explain performance gaps.
   - Better decision making – decisions are risk based.
   - Less external oversight and audits – controls are standardized using a common methodology.
3. **Implement a Consistent Reliable Methodology:** Without a consistent methodology for your internal controls program, the cost of controls can be expenses with incomplete coverage and inaccurate results. Examples of a consistent methodology include:
   - The top-down risk criteria is established with consistent risk identification.
   - The risks are properly accessed by appropriate internal controls.
   - The risks that require a response are identified.
   - The risk responses that require remediation are prioritized.
4. **Focus on Transparency, Reporting, and Monitoring:** All information on the status of risks and controls should be available for continuous reporting. If implemented effectively, communication between management and the board of directors is in place with a focus on risk mitigation and the achievement of business objectives. The benefits of a consistent and disciplined reporting structure include:
   - Availability of accurate and consistent reports.
   - Positive knowledge and reporting of risks and controls across the company.
   - Information sharing across business processes.
   - Confidence of the reliability of all risk and control information.
5. **Leverage Technology:** By eliminating information silos and redundant data entry, and taking a unique holistic approach to regulatory challenges, technology provides greater efficiency, improves collaboration, and

reduces the time and resource costs. Additional benefits that can be gained by utilizing a defined technology solution for internal controls include:

- A single universe of all risk and controls data.
- Elimination of duplicate documentation.
- The implementation of a controls self-assessment process.
- More processes, risks, and controls can be assessed and properly prioritized.
- Increase in management accountability.
- Consolidated and reliable reporting.
- The ability to produce metrics and analytics for your internal controls program.

In conclusion, the success of an internal controls strategy is dependent on communication, well-defined roles and responsibilities, standards of internal control, technology, and reporting. To address the challenges of a viable and ongoing internal controls program, standards of internal control are available.

AP TOOL 8: THE TOP TWENTY CONTROLS FOR THE AP PROCESS

About This Tool: Finance and accounting professionals know that an internal controls program should always be practical to be truly effective. This means the purpose of specific controls should be clearly understood by those who execute them for the program to be fully embraced. Additionally, controls should always be cost-effective. This means the cost of introducing and maintaining a control should not exceed the benefit to be derived or the exposure to be mitigated.

A larger number of controls may not indicate that the overall internal controls program will be effective. That's why the focus should be on the top controls or most important controls. Your accounts payable process should be periodically evaluated to determine the relevance and effectiveness of each control. A good time to review your internal controls program is usually at the start of a new fiscal year after year-end processes have been completed. Additionally, controls should be accessed if a process has been automated, there is a change to your ERP system, or if a fraud has been perpetrated.

To help build the foundation of your accounts payable internal controls program, here are the top twenty controls to consider.

1. Your company's "tone at the top" is well communicated throughout the organization and is well embedded and understood throughout the accounts payable organization.
2. All employees comply with the company's Code of Conduct and the consequences of non-compliance are well communicated through corporate policies.
3. A segregation of duties policy is established in the accounts payable organization along with supporting procedures.
4. A delegation of authority policy is in place for all company spending commitments and expenditures and has procedures in place to support the policy.
5. Monthly account reconciliations are mandatory for all general ledger accounts.
6. System access controls are reviewed on a monthly basis or after a system upgrade or organizational change.
7. Accounts payable managers are responsible for integrating effective internal controls into operations.
8. All representations and assertions regarding internal controls must be supported with the appropriate documentation and audit trails.
9. The costs and expenses for the accounts payable department are maintained under budgetary control and company policy.
10. Accounts payable uses standards of internal controls to ensure that the assets and records of the company are adequately protected from loss, destruction, theft, alteration, or unauthorized access.
11. Critical transactions within the organization's business processes must be traceable, authorized, authenticated, have integrity, and be retained in accordance with established policy such as the delegation of authority policy.
12. Background checks are conducted for all employees and contractors.
13. Critical business records and audit trails for accounts payable transactions must be maintained and retained in accordance with established company policy.
14. Accounts payable transactions and data are considered to be confidential. As a result, employees and contractors must refrain from unauthorized disclosure of sensitive or confidential information regarding suppliers and payment information.

15. All software applications that may impact the operation of the accounts payable process must have the adequacy of their internal controls verified through the user acceptance process prior to implementation.
16. Contracts that legally bind the organization or a subsidiary company to any obligation can be executed by purchasing personnel (for agreements pertinent to their areas of responsibility) or individuals duly authorized under the organization's delegation of authority policy. Legal should review and approve all contracts and legally binding documents. Right-to-audit clauses should be included in the contracts where appropriate.
17. All suppliers are validated before they are entered into the supplier master file. The validation process includes:
    - Requiring a W-9
    - Performing TIN matching with IRS services
    - Compliance screening, i.e. Office of Foreign Assets Control (OFAC), Office of Inspector General (OIG), Foreign Corrupt Practices Act (FCPA)
    - Verify supplier addresses and phone numbers
    - Supplier website and Dunn and Bradstreet (D&B) validation
18. All payments over a specified dollar amount are reviewed and approved with special attention to large international and wire payments. The dollar amount to be reviewed will depend upon risk tolerance levels within your company.
19. All intercompany payables and receivable activity is reconciled on a monthly basis.
20. All P-Cards and corporate credit cards have cardholder agreements in place in which the cardholder clearly understands their roles and responsibilities along with the consequences of non-compliance.

BENEFITS OF A PAYMENT AUDIT PROCESS

One of the places that corporations are most vulnerable when it comes to stringent internal controls is the payment process. High volumes of transactions, increased levels of operational complexity, and an often diverse range of IT platforms and systems make managing the P2P cycle challenging. Understanding which transactions are critical to review for potential risk makes monitoring controls even more difficult.

Compliance regulations of the Sarbanes-Oxley Act have further increased organizational workloads. Scarce accounts payable resources have been redeployed to assist in documenting and testing internal controls.

While organizations have made significant staffing and financial investments to prepare to meet these compliance requirements, the level of effort is not sustainable year over year, and management must look to other solutions to enable ongoing compliance with regulatory demands. The range of errors that can occur in overpayments is broad and can include:

- Duplicate payments
- Miscalculations
- Open checks/escheatment
- Supplier's pricing mistakes
- Omitted discounts
- Neglected allowances, rebates, and returns
- Non-compliance with sale agreements
- Charges for goods not received
- Charges for services not provided

The financial consequences of these payment errors can run into millions of dollars of losses each year. Undetected, these errors can cost organizations the equivalent of 1% of their procurement budgets each year.

The payment audit process actually validates effectiveness of control activities by validating if process improvement is being sustained by measuring variability and identifying defects in financial controls relating to payment processing.

As an added benefit of the payment audit process, a greater number of transactions are sampled on key processes such as supplier maintenance and payment processing. This provides an increased sample size that can reduce the need to perform additional internal testing. The payment audit process identifies control gaps and their root causes and provides gap/defect analysis report.

With a continual payment audit process, auditors can track specific data-driven measures of performance to determine whether management has implemented the agreed-upon recommendations (policy and procedure) and whether they are having the desired effect (internal control). Tracking performance over time will ensure the organization is being successful in meeting established goals (continuous process improvement) and in identifying additional actions to be taken.

An additional benefit of the payment audit process involves taking steps to actually recover the overpayments. Funds lost from payment processing errors can be detected and collected as controls are imbedded in the process and improvements are implemented.

AP TOOL 9: INTERNAL CONTROLS CHECKLIST

About This Tool: There are several tools and techniques that can be implemented within an internal controls program for an accounts payable department. The following internal controls checklist provides some examples.

Tools:

- Use standard tools to identify control objectives and activities.

Communication:

- Ensure standards are documented and communicated.
- Implement a quality control process to ensure controls can be implemented.
- Implement a team meeting structure.
- Implement status reports and a mechanism to track and elevate issues.

Project Management:

- Implement a formal project management process.
- Define roles and responsibilities.
- Specify deliverables.
- Establish leaders for process areas.

Identification of Control Deficiencies:

- Control deficiencies can be found within day to day invoice processing. Control documents should be updated as often as possible.
- Actions planned to address control deficiencies should be defined and assigned to specific owners.

Remediation and Action Tracking:

- Actions planned to address control deficiencies may require remediation plans that will require ongoing follow-up. Ensure all the steps needed to address a deficiency are defined even if several process areas or departments are impacted.
- Implement a remediation tracking process.
- Integrate remediation items into control activities and test plans.

AP TOOL 10: SAMPLE INTERNAL CONTROLS PROGRAM FOR ACCOUNTS PAYABLE FOR COMPANIES USING THE SAP ERP

About This Tool: This sample internal controls program is specific to an SAP process and includes the control objectives and activities for the supplier master and invoice processing process.

Standards of internal controls are provided for each process component of the P2P and AP process and are included in Chapters 7–18. These are generic standards which can be modified to fit your specific accounts payable process.

Process Area: Supplier Master File	
Control Objective	**Control Activity**
Access to the supplier master database is kept secure and appropriate staff update the database.	Twice a year (generally mid-year and end of the year), audit and accounting controls supervisor reviews the SAP access table for the accounts payable organization for appropriate access. The supervisor reviews the access table to ensure that recent system access changes resulting from changes in job responsibility are properly reflected. Supervisor reviews for appropriate level of access based on the job function and appropriate segregation of duties within the organization.
Inactive suppliers are deactivated in a timely manner.	Manager of audit and accounting controls runs a supplier deactivation program against the master supplier file in SAP to identify suppliers without activity (6 months for employees, 13 months for non-employee suppliers, 18 months for tax). First, this program in run in "Normal Mode" to identify inactive suppliers. After the result from the Normal Mode is reviewed for reasonableness, the program is run in Update Mode to deactivate the supplier. Deactivated suppliers are flagged in the system and a payment block is automatically placed on these suppliers.
Changes to supplier master files are accurate.	A supplier maintenance group team lead reviews a sample of additions and changes to the non-employee supplier master file to source documents daily. A minimum of 10 requests had been audited per day, and as of July 15, 2004, 10 supplier additions and 15 change requests are audited by the team lead. The team lead also follows up with the requesting party as well as the personnel who made the change, as necessary, to correct any errors identified from the review. The evidence of this review is maintained by the team lead.
Address of supplier is validated as accurate.	SAP data entry edit in the supplier maintenance interface include comparisons for the following key fields: City, State, County, and Zip Code to ensure address validity. Additionally, combinations of these fields are validated to enhance accuracy of the keyed inputs (e.g. State field is validated based on the input for City). Validation of new employee suppliers is performed by the group lead.

Process Area: Supplier Master File	
Control Objective	Control Activity
Updates to employee suppliers are accurate and complete.	SAP interfaces with PeopleSoft HR/Payroll and ESS systems for the updates to the SAP employee supplier master list. As part of the interface session initiated for the updates, standard SAP edit checks are performed on the incoming data into SAP. Edit check failures are investigated and resolved by a HR staff personnel and a spreadsheet containing the resolved errors are sent to VMG for manual input into SAP. The same edit controls apply for the manual input. HR is responsible for maintaining accurate employee data in PeopleSoft and ESS.
Supplier is paid once and only once.	SAP performs a "VIDA duplicate check" on all invoices processed. VIDA is the acronym for Supplier Number, Invoice Number, Invoice Date, and Dollar Amount. If there is a match for three of the four fields to a prior transaction, a payment block is placed on the transaction for investigation and resolution by the Audit and Accounting Controls staff personnel. This automated check is performed in SAP prior to posting.
Supplier is paid once and only once.	Periodically, a duplicate payment audit is performed by audit and accounting controls staff personnel. This audit was conducted once in 2004. Ad hoc reports are generated from SAP (through the SAP Bolt On Process), which identify potential duplicates that may have not been caught by the SAP VIDA duplicate check. Like the SAP VIDA check, this process hones in on the Supplier Number, Invoice Number, Invoice Date, and Dollar Amount to identify potential duplicates; however, duplicate Invoice Number check is based on the Invoice Root Number. The Bolt On process strips out the beginning and ending alpha characters in the Invoice Number to determine the Invoice Root Number. Checking for duplicate Invoice Root Number is a more accurate way of identifying potential duplicate invoices. Potential duplicates are reviewed and investigated and the results of the audit are maintained by the Audit and Accounting Controls.
Supplier invoice paid upon validation with goods received and purchase order.	SAP performs a three-way match (two-way match between invoice and purchase order for invoices below $5K) among the invoice, PO, and notification of goods received. This process ensures that the purchase was properly approved and the end user has received the goods prior to releasing the invoice for payment. The invoice is automatically blocked for payment in SAP if the invoice fails the three-way match. For non PO EDI, this match process does not occur, and it is the responsibility of the source groups to monitor purchasing activity that were charged to their budget and to ensure accuracy of goods receipt and appropriate authorization. Additionally, non PO EDI purchase can only be made from pre-approved catalog items.

(Continued)

	Process Area: Supplier Master File
Control Objective	**Control Activity**
Payment to contract labor suppliers do not exceed the authorized amount.	For contract labor POs, a manual verification of the total amount paid to supplier is performed by staff to ensure the amount does not exceed the authorized amount indicated in the purchase order. In the event it does, the invoice is blocked for payment until the additional amount is approved.
Supplier invoice is paid upon validation with goods received and purchase order; blocked three way match exceptions are not processed by SAP and are monitored by AP for clearing.	If the three-way match fails, the invoice is blocked for payment. The "block" can be released in two ways: (1) A supplier relations supervisor manually releases the invoice for payment via transactions FB60/FB02; or (2) SAP transaction MRBR is run daily and as needed to release the blocks. The MRBR transaction re-runs the three-way match process to identify blocked invoices that now meet the match requirements and can be released for payment. Invoice processing supervisors monitor the error queues daily and review blocked transactions weekly using standard reports, which identify blocked transactions, to ensure their timely resolution. Additionally, an aging of blocked transactions is reviewed monthly by the group managers, and monthly payment block statistics are provided to the AP director for his or her review. These reports used to monitor payment block activity are maintained by supplier relations.
Purchases submitted via Excel spreadsheet are authorized and in accordance with the company's DoA. Spreadsheet use is controlled.	File-level approval is required on all Excel spreadsheet uploads. File-level approval is based on the largest dollar document in the file and should be in accordance with the company's DoA. The appropriate approver must submit the file to accounts payable (EDI Processing) and the submitted file must be protected to prevent changes. The copy of the e-mail is maintained by EDI Processing to evidence approval, and the source group requesting the spreadsheet upload is responsible for maintaining the supporting documentation that evidence the payment obligation.
Purchases are authorized and in accordance with the company's DoA. Third-party support (invoices/contracts) is sent directly to AP for input into SAP.	The invoice, contract, or other documentation that clearly identifies the company's obligation must be provided to accounts payable for all transactions meeting the following dollar amounts: (1) Customer refunds greater than or equal to $1K, (2) Commissions greater than or equal to $1M, (3) Tax greater than or equal to $1M, and (4) Telco greater than or equal to $10M. The supporting documentation is reviewed and approved by the director of AP, or in his or her absence, the audit and accounting senior manager. The related approval and the supporting documents are sent to the Imaging group for scanning into FileNet for AP processing.

Process Area: Supplier Master File	
Control Objective	**Control Activity**
Interface, e-invoicing, and spreadsheet upload transactions are accurately and completely transmitted to SAP.	Invoices submitted via SAP Production Interface, EDI, and spreadsheet upload must pass predefined edits check for valid field and field combinations.
Transaction are accurately reflected in the general ledger; AP reconciliations for aging and GRIR are performed and reviewed in a timely manner.	A monthly reconciliation between the accounts payable sub-ledger and general ledger is performed by an audit and accounting controls manager and reviewed by the group senior manager. The reconciliation includes the following tasks: (1) review of aging of paid post-petition items, (2) GR/IR reconciliation report for goods received and not invoiced, and (3) GR/IR reconciliation for invoice received, but goods not received. The reconciliations are retained by the manager.
Transactions are processed in a timely manner.	Mailroom personnel open and date stamp and batch paper invoices by queue where invoices will be processed. Queues are used by accounts payable to manage the areas workflow. A supervisor in AP Processing reviews and monitors the invoice queues multiple times a day to ensure timely validation of invoices for processing. AP Processing staff validate the supplier information against the SAP supplier master file and the invoice information (PO#, invoice number, supplier name, and invoice date), and this monitoring ensures that the obligation is recorded and paid on a timely basis. A supervisor also reviews productivity reports for each of the processing reps to monitor workflow and backlog. This control is performed through the use of query reports and the reports are retained by the respective supervisor.
Appropriate segregation of duties exists in the AP group.	Twice a year (generally at mid-year and end of the year), audit and accounting controls supervisor reviews the SAP access table for the accounts payable organization. He or she reviews the access table to ensure that recent system access changes resulting from changes in job responsibility are properly reflected. He or she reviews for appropriate level of access based on the job function and appropriate segregation of duties within the organization. The audit and accounting controls supervisor maintains the evidence for this review.

AP TOOL 11: METRICS TO DRIVE PROCESS IMPROVEMENTS

About This Tool: Reducing costs, improving efficiency, and productivity are the three main goals for most accounts payable departments. But many companies immediately jump into the automation journey without taking a look at their accounts payable process to identify some key process improvements. It all starts with having a good understanding of the process and where to focus on. It all starts with metrics!

Many leading practice companies keep track of their metrics and use the results of their metrics program as indicators for process improvements and cost savings initiatives. Here are ten metrics to watch and suggested process improvements to make that will reduce the amount of paper and improve efficiency in your accounts paper process.

1. Percentage of Invoice Paid by Check

If your company is paying more than 50% of invoices by check, it's way too many. I suggest paying your invoices by ACH, or P-Card. Consider the cost of issuing the check, postage fees, resource fees, reconciliation costs, and the risk of check fraud.

2. Percentage of Low Dollar Invoices Paid by Check (<$100.00)

If your accounts payable department is issuing a large volume of small dollar payments, consider paying these suppliers with a P-Card. These low dollar invoices have a tremendous impact on the efficiency of your resources and certainly drive up your average cost to process an invoice.

3. Number of Manual Invoice Approvals

Many companies assign levels of authority to the job grades or levels within the organization and apply workflow to streamline the approval process. If an individual is promoted or moves to another department, his or her level of authority is automatically updated in the employee master file. This is all achieved by an automated workflow system.

4. Percent of Suppliers Using ACH Electronic Remittance

As another means to reduce paper, consider using the ACH electronic remittance process. If your company is paying a supplier via ACH, why not use this capability to reduce cost and alleviate paper?

5. Percent of Recurring Payments

If you have recurring payments, why not automatically bill your customers on a recurring basis for your products or services as another means to reduce cost?

6. Number of Escheatment Issues

If your accounts payable department is faced with ongoing escheatment issues due to uncashed suppler checks, besides looking into ACH and P-Cards for your payment process, consider outsourcing your payments process.

7. Percent of Emergency or Off-Cycle Checks Issued

Some leading practice companies charge a fee for issuing an emergency or off-cycle check. These firms also keep track of the departments or divisions that continually request an immediate payment and request that the payment is issued via a P-Card.

8. Number of Duplicate Payments

A duplicate payment can negatively impact cash flow and resources until the funds are recovered. As a best practice, many companies have implemented software tools that allow the accounts payable department to check for a duplicate invoice before the payment is made.

9. Number of Duplicate Suppliers

I suggest implementing a supplier validation process to avoid duplicating any existing suppliers in the supplier master file. This process should also include obtaining a TIN number and doing some compliance screening to ensure that the supplier is valid. Lastly, I recommend that your supplier master file is reviewed every year to ensure that suppliers with no activity for 18 months are blocked.

10. Number of Internal Control Issues

By focusing on these process improvements, the number of internal control issues in your accounts payable process will be greatly reduced.

CHAPTER THREE

Automating the AP Process

 INTRODUCTION

The emphasis on corporate cost containment and productivity enhancement during the past decade has prompted AP professionals to seek new ways to automate traditionally paper-based, labor-intensive processes.

Further, new compliance regimes have prompted a greater need to document and secure the intrinsic risks associated with the invoice and payment processes. Given these factors, accounts payable departments are turning to maturing automation solutions like purchasing cards, document imaging, approval workflow, and electronic procurement to overcome the hassles inherent to paper- and people-based processes.

Another trend in the accounts payable automation space is outsourcing certain AP tasks. Given the low value of certain tasks performed by accounts payable staff – document scanning, data extraction, and data entry, for example – these activities are becoming popular candidates for outsourcing, allowing AP employees to focus on more mission-critical tasks like invoice approval, dispute resolution, and discount capture.

Accounts payable automation solutions have been available through business process outsourcers for at least twenty years but they are recently gaining popularity as organizations comprehend the benefits of leveraging the technology and process expertise of an outsourced service provider to perform non-core activities.

"Where to start?" is one of the first questions to ask when investigating AP automation. Accounts payable professionals must decide whether a tightly focused or a comprehensive end-to-end solution would better meet their needs. AP decision makers should keep the following factors in mind when making this decision:

1. **Financial Automation Goals:** There is a solution to meet every organization's need, but identifying the ideal solution requires an organization to clearly understand what it hopes to achieve from its adoption. Organizations that have been slow to adopt other financial automation technologies but want to take an incremental step forward should consider adopting just front-end imaging as a starting point. On the other hand, organizations that are comfortable with technology and want to accelerate the pace of improvement in their invoice receipt-to-pay cycle should think about an application that delivers full circle imaging and workflow functionality.

2. **Adoption Readiness:** Every organization does not stand an equal chance of succeeding with automation. Differences in culture, financial resources, human capital, and level of senior management support mean that certain organizations are more likely to succeed. Further, even if these factors are in place, an organization still may find itself hobbled by a lack of senior management support or hemmed in by its prior technology investments. Individuals investigating AP automation should determine how their organizations stack up in each of these areas before determining what solution to implement.

3. **Process Complexity:** The higher the complexity of an accounts payable operation, the greater the payoff from automating invoice receipt and approval processing. AP professionals should consider the number of suppliers and invoice formats they receive, as well as their overall invoice volume and the complexity of their average invoice when evaluating imaging and workflow automation (IWA) solutions. The structure of their AP operation (i.e. decentralized vs. centralized) and the steps required to process, approve, and pay invoices are also critical and will have a direct bearing on the choice of solution.

4. **Accounts Payable Department Size:** Large organizations can focus on the process improvements and resulting ROI an investment in IWA will deliver, regardless of the number of staff that are performing

invoice and payment processing activities. However, small and mid-sized organizations do not always have that luxury. Small AP departments, particularly those with five or fewer employees, often face budgetary constraints that limit their solution choices. In these cases, firms looking to automate the AP process should be looking for suppliers that can deliver a foundational solution, or one targeted very specifically to their needs.

5. **Accounting Software Infrastructure:** Enterprise resource planning (ERP) and accounting systems can deliver varying levels of functionality around invoice and payment management. One of the key reasons a market has developed for best-of-breed IWA solutions is the lack of sophisticated workflow and dispute resolution capabilities offered by ERP and accounting software. A major consideration for determining an organization's selection of an IWA solution should be the process gaps or system weaknesses that are inherent to the AP or ERP software currently in use.

 ## BENEFITS OF AP AUTOMATION

Organizations that have started the process of migrating toward AP automation are achieving a range of benefits depending on the extent of their automation initiatives. While the benefits vary significantly with the type of solution implemented, companies can expect to achieve significant relief in the following areas:

 ## A SUMMARY OF AP AUTOMATION FUNCTIONALITY CONSIDERATIONS

We'll explore several of the AP automation solutions that are available in the following sections of this chapter. First, we'll review the functionality to consider when automating your AP and P2P process. The following tables provide 32 functionality considerations for: (1) Invoice Processing, (2) Invoice Payment, (3) PO Matching, (4) E-procurement, and PO Collaboration, and (5) Other Functionality. These considerations can be used to set the stage for your automation journey.

1. AP Automation Functionality to Support Invoice Processing								
1. Approval Workflows	2. Invoice Status and Tracking	3. Automated Audit Trails	4. Automated Entry of Invoices and Bulk Upload	5. Line Item Matching	6. Ability to Add Attachments (Document Sharing)	7. Automated Invoice Error Correction	8. Supplier Portals	9. Supports Digital Signatures (for Invoice Changes and Approvals)

2. AP Automation Functionality to Support Invoice Payment								
10. Offers Flexible Payment Methods	11. Supports Compliance Screening Upon Payment (OFAC, OIG, KYC, etc.)	12. Provides Payment Data and Cash Management	13. Enables Payment Reconciliation	14. Supports International and Cross Border Payments	15. Identifies Early Pay Discounts and Rebates	16. Multi-Language Support	17. Checks for Duplicate Payments and Payment Fraud	

3. AP Automation Functionality to Support PO Matching		
18. Supports Creating and Matching POs and Has "N-Way" Matching	19. Supports Communication with Suppliers and Supplier Enablement	20. Ability to Make Purchase Order Changes and PO Flip Functionality

4. AP Automation Functionality to Support E-purchasing and PO Collaboration					
21. Digital Signatures (for PO Approvals and Changes)	22. Provides or Facilitates Standard and Dynamic Discounting	23. Can Share Product Information	24. Supports Supplier Dispute Resolution and Automated Deductions	25. Facilitates Strategic Sourcing and Spend Reporting	26. Faciliates Supply Chain Financing

5. Other Functionality Considerations					
27. Easy Set-Up and Training	28. Integration with Other Tools	29. Mobile App	30. Provides Other Automation Functionality (AR, T&E, Energy and Conservation, R2R, etc.)	31. Security Has Two-Factor Authentication or User-Role Based	32. Provides Metrics and Dashboards

EXAMPLES OF AP AUTOMATION SOLUTIONS

There are several types of automation solutions for the P2P process. We'll look at the solutions available today and will highlight the benefits.

1. E-invoicing

E-invoicing not only reduces cost and improves efficiency but improves internal controls in the accounts payable process. Key benefits of E-invoicing include:

- Further reduce accounts payable costs by minimizing paper conversion.
- Receive electronic line item invoice data for more accurate matching and reporting.
- Decrease your Days Payable Outstanding (DPO) to drive early payment discounts.
- "Go Green" by doing business in a more environmentally friendly way.
- Reduce inbound calls related to invoice status.
- Eliminate issues that inevitably come with paper-based processes such as misplacing or losing paper, duplicating or overpaying invoices, or making late payments. Visibility is instantly improved with online notifications that remind approvers that an invoice needs to be processed. This improves the audit review process as well because AP departments can quickly provide access to invoices based on internal and external audit requests.

2. ERP Integration

Better ERP integration can improve automation of the entire P2P process by eliminating wasteful steps between buyers and suppliers, according to analysts, suppliers, and users who have done it. Incoming business connectors allow data to be transmitted electronically. This ensures that important information such as supplier address, PO data, receiving data, and GL chart of account data are in sync between their software and the organization's ERP or accounts payable financial system before approved invoices are interfaced back to the system of record.

3. Electronic Payment: ACH

Payment via ACH is easy to set up and use, and the process is safe and cost-effective. Getting paid electronically means cash flow is more consistent and easier to forecast. Supplier satisfaction is improved if invoices are paid electronically. Benefits include:

- Enables automated receivables and payables
- Provides additional internal controls

- Transfers funds securely to and from the organization's bank accounts
- Instills reliability and certainty
- Reduces risk of lost or fraudulent checks
- Helps protect the environment

4. Supplier Portals

Supplier portal is an interactive, enclosed Web-based environment that the organization's suppliers access after logging in. The environment is fully dynamic, meaning it can be linked to an ERP system (without being dependent on it), and continually updated. It's also available 24/7/365, allowing the organization to always have needed information available to customers, suppliers, suppliers, etc. A myriad of self-service options become available, depending on the organization's needs. Portals are ideal for providing better service, more efficiently, and for less capital expenditure. A cumbersome and manual process is automated, which reduces risk and cost. An accounts payable staff member no longer has to answer most invoice questions – the entire array of invoicing information can be seen at one's fingertips. Here are some common functions:

- Customer Service Inquiries
- Payment Inquiries
- Invoice Status Inquiries
- Order Information
- Shipment / Logistical Information
- Supplier Validation and Compliance Screening
- Supplier Information (applications, documents, etc.)
- Two-Way Communication

5. Robotic Process Automation (RPA)

Manual AP processes are repetitive, time-consuming, and typically require high levels of involvement from employees. As such, robotic process automation (RPA) is an excellent fit for the automation of AP processes. But even so, recent research by Basware and MasterCard indicates only 20% of companies use automation software internally to alleviate their accounts payable headaches.

Like other automation solutions, RPA isn't a one-size-fits-all solution for all companies, but the technology has the ability to help companies streamline their financial tasks in order create enhanced efficiency and operational control. Here are some of the challenges to consider if you are looking into an RPA solution.

Non-standard Invoicing: Invoices that companies receive from their suppliers sometimes still arrive in multiple different formats: as a paper copy, a Word document, a PDF e-mail attachment, or a fax. Because invoice formats are not always standardized, it is often a challenge for companies and automation software to handle them in the same way each time.

Unstructured Data: A company's finance team is responsible for transferring the data from various invoice formats into the company's database. The AP staff is also responsible for manually dealing with any discrepancies between the bill of lading, purchase order, and invoice as well as approving payments.

Automated Reconciliation of Matching Errors: A large, time-consuming burden for a company's AP staff is error reconciliation. This can include discrepancies in purchase amount or vendor contact information between various essential documents, such as invoices and purchase orders. By automating most of this manual matching, robotic software robots can reduce the amount of oversight and exception handling that this required of employees. This means that employees will be able to focus on more critical finance responsibilities, such as budgeting and planning.

High Scalability: Accounts payable workflows designed with RPA can be replicated or reused across different business departments and between locations, meaning that quick scalability can be easily achieved. In addition, the number of active robots can be scaled up or down with little to no additional cost.

Rapid Fiscal Close Requirements: RPA software can be used to automate data input, error reconciliation, and some of the decision-making required by a company's finance staff. Not only does the use of software robots reduce the number of errors made in closing accounts, it also means that account reconciliations can be completed much more quickly and without as much human intervention.

 ## OTHER TYPES OF AP AUTOMATION

This section describes other types of AP Automation to consider. Many organizations utilize several types of automation to streamline their end-to-end AP process.

Optical Character Recognition (OCR), Document Imaging, and Data Extraction

OCR converts an image file into machine-readable text. Data capture reads the text and converts it into useful information.

For example: An OCR engine will recognize the phrase "Purchase Order," but a data capture application will put those words into proper context to locate and extract the string of characters that represent the actual Purchase Order number on that document.

Almost all of the invoice capture recognition solutions in the market today combine both OCR and data capture tools.

All scanning and OCR solutions share the goal of improving organizations' management of their invoice receipt-to-pay processes. To address the paper problem, many accounts payable departments are turning to OCR and data capture solutions, which use an optical-sensing device and special software to read machine print.

Front-end document and data capture solutions provide greater benefits than back-end imaging. Scanning invoices at their point of receipt – either in the field or at a central location – permanently removes paper from the process and ensures that critical transaction-related documents are committed to secure storage immediately.

Back-End Invoice Capture and Archival

This is the simplest use of a scanning solution for back-end imaging and archival. Operators batch and scan paper invoices and other transaction-related documents at the end of the invoice receipt-to-pay process. Once indexing is complete, the document images are stored in an electronic repository for retrieval based on the searchable fields created. Archival imaging adds no value to the invoice approval process.

Front-End Document and Data Capture

The most advanced use of imaging technology is to scan invoices when they come in – this is called front-end imaging. Accounts payable departments can deploy an imaging and OCR and data capture solution at the front-end of the invoice receipt-to-pay cycle. While OCR performs the task of translating data from imaged invoices to computer-usable formats, data capture goes a step further by analyzing the data extracted and converting it into useful information. With front-end imaging, paper invoices are scanned then information is extracted – in industry parlance –"captured" from the invoice images. Front-end document and data capture represents a quantum leap from front-end imaging alone, because it sets up genuine improvements to the invoice receipt-to-pay cycle.

However, front-end document and data capture poses greater challenges than back-end imaging. Invoice image quality takes on greater importance due to the implications of poor quality images for the data capture process. Front-end data capture is complicated by the non-standard nature of invoices.

With a structured document, such as an employment application, certain information always appears in the same location on the page. For example, the applicant's name may always appear in the same box. In contrast, an unstructured document, such as an invoice – unfamiliar information can appear in unexpected places. Therefore, invoices are usually considered semi-structured documents.

Invoices share some of the characteristics of both types of structured and unstructured documents. On the one hand, individual suppliers' invoices feel a lot like structured documents because they have a consistent appearance from one billing period to the next. On the other hand, viewed in aggregate by an accounts payable department that receives thousands of invoices each day in a myriad of different formats, they seem more like unstructured documents. Until recently, the semi-structured nature of invoices hindered efficient data capture. OCR is already widely used by paper-intensive industries to process structured forms such as loan and employment applications. However, these solutions typically rely on templates to recognize each unique document type and guide the recognition engine to the data to be extracted. The lack of consistent structure to an invoice poses a unique problem to an accounts payable operation.

How Does OCR Work in AP?

Once invoices have been scanned and their images enhanced to optimize character recognition, the recognition engine uses scripted rules to locate, extract, and validate the desired information, regardless of its location on the invoice. Confidence rules are usually developed to manage data quality and monitor potential errors. When the software has text that it can't fully recognize the system develops a score or "confidence index" which is based on the reliability of the converted documents.

For low-confidence reads, the final step is for an accounts payable staff member to examine the recognition results of illegible scanned data. When this is complete, the information is uploaded to the ERP or accounting system. Performing document and data capture at the beginning of the invoice receipt-to-pay cycle also minimizes the time required to enter invoices into queues for processing and payment. Finally, advanced technologies that extract, index, and validate invoice data with minimal human intervention can create an automated, error-free process.

Today's best practices call for front-end image and data capture. Paper documents are scanned at receipt, either at a central processing site or a remote facility, to digitize the data they contain.

Information is then extracted using one of several types of recognition technologies:

- OCR and ICR are character-based recognition systems and are acronyms for optical character recognition and intelligent character recognition, respectively. OCR recognizes printed text, while ICR is designed to capture both machine-generated and hand-written text.
- OMR or optical mark recognition recognizes the presence of marks put in specific locations on an invoice.
- Barcode recognition is another method of electronic data capture.

 IMAGING AND WORKFLOW AUTOMATION (IWA)

Imaging and workflow automation (IWA) solutions streamline the invoice receipt-to-pay cycle by enabling organizations to convert paper invoices into digital images, store them in a Web-enabled repository for rapid retrieval, and extract data from them to enhance approval processing. IWA solutions may provide document and data capture, workflow automation, or both in order to create an end-to-end imaging and workflow solution that integrates with enterprise and line of business applications. The IWA universe includes:

Invoice Receipt Functionality

- The steps required to receive and prepare invoices for capture, including removing staples, repairing tears, photocopying small items onto 8 × 11 paper, initial data entry, and sorting (e.g. by source or cost center).
- Most solutions also require a separator page to be inserted between invoices as well as between the invoice and its attachments.
- Some providers go a step further and offer a Web-enabled interface allowing suppliers to upload invoices directly into the system.

Document and Data Capture

- The process of converting paper invoices and transaction-related documents, such as proofs of receipt, into digital images and index data.
- Document scanning and data extraction could be centralized or remote based on the organization's needs.
- Specific steps include scanning, image enhancement, indexing, validation, and data extraction based on barcodes, optical character recognition (OCR), intelligent character recognition (ICR), or manual data entry.

Supplier Portal

- The ability for suppliers to submit invoices electronically in different ways.
- Suppliers can manually enter data in the portal, perform purchase order flips (convert a PO into an invoice), and browse and add documents from accounting systems.
- Some supplier portals allow organizations to configure validation rules to check invoices at the time of submission for exceptions and missing information.

Content Management

- Refers to the delivery, storage, management, and disposition of electronic documents and index data.
- Depending on the complexity of the solution, this may include enterprise content management (ECM) or business process management (BPM) capabilities for managing the transactional content across its entire lifecycle.
- This stage also addresses the archival and retrieval as well as backup and recovery options offered as part of IWA solutions.

Workflow Management

- The routing of tasks based on individuals' roles and access rights according to pre-defined business rules.
- Ability to track and manage approval processing at the individual invoice and aggregate levels.
- Common features include automatic notifications to users when specific actions are required, reminder messages, and escalation procedures based on approval hierarchies.

Processing Efficiency

Back-end imaging and archival solutions accelerate transaction research, discrepancy resolution, and response times to supplier inquiries by allowing AP staff to retrieve invoices from an electronic repository rather than a paper filing cabinet or archive. As a front-end application, IWA solutions contribute further to processing efficiency by enabling invoices to enter processing queues more quickly and providing invoice images that can be used to accelerate approval. Maximum efficiency is achieved when imaging and workflow are used together, as review and approval tasks can be routed automatically to individuals distributed across the organization based on clearly defined and highly customizable business rules.

Lower Costs

IWA solutions drive down document storage costs by substituting electronic repositories for filing cabinets and effectively eliminating the need for long-term storage space. As the cost of electronic storage continues to fall, these savings will become more pronounced. Second, IWA solutions enable an accounts payable operation to trim its full-time equivalent (FTE) requirements. While never a pleasant topic, these savings can be substantial. Alternatively, organizations can reassign AP staff to more value-added activities. Third, IWA solutions provide a tool to eliminate late payment penalties and capture a higher percentage of prompt payment discounts.

Enhanced Visibility and Control

IWA solutions provide secure storage for invoices and support corporate policies and statutory requirements for document retention and disposal. Anytime access to invoice images facilitates reporting and analysis by eliminating the need for physical documents. In a front-end role, IWA solutions improve the speed and accuracy of decision making by allowing users to access accurate, up-to-date information from any location using a Web browser.

Regulatory Compliance

Another major benefit of IWA solutions lies in the functionality that they offer in the area of compliance management, enabling organizations to adhere to regulatory requirements and control the costs of compliance initiatives. Companies that have dealt with compliance on a departmental, or project-based, approach are now realizing the benefits of centralizing, organizing, managing, and storing all the information related to a wide array of compliance initiatives.

Imaging, Workflow, or Both?

Accounts payable managers, controllers, treasurers, and finance managers who are interested in exploring IWA solutions for the reduction of paper- and people-based processes in the AP area should have an understanding of the business case for the expanded use of IWA and evaluating and selecting an appropriate solution.

Organizations today are swimming in paper. Removing paper from corporate America has proven to be more challenging than putting men on the moon and no one is more aware of this than accounts payable professionals who constantly deal with paper documents like purchase orders, invoices, goods receipts, and other supplier-related communications.

Reporting and Analysis

- Analyzing key invoice receipt-to-pay metrics and the ability to monitor individual users' actions for quality control and load balancing.
- Typical reporting and analysis tools include the generation of standard and ad hoc reports detailing invoices pending approval, unpaid invoices past due, and average invoice processing time.
- Some solutions offer robust reporting capabilities bundled with the IWA solution, while others only allow for download of transactional data to third-party reporting tools.

DIFFERENT FLAVORS OF IMAGING AND WORKFLOW AUTOMATION

All IWA solutions share the goal of improving organizations' management of their invoice receipt-to-pay processes. However, not every solution follows the same approach or provides similar functionality at each step of the process. Therefore, accounts payable professionals should understand the major forms that IWA can take.

Back-End Document Capture and Archival

The simplest use of IWA is for back-end imaging and archival. Operators batch and scan paper documents at the end of the invoice receipt-to-pay process. AP staff then indexes the invoices manually by using a split-screen view to key information from invoice images into electronic forms.

Once indexing is complete, the document images are stored in an electronic repository for retrieval based on the searchable fields created.

Historically, AP departments have used IWA solutions in this manner to eliminate physical storage requirements, facilitate document retrieval for discrepancy resolution and audits, and improve responsiveness to supplier inquiries. However, since scanning and indexing occur after approval processing, the invoice receipt-to-pay cycle continues to follow its current manual, paper-intensive course.

Front-End Document and Data Capture

Going one step further, AP departments can deploy an IWA solution at the front end of the invoice receipt-to-pay cycle. In this scenario, paper invoices are scanned remotely or at a central processing facility upon receipt.

Once invoices have been scanned and images enhanced to optimize recognition, data is extracted from the documents using image recognition technologies like OCR and ICR. Front-end document and data capture represents a quantum leap over back-end imaging because it sets up genuine improvements to the invoice receipt-to-pay cycle.

Validation rules ensure that the data extracted is valid and accurate by directing the solution to compare specific fields against the information held in the appropriate back-end system (e.g. purchase order numbers against the purchasing system). The final step is for an AP staff member to examine and validate the recognition results.

Many solutions display the invoice image and the data that the OCR engine has extracted side-by-side on a computer screen. If there is a failed validation or low-confidence character recognition, then that field is highlighted for acceptance or correction by the staff member. When this is complete, the information is uploaded to the ERP or accounting system.

Used for front-end document and data capture, IWA solutions provide greater benefits than back-end imaging. Scanning invoices at their point of receipt – either in the field or at a central location – removes paper from the process and ensures that critical transaction-related documents are committed to secure storage immediately. Performing document and data capture at the beginning of the invoice receipt-to-pay cycle also minimizes the time required to enter invoices into queues for processing and payment.

Front-End Document and Data Capture with Workflow

In their most advanced form, IWA solutions combine front-end document and data capture with workflow capabilities to streamline and automate invoice receipt and approval processing. Workflow solutions enable AP departments to define how different types of invoices are processed. Simple invoices, such as utility bills, can be matched against the contract price, approved, and posted to the accounting system for payment automatically. Purchase order invoices can be matched against the purchase order and receipt documents and routed to the person or people who must approve them. All tasks are routed based on pre-defined business rules, and user roles and access rights can be set to match the organization's existing approval hierarchy.

Approvers are typically notified via e-mail when invoices require their review and approval. Users click on the hyperlink contained in the e-mail messages and log onto the system to view, code, and approve the invoices online. In the event that an approver does not act within a specified period of time, reminder notifications can be sent or the task can roll up to the next person in the approval chain. Similarly, most workflow solutions provide options to automatically forward tasks to backups when primary approvers are out sick or on vacation. Multiple approvers can be designated for invoices that exceed certain dollar thresholds or must be coded to multiple accounts.

Workflow-enabled IWA solutions automate more of the invoice receipt-to-pay cycle than stand-alone document and data capture solutions. They also deliver auditing, reporting, and management benefits that document and data capture solutions alone cannot provide. Workflow solutions track every action taken by every user on every invoice, providing a complete audit trail for every user and transaction. Users can respond more quickly and effectively to supplier inquiries, while supervisors gain the ability to track the status of individual invoices, view the work of individual approvers, or monitor the entire approval process. Senior managers will appreciate the ability of a workflow solution to ensure their organizations' compliance with Sarbanes-Oxley.

ELECTRONIC INVOICING

Emerging financial solutions that enable trading partners to seamlessly exchange transaction-related information and funds are about to indelibly change the invoicing and payables landscape. Enabled by new Internet tools and best-of-breed systems, a new crop of invoice networks are beginning to make significant inroads into reducing inefficiencies and driving costs out of companies' financial operations through the elimination of paper. Demand for these new networks, which facilitate real-time collaboration between buyers, suppliers and banks, is being driven by organizations' appetite for hard dollar operational savings and the opportunity for enhanced working capital management capabilities.

Electronic invoices significantly compress invoice receipt-to-payment processing cycles by eliminating mail latency and desk float. Additionally, with faster approval times, finance managers have a greater ability not only to take existing discounts but also the opportunity to create new ones. These working capital factors have sharply increased organizations' interest in automation solutions that streamline and optimize some or all of the procure-to-pay functions, including those that deliver electronic invoicing, electronic payment, and discount management capabilities.

Electronic invoicing solutions streamline the invoice receipt-to-pay cycle by enabling organizations to electronically exchange purchase orders and invoices, use sophisticated workflow tools for approval processing, and make electronic settlement against approved invoices. The various solutions featured in this report offer electronic invoicing, payments automation, or both in order to create an end-to-end solution that integrates with enterprise and other legacy business applications. We define and describe the specific components of the electronic invoicing universe as follows:

Supplier Recruitment and Enrollment: Recruitment activities typically start with supplier segmentation analysis and identifying those suppliers to target first for onboarding. The solution provider also adds value to the equation by leveraging proven best practices to develop various activation campaigns – e-mail, phone, and direct mail – for different supplier groups. The solution offers functionality to allow suppliers to enroll themselves by logging into the application to provide bank account and registration information. Alternatively, buyers can manually enter supplier information or import the same from their ERP or AP systems. In some cases, suppliers go a step further to authenticate the bank account information provided by suppliers before payments are initiated, either by verifying a canceled check or by directly calling the supplier's bank.

Invoice Generation and Delivery: This stage includes all the steps a supplier must complete in order to produce and deliver an invoice to the buyer. Electronic invoicing solutions facilitate the exchange of invoices between buyers and suppliers by supporting several methods of accomplishing this (PO flip, blank e-forms, standard template, extracting template from buyers' ERP systems, etc.). Solution providers also offer more advanced file connections via EDI, XML, CSV, etc. for high-volume suppliers or those that prefer the more hands-free approach. Some solution providers offer options to handle paper invoices as well.

Suppliers who continue to send paper invoices are asked to redirect their invoices to the solution provider, who then takes on the responsibility of converting paper documents into electronic images, and capturing and normalizing the data to suit the buyer's requirements. Each invoice, whether submitted electronically or on paper, is typically converted into a common document type for querying and filtering.

Exception Handling: Validation of invoices is a critical step to ensure that only "clean" invoices are viewed by the AP department, thereby reducing the amount of time spent on resolving exceptions. Invoices are routinely checked for duplicity and mathematical integrity. An additional layer of validation is provided by checking invoices against a set of buyer-defined criteria. This process identifies errors and exceptions in the invoices proactively at the time of invoice submission itself and notifies the infringing party to correct those errors before the invoice can be accepted and routed. These validation rules and tolerance levels can be configured and changed, as needed, by buyers based on a number of parameters including supplier category, type of spend, geographic locations, and dollar thresholds.

Workflow and Dispute Management: This is the process that buyers follow to sort, route, review, dispute, and approve invoices for payment, including workflow. Electronic invoicing solutions support multiple levels of approval and include the ability to configure reminders and escalation procedures, if no action is taken on pending tasks in a specified period of time. The systems also allow buyers and suppliers to investigate and collaboratively resolve disputes and exceptions. Comments, attachments, and other supporting documents can be added to transactions to provide further visibility into the approval and dispute-resolution process. The solutions support configurations that dictate a manual or automated workflow process for invoice and payment approval, dispute resolution, escalation procedures, and authorization protocols, all based on pre-defined criteria.

Payment Processing: The steps that buyers take to initiate, post, and execute payment, including preparation, processing, and submission of the payment file to financial institution. Most solutions offer multiple payment options including paper and electronic and allow buyers to configure payment types at the supplier level. This stage also includes integration with and posting of the payments to buyers' ERP and accounting systems. Some solutions also offer dynamic payables discounting functionality allowing buyers to configure multiple discount schemes and enabling suppliers to discount all or any of their receivables at any time, up to the maturity date. Finally, these solutions provide suppliers with complete visibility into the entire process by delivering notifications of approved invoices and scheduled payments.

Reporting and Analytics: This includes the ability of the solution to generate standard and custom queries and reports and to provide visibility across transactions to buyers and suppliers. The solutions also provide comprehensive audit trails of all actions taken within the system and supplier self-service options. Recent advancements in analytical capabilities allow managers to examine spend at various levels; including type of expense, employee, department, and region. This wealth of information gleaned from the procure-to-pay process, can not only be used to comply with regulatory requirements but also to provide valuable business intelligence for strategic spend analysis.

The electronic invoicing and electronic payments universe forms an important subset of the larger financial supply chain that includes credit facilitation, trade execution, and cash management. In the context of globalization, intensifying competition, and a trend toward deeper integration within and between trading partners, we believe that corporate managers must focus on how electronic invoicing solutions may be combined with products and services from other pieces of the financial supply chain to create complete financial automation solutions.

 ## DIFFERENT FLAVORS OF ELECTRONIC INVOICING

AP managers should understand the differences between the various electronic invoicing solutions currently available.

Web Portal Solutions: First, there are web portals, which enable either the buyer of goods or services to control the invoicing and payment process from their own systems. Web portals are available either as licensed software or through a software-as-a-service (SaaS) model.

Most supplier or web portal solutions involve one entity (buyer) providing an interface for many suppliers to present invoices and receive payments electronically. The buyer maintains an Internet presence, provides instructions and capabilities for suppliers to register, and asks them to post and monitor their invoices online. Web portal solutions typically give suppliers several options for submitting invoices directly into the buyer's ERP or legacy system, such as completing a Web form online, or "flipping" a purchase order into an invoice, or sending an electronic file.

Networked Solutions: Second, there are Internet solutions, which involve a third-party processor or bank acting as an invoice Internet network. The consolidator provides the organization with a Web-based interface that allows many buyers and suppliers to come to one location to transact with one another. The network acts as an intermediary and is focused on collecting invoices and facilitating payments from multiple buyers for multiple suppliers, eliminating the need for point-to-point or portal connections.

In addition to providing the connectivity that links buyers and suppliers, the third party also acts as the services and network provider. The network provider not only has all of the robust features of a buyer or supplier-centric solution, but also provides additional value through the shared supplier network, open to suppliers and buyers alike. Both may participate in the network, but neither controls it. Instead, buyers ask their suppliers to present invoices through the provider's Web-based solution, and suppliers ask their buyers to view and pay invoices through the network.

Rather early in the maturation of the electronic invoicing and electronic payments space, solution providers learned that buyers drive the adoption rate, and therefore the success or failure of an initiative.

CONVERGENCE OF ELECTRONIC INVOICING AND IWA

Interest in electronic invoicing goes hand-in-hand with the emergence of a different, yet similar, set of technology solutions that leverage document imaging and data extraction capabilities to streamline invoice receipt.

Buyers are usually interested in IWA for the same reasons they are drawn to electronic invoicing; it offers a way to eliminate time and waste from the invoice management process. Suppliers like that they do not have to change their processes in any way to derive the benefits of accelerated invoice processing. Though electronic invoicing and IWA solutions differ in the way they receive invoices, they are similar in that they both offer functionality for approving invoices, resolving discrepancies, and accessing up-to-date invoice and payment status information online. These features hold out the promise of reducing invoice presentment costs (including reprints), accelerating discrepancy resolution, and increasing predictability about cash inflows.

The key difference between electronic invoicing and IWA is that electronic invoicing solutions have been explicitly designed to facilitate external buyer-supplier interactions, whereas IWA solutions have evolved to meet organizations' internal needs around invoice receipt and management. But electronic invoicing and IWA both ultimately seek to eliminate paper from transactions.

However, as the Internet expands into all corners of business communication, the distinction between internal and external breaks down. This is already affecting the AP automation landscape with IWA suppliers offering supplier portals explicitly designed to facilitate buyer-supplier collaboration and enabling suppliers to submit electronic invoices and. At the same time, electronic invoicing providers are offering paper-to-electronic conversion services to clients, either directly or through their partners.

Another option that is gaining popularity is a hybrid of electronic invoicing and IWA. By leveraging the electronic invoice submission and supplier enablement services of companies that offer buyer-seller networks and combining them with the sophisticated workflow components of their existing IWA solutions, some buyer organizations are choosing a more incremental path rather than a big bang approach.

Different types of solutions will flourish for years to come, but cross-pollination is bound to occur. Ultimately, accounts payable departments will benefit from this process as AP automation solutions incorporate better options for invoice receipt, approval processing, and discrepancy resolution that provide both control and collaboration.

 ## IMPLEMENTATION OF YOUR P2P AUTOMATION SOLUTION

From the beginning, cloud-based solutions require a lower initial investment. Since there is no hardware to purchase, integration of the new system is not only less costly, but it is also less timely. Employees simply need to be trained to use the software, but there is no need for installation and troubleshooting.

Cloud-based services are maintained through a monthly or even yearly license. Cloud-hosted solutions offer unprecedented adaptability. As a company grows, or as the responsibilities of an accounts payable department increase or decrease, cloud solutions are able to effortlessly grow with the organization. Additional users or extra space and capacity simply require the purchase of additional licenses.

Since all the system upkeep is performed off-site by the cloud provider, certain costs such as maintenance and upgrades are included in the price of the license! That leaves the organization with a virtually invisible maintenance cost.

An increasingly popular feature of cloud computing technology is its ease and range of accessibility. Since data is stored remotely and delivered via the Web, users can access AP documents on the go, whether on a business trip or in the car on a mobile device. This provides a traveling staff with a simple way to access the necessary data in a secure manner.

Finally, cloud-based computing provides powerful on-demand data to help make better sense of business results. Whether there is a need to know more about cash flow, outstanding receipts, or supplier accounts, or even how decisions affect the bottom line, a cloud-hosted solution can quickly provide the information when needed.

DEVELOPING THE BUSINESS CASE

A business case is the first step in any system implementation. The complexity of the business case will be impacted by the complexity of the system. Business cases are the single-most important document in helping P2P professionals and leaders of the organization understand the business value of an investment or business opportunity.

An effective business case is a multi-purpose document that generates the support, participation, and leadership commitment required to transform an idea into reality. A business case identifies an idea, problem, or opportunity. It provides context and content around the problem and equally illustrates the desired objectives and outcomes. The problem and desired outcomes are normally defined and described in terms of the business.

SOFTWARE SOLUTIONS, SOFTWARE-AS-A-SERVICE, OR OUTSOURCING?

Accounts payable professionals investigating IWA must consider whether a software solution or a software-as-a-service (SaaS) option would be more suitable to meet their requirements. A strong case can be made for software solutions, which are implemented inside the company's firewall, as ownership provides a high degree of control, flexibility, and security. For example, customers can modify or customize the solutions to meet their business requirements, control the platforms, and adjust security parameters to their preferences.

Another option available to organizations evaluating IWA solutions is a SaaS model, where the system is hosted and maintained by the solution provider. A major benefit of SaaS solutions lies in the fact that they usually require minimal up-front investment because the buyer organization does not need to pay to license and install software. Some technology suppliers charge a small amount up front to cover implementation costs and other professional services then charge recurring fees based on the transaction volume, while others operate entirely on a per-transaction pricing structure.

AP professionals should also keep in mind that IWA services are available through business process outsourcers. The rationale for outsourcing invoice receipt-to-pay functions is the same as it is for business process outsourcing in general. It may be better for an expert service provider to perform non-strategic activities than to manage these repetitive, low-value tasks in-house. In the service model, the customer leverages the outsourcing provider's technology and expertise to offload transactional functions and gains the ability to focus more sharply on higher value, analytical activities.

In the past, finance and accounting processes were viewed as poor candidates for outsourcing due to their complexity. Today, encouraged by the success of early shared service centers and BPO initiatives, corporate managers are taking a hard look at outsourcing these functions. They are discovering that it can be a cost-effective way to shed non-essential functions without making the investments in hardware, software, and services associated with technology solutions. Advances in Internet and telephone communications have further enhanced this value proposition by enabling the delivery of services from any geographic location without loss of control for the customer.

As services delivered over the Internet, SaaS and outsourced AP automation solutions may be deployed more rapidly and cheaply than software solutions that require extensive integration with enterprise and legacy systems. This is an important consideration for buyers who are eager to bring the benefits of automation into their organizations as quickly and painlessly as possible. Another compelling advantage of SaaS and outsourced solutions is that the buyer is not burdened with the periodic expense and effort of upgrading to new versions of the solution and paying annual maintenance fees.

Each of the options outlined here has its advantages, disadvantages, and associated costs. It would be narrow-minded to believe in the existence of a silver bullet to the questions around type of solution. The solution of choice depends entirely on the individual organization's requirements. However, two factors are critical when deciding on a solution: financial stability of the supplier and the total cost of ownership. The total cost of ownership includes implementation and integration costs, functionality fit, ease of use, and the ability to adapt to a constantly evolving business landscape.

Advanced OCR will be a catalyst for adoption. Solutions that rely on template-based OCR to find and extract data from invoices have experienced mixed success. Sufficient for an AP department that receives invoices in just a handful of formats, they are inadequate for high-volume operations that see a myriad of formats every day. As a result, the application OCR for data extraction has been limited in AP departments. However, recent strides in OCR technologies and the emergence of industrial strength solutions that use full-page OCR to extract data without relying on templates are the key drivers that are unlocking adoption.

Imaging and workflow solutions and Web invoicing are cross-pollinating. Front-end imaging and workflow solutions have evolved to meet organizations' internal needs around invoice receipt and management, while Web invoicing was designed to facilitate collaboration between buyers and suppliers. As the Internet expands into all corners of business communication, the distinction between internal and external is breaking down. Both types of solutions will flourish for years to come, but cross-pollination is surely occurring. Ultimately, accounts payable departments will benefit from this process as AP automation solutions are incorporating better options for invoice receipt, approval processing, and discrepancy resolution that provide both improved internal control and external collaboration.

Front-end solutions will prevail. Accounts payable solutions are beneficial in all of their forms. However, front-end solutions preserve the benefits of back-end imaging and archival while providing additional advantages in the form of lower costs, higher processing efficiency, and enhanced visibility and control. They can be used to replicate and accelerate existing work patterns or to design entirely new electronic processes. Organizations will continue to use accounts payable automation solutions in both back-end and front-end forms, but the latter will eventually prevail.

Organizations will seek touchless processing. As automation moves to the front-end of the accounts payable process, organizations will also seek to leverage straight-through processing to the extent possible, so that AP staff and approvers can focus on more value-added tasks than reviewing each invoice. Demand will increase for solutions that facilitate this by delivering strong functionality around automated invoice matching and automatic approval of clean invoices as well as strong functionality around approval workflow to manage exceptions and the dispute-resolution process in a collaborative manner.

Impact of AP automation on discount capture. Until recently, automation efforts in the AP area were focused on the operational benefits that technology delivers. However, all this is changing. Increasingly, savvy finance managers are considering the more strategic impact of AP automation on the financial supply chain and the working capital improvements it can deliver. Innovative solutions are emerging to meet organizations' strategic objectives by offering solutions that unlock significant value from the financial supply chain through advanced features like supplier self-service, supplier on-boarding, and dynamic settlement.

Multiple solution models will coexist. There is not a single model for an IWA solution. Solutions are available in software form, as well as on an outsourced basis. Likewise, some suppliers emphasize a modular "mix and match" approach while others concentrate on providing a set solution. There is also tremendous variability in terms of solution focus. Some suppliers focus tightly on specific aspects of the invoice receipt–to-pay cycle, while others strive to provide accounts payable automation functionality as part of a larger ECM or BPM offering. Industry consolidation notwithstanding, this diversity will continue.

SECTION THREE

Dissecting the P2P Process

 INTRODUCTION

The term "procure to pay" (P2P) emerged in the 1990s and is one of a number of other buzz phrases that emerged as Internet applications became used more widely in business. Although it does not necessarily refer directly to the application of technology to the purchasing process, it is most often used in relation to applications like e-procurement and ERP purchasing and payment modules.

Following the maturation of Internet-supported supply chain processes, the case emerged for identifying opportunities to further streamline business processes across the whole of the procure-to-pay value chain. This was driven primarily by the supply chain software suppliers and consultants as well as by governments who had recognized and enthusiastically embraced concepts like e-procurement.

The corporate impact of the P2P process is significant. The P2P process is evolving from isolated functions to a single process in which purchasing and accounts payable are becoming automated and analytical functions adding value to the organization. This evolution aligns with the needs and goals of organizations in these tight economic times to reduce costs and realize productivity increases. The P2P process is no longer viewed as a "back-office" function but one of tremendous value since the process can greatly impact an organization by providing opportunities for strategic sourcing, automation, improved controls, and business partnerships which can greatly reduce risk and improve working capital. An organization's emphasis on the P2P process all starts with a strong focus on business ethics and the company's "tone at the top."

CHAPTER FOUR

What Is the P2P Process?

 INTRODUCTION

The role of the P2P professional is often defined as a business partner to other functions and divisions within an organization. P2P professionals are now faced with much broader challenges and opportunities in today's business world and are asked to take on additional responsibilities outside of the traditional chief procurement officer (CPO), strategic sourcing director, or accounts payable director. P2P professionals are asked to continually reinvent, redesign, and transform the P2P process. This is only accomplished through establishing effective business partnerships with other departments.

The P2P Process Flow

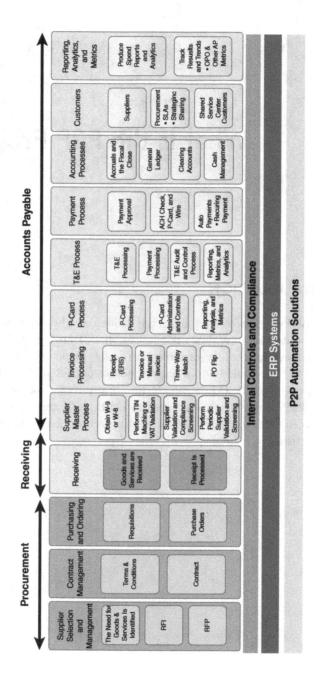

P2P BUSINESS PARTNERSHIPS, DEPENDENCIES, AND INTERDEPENDENCIES FOR SUCCESS

A business partner is an individual or company who has some degree of involvement or influence with the operational success of another department, entity, or organization. Business partners are also defined as stakeholders who are a group or organization that has interest or concern in an organization. A more effective business partnership is based upon the operational success of both departments. In some cases business partnerships are actually business dependencies for an integrated process like P2P.

Business dependency modeling is typically used to:

1. Determine the effects of change on other business processes during a business process engineering (BPE) initiative,
2. Determine the dependency of a business or organization on its suppliers and other external entities,
3. Determine the risk of exposure to your organization should the business of your suppliers (or other external entities) fail due to business problems such as failure to achieve legislative compliance.
4. Determine the importance of internal and external entities during a P2P transformation initiative.

Business dependency modeling is also used by information technology (IT) to identify the critical success factors for the business process, gather detailed information on hardware and software in use by the organization, link the technology to the business, determine the relationships and dependencies in the business, and analyze the dependencies and assess risks.

Within the manufacturing arena, academics use the term "task interdependence" to describe the manner in which different business units are reliant on one another during the production phase.

AP TOOL 12: DEPENDENCIES AND INTERDEPENDENCIES WITHIN THE P2P PROCESS

About This Tool: The following table outlines the dependencies and interdependencies for the P2P process by the three main components: procurement, receiving, and accounts payable.

We have also included a category called "other factors to consider." This category includes other factors that will impact the P2P process that will be explored in future sections.

Dependency	Procurement	Receiving	Accounts Payable
	■ Contract ■ Purchase Order ■ Suppler Master File	■ Receipt ■ ERS ■ Purchase Order ■ Supplier Master File	■ Supplier Master ■ EDI ■ E-invoice ■ Check Request ■ Check Payment ■ ACH ■ E-payment ■ Supplier Portal ■ Blocked Invoice ■ Debit Balance ■ Credit Memo ■ PO Flip
Interdependency	■ Business Need for Goods or Services ■ Proposal, RFI, RFP	■ Purchase Order ■ Suppler Master File	■ Contract ■ Purchase Order Receipt ■ ERS ■ Purchase Order ■ Supplier Master File
Other Factors	■ Internal Controls and Compliance ■ ERP Systems ■ P2P Automation	■ Internal Controls and Compliance ■ ERP Systems ■ P2P Automation	■ Internal Controls and Compliance ■ ERP Systems ■ P2P Automation

CHAPTER FIVE

Transforming the P2P Process

 INTRODUCTION

More and more companies are recognizing the value of end-to-end business process management as it breaks down functional and organizational silos to enable a more holistic approach to enterprise performance management. Of the common sets of end-to-end processes – which include: source to contract (S2C), procure to pay (P2P), order to cash (O2C), record to receipt (R2R), and hire to retire (H2R), P2P is most often identified as the priority for transformation and optimization.

There are two key drivers for this trend.

1. Compared to other end-to-end processes, P2P activities are typically more common across the organization, making them somewhat easier to standardize.
2. The business case for transforming P2P is frequently the most compelling. Through process standardization, workflow automation, system integration, and rigorous compliance enforcement, companies have been able to achieve rapid and significant spend and operating cost savings while simultaneously gaining the ability to better manage risk.

AP TOOL 13: CURRENT STATE ANALYSIS

About The Tool: Many global organizations have experienced significant challenges when combining their procurement and accounts payable functions to form truly integrated procure-to-pay (P2P) process models.

Key Point: Disconnects between supply chain and finance, the two larger areas responsible for procurement and accounts payable respectively, are not a new phenomenon. Inherently, business drivers of the two functions are different: supply chain aims to create processes which reduce cost and deliver goods and services in a timely manner, while finance strives to establish processes that improve control, simplify accounting, optimize working capital, and ensure proper purchase order authorization.

Current State Analysis Template

Leading Practice	Current State	Gaps
■ Have very clear and developed executive sponsorship (champions) of procurement initiatives to echo goals of process improvements, reporting, and compliance. ■ Department level reports to help managers to monitor spend commitments and budgets.	■ Limited goals to promote strategic importance of process improvements, reporting, and compliance to policy. ■ Limited communications to departments about policies and process improvement opportunities. ■ Reports have not been developed to support AP's monitoring of service level agreements (SLA's).	■ Due to decentralized departmental structure, client procurement has difficulty in driving compliance. ■ Gap in executive sponsorship of procurement policies. ■ Inability to monitor spend and compliance to policy via current systems.
■ Maintain a central repository with dynamically updated documentation to ensure changing documents are widely accessible to staff for reference. ■ Publish goals and metrics for spend under procurement review.	■ Procurement documentation, policies, and procedures exist but are not necessarily the most up-to date nor are stored centrally or widely available to client staff for reference. ■ Limited spend savings and procurement visibility goals.	■ Current procurement documentation not readily accessible and stored in a central location leading to inefficiencies for referencing procurement policies and procedures. ■ Develop metrics and goals for spend under review and expected P2P savings.

Leading Practice	Current State	Gaps
■ Have processes (supported by policies) in place to measure requisition to PO cycle times. ■ Have a means in place to recognize and address performance enhancement opportunities.	■ There are limited processes to track and enforce procurement compliance and governance. ■ Limited metrics to measure progress. ■ Process effectiveness not measured.	■ Inability to measure Procurement efficiency metrics and identify improvement opportunities. ■ Policies are not optimized to enforce compliance to processes.

 ## VISIONING AND TRANSFORMATION ROADMAP

Many global organizations have experienced significant challenges when combining their procurement and accounts payable functions to form truly integrated P2P process models.

Disconnects between supply chain and finance, the two larger areas responsible for procurement and accounts payable respectively, are not a new phenomenon. Inherently, business drivers of the two functions are different: supply chain aims to create processes that reduce cost and deliver goods and services in a timely manner, while finance strives to establish processes that improve control, simplify accounting processes, optimize working capital, and ensure proper purchase order authorization.

In addition to these functional alignment challenges, internal customer adoption can undermine even the best P2P implementations. As a result, companies must effectively manage service with control/cost savings.

Developing a well-integrated P2P model goes beyond optimization at the transaction or improving processing efficiency. In order for companies to truly transform their P2P model, there should be a clear alignment across an enterprise, not just procurement and accounts payable, for its P2P strategy must be the central driver for any transformation effort to be successful.

The full value of a P2P transformation is much more than just transaction efficiency. To that end, the area of sourcing through improvements in spend aggregation analysis and focused category management (e.g. strategic sourcing) can unlock significantly greater value than initial savings achieved from PO and invoice transaction optimization efforts.

AP TOOL 14: P2P TRANSFORMATION ROADMAP

About This Tool: Many companies are at different stages of maturity across the sourcing, purchasing, and invoice processing dimensions. However, following are the P2P strategic elements, which can be deployed irrespective of maturity:

1. **Governance:** Structured oversight provides a mechanism for evaluating funding requests or process changes and arbitrating issues within the P2P process. Governance models typically include an advisory panel that provides recommendations on how to enhance the performance of people, process, and technology.
2. **Performance Measures:** Performance measures help to inform strategy by identifying process opportunities (e.g. invoice processing exceptions) and areas where technology investment can be best leveraged. Performance measures also provide a means to share data across P2P functions.
3. **Competencies:** As P2P operations mature, the required organizational skills and competencies change. Being proactive and planning for shifting competencies in P2P strategy is critical.
4. **Roles:** Armed with more data and fewer transactional duties, maturing P2P organizations can offer more value as their roles change. Preparing for this change in role is also a key component of strategy.

 ## AP TOOL 15: OTHER RECOMMENDATIONS FOR P2P TRANSFORMATION

About This Tool: Other recommendations for a successful P2P transformation include the following items.

---

1. **Cross-Functional Management Team:** A cross-functional management team is needed to drive improvement in P2P initiatives.
2. **Collaboration:** Each stage of process maturity requires improvements in the process, increased collaboration, and transparency.
3. **Coordinated Processes:** Integrated P2P processes include specific acknowledgement of the need, forecasting processes, collaboration and standardization on specifications, supplier performance measurement systems, and approval systems.
4. **Continuous Process Improvement:** Improvement is a continuous process – it may take several years to drive to a fully integrated P2P system.

5. Change Management Processes: Change management is an important component of the process – training and understanding are critical to success.

 ## AP TOOL 16: MANAGING CHANGE

About This Tool: The experts agree that change management is a key factor to consider for a P2P transformation initiative since the transformation will result in significant process and system changes. One of the major challenges within change management is assessing the readiness for change within the organization. Unfortunately, this does not always happen and the risks associated with the change are not properly addressed and the success of the initiative is impacted.

The Association of Change Management Professionals (ACMP), PROSCI, the Innovation and Organizational Change Management Institute (IOCMI), and others view change management from an organizational perspective. While each group has its own approaches, frameworks, and language, these groups all address the human side of change in organizational contexts.

The clearest definition of this type of organizational change management (OCM) is provided by Sheila Cox of Performance Horizons who states: "Organizational change management ensures that the new processes resulting from a project are actually adopted by the people who are affected."[1]

The goal of assessing change readiness is to identify specific issues and then plan for and address those issues so that the risks associated with change are minimized. The risks if change is not properly and thoroughly addressed are:

1. Performance improvement is not achieved.
2. Performance improvement is delayed.
3. Performance improvement costs are higher than expected.

---

[1]Bart Perkins, "What Is Change Management? A Guide to Organizational Transformation," April 12, 2018, CIO, accessed on September 8, 2020, https://www.cio.com/article/2439314/change-management-change-management-definition-and-solutions.html.

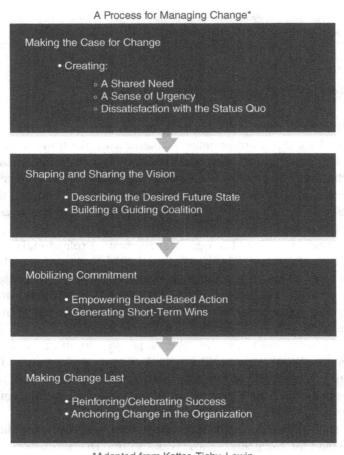

A Process for Managing Change*

Making the Case for Change

 • Creating:

  ○ A Shared Need
  ○ A Sense of Urgency
  ○ Dissatisfaction with the Status Quo

Shaping and Sharing the Vision

 • Describing the Desired Future State
 • Building a Guiding Coalition

Mobilizing Commitment

 • Empowering Broad-Based Action
 • Generating Short-Term Wins

Making Change Last

 • Reinforcing/Celebrating Success
 • Anchoring Change in the Organization

*Adapted from Kotter, Tichy, Lewin.

 ## AP TOOL 17: P2P TRANSFORMATION METRICS

About This Tool: The Everest Group recommends that one of the critical success factors to achieving the transformation is the establishment of a metrics framework. The following diagram presents a P2P metrics framework that starts with clearly defined business objectives that are measured by a small set of outcome-based metrics to reflect the overall efficiency and effectiveness of the P2P process. The diagnostic measures are designed to identify specific process breakdowns and improvement opportunities, and are tracked and reported at the operational level.

P2P Objectives	Improve efficiency	Maximize value creation	Prevent value leakage	Ensure stakeholder satisfaction
P2P Outcome Metrics	P2P Transaction Cost per Invoice	% of Early Payment Discount Captured	% of Contracted Saving Realized	Level of Customer & Vendor Satisfaction
P2P Diagnostic Measures (not exhaustive)	% of Payment on E-Invoices; % Payment on P-Card; % of Invoices Requires Correction; % of Invoices Require Manual Processing; PO Processing Cycle Time; Number of Paid Invoices per P2P FTE	% of Invoices Paid on Time/Late Penalties Incurred; Invoice Processing Cycle Time	% Payment on Contract; % Payment Thru POs; % of Incorrect/Duplicated Payments; % of Spend Thru Preferred Vendors; % of Spend Thru Catalogs	Requisition Conversion Time; Average Query Response/Resolution Time

The Everest Group recommends that companies follow a structured approach to develop a holistic P2P performance management framework:

1. **Define common metrics** and clearly delineate objectives, descriptions, and interdependencies with other performance measures
2. **Establish a standard methodology and systems** to track and report performance; key components include:
   - Measurement scope, parameters, method, data source, and frequency
   - Benchmarking methodology and data source
   - Reporting dashboards, frequency, and forum
3. **Assign accountability for:**
   - Measuring and tracking performance metrics
   - Benchmarking and reporting overall P2P performance
   - Identifying and prioritizing continuous improvement (CI) opportunities
   - Reviewing and approving CI projects
   - Implementing and monitoring CI initiatives
   - Calibrating performance metrics based on evolving business objectives

AP TOOL 18: STREAMLINING YOUR P2P PROCESS WITHOUT AUTOMATION

About This Tool: Now I'll take a purely strategic approach to the implementation of new cost reduction ideas and techniques for your P2P process. I'll focus on the following three areas in the order of suggested implementation times.

1. Streamlining your supplier master file
2. Building a supplier management process
3. Transforming your P2P organization

Streamlining Your Supplier Master File

A comprehensive supplier master cleansing process streamlines operations for both accounts payable and procurement. This supplier master cleanup is typically performed as part of a system conversion process, but should be performed annually to enhance internal controls, foster processing efficiencies, prevent duplicate payments, and reduce costs.

Suggested Implemented Times

I suggest that efforts to streamline your supplier master file are ongoing but a formal program should be implemented on a quarterly to annual basis.

The cleansing should incorporate the identification of inactive suppliers for purge, flagging duplicate suppliers for removal, isolating multiple remittance addresses for possible consolidation, implementing consistent supplier name and address conventions, commoditizing the supplier base, and establishing corporate linkage to support a strategic sourcing initiative. Following are the steps I recommend as part of this cleanup process:

1. Identify inactive suppliers
2. Remove duplicate supplier
3. Consolidate multiple remittance addresses
4. Pursue a strategic sourcing strategy
5. Building a supplier management process

Identify Inactive Suppliers

The identification and periodic blocking or segregation of inactive suppliers increases processor keying speed, reduces errors, and will likely enhance system response time. The recommended timeframe is to focus on suppliers with no invoice activity within the prior 18 months. This covers seasonality and retains those suppliers that invoice once-a-year.

Remove Duplicate Suppliers

In efforts to prevent duplicate suppliers from reappearing, we recommend that the supplier creation process require a look-up by the supplier address prior to adding new suppliers. This will minimize adding redundant suppliers at the source, particularly when the names or initials would be keyed slightly differently. We also recommend using coding standards when setting up a new supplier, which will also prevent setting up duplicate suppliers.

Consolidate Multiple Remittance Addresses

Many larger suppliers will have multiple remittance locations. These addresses are often geographically placed to expedite the flow of funds into the supplier's operation, or can be a function of the supplier's ownership structure. Suppliers with significant remittance addresses often include those operating in the areas of telecom, waste management, industrial parts, post offices, and technology.

Pursue a Strategic Sourcing Strategy

Given that the average Fortune 1000 company buys approximately 400–500 commodities and maintains a global supplier base of over 50,000 suppliers, this means that there is an average of over 100 suppliers per commodity. This is clearly not optimal from the procurement or accounts payable standpoint. Those organizations that have successfully optimized their supply base have addressed the following challenges:

1. The procurement organization has the necessary systems and the support of senior management to capture global spending, and routinely quantifies the financial savings from sourcing projects.
2. Preferred supplier agreements are in place for 80% or more of the organization's common purchases.
3. The proper structure and/or incentives have been implemented to ensure employees use preferred suppliers.

Building a Supplier Management Process

Now that we've addressed the methodology for streamlining your supplier master file, I'd like to introduce the concept of a supplier management process. This process is enabled by the supplier management lifecycle. The lifecycle identifies key leverage points for accounts payable and procurement to team together throughout the supplier management process. The accounts payable and procurement teams have an amazing opportunity to share information, work more efficiently with the organization's suppliers, and establish a system to support smooth procurement, delivery, and payment processes.

Suggested Implemented Times

Building a supplier management process and establishing the suggested end-to-end process throughout the P2P process can take over one year to fully implement. However, some of the suggested components of the supplier management lifecycle may be quicker to implement on an individual basis.

Transforming Your P2P Organization

Now that we've streamlined our supplier master file, and have a supplier management process in place, let's discuss the transformation of the P2P organization. Transformation of the P2P process is most often identified as the priority optimization for the following reasons.

1. Compared to other processes, P2P activities are typically more common across the organization, making them somewhat easier to standardize.
2. Through process standardization, workflow automation, system integration, and rigorous compliance enforcement, companies have been able to achieve rapid and significant spend and operating cost savings while simultaneously gaining the ability to better manage risk and improve internal controls.
3. The business owners of the P2P process are usually finance and procurement. Both functions have different goals. Finance focuses on processes which improve control, simplify accounting, optimize working capital, and ensure proper purchase order authorization. Purchasing wishes to create processes that reduce cost and deliver goods and services in a timely manner. Combining these goals into a single set of metrics can result in a tremendous cost saving initiative.

Suggested Implemented Times

Transforming your P2P organization and process can take over one to three years depending on the maturity levels of the organization.

Scott Madden, a management consulting firm, has found that most companies are at different stages of maturity across the sourcing, purchasing, and invoice processing dimensions. However, the following strategic elements can be deployed irrespective of maturity:

1. **Governance:** Structured oversight provides a mechanism for evaluating funding requests or process changes and arbitrating issues within the P2P process. Governance models typically include an advisory panel that provides recommendations on how to enhance the performance of people, process, and technology.
2. **Performance Measures:** Performance measures help to inform strategy by identifying process opportunities and areas where technology investment can be best leveraged. Performance measures also provide a means to share data across P2P functions and establish a common set of metrics to focus on cost savings goals.
3. **Competencies:** As P2P operations mature, the required organizational skills and competencies change. Being proactive and planning for shifting competencies in P2P strategy is critical.
4. **Roles:** Armed with more data and fewer transactional duties, maturing P2P organizations can offer more value as their roles change.

▪ AP TOOL 19: HOW TO BEGIN YOUR P2P AUTOMATION JOURNEY

About This Tool: P2P automation is defined as using technology to streamline part or all of the procurement process. The objectives of P2P Automation are to:

- Create paperless procurement environments
- Reduce the time required for each step of the procurement process
- Increase the number of transactions received or sent electronically
- Increase the visibility of information, including company spend
- Eliminate or reduce the use of manual processes

To determine how to begin your P2P automation journey, take a look at the most common components of the procurement process.

- **Requisitioning:** The objective of automation of the requisition function is to provide a method for the operations staff to complete the requisitions electronically, often selecting items from a limited catalog or template of items that they are permitted to order.
- **Requisition Approval:** Most organizations require approval prior to a purchase being made. In a manual environment, this requires completing a form to request goods, and forwarding that form to the approvers. Workflow automation solutions allow for these invoices to be routed electronically, reducing approval time.
- **Issuance of Purchase Orders:** Once a requisition is approved, a purchase order is issued to a supplier. Without automation, purchase orders are called in to suppliers or faxed. In a highly automated organization, purchase orders are sent electronically with acknowledgments being returned electronically from the supplier.
- **Receiving Invoices:** The most common way for invoices to be submitted from suppliers is by mail. Upon receipt, invoices are manually entered. In automated AP departments, invoices can be received electronically using a method such as EDI or e-payables. Invoices that are received manually can still be scanned and have information extracted using advanced data capture, creating a fully electronic environment.
- **Matching Invoices:** Once received, invoices should be matched to purchase orders and receipts so that an invoice is paid based on actual goods received, at the price negotiated with the supplier. Supplier over-billing or billing in error is common, yet not all organizations use the three-way matching process to prevent overpayments.

- **Issuing Payments:** A combination of ACH and procurement cards are quickly increasing the volume of payments processed electronically, steadily reducing the number of checks issued by many organizations.

The world of financial transaction processing has evolved from moving the problem behind the curtain into a shared service organization. Today's companies are focused on process improvements and efficiencies that reduce cost in these difficult economic times.

The P2P process is evolving from a manual clerical "cost-center" process to an automated and analytic process that enables visibility to the spending for the organization and highlights opportunities for cost reduction through strategic sourcing and other initiatives. The P2P process continues to be the backbone of all organizations. Today's technology options provide several alternatives for automation. The challenge is to select the focus for automation, develop the business case, and select the best solution provider to team with your company.

The focus on P2P transformation has resulted in integrated processes with few silos and bottlenecks. Many organizations measure the performance of an end-to-end P2P process. Common goals and metrics support an ongoing P2P transformation with a focus on cost savings, cycle time, and customer service.

Due to the need for enhanced reporting and data accuracy, AP is no longer looked upon as a "back-office function" and has evolved to a team focused on supplier analytics and spend analysis.

The implementation of these strategic initiatives results in several operational and cost saving benefits. An integrated supplier management process in a transformed P2P organization sets the foundation for the identification of process and automation efficiencies. However, as with a strategic initiative, I suggest establishing a business plan with clear timelines and goals – aiming for the quick wins and acknowledging the leading practices that are already in place.

CHAPTER SIX

Structuring the AP Organization

 ## INTRODUCTION

Increased productivity remains a key focus in the ongoing tight economic conditions. Process improvements and automation are the leading tools in productivity gains for the AP process. This means that AP is evolving from a manual clerical "cost-center" process to a touchless, automated, and analytical process which enables cost reductions. Today's AP department also provides the data for better cash management and the intelligence for dollar savings through enhanced visibility to the purchasing process resulting in overall AP process improvements.

AP provides several benefits by performing due diligence related to supplier setup and timely invoice processing, assuring that payments are processed based on terms and providing a high level of customer service.

One of the hallmarks of good leaders is the ability to inspire subordinates to be productive, honorable, and quality-oriented. This requires passion, without which true leadership is impossible. The best leaders influence their employees to actively contribute to achieving the organization's mission by showing them where they fit into the big picture; empowers them to excel by example and setting the highest standards for quality and integrity; and encourages them to take their skills and careers to the next level of maturity by guiding them, coaching them, and making opportunities for growth available to them.

This can be especially challenging in times of limited resources and the need to do more with less. However, such environments present the ideal opportunity to demonstrate creative leadership that generates renewed enthusiasm and energy within an AP department.

 ## THE FINANCE AND ACCOUNTING ORGANIZATION

The finance and accounting organization usually reports to the corporate controller. The size of the company and the levels within an organization will define how this organization is structured. Here's an example of a typical organizational chart for the finance and accounting organization.

THE FINANCE AND ACCOUNTING ORGANIZATIONAL CHART (EXAMPLE)

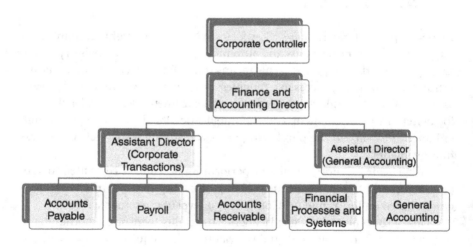

Key Point: The AP department plays a critical role within an organization as it is a last point of control before a payment is made and sent to a supplier.

The AP profession is no longer looked upon as a "necessary" stepping stone in a career path of an accounting professional. Today's AP professional is now considered to be an analyst and an influencer of the direction of their company's P2P process since data is readily available.

Today's AP professional is less focused on the tactical day-to-day "world" and is now asking the following questions to become more strategic as the function provides untapped value to a company.

- How can AP become a profit center?
- How can we capture available discounts?
- How can we effectively leverage multiple payment options?
- How can we implement dynamic discounting? How can we identify new discount opportunities?
- How can we reduce cost and reduce manual processes?
- How can we impact days payable outstanding (DPO) with automated payment processes?
- How can we reduce cost through automated workflow processes?
- Can we improve our escheatment processes?
- How can we focus on analysis vs. processing invoices with more automation?

ORGANIZATIONAL CHART FOR AN AP DEPARTMENT (EXAMPLE)

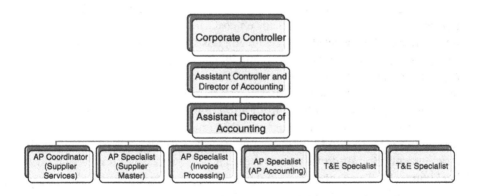

HISTORY OF THE TRANSITION

For at least three decades, many companies have been focused on reducing costs and improving productivity in their corporate transaction processing areas. These companies focused on traditional "back office" processes such as accounts payable (AP), payroll, travel and entertainment (T&E), fixed asset accounting, and accounts receivable (AR).

Over the years there has been an evolution of transitioning financial transaction processes to financial management centers; next to shared service centers; and finally to an outsourced model. Today, companies are now focused on process improvements and automation initiatives to garner additional efficiencies and cost reduction opportunities.

Key Point: Many companies look upon centralization and the movement to shared services as a necessary step to take before considering automation. This is because centralizing the AP process and implementing a shared services model can identify best practices that can eliminate process inefficiencies. A few companies consider automation as a first step toward cost reduction and process efficiency without considering centralization or a shared services model, or only partial centralization. These are usually service organizations with widely distributed offices, or smaller companies that do not have multiple locations and divisions.

 ABOUT SHARED SERVICES

The movement of the AP process to a shared service center creates an opportunity to allocate transaction processing costs back to the organization. The allocation model places an additional focus on cost, since business units will question any increase. This model also places an emphasis on reporting and metrics since savvy business units may ask for additional value-added services such as spend analysis and purchase order compliance. Automating the AP process provides organizations with the tools to better analyze spending and compliance.

The AP process is evolving from a manual clerical "cost-center" process to an automated and analytic process that enables visibility to the spending for the organization and highlights opportunities for cost reduction through strategic sourcing and other initiatives. The AP process continues to be the backbone of all organizations. Today's technology options provide several alternatives for automation. The challenge is to select the focus for automation, develop the business case, and select the best solution provider to team with your company. Lastly, it's critical to define and provide the critical skills that the new AP analyst will need to be successful in today's environment. These skills will include: an immediate Excel knowledge base, financial analysis, problem solving, knowledge of financial ratios and foundational six sigma skills.

ORGANIZATIONAL CHART FOR A SHARED SERVICES STRUCTURE (EXAMPLE)

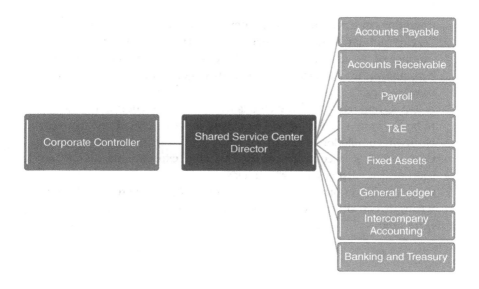

SHARED SERVICES AND SERVICE-LEVEL AGREEMENTS (SLAS)

Many organizations ask their shared service organizations to provide a service-level agreement (SLA). An SLA is a negotiated agreement between two parties where one is the customer and the other is the actual service provider. An SLA should contain operating norms, which describe how the process is governed, managing, and controlled.

Key Point: An SLA should also include a set of operating metrics that are reported on a monthly or basis. As an example, a good set of metrics for accounts payable is: cost per invoice, days payable outstanding, invoices paid on time, outstanding credit balances, paid credits, and number of suppliers on the supplier master. We'll review the SLA process in more detail in Chapter 8 on contract management.

The Shared Service and Outsourcing Network (SSON) recommends the inclusion of the following items in the SLA process.

1. The processes to be included and the products and services of those processes.
2. A list of the processes which are out of scope at this point – to manage customer expectations.
3. Conditions of service availability: hours of opening, days of operation
4. Service standards: times for delivery of services should be recorded in number of working days (rather than say 24 or 48 hours) to manage expectations and be clear about closures of operations for bank holidays or weekends.
5. A R-A-C-I matrix – to show who is Responsible, Accountable, and needs to be Consulted and Informed regarding process steps. This ensures role clarity in completion of tasks.
6. Cost versus service trade-offs, to manage expectations about "work arounds" or "just as a favor" requests.
7. Clear escalation procedures and timelines so that when something goes wrong it can be resolved by the right person, in the right role, at the right time.

SECTION FOUR

How Procurement and Receiving Impact AP

 INTRODUCTION

Procurement and AP are often viewed as less attractive areas for organizations to focus on improving. Because of this, a lot of organizations are not realizing the benefits of procurement and AP working together toward a common goal. As two separate functions working in their own silos, procurement and AP are individually moving the dial in a positive direction when it comes to saving costs and improving process efficiencies. However, these improvements are minimal in comparison to the opportunities that present themselves through true alignment.

According to SpendMatters, "Like most worthy goals, reaching this perfect world is easier said than done. It is common to have AP and purchasing report up to different division managers. These divisions often have different philosophies in handling supplier relationships as well. This creates friction and tension between the two teams, and in extreme situations, results in unhealthy organizational rivalries.

"So what needs to happen for AP and purchasing to align? Regulations have already helped address this issue in the form of Sarbanes-Oxley. This has forced companies to deal with issues both AP and purchasing have known about for years:

- Inconsistent supplier master data setup
- Poor communication to resolve issues

- Frustrating invoice errors
- Overlapping AP and purchasing roles that create conflict
- Late payments to suppliers that dilute discounts negotiated by purchasing
- Off the record purchases off the purchasing radar"[1]

The receiving department is responsible for processing receipts of goods often used for production and resale. The receipt should indicate the correct purchase, quantity, and price. Aligning procurement and receiving is critical to ensure the timely and accurate processing of invoices, the avoidance of clearing account variance, and the correct recording of liabilities.

---

[1]"Aligning Accounts Payable and Purchasing," Guest Contributor, Spend Matters, September 26, 2014, accessed August 1, 2020, https://spendmatters.com/2014/09/26/aligning-accounts-payable-and-purchasing/.

CHAPTER SEVEN

7

Supplier Selection and Management

 INTRODUCTION

The P2P process starts with the supplier selection and management process. The supplier management lifecycle is a process driver for both the P2P and procurement processes. This process is also defined by the six phases of the supplier management lifecycle, which is explored in the process insights section following the process flow depicted in the following section.

Supplier Selection and Management Process Flow

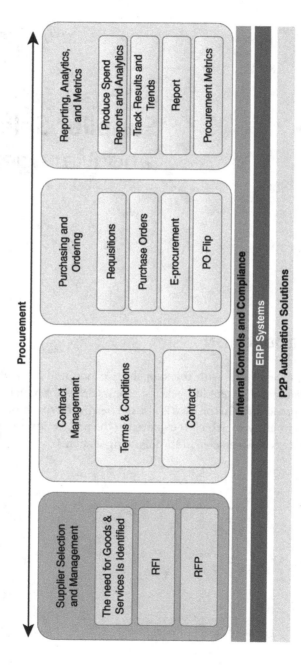

SUPPLIER SELECTION AND MANAGEMENT PROCESS INSIGHTS

There are six key phases in the supplier management lifecycle as defined below. Refer to AP Tool 20 for an in-depth review of each phase.

1. **Qualification:** Defining the qualification criteria for your organization's suppliers.
2. **Sourcing:** Inviting suppliers to participate in a pre-qualification or request for proposal process.
3. **Onboarding:** Ensuring contractual compliance with your company's requirements and defining what documents are required, optional, or unnecessary.
4. **Doing Business:** Includes the transactional validation in regulated and non-regulated environments such as commodity-based, geographical, and specific business units. Transactions including purchase orders, processing receipts, and paying invoices.
5. **Managing Performance:** Involves collecting, analyzing, and acting upon established supplier performance across the P2P process.
6. **Probation or Exit:** Ensures that you have defined "exit criteria" for suppliers with SLA or compliance issues.

AP TOOL 20: THE TOP TEN BEST PRACTICES IN THE SUPPLIER MANAGEMENT LIFECYCLE

About This Tool: This topic focuses on the "top ten" best practices in supplier management. We have mapped the best practice to the applicable process with the supplier management lifecycle. They are summarized in the following table.

Qualification

1. Establish a supplier qualification process

Sourcing

2. Request for proposal (RFP) and request for information (RFI)

3. Utilize an objective supplier evaluation and selection process

Onboarding

4. Obtain a W-9 form for domestic suppliers and a form W-8 for foreign suppliers

5. Perform TIN Matching

6. Perform initial compliance screening

Doing Business

7. Perform ongoing compliance screening

8. Fine-tune your supplier master

Managing Performance

9. Establish supplier service-level agreement reviews

Probation or Exit

10. Continuous monitoring

BEST PRACTICE #1: ESTABLISH A SUPPLIER QUALIFICATION PROCESS

Responsibility: Procurement

Leading companies recognize the importance of comprehensive supplier qualification processes but struggle to communicate qualification requirements to potential suppliers, create baselines for evaluating supplier risk levels, and ensure material conformance to specific requirements.

Some procurement functions adopt qualification standards to evaluate product quality during supplier qualification. International standards, such as ISO 9000 or TS-16949, promote broad participation and qualification of suppliers and create selection criteria for several processes including design control, inspections, equipment testing, handling, storing, packaging, and delivery.

Recognized qualification standards such as ISO 9000 outline management processes and enable high-quality production, but may prove too general for industry specifications. As a result, companies often create supplementary criteria to ensure comprehensive supplier evaluations and applicability to specific industry needs. Best practices for the supplier qualification process include:

- Deploy electronic tools to manage qualification data
- Establish and measure supplier safety risk levels
- Verify product quality levels
- Register new suppliers

BEST PRACTICE #2: REQUEST FOR PROPOSAL (RFP) AND REQUEST FOR INFORMATION (RFI)

Responsibility: Procurement and Business Management

Initiate a requirement that a request for proposal (RFP) is completed for each new supplier. In some cases a request for information (RFI) may be initiated to gather information about the supplier and to obtain additional details the functionality of specific solutions.

The Request for Information (RFI) Versus the Request for Proposal (RFP)

After the business case has been approved, the RFP or RFI process starts. Some organizations may choose to initiate an RFI, which focuses on obtaining information from the solution providers. The RFI is not as formal as the RFP process but may require similar information.

The Request for Proposal (RFP)

An RFP is a document that reflects the detailed requirements by a prospective buyer in order to receive supplier offerings. Usually dedicated to the evaluation of IT solutions, an RFP is issued to select any kind of products (tangibles) and services (non-tangibles).

All RFPs should include a cover letter or e-mail specifying the deadline (date and time) for the responses. The cover letter or e-mail should also specify the format that is required for all responses. Some organizations request electronic submissions and may outsource the management of their RFP process to a third party. Some companies may request hard copies.

When establishing your RFP process, it's important to provide the supplier with a timeline. The timeline should include the following items:

1. Deadline for acknowledgment of participation in the RFP process
2. Deadline for supplier questions
3. Date for follow-up with supplier references (organizations request at least three to five references and often request a reference within their industry)
4. Date for electronic responses
5. Deadline for hard copy responses
6. Selection of finalists
7. Finalist presentations
8. Final decision

BEST PRACTICE #3: UTILIZE AN OBJECTIVE SUPPLIER EVALUATION AND SELECTION PROCESS

Responsibility: Procurement and Business Management

Use a standard template for the decision-making process. Most companies select three finalists to participate in a final presentation in which procurement and business management can participate and ask pertinent questions.

AP Tool 15: Eight Factors to Consider in the Supplier Selection Process

About This Tool: Besides the completion of the supplier scorecard, there are other factors to consider when finalizing your selection as included below.

1. The professionalism exhibited in all aspects by the supplier.
2. Quality standards that the supplier has achieved.
3. The supplier being able to deliver the solution on time.
4. Whether the supplier has the resources to handle your system implementation, or whether the supplier normally outsources the implementation to another firm.
5. Project management and implementation support required by your organization. Are additional resources needed?
6. The contract, costs, and payment terms offered.
7. The identification of additional value added services.
8. Supplier's references and current clients, particularly if they are in a similar industry or business sector to your organization.

BEST PRACTICE #4: OBTAIN A W-9 FORM FOR DOMESTIC SUPPLIERS AND A FORM W-8 FOR FOREIGN SUPPLIERS

Responsibility: Accounts Payable

The Foreign Account Tax Compliance Act (FATCA) established a new regime under Chapter 4 of the Internal Revenue Code for documentation of foreign entity payees and withholding from payments in the absence of certain documentation. These requirements are in addition to the documentation, withholding, and reporting required under Chapter 3 of the Code. FATCA compliance will be phased in, starting in 2013.

Some FATCA requirements will affect payers that make the types of payments reportable on Form 1099-MISC and Form 1042-S. Payers will need to update their procedures to ensure compliance with both sets of documentation and withholding requirements: the new rules for FATCA, and the previously existing rules for withholding at source on certain payments to nonresident alien individuals, foreign corporations, and other foreign entities.

BEST PRACTICE #5: PERFORM TIN MATCHING

Responsibility: Accounts Payable

When it comes to TIN matching, the name says it all. It's when businesses match a payee's tax identification number (TIN) against Internal Revenue Service (IRS) records. However, companies can encounter errors during the TIN matching process that could put the accounts payable process at risk of noncompliance with tax regulations.

The TIN is a nine-digit number assigned to individuals or companies by the IRS for tax purposes. There are five types of TINs: an employee identification number (EIN), social security numbers, individual taxpayer identification numbers (ITINs), adoption taxpayer identification numbers (ATINs), and preparer taxpayer identification numbers (PTINs).

Businesses are required to apply for an EIN for tax purposes. For individuals operating as a sole proprietor, a social security number, which is assigned by the Social Security Administration, is acceptable to use as a TIN.

Payers are required by the IRS to annually file a 1099 tax form for each payee; the form reports the annual income and tax withheld. TIN matching verifies that the tax identification of a business or individual matches the IRS database. Accounts payable usually obtains the TIN of a business or individual during the onboarding process by requiring a W-9, a tax form for the Request for Taxpayer Identification Number and Certification.

The concept of TIN matching sounds straightforward, but your accounts payable needs to have protocols for handling common problems that come up in the TIN matching process. Otherwise, mishandling the issues will put your company at risk for tax noncompliance or fines.

BEST PRACTICE #6: PERFORM INITIAL COMPLIANCE SCREENING

Responsibility: Accounts Payable

The Supplier Compliance Roadmap will provide much more detail of all the compliance requirements to consider when both setting up a new supplier on the master file and when completing the ongoing screening process. Here are some recommendations for the basic screening process.

> **OFAC** – Office of Foreign Asset Control
> **BIS** – Bureau of Industry and Security
> **SDNs** – Specially Designated Nationals (SDNs) are considered enemies of the United States. They can be either organizations or individuals who are involved in drug trafficking, terrorism, or other illegal activities.

BEST PRACTICE # 7: PERFORM ONGOING COMPLIANCE SCREENING

Responsibility: Account Payable

The OFAC, BIS, and SDN lists are updated regularly. This means that a supplier that was screened during the initial setup may appear on a "watch list" during this phase of the lifecycle.

As a best practice, the compliance screening should be performed on a quarterly basis. However, some organizations have linked their compliance screening efforts to a "Monthly Letter of Commitment" that was implemented at the CEO level. This is a great example of linking compliance efforts to the "tone at the top."

BEST PRACTICE #8: FINE-TUNE YOUR SUPPLIER MASTER

Responsibility: Accounts Payable and Procurement

An effort to fine-tune or "clean up" your supplier master should be initiated annually.

AP TOOL 21: FIVE STEPS TO USE WHEN "FINE-TUNING" YOUR SUPPLIER MASTER FILE

Eliminate Inactive Suppliers

The periodic elimination of an inactive supplier increases processor keying speed, reduces errors, and will likely enhance system response time. The recommended timeframe for purging suppliers are those with no invoice activity within the prior 18 months (covers seasonality and retains those suppliers billing once-a-year). The timeframe retained should coincide with the paid invoice data that is retained for online inquiry. Most ERP systems have the capability to purge inactive suppliers, but due to infrequent use, the system staff may not be confident in its usage. For invoice processors, removing inactive suppliers speeds keying by offering fewer supplier choices, and reduces the potential for selecting an outdated or incorrect supplier number. From a system response time, reducing the supplier base can significantly reduce the run-time for any report that extracts data from the supplier master file. It is critical to check with your purchasing counterparts as suppliers that are linked to open purchase orders on file often cannot be purged.

Remove Duplicate Suppliers

Duplicate suppliers are an exposure for any accounts payable organization, but represent an increased risk for an organization that has absorbed multiple locations and/or systems into a centralized operation. Duplicate suppliers increase the likelihood of duplicate payments, and intensify the difficulty in compiling a comprehensive spend profile for supplier negotiations (i.e. "IBM," "I.B.M.," or "International Business Machines," etc.).

In efforts to prevent duplicate suppliers from reappearing, we recommend that the supplier creation process require a lookup by the supplier address prior to adding new suppliers. This will minimize adding redundant suppliers at the source, particularly when the names or initials would be keyed slightly differently.

Perform a Comparison of Your Supplier Master File Against Your Employee Master File

As part of the annual fine-tuning process, we recommend that you compare your supplier master file against your employee master file. This comparison should include a review of the following fields:

- Supplier Name and Employee Name
- Supplier TIN/EIN and Employee SSN
- Supplier Address and Employee Address
- Supplier ACH Account and Employee ACH Account
- Supplier Phone Number and Employee Phone Number

Consolidate Multiple Remittance Addresses

Many of your larger suppliers will have multiple remit-to locations. These addresses are often geographically placed to expedite the flow of funds into the supplier's operation, or can be a function of the supplier's ownership structure. Those suppliers with significant remittance addresses often include those operating in the areas of telecom, waste management, industrial parts, post offices, computers, and more.

Many companies have been successful in persuading suppliers to accept all payments to one remittance address (regardless of division). The savings can be fairly significant for both parties, as the supplier realizes administrative savings by having fewer people handling incoming remittances. An additional benefit is the ability to more easily capture all payment activity through one supplier number for use in negotiating company-wide purchasing agreements. This is an initiative best pursued with procurement, as they can potentially make the one remittance address a condition of doing business with your company.

Pursue Strategic Sourcing

When the supplier master tune-up has been completed, this is a good opportunity to pursue a strategic sourcing initiative. With few exceptions, Fortune 1000 organizations are burdened with an oversized base of suppliers. Given that the average Fortune 1000 company buys approximately 400–500 commodities and maintains a global supplier base of over 50,000 suppliers, this means that there is an average of over 100 suppliers per commodity. This is clearly not optimal from a procurement or accounts payable standpoint. Those organizations that have successfully optimized their supply base have addressed the following challenges:

Senior management understands and supports the quantified impact that an aggressive strategic sourcing program has on earnings per share;

The procurement organization has created the necessary systems to capture global spending, and routinely quantifies the financial savings from sourcing projects;

Preferred supplier agreements are in place for 80% or more of the organization's common purchases; and

The proper structure and/or incentives have been implemented to ensure employees buy only from preferred suppliers, and that negotiated prices are adhered to.

The steps for the strategic sourcing process are defined in the following diagram.

The Strategic Sourcing Process

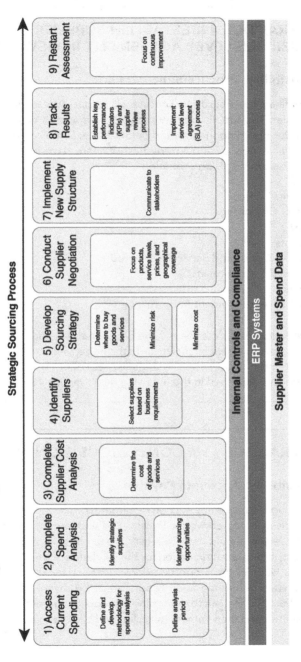

Strategic Sourcing Process

1) Access Current Spending
- Define and develop methodology for spend analysis
- Define analysis period

2) Complete Spend Analysis
- Identify strategic suppliers
- Identify sourcing opportunities

3) Complete Supplier Cost Analysis
- Determine the cost of goods and services

4) Identify Suppliers
- Select suppliers based on business requirements

5) Develop Sourcing Strategy
- Determine where to buy goods and services
- Minimize risk
- Minimize cost

6) Conduct Supplier Negotiation
- Focus on products, service levels, prices, and geographical coverage

7) Implement New Supply Structure
- Communicate to stakeholders

8) Track Results
- Establish key performance indicators (KPIs) and supplier review process
- Implement service level agreement (SLA) process

9) Restart Assessment
- Focus on continuous improvement

Internal Controls and Compliance

ERP Systems

Supplier Master and Spend Data

BEST PRACTICE #9: ESTABLISH SUPPLIER AND SERVICE-LEVEL AGREEMENT REVIEWS

Responsibility: Procurement

A well-defined supplier review process will help to access the performance of a supplier. The supplier review should be conducted on an annual basis and includes the components listed below. **Note:** Some companies perform the supplier review on a quarterly basis if there have been performance issues or the supplier is on probation.

- Customer Service
- Contract Compliance
- Pricing
- Discounts
- Quality of Goods and Services Delivered
- Supplier Risk Assessment
- Financial
- Service Level Agreement Performance

Two factors will determine if the supplier status should be moved to probation or exit. These factors include the negative outcome of a supplier review (as noted above) and the negative results of the continuous monitoring process described in the following Best Practice #10.

BEST PRACTICE #10: CONTINUOUS MONITORING

Responsibility: Accounts Payable

The continuous supplier transaction monitoring process includes a review of the controls as noted above for the supplier onboarding phase of the lifecycle. The review should entail selecting a sample of suppliers and reviewing the supporting documentation for the validation of a new supplier . . . as well as validation of the supporting documentation for changes of address.

All system-generated audit reports must be reviewed – not only for segregation of duties, but to determine if a supplier address has been fraudulently altered and then immediately changed back to the original address.

What Are Examples of Suspicious Invoice Attributes?

The continuous monitoring process should include a review of the invoice attributes throughout the process to determine if specific suppliers may have fraudulent activities. Common suspicious attributes include:

Consecutive invoice numbering. An individual supplier with consecutive invoice numbering is a red flag because it is unlikely that the supplier is providing goods and services to another customer.

First payment is small relative to average. If the first payment issued to a supplier is unusually small relative to the average payment for its product or service, this transaction should be assigned "risk points." Many fraudulent suppliers are established based on a $50–$100 initial invoice. Larger invoices will follow once the supplier is added to the supplier master file.

Benford's Law anomalies. Benford's Law is a well-known audit technique used to flag questionable patterns of activity. Intuitively, one would expect a range of numbers to begin with each digit 10% of the time (10% for 0, 10% for 1, 10% for 2, etc.). Benford discovered that when testing groups of transactions from various unrelated sources, a mathematical phenomenon confirms that about 30% of the numbers have 1 as the first digit, 18% have 2, and only 5% have 9. If the numbers for an individual supplier do not conform to this established pattern (+/– a certain percentage), it may indicate that the non-conforming transactions are fraudulent

Unusual spending increases. Suppliers that have experienced significant year-over-year increases in spending levels should be analyzed to ensure that fraudulent activities are not occurring.

What Are the Benefits of Continuous Monitoring?

Continuous monitoring on a real-time basis quickly identifies a potentially fraudulent supplier and validates that supplier master set-up controls are working properly. If there is a concern about a specific supplier, it is important to raise the issue with your internal controls or internal audit department after performing an evaluation of internal controls within the P2P process. This process will determine if the control is operating as defined. If a control weakness is identified, immediately adjust the control and increase the sample size of the test.

ANOTHER LOOK AT SUPPLIER MASTER FILE MANAGEMENT BEST PRACTICES

Now that we've described the top ten best practices in supplier management, we'll focus on the details of supplier validation. The basic components of a supplier validation process are depicted in the graphic below. We have identified nine components that should be considered during the supplier validation lifecycle and to ensure supplier management compliance.

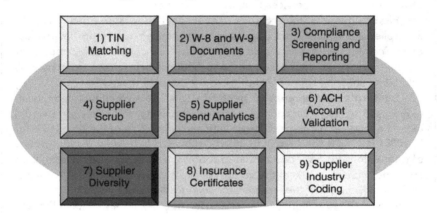

What Is TIN Matching?

TIN Matching is service provided by the IRS through their eServices offering. As noted as a best practice, it is important to match the TIN provided on the supplier's W-9 with the TIN on file with the IRS. The matching can either be performed in an interactive session or by bulk loading your supplier master file.

Benefits:
- Ensures 1099 accuracy.
- Eliminates B-Notices.
- Provides fraud prevention since the matching process ensures suppliers are "legitimate."
- The TIN Matching process can identify duplicate suppliers and can be a catalyst for cleaning up your supplier master file.

What Is the Importance of W-8 and W-9 Documents?

The W-8 form is required for all foreign suppliers. There are many variations of the W-8 form such as W-8BEN and W-8ECI. In summary, the W-8 is an IRS form that grants an exemption from certain US information return reporting and backup withholding regulations.

The W-9 applies to a person or supplier who is required to file an information return with the IRS and must obtain the correct taxpayer identification number (TIN) to report. For example: income paid, real estate transactions, mortgage interest paid, acquisition or abandonment of secured property, cancellation of debt, or contributions you made to an IRA. The W-9 is the audit trail to provide substantive proof for the items listed here:

1. Certify that the TIN you are giving is correct (or you are waiting for a number to be issued);
2. Certify that the supplier is not subject to backup withholding; or
3. Claim exemption from backup withholding if the supplier is a US exempt payee. If applicable, you are also certifying that as a US person, your allocable share of any partnership income from a US trade or business is not subject to the withholding tax on foreign partners' share of effectively connected income.

Benefits:
- Provides an audit trail that reflects your supplier's TIN information
- Provides proof of exemption from backup withholding
- Backup documentation for an erroneous B-Notice and during an IRS audit

Why Is the "Supplier Scrub" Process So Important?

To keep your supplier master in control, we recommend a periodic "scrub" of supplier master file records. Performing the scrub process on a quarterly basis is a recommended best practice, but many companies perform the process on an annual basis when they fine-tune their supplier master file. However, the frequency of the review process can be determined by a merger and acquisition activity or a recent supplier fraud. The supplier scrub should include the following components.

Recommended Supplier Scrub Components:
- Duplicate Supplier Names
- Suppliers with Duplicate Street Addresses
- Suppliers with Duplicate PO Boxes
- Suppliers with Duplicate Phone or FAX Numbers
- Suppliers with Duplicate TINs

Benefits:
- Provides enhanced internal controls for your supplier master file
- Identifies duplicate and potentially fraudulent suppliers

What Are Some Key Supplier Spend Analytics?

Spend analytics focuses on the analysis of accounts payable transactions by dollar distribution and the stratification of spending levels. Key analytics include:

Suppler Analytics:
- Top 30 Suppliers with Invoice Amounts of $0–150
- Top 30 Suppliers with Invoice Amounts of $0–50
- Top 30 Suppliers with Invoice Amounts of $50–100
- Top 30 Suppliers with Invoice Amounts of $100–150
- Invoice Payment Dollar Distribution
- Accounts Payable Year-to-Year Analysis
- Accounts Payable Transactions by Month
- Top 50 Suppliers by Transaction
- Top 50 Suppliers by Dollars

Benefits:
- Identifies transactional volumes
- Provides the analysis to develop a sourcing strategy
- Identifies maverick spending
- Spotlights accounts payable productivity
- Highlights opportunities for invoice automation, summary billing, and the implementation of P-Cards

Validating Your Supplier's Bank Account

ACH account validation is the most efficient if ACH account information is maintained in the supplier master file. Accounts payable should verify the ACH account number with the bank to confirm the account number provided by the supplier. In many cases, banks use the same ABA or check routing number as their ACH number. As an additional verification, we advise comparing employee master against supplier master bank accounts to determine if there are any matches which could indicate a potential fraud. A quarterly comparison is a best practice.

Benefits:
- Prevents payment fraud and ensures that funds are disbursed to the correct supplier bank account
- Provides an enhancement to current payment controls

Case Study: Condé Nast Pays a Fraudulent Supplier

The fraud was first reported by Forbes in early April 2011 after Conde Nast filed a forfeiture lawsuit with the U.S. Attorney's office in New York to try to regain the money. The lawsuit indicates that Andy Surface, the scammer, opened a bank account in Texas in the name of Quad Graph. Conde Nast works with Quad/Graphics, a publicly traded company that prints Conde Nast magazines. Surface sent an email to Conde Nast with an electronic payment authorization PDF form attached, instructing payments to be made to the Quad Graph account. A Conde Nast employee accepted the email as legitimate, and signed and faxed back the form, allowing its bank to make electronic transfer payments to the fraudulent account.[1]

Surface's account had received $8 million from Conde Nast over a six-week stretch before the scam was revealed. The publishing company quickly contacted federal authorities, who froze the account before Surface was able to withdraw the money. This incident illustrates how simple it is to commit cybercrime for potentially huge gains, with a simple e-mail and social engineering tactics and why controls need to be in place for both the supplier onboarding process and the payment process. (See Chapter 15 for additional details and suggested controls.)

What Is a Supplier Diversity Program?

Many companies have supplier diversity programs. These programs, also referred to as minority-owned business enterprise or MBE programs are intended to help large corporations do business with smaller companies owned by African, Hispanic, and Asian Americans.

A supplier diversity program is a proactive business program which encourages the use of minority-owned, women-owned, veteran-owned, LGBT-owned [1], service-disabled veteran-owned, historically underutilized business, and Small Business Administration (SBA) – defined small business concerns [1] as suppliers. It is not directly correlated with supply chain diversification, although utilizing more vendors may enhance supply chain diversification. Supplier diversity programs recognize that sourcing products and services from previously underused suppliers helps to sustain and progressively transform a company's supply chain, thus quantitatively

---

[1]Stu Sjouwerman, "Conde Nast Caught in $8 Million Spear-Phishing Scam," KnowBe4, April 21, 2020, accessed July 16, 2020, https://blog.knowbe4.com/bid/252040/conde-nast-caught-in-8-million-spear-phishing-scam.

reflecting the demographics of the community in which it operates by recording transactions with diverse suppliers.[2]

What Are Examples of Best Practices for Supplier Diversity Programs?

The effectiveness of supplier diversity programs varies widely, depending on whether the company wants to use theirs as a strategic means to lower their bottom-line costs and improve profitability, or only as a public relations vehicle to demonstrate corporate social responsibility. Here are some of the characteristics of the best practices for supplier diversity programs:

1. Clearly documented commitment from the company's CEO
2. Specific annual goals for purchasing from minority owned businesses
3. Attainment of the goals tied to the compensation and performance plans of senior management
4. Inclusion of supplier diversity in a strategic plan for diversity
5. Head of the supplier diversity program is at the senior management level or above, and has control over corporate purchasing
6. Consideration of minority owned businesses included as a formal part of the contracting procurement process
7. Second-tier subcontracting to minority owned businesses also included as part of that process and written into the prime supplier's contract
8. A comprehensive database of minority owned businesses that is actively maintained and integrated into the purchasing process
9. Purchasing system that tracks supplier diversity performance and can target specific contracts for additional focus, outreach, or consideration
10. Visibility on the company's Internet website, including program details, contacts, and list of products and services purchased
11. Strategic partnerships with ethnic chambers, publishers, and other organizations that can assist in outreach

 AP TOOL 22: SUPPLIER DIVERSITY

About This Tool: Supplier diversity is a business program that encourages the use of: diverse-owned, women-owned, veteran-owned, LGBT-owned,

---

[2]Supplier Diversity, Wikipedia, accessed July 16, 2020, https://en.wikipedia.org/wiki/Supplier_diversity#:~:text=APercent20SupplierPercent20DiversityPercent20programPercent20is,small Percent20businessPercent20concernsPercent20asPercent20suppliers.

service-disabled veteran–owned, historically underutilized business, and SBA-defined small business suppliers as suppliers. As corporate social responsibility becomes more widely discussed, more organizations are asking purchasing departments to increase supplier diversity spend. Industry terms, certifications, and ownership classifications are provided in the following table.

Industry Terms, Certifications, and Ownership Classifications

Small Business Concern

The term "small business" means a business as defined pursuant to Section 3 of the Small Business Act and relevant regulations issued pursuant thereto. Generally, this means a small business organized for profit that is independently owned and operated, is not dominant in the field of operations in which it is bidding, and meets the size standards as prescribed in government regulations.

Large Business Concern

A business concern that exceeds the small business size code standards established by the SBA as set forth in the Code of Federal Regulations, Title 13, and Part 121.

Foreign Business

A business concern organized under the law of a country other than the United States, its territories or possessions and is not incorporated in the United States.

Non-profit Organization

Any organization not conducted or maintained for the purpose of making profit. Included in this category are sheltered workshops, universities, colleges, and local, state, and federal governments, NISH (Creating Employment Opportunities for People With Severe Disabilities), and NIB (National Industries for the Blind).

Historically Black College/University or Minority Institution (HBCU/MI)

Historically Black Colleges and Universities (HBCUs) are institutions that were established before 1964 and have a principal mission that was, and is, the education of Black Americans and that meet the requirements set forth in the Code of Federal Regulations (CFR), Title 34, and Part 608. Minority Institutions (MIs) are institutions that substantially increase the higher education opportunities for minority and/or low-income students education and meet the requirements set forth in Title 34 of the CFR, Part 607.2.

Ownership

Minority-Owned or Minority Business Enterprise (MBE)

A business concern that is at least 51% owned by one or more minorities; or, in the case of any publicly owned business, at least 51% of the stock is owned by one or more minorities; and whose management and daily business operations are controlled by one or more minorities.

SBA-Certified Small Disadvantaged Business Concerns (SDB)

A business certified by the SBA as a socially and economically small disadvantaged business. SBA certified SDB's include all SBA-8(a) certified SDBs (see following). SDBs must provide a copy of their certification letter from the SBA or a copy of their Central Contractor Registration profile showing SDB certification to a company procurement representation representative.

Self-Certified Small Disadvantaged Business Concern (SDB)

A "for profit" business concern: that qualifies as "small" per the SBA Table of Small Business Size Standards Matched to North American Industry Classification System Codes, and that is at least 51% unconditionally owned by one or more US citizens who are socially and economically disadvantaged individuals, and whose management and daily business operations are controlled by one or more US citizens who are socially and economically disadvantaged individuals, and the personal net worth of each individual claiming economic disadvantage is less than $750,000 (except for tribes, Alaskan Native Corporation-Owned Concern (ANCs), Community Development Corporation-Owned Concern (CDCs), and Native Hawaiian Corporation-Owned Concern (NHOs). Note: ANCs, NHOs, or CDCs, must meet the "ownership," "management," and "control" criteria in Title 13 of the Code of Federal Regulations, Part 124.109, 124.110, and 124.111, respectively.

SBA-8(a) Small Disadvantaged Business Concerns (SDB)

A business certified by the SBA as a socially and economically small disadvantaged business for consideration of government set-aside contracting opportunities and business development. SDB-8(a)s must include a copy of their certification letter from the SBA or a copy of their Central Contractor Registration profile showing SDB certification to a company procurement representative.

HUBZone Small Business Concerns

A business concern located in a "historically underutilized business zone," owned and controlled by one or more US Citizens, and at least 35% of its employees must reside in a HUB Zone. It must appear on the list of Qualified HUBZone Small Business Concerns maintained by the SBA.

Women-Owned or Women Business Enterprise

A business concern that is at least 51% owned by one or more women, or, in the case of any publicly owned business, at least 51% of the stock is owned by one or more women, and whose management and daily business operations are controlled by one or more women.

Women-Owned Small Business Concerns (WOSB)

A small business concern that is at least 51% owned by one or more women, or in the case of any publicly owned business, at least 51% of the stock is owned by one or more women, and whose management and daily business operations are controlled by one or more women.

Veteran (V)

A person who served in the active military, naval, or air service, and who was discharged or released there from under conditions other than dishonorable as defined in title 38 of the U.S.C., section 101 (2).

Service-Disabled Veteran (SDV)

A veteran with a "service connected" disability, which means a disability that was incurred or aggravated, in the line of duty in the active military, naval, or air service as defined in Title 38, of the U.S.C., section 101 (16).

Veteran-Owned Small Business Concerns (VOSB)

A small business concern that is at least 51% owned by one or more veterans, or in the case of any publicly owned business, at least 51% of the stock is owned by one or more veterans, and whose management and daily business operations are controlled by one or more veterans.

Service-Disabled Veteran–Owned Small Business Concerns (SDVOSB)

A small business concern that is at least 51% owned by one or more service-disabled veterans, or in the case of any publicly owned business, at least 51% of the stock is owned by one or more service-disabled veterans, and whose management and daily business operations are controlled by one or more service-disabled veterans or a permanent caregiver of a service-disabled veteran with permanent and severe disability.

Ethnicity/Minority Categories

Asian Pacific American

Persons with origins from Burma, Thailand, Malaysia, Indonesia, Singapore, Brunei, Japan, China (including Hong Kong), Taiwan, Laos, Cambodia (Kampuchea), Vietnam, Korea, The Philippines, US Trust Territory of the Pacific Islands (Republic of Palau), Republic of the Marshall Islands, Federated States of Micronesia, the Commonwealth of the Northern Mariana Islands, Guam, Samoa, Macao, Fiji, Tonga, Kiribati, Tuvalu, or Nauru.

African American

Persons having origins in any of the black racial groups of Africa.

Hispanic American

Persons of Cuban, Mexican, Puerto Rican, South or Central American, or other Spanish culture or origin, regardless of race.

Native American

American Indians, Eskimos, Aleuts or Native Hawaiians.

Subcontinent Asian American

Persons with origins from India, Pakistan, Bangladesh, Sri Lanka, Bhutan, the Maldives Islands, or Nepal

Obtaining Insurance Certificates from Your Suppliers

An insurance certificate is a document issued by an insurance company/broker that is used to verify the existence of insurance coverage under specific conditions granted to listed individuals. More specifically, the document lists the effective date of the policy, the type of insurance coverage purchased, and the types and dollar amount of applicable liability.

Benefits:
- Provides the insurance coverage of the supplier
- Highlights a potential risk for under-insured suppliers

Suppliers and Industry Codes

The North American Industry Classification System or NAICS is used by business and government to classify business establishments according to type of economic activity (process of production) in Canada, Mexico, and the United States. It has largely replaced the older Standard Industrial Classification (SIC) system; however, certain government departments and agencies, such as the US Securities and Exchange Commission (SEC), still use the SIC codes.

Benefits:
- Industry coding enables spend analysis, and identifies opportunities for strategic sourcing across your supplier master file.
- Industry coding can be combined with commodity coding as a prerequisite of strategic sourcing which is considered one of the ten best practices for supplier management. Strategic sourcing analysis identifies opportunities to leverage pricing with your suppliers and can help reduce the number of suppliers in your master file.

 ## AP TOOL 23: EIGHT CRITICAL SUPPLIER MASTER PRACTICES

About This Tool: The supplier master file is an integral part of the procurement and accounts payable control environments. Responsibilities for the supplier master, including the set-up and maintenance process, generally resides with the accounts payable department.

A well-maintained supplier master file helps prevent failure of system controls, process inefficiencies, and inaccurate management reporting. Failure of system controls can result in duplicate and erroneous payments, missed earned discounts, uncashed checks, unapplied credits, tax reporting errors, pricing errors, and fraud. P2P consultants have identified eight critical practices that should be in place when establishing the process and controls for supplier master files:

1. Define Ownership
2. Engage System Access Controls
3. Establish Clear Supplier Setup Procedures
4. Enforce New Supplier Approval Practices
5. Determine When Multiple Supplier Records Will Be Allowed

6. Manage One-Time Supplier Accounts Separately
7. Apply Consistent Naming Conventions
8. Enforce Data Validation

The following table provides more detail for these important practices.

Eight Critical Supplier Master Practices

1. **Define Ownership.** Defining a data owner helps ensure accountability and responsibility for the accuracy and integrity of the supplier master file. Ideally the supplier master file data owner should be someone with sufficient accounts payable process and procedures experience.

2. **Engage System Access Controls.** Many accounts payable software packages have the ability to limit access to the supplier master file based on user IDs, passwords, and other controls. Password standards can be defined on password length, complexity, frequency of required change, and other restrictions. Access can be granted to read-only, or change and update supplier master file data.

3. **Establish Clear Supplier Setup Procedures.** The policies and procedures for supplier setup should be clearly documented. The use of a standard form or format will help ensure consistency and compliance with policies and procedures and naming conventions.

4. **Enforce New Supplier Approval Practices.** Sufficient due diligence procedures should be in place requiring review and evaluation of new supplier criteria (financial and operational) prior to accepting a new supplier.

5. **Determine When Multiple Supplier Records Will Be Allowed.** While it is preferred to have each supplier listed only once in the supplier master file, policies and procedures should outline when and under what circumstances it is allowable to have multiple records.

6. **Management One-Time Supplier Accounts Separately.** Allowing the use of one-time suppliers increases the risk of duplicate payments and should be discouraged. However, if it is necessary to accommodate one-time suppliers, then it should be done only under close review and limitations (dollar amount and volume of transactions).

7. **Apply Consistent Naming Conventions.** One of the simplest way to help ensure accuracy and integrity of the supplier master file is to establish naming conventions and make sure that everyone responsible for data entry is adequately trained on entering and maintaining suppliers.

8. Enforce Data Validation. While many accounts payable software packages contain data validation editing to help ensure the accuracy of data input to the system, a suggested best practice is to have a quality assurance function where someone separate from data entry review key data entry fields for accuracy prior to updating the supplier master file.

AP TOOL 24: MANAGING THE SUPPLIER MASTER FILE

About This Tool: The supplier master file isn't just a key source of corporate information. It's also a core business asset that directly impacts the effectiveness of procure-to-pay transactional controls. Here are suggested best practices.

Managing Your Supplier Master File

1. Maintain Systems and Policies on a Regular Basis. Since suppliers' names and addresses change, it is important for the supplier master file data owner to ensure updates are made on a timely basis. Reviews should be at least on an annual basis to look for inactive, duplicate, and incomplete supplier information. A basic fraud detection technique is to compare employee address files to supplier remit-to address files and look for matches that could potentially indicate a fraudulent supplier.

2. Remove Old/Unused Suppliers from the System. It is considered a best practice to keep the supplier master file up to date. However, it is important to understand the limitations and requirement of the organization's accounts payable system prior to deleting any suppliers, especially if the system links to archived transactional records. A best practice used by several Fortune 500 companies to review and purge duplicate supplier records on an annual basis when there has been no activity for 18 months.

3. Retaining the Right Records. Develop a record retention policy that is incompliance with federal, state, and local legal and regulatory requirements. Ensure that the supplier master file is in compliance with this policy.

STANDARDS OF INTERNAL CONTROL: SUPPLIER SELECTION AND MANAGEMENT

Internal Control	Type of Internal Control	Risks Mitigated
7.A Purchasing Strategies. Sourcing strategies, supplier selections, and contract negotiations processes should be developed and documented. **Refer to risks: 7-1, 7-2, 7-3, 7-4**	**Preventive** **Organizational**	**7-1 Unapproved Suppliers.** A purchase may be made from an unapproved supplier. **7-2 Export control violations, related party transactions, or conflict of interest situations may occur.** The potential for errors and irregularities is substantially increased. **7-3 Goods purchased may not meet quality standards.** Unauthorized prices or terms may be accepted. **7-4 Unable to Leverage Purchasing Power.** The company will not have sufficient information to conduct meaningful negotiations and utilize its full purchasing power.
7.B Documented Supplier Selection. Purchasing has established and follows documented policies and procedures to qualify and evaluate suppliers based on established criteria prior to becoming approved. **Refer to risks: 7-1, 7-2, 7-3, 7-4, 7-5**	**Preventive** **Organizational** **Policy** **Procedure**	**7-1 Unapproved Suppliers.** A purchase may be made from an unapproved supplier. **7-2 Export control violations, related party transactions, or conflict of interest situations may occur.** The potential for errors and irregularities is substantially increased.

(Continued)

Internal Control	Type of Internal Control	Risks Mitigated
		7-3 Goods purchased may not meet quality standards. Unauthorized prices or terms may be accepted.
		7-4 Unable to Leverage Purchasing Power. The company will not have sufficient information to conduct meaningful negotiations and utilize its full purchasing power.
		7-5 Material Planning Issues. Materials may be received early or late resulting in business interruption or excess levels of inventory.
7.C Purchasing from Approved Suppliers. Purchases must be made from an approved supplier database/list in accordance with local procedures. A formal process should be in place to approve purchases from suppliers not on the approved database. The supplier database must be reviewed, updated, and purged of inactive suppliers (i.e. suppliers with no activity for 18–24 months) at least annually. Suppliers should be added to the supplier database upon completion of supplier selection process and financial review. **Refer to risks: 7-1, 7-2, 7-3, 7-4**	Preventive Organizational Policy Procedure	**7-1 Unapproved Suppliers.** A purchase may be made from an unapproved supplier.
		7-2 Export control violations, related party transactions, or conflict of interest situations may occur. The potential for errors and irregularities is substantially increased.
		7-3 Goods purchased may not meet quality standards. Unauthorized prices or terms may be accepted.
		7-4 Unable to Leverage Purchasing Power. The company will not have sufficient information to conduct meaningful negotiations and utilize its full purchasing power.

Internal Control	Type of Internal Control	Risks Mitigated
7.D Global and Regional Contracts. Where global, regional, or geographic contracts are in place (e.g. Information Technology), that contract will be leveraged by all affected operating units. **Refer to risks: 7-1, 7-2, 7-3, 7-4**	Preventive Organizational Policy Procedure	**7-1 Unapproved Suppliers.** A purchase may be made from an unapproved supplier. **7-2 Export control violations, related party transactions, or conflict of interest situations may occur.** The potential for errors and irregularities is substantially increased. **7-3 Goods purchased may not meet quality standards.** Unauthorized prices or terms may be accepted. **7-4 Unable to Leverage Purchasing Power.** The company will not have sufficient information to conduct meaningful negotiations and utilize its full purchasing power.
7.E Business Interruption Contingency Plans. Supplier and sourcing strategies must take into consideration contingency plans to address or minimize risk of business interruption. These plans should be regularly reviewed and simulated. **Refer to risk: 7-5**	Preventive Organizational Policy Procedure	**7-5 Material Planning Issues.** Materials may be received early or late resulting in business interruption or excess levels of inventory.
7.F Supplier Performance Monitoring. Suppliers must be periodically monitored in accordance with Business Unit policy to ensure that	Detective Preventive Organizational Policy Procedure	**7-3 Goods purchased may not meet quality standards.** Unauthorized prices or terms may be accepted. **7-5 Material Planning Issues.** Materials may be received early or late resulting in business interruption or excess levels of inventory.

(Continued)

Internal Control	Type of Internal Control	Risks Mitigated
actual performance meets the Quality, Delivery, Product/Technology, Service and Support, and Cost expectations. **Refer to risks: 7-3, 7-5, 7-6**		**7-6 Supplier base doesn't meet the needs of the company.** Lose opportunity to revise supplier base to better meet the needs of the company.
7.G Supplier Master Updates and Periodic Screening: Regulatory Compliance and TIN Matching. (1) The actual update of approved supplier master/ lists must be performed by individuals not involved in supplier selection process. (2) The appropriate compliance screening must be completed to ensure that the organization is protected. Compliance screening should include: Office of Foreign Asset Control (OFAC), Bureau of Industry and Security (BIS), Office of Inspector General (OIG) (health care), System for Award Management (SAMS), and Foreign Corrupt Practices Act (FCPA). (3) All new suppliers must provide a tax identification number (TIN) and a W-9 which will be verified with IRS records. (4) Periodic compliance screening and TIN matching should take place on a monthly to quarterly basis to ensure that there are no issues with previously screened suppliers. **Refer to risks: 7-1, 7-2, 7-3, 7-5, 7-7, 7-8**	Detective Preventive Organizational Policy Procedure	**7-1 Unapproved Suppliers.** A purchase may be made from an unapproved supplier. **7-2 Export control violations, related party transactions, or conflict of interest situations may occur.** The potential for errors and irregularities is substantially increased. **7-3 Goods purchased may not meet quality standards.** Unauthorized prices or terms may be accepted. **7-4 Unable to Leverage Purchasing Power.** The company will not have sufficient information to conduct meaningful negotiations and utilize its full purchasing power. **7-5 Material Planning Issues.** Materials may be received early or late resulting in business interruption or excess levels of inventory. **7-7 Regulatory Compliance Fines.** The company may be faced with significant fines from non-compliance with regulatory requirements. **7-8 Fraudulent Suppliers.** Fraudulent suppliers may be established on the company's supplier master file.

CHAPTER EIGHT

Contract Management

 INTRODUCTION

The term "contract" often refers to a written agreement, typically including some or all of the following elements as included below.

1. Introductory material (sometimes known as "recitals" or "whereas provisions")
2. Definitions of key terms
3. A statement of the purpose or purposes of the agreement
4. The obligations of each party (and conditions that may trigger obligations)
5. Assurances as to various aspects of agreement (sometimes phrased as warranties, representations, or covenants)
6. A signature block
7. Exhibits or attachments

"Contract" is a noun, but it can be used as a verb, too. When you contract with a supplier or contractor, you participate in a process that typically involves three phases.

■ **Phase 1: Contemplating the deal.** The parties each assess the prospective arrangement and its risks.

■ **Phase 2: Reaching an agreement.** During this phase the parties negotiate and agree on the terms, usually formalized in a written contract or some other documented evidence of the arrangement.

■ **Phase 3: Performance and enforcement.** Once the contract is in place, the parties are legally required to perform their mutual obligations. If one party fails to perform, the other can sue to enforce the deal. Service-level agreements or SLAs are usually agreed upon and implemented to ensure performance.

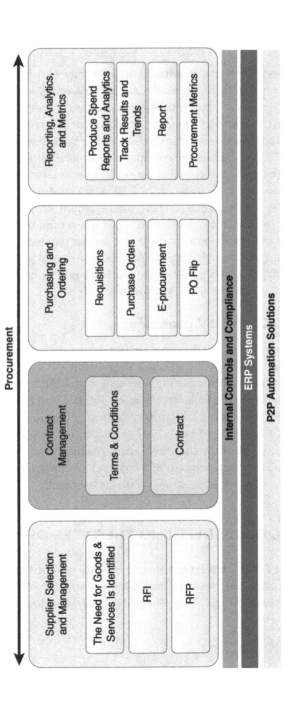

Contract Management Process Flow

CONTRACT MANAGEMENT PROCESS INSIGHTS

Companies today face many obstacles when it comes to effective contract automation and management. Manual and outdated systems, non-standard terms and a lack of consistent procedures are just a few. In order to control contracting costs and improve performance, companies need a system that manages all phases of the contract lifecycle: from offer development to go-live to amendments and renewals. Contract lifecycle management must also integrate seamlessly with pricing execution and enable convenient analysis and decision making.

Contracts are the foundation of B2B relationships, yet many companies still lack effective contract lifecycle management processes. They manage contract authoring and execution using simple templates, spreadsheets, and "track changes" functionality. Without an automated workflow, contract approvals can be delayed, putting revenue at risk and jeopardizing business relationships. Lack of visibility into contract milestones and other obligations can also impair business performance.

The Basic Contract Agreement

A contract agreement is a document between two or more parties that outlines the responsibilities of each party and states what value or payment they will exchange for the performance of those obligations. Although a valid contract sometimes can be made verbally, the safest practice is to get terms in writing.

The basic elements of a contract are an offer, an acceptance and an exchange of something of value. To be valid, a contract must outline each of these elements and show that the parties reached an agreement. By understanding the basic requirements of a contract and paying attention to writing terms clearly, you can write simple contracts yourself.

 AP TOOL 25: DEFINING THE TYPES OF CONTRACTS

About This Tool: Contract types are generally grouped into two broad categories: fixed price contracts and cost-reimbursement contracts. The details for these two types of contracts are reflected in the table below.

Contract Type	Description	Variations
Fixed Price Contracts	**Fixed Price Contracts** ■ The contract price is not subject to any adjustments. ■ Places upon the contractor maximum risk and full responsibility for all costs and resulting profit. ■ A fixed-price contract provides a maximum incentive for the contractor to control costs and perform effectively. **Firm-Fixed-Price Contracts** ■ These contracts are used when a sealed bid is required. ■ This type of fixed-price contract may also be used when acquiring supplies and services or for acquiring commercial items.	1. **Economic Price Adjustments** ■ Revision of prices for specific contingencies. ■ Adjustments based upon increases or decreases from an agreed upon level in either published or established market prices for specific items. ■ Adjustments based upon actual increases or decreases in the price of specific items of cost or specific labor that the contractor incurs. ■ Adjustments based upon increases or decreases in the specific labor or material cost standards or indexes, such as Bureau of Labor Standards indices. 2. **Fixed Price Incentive (FPI) Contracts** ■ An FPI contract specifies a target cost, a target profit, a price ceiling, and a profit adjustment formula. The FPI contract provides a profit motive for the contractor to perform efficiently from a cost perspective. If the supplier completes the contract while incurring less cost than was originally anticipated, the supplier will receive more profit.

(Continued)

Contract Type	Description	Variations
		■ Used when a firm-fixed-price contract is not appropriate. ■ Used when supplies/ services can be acquired at lower costs, with improved delivery or improved technical performance.
Cost-Reimbursement Contracts	**Cost-Reimbursement Contracts** ■ Provides for payment of allowable incurred costs, to the extent prescribed in the contract. ■ Establishes an estimate of total costs for the purpose of obligating funds and establishes a ceiling that the supplier may not exceed, except at his or her own risk. ■ Cost-reimbursement contracts place the least cost and performance risk on the supplier. ■ Cost-reimbursement contracts are suitable for use only when uncertainties involved in contract performance do not permit costs to be estimated with sufficient accuracy to use and type of fixed price contract. ■ Used for research and development contracts. Prohibited for the acquisition of commercial items. **An Example of a Cost Contract: Cost Plus Fixed Fee (CPFF)** ■ **CPFF**=Cost plus fixed fee. A detailed breakdown of estimated costs, both direct and indirect is provided, and the customer will allow certain specific dollar amount for profit and fee. ■ The supplier is allowed to invoice for actual costs incurred, or for actual costs paid for and due for reimbursement (depending on the contract terms), and each invoice may include a proportion of the fixed fee. ■ The supplier will not be allowed to bill for costs that exceed the agreed-on estimate without the advance approval which is not always granted.	1. **Cost Plus Incentive Fee** 2. **Cost Plus Award Fee** 3. **Time and Materials** ■ Direct labor hours at specified hourly rates. ■ Materials at cost. ■ Used only when not possible to estimate accurately the extent or duration of the work or to anticipate costs with any reasonable degree of confidence.

Contract Type	Description	Variations

Other Types of Contracts

Letter Contracts

- Written preliminary contractual instruments that authorize the contractor to begin immediately manufacturing supplies or performing services.
- A letter contract may be used when (1) the customer's interests demand that the contractor be given a binding commitment so that work can start immediately and (2) negotiating a definitive contract is not possible in sufficient time to meet the requirement.

Indefinite Delivery Contracts

- There are three types of indefinite delivery contracts: (1) definite quantity contracts, (2) requirements contracts, and (3) indefinite quantity contracts.

1. **Definite Quantity Contracts**

   Provides for the delivery of a definite quantity of specific supplies and service for a fixed period. Deliveries or performance to be scheduled at designated locations upon order. A definite quantity contract may be used when it can be determined in advance that a definite quantity of supplies or services will be required during the contract period; and the supplies or services are regularly available or will be available after a short lead time.

2. **Requirements Contract:**

   A requirements contract provides for filling all actual purchase requirements of designated customer activities for supplies or services during a specified contract period, with deliveries or performance to be scheduled by placing orders with the supplier. A requirements contract may be appropriate for acquiring any supplies or services when the customer anticipates recurring requirements but cannot predetermine the precise quantities of supplies or services that designated customer activities will need during a definite period.

3. **Indefinite Quantity**

   An indefinite quantity contract provides for an indefinite quantity, within stated limits, of supplies or services during a fixed period. Quantity limits may be stated as number of units or as dollar values.

AP TOOL 26: TEN RECOMMENDATIONS FOR ESTABLISHING CONTRACTS

About This Tool: Here are ten recommendations to use when creating and executing a contract.

1. **Get it in writing.**

    Although oral agreements are legal and binding in many situations, they're often difficult to enforce in court (and in some situations, they aren't enforceable at all). In the business world, most agreements should be in writing even if the law doesn't require it. A written agreement is less risky than an oral agreement, because you have a document that clearly spells out each party's rights and obligations in case of confusion or disagreement.

2. **Keep it simple.**

    Contrary to what most lawyers think, you don't need a lot of "heretofore" and "party of the first part" legalese to make a contract enforceable. Instead, create short, clear sentences with simple, numbered paragraph headings that alert the reader to what's in the paragraph.

3. **Deal with the right person.**

    Don't waste time negotiating a business agreement with a junior person who has to okay everything with the boss. If you sense that this is happening, politely but firmly request to be put in touch with the person in charge. Make sure the person you negotiate with has the authority to bind the business and has a vested interest in making sure the business performs its obligations under the agreement. If you're not sure who that is, ask. In a smaller business, it might be one of the owners; in a larger organization it might be a chief executive officer or chief operating officer.

4. **Identify each party correctly.**

    You'd be surprised how often businesspeople get this wrong and how important it is. You need to include the correct legal names of the parties to the contract so it's clear who is responsible for performing the obligations under the agreement (and against whom you have legal rights if things go wrong). For instance, if a business is organized as an LLC or a corporation, identify it by its correct legal name – including the Inc. or LLC suffix – not by the names of the people who are signing the agreement for the business.

5. **Spell out all of the details.**

The body of the agreement should spell out the rights and obligations of each party in detail. Don't leave anything out; if you discuss something verbally and shake on it but it's not in the contract, it will be next to impossible to enforce. In the world of contract law, judges (with a few exceptions) may only interpret a contract from its "four corners," not from what the parties said to each other. If you forget to include something, you can always create a short written amendment. Or, if you haven't signed the agreement, you can handwrite the change into the contract. If parties initial the change, it becomes part of the contract.

6. **Specify payment obligations.**

Specify who pays whom, when the payments must be made, and the conditions for making payments. As you might guess, money is often a contentious issue, so this part should be very detailed. If you're going to pay in installments or only when work is completed to your satisfaction, say so and list dates, times, and requirements. Consider including the method of payment as well.

7. **Agree on circumstances that terminate the contract.**

It makes sense to set out the circumstances under which the parties can terminate the contract. For instance, if one party misses too many important deadlines, the other party should have the right to terminate the contract without being on the hook legally for breaching (violating) the agreement.

8. **Agree on a way to resolve disputes.**

Write into your agreement what you and the other party will do if something goes wrong. You can decide that you will handle your dispute through arbitration or mediation instead of going to court, which takes up a lot of time and money.

9. **Pick a state law to govern the contract.**

If you and the other party are located in different states, you should choose only one of your state's laws to apply to the contract to avoid sticky legal wrangling later. In addition, you may want to specify where you will mediate, arbitrate, or bring legal actions under the contract. This will simplify your life if a dispute does crop up.

10. **Keep it confidential.**

Often, when one business hires another to perform a service, the other business will become privy to sensitive business information. Your agreement should contain mutual promises that each party will keep strictly confidential any business information it learns of while performing the contract.

Automating the Contract Management Process

Automating all phases of the contract lifecycle improves end-to-end visibility while enabling businesses to speed approval cycles and reduce performance risks. Greater visibility into contract processes significantly reduces the risk and exposure that complex agreements typically introduce.

Measuring Suppliers – The Service-Level Agreement (SLA) Process

An important step in the decision-making process is to establish a set of SLAs and internal control requirements that will establish performance expectations for the BPO.

A service-level agreement (SLA) is a negotiated agreement between two parties where one is the customer and the other is the actual service provider. This can be a legally binding formal or informal contract. An SLA should contain operating norms, which describe how the process is governed, managed, and controlled.

An SLA should also include a set of operating metrics that are reported on a monthly or basis. As an example, a good set of metrics for accounts payable is: cost per invoice, days payable outstanding, invoices paid on time, outstanding credit balances, paid credits, and number of suppliers on the supplier master file.

Contracts between the service provider and other third parties are often (incorrectly) called SLAs – because the level of service has been set by the (principal) customer, there can be no "agreement" between third parties; these agreements are simply a "contract."

SLAs have been used since the late 1980s by fixed line telecom operators as part of their contracts with their corporate customers. This practice has spread such that now it is common for a customer to engage a service provider by including a service-level agreement in a wide range of service contracts in practically all industries and markets. Internal departments (such as IT, HR, and real estate) in larger organizations have adopted the idea of using service-level agreements with their "internal" customers — users in other departments within the same organization. Other examples of when to use SLAs are included below.

SLA Performance Components

SLAs usually include the performance components that are listed below.

1. A definition of services
2. Performance measurement and metrics
3. Problem management expectations and cycle times
4. Roles and responsibilities
5. Warranties
6. Disaster recovery plans
7. Termination of agreement
8. Escalation clauses and cycle times

The Types of SLAs

1. **Customer-based SLA:** An agreement with an individual customer group, covering all the services they use. For example, an SLA between a supplier (IT service provider) and the finance department of a large organization for the services such as finance system, payroll system, billing system, procurement/purchase system, etc.
2. **Service-based SLA:** An agreement for all customers using the services being delivered by the service provider. Examples are provided here:
   a. A car service station offers a routine service to all the customers and offers certain maintenance as a part of offer with the universal charging.
   b. A mobile service provider offers a routine service to all the customers and offers certain maintenance as a part of offer with the universal charging.
   c. An e-mail system for the entire organization. There are chances of difficulties arising in this type of SLA as the level of the services being offered may vary for different customers (for example, head office staff may use high-speed LAN connections while local offices may have to use a lower speed leased line).
3. **Multilevel SLA:** The SLA is split into the different levels, each addressing different sets of customers for the same services within the same SLA.
4. **Corporate-level SLA:** The corporate-level SLA covers all the generic service-level management (often abbreviated as SLM) issues appropriate to every customer throughout the organization. These issues are likely to be less volatile and SLA reviews are less frequently required.

Developing an SLA Program

The following twelve questions should be considered when establishing an SLA program with a supplier.

1. Does the firm have a standard set of metrics?
2. Does the firm have an SLA process?
3. Previous experience and track record.
4. Obtain the SLAs and determine if they meet your needs and that they help achieve business objectives.
5. What corrective action is taken if the SLAs are not accomplished?
6. Suggest periodic status review meetings.
7. Does the contract have an "exit clause" for non-performance?
8. How is the process managed?
9. How are system or process changes addressed?
10. Is communication an issue?
11. What is the timeframe for implementation?
12. How is the implementation managed?

Additionally, the Shared Service and Outsourcing Network (SSON) recommends that the following items are included in the SLA process.

1. The processes to be included and the products and services of those processes.
2. A list of the processes which are out of scope at this point – to manage customer expectations.
3. Conditions of service availability – hours of opening, days of operation.
4. Service standards – times for delivery of services should be recorded in number of working days (rather than say 24 or 48 hours) to manage expectations and be clear about closures of operations for bank holidays or weekends.
5. A R-A-C-I matrix – to show who is Responsible, Accountable, needs to be Consulted, and Informed, regarding process steps. This ensures role clarity in completion of tasks.
6. Cost versus service trade-offs, to manage expectations about "workarounds" or "just as a favor" requests.
7. Clear escalation procedures and timelines so that when something goes wrong it can be resolved by the right person, in the right role, at the right time.

STANDARDS OF INTERNAL CONTROL: CONTRACT MANAGEMENT

Internal Control	Type of Control	Risks Mitigated
8.A Define the Contract Policy and Approval Process. Establish a signature approval process for all company commitment and contracts. Usually, the legal department approves all contracts before implementation. **Refer to risks: 8-1, 8-2, 8-3, 8-4**	Manual Policy Preventive Procedure	**8-1 Unapproved and Fraudulent Suppliers.** Contracts are initiated for fraudulent and unapproved suppliers without adhering to company policies. **8-2 Pricing Issues.** Pricing for goods and services is incorrect causing financial exposure to the company and incorrect payments to suppliers. **8-3 Supplier Management Review Process.** Supplier performance is not tracked or reported in a timely manner and supplier issues are not identified nor corrected in a timely manner. **8-4 Audit and Performance of Third Parties.** Performance of third parties cannot be reviewed or audited. Using third parties can prove to be extremely beneficial in terms of cost and time savings, but they do come with added operational and compliance risks.
8.B Define Contract Types and Usage. A fixed price contract is applicable for most standard materials, but not quite so relevant for procuring certain kinds of services.	Manual Policy Preventive Procedure	**8-1 Unapproved and Fraudulent Suppliers.** Contracts are initiated for fraudulent and unapproved suppliers without adhering to company policies.

(Continued)

Internal Control	Type of Control	Risks Mitigated
A cost-reimbursement plus percentage fee contract is far more difficult to administer than is a unit-price contract, but may be more appropriate in specific circumstances. **Refer to risks: 8-1, 8-2, 8-4**		**8-2 Pricing Issues.** Pricing for goods and services is incorrect causing financial exposure to the company and incorrect payments to suppliers.
		8-4 Audit and Performance of Third Parties. Performance of third parties cannot be reviewed or audited. Using third parties can prove to be extremely beneficial in terms of cost and time savings, but they do come with added operational and compliance risks.
8.C Define Controls for Pricing Structures. A variety of contract-pricing mechanisms are used in procurement. Each structure has its advantages and disadvantages in different circumstances. The specific pricing alternatives considered are: Fixed price Unit price Target price Cost-reimbursement with incentive fees Cost-reimbursement with fixed or percentage fees. **Refer to risk: 8-2**	Manual Policy Preventive Procedure	**8-2 Pricing Issues.** Pricing for goods and services is incorrect causing financial exposure to the company and incorrect payments to suppliers.

Internal Control	Type of Control	Risks Mitigated
8.D Use Approved Company Templates for Contracts. Use an approved company templates for all contracts. **Refer to risks: 8-1, 8-2, 8-3, 8-4**	Manual Policy Preventive Procedure Organizational	**8-1 Unapproved and Fraudulent Suppliers.** Contracts are initiated for fraudulent and unapproved suppliers without adhering to company policies. **8-2 Pricing Issues.** Pricing for goods and services is incorrect causing financial exposure to the company and incorrect payments to suppliers. **8-3 Supplier Management Review Process.** Supplier performance is not tracked or reported in a timely manner and supplier issues are not identified nor corrected in a timely manner. **8-4 Audit and Performance of Third Parties.** Performance of third parties cannot be reviewed or audited. Using third parties can prove to be extremely beneficial in terms of cost and time savings, but they do come with added operational and compliance risks.
8.E Assign Service-Level Agreements (SLAs) for Contracts. An SLA should also include a set of operating metrics that are reported on a monthly basis. As an example, a good set of metrics for AP is: cost per invoice, days payable outstanding, invoices paid on time, outstanding credit balances, missed discounts, paid credits, and number of suppliers on the supplier master. **Refer to risk: 8-3**	Detective Manual Policy Preventive Procedure Organizational	**8-3 Supplier Management Review Process.** Supplier performance is not tracked or reported in a timely manner and supplier issues are not identified nor corrected in a timely manner.

(Continued)

Internal Control	Type of Control	Risks Mitigated
8.F Implement "Right to Audit" Clauses. In the ever-evolving business of specialization and the desire for continued growth, many companies are utilizing third-party specialists to assist with various revenue streams. Using third parties can prove to be extremely beneficial in terms of cost and time savings, but they do come with added risks. Having a Right to Audit clause and acting on it annually will help mitigate those added risks. **Refer to risk: 8-4**	Manual Policy Preventive Procedure	**8-4 Audit and Performance of Third Parties.** Performance of third parties cannot be reviewed or audited. Using third parties can prove to be extremely beneficial in terms of cost and time savings, but they do come with added operational and compliance risks.
8.G Supplier Management Review Process. To ensure that SLAs are reported and action is taken on potential issues, a supplier management review process establishes a schedule (monthly, quarterly, and annually) to formally review supplier performance. **Refer to risk: 8-3**	Detective Manual Policy Preventive Procedure	**8-3 Supplier Management Review Process.** Supplier performance is not tracked or reported in a timely manner and supplier issues are not identified nor corrected in a timely manner.

CHAPTER NINE

Purchasing and Ordering

 INTRODUCTION

We explored various definitions for procurement and purchasing when we introduced the concept of procure to pay (P2P). Procurement can also be defined at the act of obtaining or buying goods and services. The process of procurement is often considered to be a key part of a company's strategy in the establishment of key strategic sourcing relationships and cost saving opportunities. Additionally, automated procurement processes can improve efficiency and visibility to suppliers and spend activity.

Key Point: In fact, many P2P professionals often refer to procurement as an "art." The procurement process includes the preparation and processing of a demand as well as the end receipt and approval of payment. It often involves the processes listed here.

Procurement Process Steps
1. Purchase planning
2. Standards determination
3. Specifications development
4. Supplier research and selection

5. Value analysis
6. Financing
7. Price negotiation
8. Making the purchase
9. Supply contract administration
10. Inventory control and stores
11. Disposals and other related functions

AP TOOL 27: FIVE STEPS IN AN ELECTRONIC PROCUREMENT PROCESS

About This Tool: Electronic procurement streamlines the purchasing process by enabling organizations to connect to supplier catalogs, generate requisitions, use sophisticated workflow tools for approval processing and deliver purchase orders to suppliers electronically.

1. **Purchase Requisition:** The first step in electronic procurement is the integration with online supplier catalogs, which list approved products and display negotiated pricing and contract terms. This catalog is then managed, as product availability or prices change, and new items are added. Using the requisitioning functionality, buyers can log into the procurement system to search for products and services, compare multiple items, save favorite searches, easily access frequently purchased items, and order the items they need.

2. **Requisition Approval:** Once a purchase requisition is created, it is routed for approval based on the business rules and criteria configured by the organization. E-procurement solutions allow multiple levels of approval to model their clients' organization charts. Approval workflows can be designed based on category of spend (one person approves office supplies, while another reviews electronic items), dollar thresholds (all items over a certain dollar amount have to be approved by two users),

business unit, geographic location, supplier categories, or any other custom parameters.

3. **Workflow Management:** Workflow management involves the definition and management of user roles, rights, and permissions. Administrators can specify which users can create requisitions, what their spend limits are and which approvers are responsible for what items or dollar thresholds, to name a few. Most solutions offer an intuitive and easy-to-use interface to manage the workflow administration process either through drag and drop functionality, templates, or simple menu-driven features. Alerts and notifications go hand in hand with workflow management.

4. **Purchase Order Delivery:** This stage includes the creation of purchase orders from approved requisitions and the transmission of the orders from buyers to suppliers. Most solutions support the batching of multiple orders to a single supplier or conversely the creation of multiple purchase orders to be delivered to different suppliers from a single requisition. Suppliers can also use the portal to accept the POs and send advance shipment notices (ASNs) and notifications when items are actually shipped to buyers.

5. **Receiving and Reconciliation:** Most e-procurement solutions address more than just the ordering process by including functionality that covers invoice management and receiving as well. On the supplier side, e-procurement solutions facilitate the flipping of purchase orders into invoices and the delivery of invoices to the buyer. On the buyer side, they automate the goods receipt and reconciliation process.

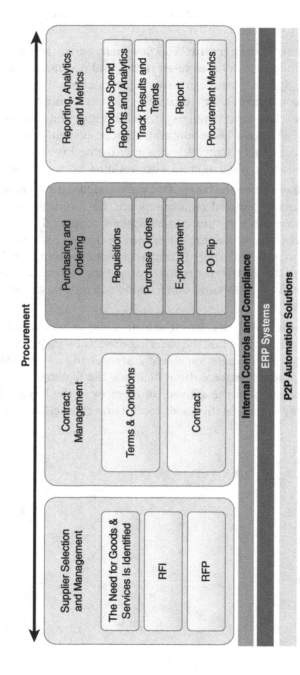

Purchasing and Ordering Process Flow

PURCHASING AND ORDERING PROCESS INSIGHTS

Contract Management

Contract management includes negotiating the terms and conditions in contracts and ensuring compliance with any applicable regulations, as well as documenting and agreeing on any changes that may arise during negotiations. Contract management is a strategic process that can result in large benefits in both operational efficiency and reducing risk.

Procurement professionals understand that contract negotiations often center on one of the triple constraints of time, money, or scope. In today's global market, these areas may contain elements that are not negotiable, such as adherence to compliance standards, partner location, and even the software used for warehouse automation or customer management.

The economy encouraged business to focus on cost reduction, and the first to feel this impact is the purchasing department. Discover popular methods and strategies for local and global sourcing with these free resources that provide guidance on contract and supplier management.

There are two types of procurement that drive the contract management process: indirect procurement and direct procurement.

Indirect procurement is the sourcing of all goods and services for an organization that supports its non-manufacturing or production processes. Indirect procurement is also defined as the goods and services which are commonly bought for consumption by internal stakeholders (functions or business units). The categories of indirect procurement categories include:

1. Marketing related services (advertising)
2. Professional services (consultants and advisory services)
3. Travel agencies
4. IT related services and support (hardware and software)
5. HR related services (recruitment agencies and training)
6. Facilities and office services (Telecom, furniture, cleaning, catering, and printers)
7. Utilities (gas, electricity, and water)

Within the retail industry, **indirect procurement** is often called **goods not for resale**, non-core procurement, or non-common procurement.

Goods for resale is a category of finished items that are sold to a retailer by a manufacturer or distributer and are eventually intended to be sold to consumers for profit. These are not considered end-user goods at the time of purchase by the retailer because they are still in the distribution phase. This is an important distinction because any sales tax paid by the retailer for these goods is considered a cost of doing business and can qualify as a tax reduction.

Direct procurement spend is a significant component of cost of goods sold (COGS), in excess of 30% of total costs for most infrastructure and manufacturing firms. Optimization of costs associated with "direct" materials and services, therefore, can have a significant impact on profitability and working capital management.

1. Risk is kept to a minimum.
2. Long-term supply has been assured with preferred suppliers.
3. Relationships have been built and developed over time.
4. Processes have been engrained into the core business.
5. Senior executives and board members acknowledge the value of the supply chain in light of business objectives.

The Purchase Requisition

A purchase requisition is a form used by businesses, nonprofit agencies, and government offices to coordinate organizational requests for purchases of goods and services. These forms make the process of purchasing items within an organization standard and streamlined.

A requisition order is a form that a department must submit to whichever department controls the financial activities of the business. Although individual forms vary by business, requisition orders generally require certain information, including the department requesting materials, the exact number of supplies requested, a general description of those supplies, the legal name of the supplier, and the expected price of the purchase. A requisition order is either approved or denied by the financial department of the business.

Most purchase requisitions have common components such as an area where a number of items to be purchased are listed. Depending on the structure of the organization, a signature or authorization from a key staffer with budgetary authority is usually necessary. Also, the form often has designated areas for office use that only the purchasing department may use for notes or internal communication.

AP TOOL 28: FOUR BEST PRACTICES TO CONSIDER FOR THE PURCHASE REQUISITION PROCESS

About This Tool: Requisition orders most often are submitted so a department may get approval to purchase needed materials from an entity operating outside of the business. However, sometimes one department of a business wishes to purchase equipment or materials from another department; in such cases, many businesses require that the purchasing department submit an interdepartmental requisition order. Interdepartmental requisition orders can be helpful to the financial or accounting office in large businesses where departments have separate operating budgets.

1. Many purchase requisition processes are automated and are part of the company's ERP system. In many cases a workflow process is embedded into the process and as part of the workflow; those with budgetary or signing authority (as mentioned earlier) are automatically mapped to the workflow.
2. As an additional best practice, many companies assign delegation of authority directly to job level which is maintained in the employee master file. The delegation of authority approvals for a procurement activity may start when the contract is initiated. Additional approvals may be required based on the type and level of expenditure or company commitment.
3. A purchase requisition needs to have an area that lists items to be ordered. This list would also require unit prices and the quantities requested. There may also be an area designated for account information such as which budget would be affected by the purchase and other accounting information. This "pre-coded" information prevents accounting errors and alleviates additional approvals for exception spending.
4. For small purchase orders, it often is standard procedure for departments to buy materials directly from retailers using a P-Card and skip the process of requisition and purchase orders altogether. Usually, businesses and organizations require a requisition order when a proposed purchase exceeds a certain monetary value. For example, Tufts University requires a requisition order for most purchases in excess of $2,000. Other businesses require requisition orders for much smaller purchases.

THE CATALOG PROCUREMENT MODEL

The term "catalog" is a list of items available for purchase with specific part numbers and descriptions. An e-catalog is an electronic document which carries the product specifications, listings, and information in detail. A successful catalog management improves the working relationship between the customer and supplier; in addition, it automatically provides a passage to sourced products, suppliers, and the ordering process. A robust e-catalog provides product reviews and specific industry information and updates. The benefits of a catalog procurement model are:

1. Suppliers create value added catalog content.
2. Drives, monitors, and maintains all communication between all the involved parties.
3. Performs the content validation against data formats, business logic, and coding structures.
4. Monitors all catalog management processes.
5. Updates the list at the instant a new product is in market by making it available for the customer.
6. Provides a comparison of product features, advising related products and alternative products and services to customers.
7. Online catalogs are also more easily searchable and help instant recovery.
8. It generates the opportunity to receive the purchase orders online which will lead to cost savings and increased working capital.
9. It increases the accuracy of the orders placed because it reduces the time which was previously used to confirm the quotes and prices; in short, we can say it reduces the conversation time by presenting the product details and specifications in full length.
10. Supports an automated e-procurement environment.
11. Accurately showcased online catalogs reduce the error rate of mismatches between the invoice and the purchase order.
12. The catalog management solution can improve the efficiency within an organization's existing procurement process which includes process design, change management, and communication

When a company has an open procurement model, employees or purchasing departments have the freedom to purchase goods and services from numerous suppliers, which makes it virtually impossible to control rogue spending and enforce company compliance with procurement guidelines. Open procurement also prohibits supplier rebates and inhibits their ability to negotiate deals which are awarded when volume purchase agreements are in place.

Key Point: A catalog procurement model boosts contract spending and enforces compliance with procurement guidelines by providing a list of items by approved suppliers where employees can purchase goods. A catalog procurement system helps automate, simplify, and accelerate the procure-to-pay process for goods and services.

Defining a Punchout Catalog

Let's deep dive into procurement catalogs to find out how they work to streamline the P2P process. Punchout catalogs allow buyers to access a supplier's e-commerce website, be automatically logged in, search the catalog, configure items, add them to the shopping cart, and return the cart as a pending purchase order back to the procurement system. In short, a punchout catalog website is a standard e-commerce website with the ability to communicate directly with a procurement system and return a pending purchase order back to the buyer so they don't need to enter product information in the procurement system. This saves purchasing personnel valuable time since they don't need to enter the product information.

Punchout catalogs also save time by eliminating all the maintenance and data entry of catalog upkeep. Punchout catalogs are maintained by the supplier and do not require constant upkeep from procurement. Companies attempting to eliminate rogue spending and enforce compliance need to investigate catalog procurement models and how these models work to provide a seamless P2P process.

Order Management and Purchase Order Matching

Once the requisition order has been approved, a purchase order is issued to the supplier for requested goods or services. Purchase orders should include certain information, such as the name of the purchasing office, supplies being purchased, ship-to address, payment terms, invoicing instructions, and purchase order number. To assist in record keeping, purchase orders will have the same number as the requisition order that generated them.

A purchase order is a written authorization requesting a supplier to furnish goods to a purchaser. It is an offer from the purchaser to buy certain articles. The offer is accepted by the seller when they supply the requested items. A contract is formed and the seller can expect payment in return for the delivered goods.

A purchase order is a legal authorization for a supplier to supply a product to a purchaser and a promise by the purchaser to pay for the product at a stated time. Purchase orders allow both parties to book the transaction into their scheduling and cash projections. They also help to eliminate misunderstandings regarding numbers of units, specific models ordered, prices, and delivery requirements. Because POs are legal documents, the supplier can borrow a portion of the expected payment based on the promise implied by the purchase order.

A purchase order sets forth the descriptions, quantities, prices, discounts, payment terms, date of performance or shipment, other associated terms and conditions, and identifies a specific seller.

A purchase requisition is not a purchase order and therefore should never be used to purchase goods or services or be used as an authorization to pay an invoice from a supplier or service provider. A purchase requisition is owned by the originating department and should not be changed by the purchasing department without obtaining approval from the originating department. This important distinction (e.g. essential control) is not clearly defined in some of the more popular integrated procurement software systems on the market today.

The purchase requisition is a precise document generated by an internal or external organization to notify the purchasing department of items it needs to order, their quantity, and the timeframe that will be given in the future. It may also contain the authorization to proceed with the purchase. A purchase requisition is a request sent to the purchasing department to procure goods or services. It is originated and approved by the department requiring the goods or services. Typically, it contains a description and quantity of the goods or services to be purchased, preferred make, a required delivery date, account number, and the amount of money that the purchasing department is authorized to spend for the goods or services. Often, the names of suggested supply sources are also included.

As part of an organization's internal financial controls, the accounting department may institute a purchase requisition process to help manage requests for purchases. Requests for the creation of purchase of goods and services are documented and routed for approval within the organization and then delivered to the accounting group.

Responsibility for Managing and Tracking Purchase Orders

Typically an accounts payable staff member is assigned responsibility for purchase order management, referred to commonly as the purchase order coordinator.

In some industrial (e.g. production line) environments, the purchasing department may be assigned responsibility for requesting and purchasing goods. This is especially true for raw material purchases where the purchasing department is also responsible for inventory management.

A purchase from a taxation point of view is also a cost that depletes profits that reduces a tax liability. The onus lies with the originator to prove the cost incurred is for generating income or to better a service to promote a sale that fulfills an objective, whilst ensuring valuable resources are best used and not wasted in the interest of the company.

Purchase Order Management

Purchase order management is an internal business accounting function. Companies use a purchasing process to acquire inventories, operational assets, and other items needed to produce goods or services. Purchase orders represent an internal document that gives specific authorization for purchasing different resources.

Larger companies usually have a more well-defined purchase order process than smaller businesses. Large companies create purchase order management policies to ensure employees follow standard operating procedures for this process.

Business owners usually designate purchase order authority or delegation of authority to specific individuals in the business. Business owners, directors, and executive-level managers often allow operational managers to approve purchase orders for their department. Purchase orders for significant dollar amounts, such as several thousand dollars, are the only purchase orders needing an executive's authorization. Business owners and executive managers delegate this ability to ensure the company's business operations can continue without excessive oversight.

Companies may use a purchase order management system that requires a review of several suppliers or suppliers. This requirement ensures the company gets the lowest possible cost for economic resources. Manufacturing, production, and construction companies commonly use a bid/proposal purchase order system. A bid/proposal system allows suppliers to present a company with specific information relating to economic resource purchases. Suppliers will outline the cost for each item, delivery process available, and time needed to complete all services listed on the bid/proposal. This process alleviates the company from doing copious amounts of footwork relating to economic resource acquisition.

1. When a decision is made to purchase goods, the purchase is described in detail in the PO. The information includes number of units, identifying catalog or style numbers, description of the product, model number, unit price, total price, delivery instructions, expected date of delivery, and contact information of key people involved in the transaction.
2. The PO allows the procurement department of a company to track purchases and keep other departments in the company informed about what is on order and when it is expected to be delivered.
3. This is particularly important in large companies that must keep track of many orders of supplies and equipment. POs are also used by some companies in hiring temporary staff and consultants.

STANDARDS OF INTERNAL CONTROL: PURCHASING AND ORDERING PROCESS

Internal Control	Type of Control	Risks Mitigated
9.A Segregation of Duties. All purchasing (ordering) responsibilities must be segregated from accounts payable/ payment, receiving, and accounting activities. **Refer to risks: 9-1, 9-2, 9-5, 9-6, 9-7, 9-9, 9-11, 9-12**	**Preventive** **Organizational**	**9 -1 Unauthorized Purchase Orders.** A purchase order may be: a. Unauthorized or improperly authorized. b. Made from an unauthorized supplier. c. Ordered and received by an unauthorized individual. **9-2 Import and export control violations, related party transactions, or conflict-of-interest situations may occur.** The potential for errors and irregularities is substantially increased. **9-5 Records may be misused or altered by unauthorized personnel to the detriment of the company and its suppliers.** **9-6 Goods and services may be received but not reported or reported inaccurately.** Unrecorded liabilities and misstated inventory and cost of sales may occur. **9-7 Goods purchased may not meet quality standards.** Unauthorized prices or terms may be accepted. **9-9 Duplicate Payments.** Duplicate payments may occur, or payments may be made for the wrong amount or to unauthorized or nonexistent suppliers. **9-11 Errors in Recording.** Purchases and/or payments may be recorded at the incorrect amount, to the wrong account, or in the wrong period. **9-12 Incorrect Payments.** Payment may be made for goods or services never received.

(Continued)

Internal Control	Type of Control	Risks Mitigated
9.B Written Purchasing Policies. Purchasing policies and procedures are established, communicated, and followed. Refer to risks: 9-1, 9-2, 9-4, 9-6, 9-7, 9-9, 9-10, 9-11	Policy Preventive Procedure Organizational	**9-1 Unauthorized Purchases.** A purchase order may be: a. Unauthorized or improperly authorized. b. Made from an unauthorized supplier. c. Ordered and received by an unauthorized individual. **9-2 Import and export control violations, related party transactions, or conflict-of-interest situations may occur.** The potential for errors and irregularities is substantially **9-4 Records may be lost or destroyed.** **9-6 Goods and services may be received but not reported, or reported inaccurately.** Unrecorded liabilities and misstated inventory and cost of sales may occur. **9-7 Goods purchased may not meet quality standards.** Unauthorized prices or terms may be accepted **9-9 Duplicate Payments.** Duplicate payments may occur, or payments may be made for the wrong amount or to unauthorized or nonexistent suppliers. **9-10 Records may not be available for external legal, tax, or audit purposes.** **9-11 Errors in Recording.** Purchases and/or payments may be recorded at the incorrect amount, to the wrong account, or in the wrong period.

Internal Control	Type of Control	Risks Mitigated
9.C System Access Controls. All purchase orders or access to ERP systems must be safeguarded and internal control procedures for processing and approval must be in place to prevent unauthorized use. **Refer to risks: 9-1, 9-2, 9-4, 9-5, 9-6, 9-9, 9-10, 9-12**	Detective Preventive Organizational Policy Procedure	**9-1 Unauthorized Purchases.** A purchase order may be: a. Unauthorized or improperly authorized. b. Made from an unauthorized supplier. c. Ordered and received by an unauthorized individual. **9-2 Import and export control violations, related party transactions, or conflict-of-interest situations may occur.** The potential for errors and irregularities is substantially **9-4 Records may be lost or destroyed.** **9-5 Records may be misused or altered by unauthorized personnel to the detriment of the company and its suppliers.** **9-6 Goods and services may be received but not reported or reported inaccurately.** Unrecorded liabilities and misstated inventory and cost of sales may occur. **9-9 Duplicate Payments.** Duplicate payments may occur, or payments may be made for the wrong amount or to unauthorized or nonexistent suppliers. **9-10 Records may not be available for external legal, tax, or audit purposes.** **9-12 Incorrect Payments.** Payment may be made for goods or services never received.
9.D Purchase Price Negotiation. To assure the company's competitive advantage, prices will be negotiated through cost analysis (e.g. target costing), bidding, or industry cost benchmarking. **Refer to risks: 9-2, 9-5, 9-7**	Detective Preventive Organizational Policy Procedure	**9-2 Import and export control violations, related party transactions, or conflict-of-interest situations may occur.** The potential for errors and irregularities is substantially increased. **9-5 Records may be misused or altered by unauthorized personnel to the detriment of the company and its suppliers.** **9-7 Goods purchased may not meet quality standards.** Unauthorized prices or terms may be accepted

(Continued)

Internal Control	Type of Control	Risks Mitigated
9.E Contracts Based on Supplier Selection Process. Oral or written contracts, memorandums of understanding, and statements of intent that may financially obligate the company must not be done prior to the completion of the selection process without proper approvals. **Refer to risks: 9-1, 9-2, 9-5, 9-6, 9-7, 9-9, 9-10**	Detective Preventive Organizational Policy Procedure	**9-1 Unauthorized Purchases.** A purchase order may be: a. Unauthorized or improperly authorized. b. Made from an unauthorized supplier. c. Ordered and received by an unauthorized individual. **9-2 Import and export control violations, related party transactions, or conflict-of-interest situations may occur.** The potential for errors and irregularities is substantially increased. **9-5 Records may be misused or altered by unauthorized personnel to the detriment of the company and its suppliers.** **9-6 Goods and services may be received but not reported or reported inaccurately.** Unrecorded liabilities and misstated inventory and cost of sales may occur. **9-7 Goods purchased may not meet quality standards.** Unauthorized prices or terms may be accepted. **9-9 Duplicate Payments.** Duplicate payments may occur, or payments may be made for the wrong amount or to unauthorized or nonexistent suppliers. **9-10 Records may not be available for external legal, tax, or audit purposes.**

Internal Control	Type of Control	Risks Mitigated
9.F No Payments in Advance. Payment in advance should be avoided if possible. A procedure should be established and followed when it is necessary to make payments in advance of the shipment or receipt of material to prevent overpayment. No advance payments can be made unless they are part of the purchase order terms. **Refer to risks: 9-6, 9-9, 9-11**	Preventive Organizational Policy Procedure	**9-6 Goods and services may be received but not reported or reported inaccurately.** Unrecorded liabilities and misstated inventory and cost of sales may occur. **9-9 Duplicate Payments.** Duplicate payments may occur, or payments may be made for the wrong amount or to unauthorized or nonexistent suppliers. **9-11 Recording Errors.** Purchases and/or payments may be recorded at the incorrect amount, to the wrong account, or in the wrong period.

(*Continued*)

Internal Control	Type of Control	Risks Mitigated
9.G Order Audit Trail. All orders/ transactions must be uniquely identifiable and traceable and periodically accounted for. **Refer to risks: 9-3, 9-4, 9-5, 9-6, 9-9, 9-10, 9-11, 9-12**	Detective Preventive Organizational Policy Procedure	**9-3 Incorrect liabilities and payments.** Rather than being returned or refused, the following items may be received and ultimately paid for: a. Unordered goods or services. b. Excessive quantities or incorrect items. c. Canceled or duplicated orders. **9-4 Records may be lost or destroyed**. **9-5 Records may be misused or altered by unauthorized personnel to the detriment of the company and its suppliers.** **9-6 Goods and services may be received but not reported or reported inaccurately.** Unrecorded liabilities and misstated inventory and cost of sales may occur. **9-9 Duplicate Payments**. Duplicate payments may occur, or payments may be made for the wrong amount or to unauthorized or nonexistent suppliers. **9-10 Records may not be available for external legal, tax, or audit purposes.** **9-11 Purchases and/or payments may be recorded at the incorrect amount, to the wrong account, or in the wrong period.** **9-12 Payment may be made for goods or services never received.**

Internal Control	Type of Control	Risks Mitigated
9.H Invoice Forwarding. Purchase orders/ transactions must instruct suppliers to forward their billings directly to accounts payable in a manual process. **Refer to risks: 9-3, 9-4, 9-5, 9-6, 9-9, 9-10, 9-11**	**Preventive** **Organizational** **Policy** **Procedure**	**9-3 Incorrect liabilities and payments.** Rather than being returned or refused, the following items may be received and ultimately paid for: a. Unordered goods or services. b. Excessive quantities or incorrect items. c. Canceled or duplicated orders. **9-4 Records may be lost or destroyed.** 9-5 Records may be misused or altered by unauthorized personnel to the detriment of the company and its suppliers. **9-6 Goods and services may be received but not reported or reported inaccurately.** Unrecorded liabilities and misstated inventory and cost of sales may occur. **9-9 Duplicate Payments.** Duplicate payments may occur, or payments may be made for the wrong amount or to unauthorized or nonexistent suppliers. **9-10 Records may not be available for external legal, tax, or audit purposes.** **9-11 Purchases and/or payments may be recorded at the incorrect amount, to the wrong account, or in the wrong period.**

(*Continued*)

Internal Control	Type of Control	Risks Mitigated
9.I Purchase Order Distribution. Purchase order information must be made available via the ERP system and should be assessable to the receiving and accounts payable departments. Accounts payable and receiving must be notified of changed or canceled purchase orders in a timely manner. **Refer to risks:** **9-3, 9-5, 9-6, 9-7, 9-8, 9-9, 9-11, 9-12, 9-14**	**Preventive** **Organizational** **Policy** **Procedure**	**9-3 Inaccurate liabilities and payments.** Rather than being returned or refused, the following items may be received and ultimately paid for: a. Unordered goods or services. b. Excessive quantities or incorrect items. c. Canceled or duplicated orders. **9-5 Records may be misused or altered by unauthorized personnel to the detriment of the company and its suppliers.** **9-6 Goods and services may be received but not reported or reported inaccurately.** Unrecorded liabilities and misstated inventory and cost of sales may occur. **9-7 Goods purchased may not meet quality standards.** Unauthorized prices or terms may be accepted. **9-8 Material Planning Issues.** Materials may be received early or late resulting in business interruption or excess levels of inventory. **9-9 Duplicate Invoices.** Duplicate payments may occur, or payments may be made for the wrong amount or to unauthorized or nonexistent suppliers. **9-11 Purchases and/or payments may be recorded at the incorrect amount, to the wrong account, or in the wrong period.** **9-12 Payment may be made for goods or services never received.** **9-13 Loss of intellectual property.** **9-14 Unauthorized Receipt.** A purchase order may be received by an unauthorized individual.

Internal Control	Type of Control	Risks Mitigated
9.J Product Return Procedures. Procedures must be established to ensure proper approval, recording, and follow-up of all return items (due to poor quality, improper specifications, etc.). **Refer to risks: 9-4, 9-5, 9-7, 9-9, 9-10, 9-11, 9-12**	Management Review Preventive Organizational Policy Procedure Supervisory	**9-4 Records may be lost or destroyed.** **9-5 Records may be misused or altered by unauthorized personnel to the detriment of the company and its suppliers.** **9-7 Goods purchased may not meet quality standards.** Unauthorized prices or terms may be accepted. **9-9 Duplicate Payment.** Duplicate payments may occur, or payments may be made for the wrong amount or to unauthorized or nonexistent suppliers. **9-10 Records may not be available for external legal, tax, or audit purposes.** **9-11 Purchases and/or payments may be recorded at the incorrect amount, to the wrong account, or in the wrong period.** **9-12 Payment may be made for goods or services never received.**
9.K Evaluation of Purchasing Process. Purchasing process should be evaluated consistent with supplier management processes. **Refer to risks: 9-7, 9-8**	Management Review Preventive Organizational Policy Procedure Supervisory	**9-7 Goods purchased may not meet quality standards.** Unauthorized prices or terms may be accepted. **9-8 Material Planning Issues.** Materials may be received early or late resulting in business interruption or excess levels of inventory.

(Continued)

Internal Control	Type of Control	Risks Mitigated
9.L Safeguarding Intellectual Property. Procedures governing the review and approval of contracts should address the safeguarding of the company's intellectual property including patents and trademarks. **Refer to risks: 9-4, 9-5, 9-10, 9-12, 9-13**	Preventive	**9-4 Records may be lost or destroyed.** **9-5 Records may be misused or altered by unauthorized personnel to the detriment of the company and its suppliers.** **9-10 Records may not be available for external legal, tax, or audit purposes.** **9-12 Payment may be made for goods or services never received.** **9-13 Loss of intellectual property.**
9.M Blanket Purchase Orders. A "not to exceed" limit and duration must be specified on each blanket purchase order. **Refer to risk: 9-8**	Preventive	**9-8 Material Planning Issues.** Materials may be received early or late resulting in business interruption or excess levels of inventory.

Internal Control	Type of Control	Risks Mitigated
9.N Independence and Purchasing. Independence between purchasing agent/buyer and supplier must be maintained. This can be accomplished through periodic buyer rotation, or participation in corporate contracts, or use of commodity teams. The company's code of conduct should be distributed to all suppliers. **Refer to risks: 9-1, 9-2, 9-3, 9-4, 9-5, 9-7**	Policy Preventive Procedure Organizational	**9-1 Unauthorized Purchases.** A purchase order may be: a. Unauthorized or improperly authorized. b. Made from an unauthorized supplier. c. Ordered and received by an unauthorized individual. **9-2 Import and export control violations, related party transactions, or conflict-of-interest situations may occur.** The potential for errors and irregularities is substantially increased. **9-4 Records may be lost or destroyed.** **9-5 Records may be misused or altered by unauthorized personnel to the detriment of the company and its suppliers.** **9-7 Goods purchased may not meet quality standards.** Unauthorized prices or terms may be accepted. Purchases and/or payments may be recorded at the incorrect amount, to the wrong account, or in the wrong period.

(Continued)

Internal Control	Type of Control	Risks Mitigated
9.O Requisitioning Procedures. Purchase requirements (e.g. purchase orders, blanket orders, contracts, etc.) must be initiated by the requesting department and be properly approved, within approver's limits, before a purchase request is made. Purchase orders must not be split to get around approval limits. **Refer to risks: 9-1, 9-2, 9-3, 9-5**	Policy Preventive Procedure Organizational	**9-1 Unauthorized Purchases.** A purchase order may be: a. Unauthorized or improperly authorized. b. Made from an unauthorized supplier. c. Ordered and received by an unauthorized individual. **9-2 Import and export control violations, related party transactions, or conflict-of-interest situations may occur.** The potential for errors and irregularities is substantially increased. **9-3 Inaccurate Payments and Liabilities.** Rather than being returned or refused, the following items may be received and ultimately paid for: a. Unordered goods or services. b. Excessive quantities or incorrect items. c. Canceled or duplicated orders. **9-5 Records may be misused or altered by unauthorized personnel to the detriment of the company and its suppliers.** Purchases and/or payments may be recorded at the incorrect amount, to the wrong account, or in the wrong period.

Internal Control	Type of Control	Risks Mitigated
9.P Low Value Requisitions. Authorization limits must be established for individuals making low-value purchases through special procurement processes (e.g. P-Cards, catalogs, procurement cards, etc.). **Refer to risks: 9-1, 9-3, 9-5**	Policy Preventive Procedure Organizational	**9-1 Unauthorized Purchases.** A purchase order may be: a. Unauthorized or improperly authorized. b. Made from an unauthorized supplier. c. Ordered and received by an unauthorized individual. **9-3 Incorrect Payments and Liabilities.** Rather than being returned or refused, the following items may be received and ultimately paid for: a. Unordered goods or services. b. Excessive quantities or incorrect items. c. Canceled or duplicated orders. **9-5 Records may be misused or altered by unauthorized personnel to the detriment of the company and its suppliers.** Purchases and/or payments may be recorded at the incorrect amount, to the wrong account, or in the wrong period.

(Continued)

Internal Control	Type of Control	Risks Mitigated
9.Q Purchase Order Revisions. Purchase order revisions for price or quantity that cause increases that exceed buyer's approval level must be approved in compliance with local procedures. **Refer to risks: 9-1, 9-2, 9-3, 9-5, 9-7, 9-8**	**Policy** **Preventive** **Procedure** **Managerial Reviews** **Organizational** **Supervisory**	**9-1 Unauthorized Purchases.** A purchase order may be: a. Unauthorized or improperly authorized. b. Made from an unauthorized supplier. c. Ordered and received by an unauthorized individual. **9-2 Import and export control violations, related party transactions, or conflict-of-interest situations may occur.** The potential for errors and irregularities is substantially increased. **9-3 Incorrect Payments and Liabilities.** Rather than being returned or refused, the following items may be received and ultimately paid for: a. Unordered goods or services. b. Excessive quantities or incorrect items. c. Canceled or duplicated orders. **9-5 Records may be misused or altered by unauthorized personnel to the detriment of the company and its suppliers.** **9-7 Goods purchased may not meet quality standards. Unauthorized prices or terms may be accepted.** **9-8 Material Planning Issues.** Materials may be received early or late resulting in business interruption or excess levels of inventory.

Internal Control	Type of Control	Risks Mitigated
9.R After-the-Fact Purchase Orders. After-the-fact POs are identified, tracked, and followed up regularly. **Refer to risks 9-1, 9-3, 9-5, 9-7, 9-8**	Detective Preventative	**9-1 Unauthorized Purchases.** A purchase order may be: a. Unauthorized or improperly authorized. b. Made from an unauthorized supplier. c. Ordered and received by an unauthorized individual. **9-3 Incorrect Payments and Liabilities.** Rather than being returned or refused, the following items may be received and ultimately paid for: a. Unordered goods or services. b. Excessive quantities or incorrect items. c. Canceled or duplicated orders. **9-5 Records may be misused or altered by unauthorized personnel to the detriment of the company and its suppliers.** **9-7 Goods purchased may not meet quality standards.** Unauthorized prices or terms may be accepted. **9-8 Material Planning Issues.** Materials may be received early or late resulting in business interruption or excess levels of inventory.

CHAPTER TEN

Receiving

INTRODUCTION

The outcome of the receiving process is to accurately reflect goods and services received by the organization in a timely manner with accurate pricing, part numbers, purchase order number, and quantity.

An incorrect receiving transaction can cause a reconciliation issue with accounts payable clearing accounts that capture the goods received/invoices received process. The receiving transaction is also a component of the two-way and three-way match process which is used to accurately process an invoice. The other components include the purchase order and invoice.

Good receiving is critical because when you move product faster with fewer employees, employee productivity is higher, you use less warehouse space, and you reduce the number of touches on items, which reduces opportunities to inadvertently damage them. Finally, good receiving practices enable the timely and accurate processing of invoices and supplier payments.

Receiving Process Flow

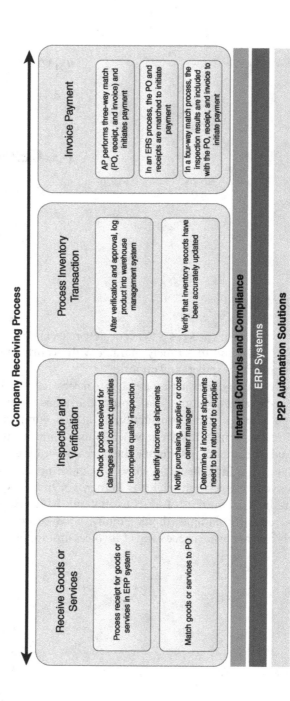

Company Receiving Process

Receive Goods or Services
- Process receipt for goods or services in ERP system
- Match goods or services to PO

Inspection and Verification
- Check goods received for damages and correct quantities
- Incomplete quality inspection
- Identify incorrect shipments
- Notify purchasing, supplier, or cost center manager
- Determine if incorrect shipments need to be returned to supplier

Process Inventory Transaction
- After verification and approval, log product into warehouse management system
- Verify that inventory records have been accurately updated

Invoice Payment
- AP performs three-way match (PO, receipt, and invoice) and initiates payment
- In an ERS process, the PO and receipts are matched to initiate payment
- In a four-way match process, the inspection results are included with the PO, receipt, and invoice to initiate payment

Internal Controls and Compliance

ERP Systems

P2P Automation Solutions

RECEIVING PROCESS INSIGHTS

This section provides insights in the receiving process and recommends best practices for warehousing received goods. These best practices will help to mitigate the risk of incorrect receiving processes and will reduce the potential for fraud.

Best Practices for the Warehousing Process

1. **Utilize Good Labeling.** Good receiving starts with good labeling. Get your suppliers to correctly label materials before they arrive at your warehouse. Make sure the labels can be read by both human and data capture devices. It goes without saying that you need to ensure that your warehouse has the proper data scanners in the receiving locations where you need them.

   Depending on your receiving system, the labeling standard you use, and your suppliers' willingness to customize printing for you, here are some of the data that you may want to include on your labels:
   1. Shipper/supplier information (company name, telephone number)
   2. Purchase order number
   3. Pallet labels and quantity
   4. Case labels and quantity
   5. Product number and description
   6. Package count
   7. Part/unit labels or markings (each item in the case should have a unique product ID)
2. **Use an Industry Standard for Labeling.** With labeling, stick with an industry standard. Suppliers will be more likely to comply or, better yet, already use one of the standards with some of their other customers. In this case, your request will be easier to meet.
3. **Implement a Well-Labeled Warehouse.** An effective labeling component of your receiving system also includes a well-labeled warehouse. Identify areas, aisles, rack bays, and shelves with large, easy-to-read location labels. Use large barcode-readable "license plate" labels viewable from 30–40 feet to identify warehouse locations.
4. **Adhere to Rigid Labeling Policies.** Create and adhere to some rigid labeling policies in your warehouse and you will reduce your error rates. Here are seven policies that will help you:
   1. Require that suppliers (or your staff) label every case and pallet to identify it.

2. Scan the label to confirm that you are moving the correct product.

3. If products are not labeled by your supplier, you need to enable the receiving team to handle printing on your end. This means having the correct information and output devices so they can print and apply the labels as needed.

4. Mark all storage locations.

5. Replace damaged location tags.

6. Make sure labels are readable when shelved. Train "put-away" staff to shelve with labels facing outward.

7. If you remove items from cartons or change their location or quantity, print new labels with the updated information.

5. **Implement and Enforce Supplier Compliance Standards.** Before a correctly labeled carton ever arrives at your warehouse, you need to collaborate with your suppliers and map out a plan for efficiency and success. Your suppliers can help or hurt you. How your suppliers ship product to you strongly affects the fate of your receiving operation and even the profit of your company.

6. **Supplier Compliance Standards "Playbook."** As a standard of compliance, specify to the supplier how you want to receive the product (pallets, cartons). Make sure your warehouse management system (WMS) can accommodate various units of measure for each product. Create, adopt, publish, and enforce supplier compliance procedures internally within your organization as well as with suppliers. Decide the details (how, what, and when) and require suppliers to sign off on your playbook. Some of the things that you may want to specify include: request that suppliers label the outer carton with the PO number, product or style number, carton count, and bar code; request that suppliers add pallet tags that be easily scanned to identify pallets, boxes, or individual products. Figure out what you want and formalize it in a written document. For example, if you want single-SKU cartons whenever possible, specify this in your manual.

7. **Compliance Standards as End User Licensing Agreement.** Think of your compliance procedures as an End User Licensing Agreement. Every consumer software user has experience clicking on a button acknowledging that they have agreed to whatever terms-of-use agreement a software developer has created. Obtain written acknowledgment from suppliers that they have read and will adhere to your compliance procedures. Part of your procedures should include details on the penalties and remediation steps should things go awry. This includes creating and instituting a charge-back program that is acceptable to both you and your suppliers.

8. **Implement a Supplier Scorecard and Quality Assurance.** There are a lot of scorecards in life and you should be regularly tracking your supplier's performance or lack thereof. If they fail to follow the mutually agreed-on procedures, you need to track and record shortcomings. Work with suppliers to solve problems. If they are reluctant to improve and unwilling to eliminate or otherwise reduce the error rate, you might just have to fire them. Remember, you are in business to make money, not to throw away some of your gross margin because a supplier isn't doing what they agreed to do. You need to make supplier quality assurance a regular practice. One idea is rank them on a dependability scale. Knowing that certain suppliers will be less dependable, receiving staff will be able to give their shipments more attention.

9. **Automating the Receiving Process.** If your current and projected business volume calls for it, the only thing stopping you from integrating technology is your capital investment budget. The technology blueprint that you ultimately install, from docking technology and material handling equipment, to data entry and data management systems, should be both flexible and efficient.

   Radio frequency (RF) terminals and systems have evolved at a rapid pace in recent years. Prices have dropped sharply and you have a wide variety of basic as well as advanced options for scanning readers and transmitting stations. If you aren't currently using wireless, you might want to revisit next year's capital budget and see if you can insert a "system upgrade to RF" line item. Label printer prices have similarly dropped.

   Warehouse management system have dropped in cost as their functionality has risen. Some automation options include:
   1. Receive against multiple purchase orders simultaneously.
   2. Receive by purchase order, by product, or without a purchase order.
   3. Assign inventory to a location for put-away.
   4. Store products in unique or multiple locations based on bin/inventory characteristics.
   5. Update inventory levels automatically upon receipt.
   6. View receipt details for single receipt or all receipts from a single supplier.

Improving the Physical Layout of the Receiving Process

1. Receiving locations designated for tracking product.
2. Organized use of dock, receiving, and staging spaces for put-away.

3. Sufficient space when and where bottlenecks occur.
4. Delivery capacity. Do you have enough bays/doors?
5. Dock door levelers.
6. Availability of conveyors (if your automation system requires them).
7. Availability of pallets for receipts and the material handling equipment to move them.

Examples of Receiving Process Metrics

Receiving Process Performance Metrics

1. **On-Time Receiving** – Items Received into Inventory Within X Timeframe
2. **Supplier Quality Control** – Adhere to Supplier Compliance Scorecard
3. **Units Received** – Per Hour/Day/Week/Month
4. **Receiving Process Cycle Time** – Time of Receipt to Stock
5. **Receiving Process Quality** – Percent of Receipt Matches to POs

STANDARDS OF INTERNAL CONTROLS: RECEIVING PROCESS

Internal Control	Type of Control	Risks Mitigated
10.A Physical Segregation of Receiving Department. The receiving department should be physically segregated from the production facilities and shipping. Where segregation is not feasible, compensating controls must be established. **Refer to risks: 10-1, 10-2, 10-3**	Compensating Manual Preventive Organizational	**10-1 Unauthorized Purchases.** A purchase may be: a. Unauthorized or improperly authorized. b. Made from an unauthorized supplier. c. Ordered and received by an unauthorized individual. **10-2 Related party transactions or conflict-of-interest situations may occur.** The potential for errors and irregularities is substantially increased. **10-3 Incorrect Payments, Liabilities, and Inventory Levels.** Rather than being returned or refused, the following items may be received and ultimately paid for: a. Unordered goods or services. b. Excessive quantities or incorrect items. c. Canceled or duplicated orders.

Internal Control	Type of Control	Risks Mitigated
10.B Segregation of Duties. The receiving function must be separated from the buying function, invoice processing, accounts payable, and general ledger functions. **Refer to risks: 10-1, 10-2, 10-3, 10-5, 10-6, 10-7, 10-8**	**Compensating** **Manual** **Preventive** **Organizational**	**10-1 Unauthorized Purchases.** A purchase may be: a. Unauthorized or improperly authorized. b. Made from an unauthorized supplier. c. Ordered and received by an unauthorized individual. **10-2 Related party transactions or conflict-of-interest situations may occur.** The potential for errors and irregularities is substantially increased. **10-3 Incorrect Payments, Liabilities, and Inventory Levels.** Rather than being returned or refused, the following items may be received and ultimately paid for: a. Unordered goods or services. b. Excessive quantities or incorrect items. c. Canceled or duplicated orders. **10-5 Records may be misused or altered by unauthorized personnel to the detriment of the company and its suppliers.** **10-6 Goods and services may be received but not reported or reported inaccurately.** Unrecorded liabilities and misstated inventory and cost of sales may occur. **10-7 Goods purchased may not meet quality standards.** Unauthorized prices or terms may be accepted. **10-8 Purchases and/or payments may be recorded at the incorrect amount, to the wrong account, or in the wrong period.**

(Continued)

Internal Control	Type of Control	Risks Mitigated
10.C Access to Receiving Department. Access to the receiving department must be restricted to authorized personnel only. **Refer to risks: 10-1, 10-2, 10-3, 10-4, 10-5, 10-6**	Manual Preventive Organizational	**10-1 Unauthorized Purchases.** A purchase may be: a. Unauthorized or improperly authorized. b. Made from an unauthorized supplier. c. Ordered and received by an unauthorized individual. **10-2 Related party transactions or conflict-of-interest situations may occur.** The potential for errors and irregularities is substantially increased. **10-3 Incorrect Payments, Liabilities, and Inventory Levels.** Rather than being returned or refused, the following items may be received and ultimately paid for: a. Unordered goods or services. b. Excessive quantities or incorrect items. c. Canceled or duplicated orders. **10-4 Records may be lost or destroyed.** **10-5 Records may be misused or altered by unauthorized personnel to the detriment of the company and its suppliers.** **10-6 Goods and services may be received but not reported or reported inaccurately.** Unrecorded liabilities and misstated inventory and cost of sales may occur.

Internal Control	Type of Control	Risks Mitigated
10.D Receiving Policy. All incoming material, merchandise, and supplies must be processed by the designated receiving location at each facility, unless otherwise arranged and approved in accordance with local policy. **Refer to risks: 10-1, 10-2, 10-4, 10-5**	Policy **Preventive** **Procedure**	**10-1 Unauthorized Purchases.** A purchase may be: a. Unauthorized or improperly authorized. b. Made from an unauthorized supplier. c. Ordered and received by an unauthorized individual. **10-2 Related party transactions or conflict-of-interest situations may occur.** The potential for errors and irregularities is substantially increased. **10-4 Records may be lost or destroyed.** **10-5 Records may be misused or altered by unauthorized personnel to the detriment of the company and its suppliers.**

(Continued)

Internal Control	Type of Control	Risks Mitigated
10.E Acceptance of Goods Received. The receiving location will accept only those goods with an approved purchase order or if its equivalent has been prepared. All other receipts should be returned to the supplier or investigated for propriety in a timely manner. **Refer to risks: 10-3, 10-4, 10-5, 10-6, 10-7**	Policy Preventive Procedure	**10-3 Incorrect Payments, Liabilities, and Inventory Levels.** Rather than being returned or refused, the following items may be received and ultimately paid for: a. Unordered goods or services. b. Excessive quantities or incorrect items. c. Canceled or duplicated orders. **10-4 Records may be lost or destroyed.** **10-5 Records may be misused or altered by unauthorized personnel to the detriment of the company and its suppliers.** **10-6 Goods and services may be received but not reported or reported inaccurately.** Unrecorded liabilities and misstated inventory and cost of sales may occur. **10-7 Goods purchased may not meet quality standards.** Unauthorized prices or terms may be accepted.
10.F Receipt Documentation. Each designated receiving location must account for and provide evidence of a receiving transaction for all material, merchandise, or supplies accepted by the receiving location. Evidence must exist of goods returned or moved to other areas. **Refer to risks: 10-2, 10-6, 10-7**	Detective Policy Preventive Procedure	**10-2 Related party transactions or conflict-of-interest situations may occur.** The potential for errors and irregularities is substantially increased. **10-6 Goods and services may be received but not reported or reported inaccurately.** Unrecorded liabilities and misstated inventory and cost of sales may occur. **10-7 Goods purchased may not meet quality standards.** Unauthorized prices or terms may be accepted.

Internal Control	Type of Control	Risks Mitigated
10.G Receipt Recording. Receiving transactions will not be generated without actual receipt of goods or services and adequate proof of delivery. **Refer to risks:** 10-3, 10-6	Detective Policy Preventive Procedure	**10-3 Incorrect Payments, Liabilities, and Inventory Levels.** Rather than being returned or refused, the following items may be received and ultimately paid for: a. Unordered goods or services. b. Excessive quantities or incorrect items. c. Canceled or duplicated orders. **10-6 Goods and services may be received but not reported or reported inaccurately.** Unrecorded liabilities and misstated inventory and cost of sales may occur.
10.H Receiving Procedures. In the absence of an effective supplier qualification and performance-monitoring program, incoming goods must be evaluated for damage and shortages. Goods must be counted, weighed, or measured on a sample basis to determine the accuracy of supplier's shipments. All discrepancies and damage must be documented, tracked, and appropriately resolved with the supplier. **Refer to risks: 10-2, 10-3, 10-4, 10-6, 10-7**	Detective Policy Preventive Procedure	**10-2 Related party transactions or conflict-of-interest situations may occur.** The potential for errors and irregularities is substantially increased. **10-3 Incorrect Payments, Liabilities, and Inventory Levels.** Rather than being returned or refused, the following items may be received and ultimately paid for: a. Unordered goods or services. b. Excessive quantities or incorrect items. c. Canceled or duplicated orders. **10-4 Records may be lost or destroyed.** **10-6 Goods and services may be received but not reported or reported inaccurately.** Unrecorded liabilities and misstated inventory and cost of sales may occur. **10-7 Goods purchased may not meet quality standards.** Unauthorized prices or terms may be accepted

(Continued)

Internal Control	Type of Control	Risks Mitigated
10.I Receiving Information. Receiving transaction information and electronic copies of documentation (BOL, packing slip, etc.) must be maintained in the receiving department and made available to purchasing and accounts payable for supplier payment processing on a timely basis. **Refer to risks: 10-2, 10-6, 10-7**	Detective Policy Preventive Procedure	**10-2 Related party transactions or conflict-of-interest situations may occur.** The potential for errors and irregularities is substantially increased. **10-6 Goods and services may be received but not reported or reported inaccurately.** Unrecorded liabilities and misstated inventory and cost of sales may occur. **10-7 Goods purchased may not meet quality standards.** Unauthorized prices or terms may be accepted
10.J Supply Chain Inspection. In the absence of an effective supplier qualification and performance-monitoring program, incoming goods must be promptly inspected and tested for damage, quality characteristics, product specifications, etc., by the appropriate supply chain personnel. **Refer to risks: 10-4, 10-7**	Detective Management Review Supervisory	**10-4 Records may be lost or destroyed.** **10-7 Goods purchased may not meet quality standards.** Unauthorized prices or terms may be accepted

Internal Control	Type of Control	Risks Mitigated
10.K Safeguarding Receiving Information. Receiving transaction information must be adequately safeguarded from theft, destruction, or unauthorized use. Receiving transactions must be uniquely identifiable, traceable, and accounted for periodically. Access to the receiving screens must be controlled and password protected. **Refer to risks: 10-1, 10-2, 10-4, 10-5**	Policy Preventive Procedure	**10-1 Unauthorized Purchases.** A purchase may be: a. Unauthorized or improperly authorized. b. Made from an unauthorized supplier. c. Ordered and received by an unauthorized individual. **10-2 Related party transactions or conflict-of-interest situations may occur.** The potential for errors and irregularities is substantially increased. **10-4 Records may be lost or destroyed.** **10-5 Records may be misused or altered by unauthorized personnel to the detriment of the company and its suppliers.**
10.L Safeguarding of Received Goods. Incoming goods must be secured and safeguarded upon receipt. High value parts, such as microprocessors, must be safeguarded during the receiving process. **Refer to risk: 10-1**	Policy Preventive Procedure	**10-1 Unauthorized Purchases.** A purchase may be: a. Unauthorized or improperly authorized. b. Made from an unauthorized supplier. c. Ordered and received by an unauthorized individual.

(Continued)

Internal Control	Type of Control	Risks Mitigated
10.M Changes to Receiving Records. Changes required to correct errors in original receiving transactions may be generated only by authorized personnel as specified by local policy. **Refer to risks: 10-1, 10-2, 10-4, 10-5, 10-6, 10-7, 10-8**	Policy Preventive Procedure Organizational	**10-1 Unauthorized Purchases.** A purchase may be: a. Unauthorized or improperly authorized. b. Made from an unauthorized supplier. c. Ordered and received by an unauthorized individual. **10-2 Related party transactions or conflict-of-interest situations may occur.** The potential for errors and irregularities is substantially increased. **10-4 Records may be lost or destroyed.** **10-5 Records may be misused or altered by unauthorized personnel to the detriment of the company and its suppliers.** **10-6 Goods and services may be received but not reported or reported inaccurately.** Unrecorded liabilities and misstated inventory and cost of sales may occur. **10-7 Goods purchased may not meet quality standards.** Unauthorized prices or terms may be accepted. **10-8 Purchases and/or payments may be recorded at the incorrect amount, to the wrong account, or in the wrong period.**

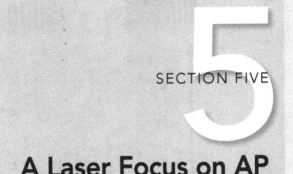

SECTION FIVE

A Laser Focus on AP

 INTRODUCTION

We define the AP process as a strategic, value-added accounting function that performs the primary non-payroll payment functions in an organization. As such, the AP operation plays a critical role in the financial cycle of the organization. AP enables an organization to accomplish its objectives by bringing a systematic, disciplined approach to evaluate and improve the effectiveness of the entire payables process.

In addition to the traditional AP activities whereby liabilities to third-party entities (suppliers, suppliers, tax authorities, etc.) are recognized and paid based on the credit policies agreed to between the company and its suppliers, today's AP departments have taken on much wider roles including fraud prevention, cost reduction, workflow system solutions, cash-flow management, internal controls, and supplier (supply chain) financing.

The AP process is a business process that represents an organization's obligation to pay off a short-term debt to its creditors. AP also refers to short-term debt payments to suppliers and banks. The AP process is significantly impacted by other components within the P2P process.

The components of the AP process will be explored in this section and standards of internal controls are provided for each component. Each component is depicted in the following process flow.

Accounts Payable

Supplier Master	Invoice Processing	P-Card Process	T&E Processing	Payment Process	Accounting Processes	Customers	Reporting, Analytics, and Metrics
Obtain W-9 or W-8	Three Way Match	P-Card Processing	Payment Processing	Payment Approval	Accruals and the Fiscal Close	Suppliers	Produce Reports and Analytics
Perform TIN Matching or VAT Validation	E-invoice	P-Card Administration and Controls	T&E Audit and Control Process	ACH, P-Card, and Wires	General Ledger	Procurement • SLAs • Strategic Sourcing	Track Results and Trends
Supplier Validation and Compliance Screening	Manual Invoice	Reporting, Analytics, and Metrics	Reporting, Metrics, and Analytics	Manual Checks	Cash Management	Shared Service Center	
Perform Periodic Supplier Validation and Screening	Receipt (ERS)			Auto Payments • Recurring Payments	Clearing Accounts		
	PO Flip						

Internal Controls and Compliance

ERP Systems

AP Automation Solutions

CHAPTER ELEVEN

The Supplier Master File

 INTRODUCTION

When a member of the accounts payable team for a Fortune 50 company decided to bilk her employer, her knowledge of internal controls helped her to stay under the radar. She started by setting her brother up as a corporate supplier and then paid invoices to the fake firm for $9,999 weekly – just one dollar shy of the $10,000 limit requiring a second authorization signature. The well-constructed scam put her on track to net more than $500,000 a year.

To complicate the problem, much of what companies lose to fraud is never recovered. The cost of prosecution can be high and often exceeds the amount of the loss. Guilty individuals who are found guilty may be unable to make restitution. In addition, your company's reputation among shareowners and customers can be damaged if word gets out – making it appear that you have inadequate internal controls and have failed to be a good financial steward. So, that means prevention is the best solution of all.

With final power over the payments that go out the door and to whom, your accounts payable organization is uniquely positioned to be strategic contributors in the fight against fraud. And by doing so, your accounts payable team can become a more visible and strategic player in the overall operations of their company.

Key Point: Correct data in the supplier master file process supports accurate invoice processing. If the supplier master data is accurate, then we have confidence that supplier payments will be correct.

AP TOOL 29: SUPPLIER MASTER FILE PROCESS BEST PRACTICES

About This Tool: How can you make certain your suppliers are real and that the invoices you receive aren't fraudulent? The list includes ten important actions your accounts payable team can take up front to tighten up your supplier set-up process, and the critical steps you can take on an ongoing basis to for monitoring supplier invoices.

Tip 1: Require supplier profile forms.

The very first step in helping you weed out fraudulent shell companies and phantom suppliers is to require profile forms from all suppliers or use a supplier portal. Ask for the basics, including sales tax certificates, applicable business licenses, a physical business address, daytime phone number, and other verifiable confirmable data. It is also important to ask for the names of key officers so you can screen for any conflicts of interest.

Tip 2: Establish controls.

In addition to a profile form, it's important to have control points for each of your suppliers before the first payment goes out the door. Make certain you require and receive a completed W-9 form from each of your suppliers before the first payment is made. Use the IRS Tax Identification Number (TIN) online matching service to validate the information provided so you can confirm the supplier exists and has a valid TIN. This validation process will also help prevent B-Notices when you process your 1099s.

Tip 3: Look for initials.

When a supplier uses initials in a company name, it is often a red flag for fraud. Why? It is simply harder to track the supplier down. Experienced fraudsters know this trick well. So, be on the lookout for suppliers who use initials as their company name.

Tip 4: Beware of post office box addresses.

The use of a post office box can indicate an attempt to obscure a physical address or to divert company funds to a personal mailbox. While a post office box address alone isn't an indicator of fraud, it is yet another parameter you should consider as you establish suppliers in your system. Note that box numbers with one to four digits (typically used by independent mailbox providers) can be more indicative of risk than a traditional five-digit US Postal Service box number.

Key Point: Take a close look when "change of address" requests are received. Some experienced fraudsters will use one address initially to get established in your system, and then submit an address change order to divert the funds elsewhere once they are established in your supplier master file. So take a close look when "change of address" requests are received. Of course, electronic payments will alleviate the need to mail checks.

Tip 5: Search for high-risk zip codes.

Statistics show fraudulent transactions are more likely than average to be correlated with certain zip codes. Locations in New York, New Jersey, California, Florida, and border towns near Mexico are among those that often represent a higher risk. Your bank or credit-card company should be able to provide you with a current list of zip codes that may warrant a closer look.

Tip 6: Identify high-risk countries with a history of scam activity.

We've all heard of the e-mail scams based in Nigeria that bilk unsuspecting victims who agree to helping a wealthy foreigner move his fortunes to the United States. Flag them for review prior to payment and check the Office of Foreign Asset Control (OFAC) and Foreign Corrupt Practices Act (FCPA) violations. If you support the health care industry, be sure to validate your suppliers with the Office of Inspector General (OIG) for possible Medicare and Medicaid fraudsters. Continue monitoring your supplier master file since compliance lists are updated on a regular basis.

Tip 7: Beware of consecutive invoices numbering.

Have any of your suppliers submitted invoices with consecutive numbering? That means it is unlikely they are providing goods or services to other customers, unless they have set aside a series bank of numbers just for you.

Tip 8: Size matters: review small first-time payments.

Suppliers who want to test your internal controls will often submit a small initial invoice for a small dollar value, following it with larger invoices. Once they are firmly established in your supplier master file, they will begin to issue invoices for larger amounts. If the first payment issued to a supplier is unusually small relative to the average payment for similar products or services from other suppliers, it is an indicator of a potential risk.

Tip 9: Apply Benford's Law of Anomalies.

Benford's Law is an audit technique that can serve as a great tool in helping you uncover fraudulent financial activity. It is based on the discovery that for many kinds of numerical data, there is a pattern to be found in the numbers used for the first digits of any number.

While logic would say the first digit of an invoice amount could be any number so there should be an even spread among the first numbers used in an invoice amount, but in actual practice that's not the case. Benford's Law says that the larger the digit, the less likely it will be the first number in an invoice amount. The number 1 is by far the most frequent first digit number in an invoice amount (found in roughly one-third of all entries), while the number 9 is found to be the first digit number only 5% of the time.

Tip 10: Look for unusual spending increases.

Are certain suppliers billing you at significantly higher levels than before? Do their invoice amounts fall outside the norm for other suppliers in the same category? If that's the case, this could be a sign that fraudulent invoices are being submitted. Take time to dig into the background and take a closer look at those suppliers.

Supplier fraud is no accident; so, why should preventing it be? The best approach is proactive, early detection so you can avoid significant losses. Establish strong internal controls for adding new suppliers to your database; and, monitor your payables activity on an ongoing basis. Doing so can give you a competitive edge for combating fraud and help you stem its impact on your company's bottom line.

Tip 11: Perform TIN matching.

TIN matching is part of a suite of Internet based pre-filing e-services that allows "authorized payers" the opportunity to match 1099 payee information against IRS records prior to filing information returns.

An authorized payer is one who has filed forms 1099-B, 1099-DIV, 1099-INT, 1099-K, 1099-MISC, 1099-OID, or 1099-PATR with the IRS in at least one of the two past tax years.

Interactive TIN matching will accept up to 25 payee TIN/Name combinations on-screen while bulk TIN matching will allow up to 100,000 payee TIN/Name combinations to be matched via a text file submission.

Both programs will:

- match the payee name and TIN with IRS records;
- decrease backup withholding and penalty notices; and
- reduce the error rate in TIN validation.

Individuals who are authorized to act for the federal, state, local, or tribal government must first register to use e-services and select a username, password, and PIN. Then they can register to use TIN matching from the suite of e-service products available.[1]

(Refer to Chapter 7, Supplier Selection and Management and Chapter 22, Independent Contractors and the 1099 Process.)

---

[1]IRS, Taxpayer Identification Number (TIN) On-Line Matching, accessed July 22, 2020, https://www.irs.gov/government-entities/indian-tribal-governments/taxpayer-identification-number-tin-on-line-matching-1.

The Supplier Master Process Flow

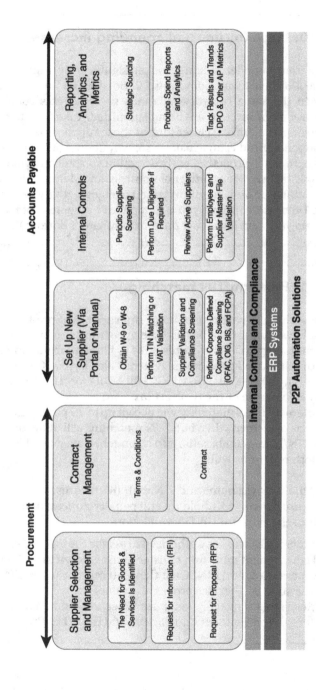

Supplier Master File Process Insights

The Supplier Master File Cleansing Process

A comprehensive supplier master file cleansing process streamlines operations for both accounts payable and procurement. This supplier master file cleanup is typically performed as part of a system conversion process, but should be performed annually to enhance internal controls and foster processing efficiencies.

The cleansing should incorporate the identification of inactive suppliers for purge, flagging duplicate suppliers for removal, isolating multiple remittance addresses for possible consolidation, implementing consistent supplier name and address conventions, commoditizing the supplier base, and establishing corporate linkage to support a strategic sourcing initiative. Below are the steps I recommend as part of this clean-up process:

1. Identify inactive suppliers
2. Remove duplicate supplier
3. Consolidate multiple remittance addresses
4. Pursue strategic sourcing

Four Steps to a Streamlined Supplier Master File

1. Identify Inactive Suppliers

The identification and periodic blocking or segregation of inactive suppliers increases processor keying speed, reduces errors, and will likely enhance system response time. The recommended timeframe is to focus on suppliers with no invoice activity within the prior 18 months. This covers seasonality and retains those supplier that invoice once a year.

For invoice processors, isolating inactive suppliers speeds keying by offering fewer supplier choices, and reduces the potential for selecting an outdated or incorrect supplier number. From a system response time, reducing the supplier base can significantly reduce the run-time for any report that extracts data from the supplier master file. It is critical to check with your purchasing counterparts as suppliers often cannot be segregated because they are linked to open purchase orders on file.

2. Remove Duplicate Suppliers

Duplicate suppliers are an exposure for any accounts payable organization, but represent an increased risk for an organization that has absorbed multiple locations and/or systems into a centralized operation. Duplicate suppliers increase the likelihood of duplicate payments and intensify the difficulty in compiling a comprehensive spend profile for supplier negotiations (i.e. "IBM," "I.B.M.," "International Business Machines," etc.).

In efforts to prevent duplicate suppliers from reappearing, we recommend that the supplier creation process require a lookup by the supplier address prior to adding new suppliers. This will minimize adding redundant suppliers at the source, particularly when the names or initials would be keyed slightly different. We also recommend using coding standards when setting up a new supplier this will also prevent setting up duplicate suppliers.

3. Consolidate Multiple Remittance Addresses

Many larger suppliers will have multiple remittance locations. These addresses are often geographically placed to expedite the flow of funds into the supplier's operation, or can be a function of the supplier's ownership structure. Suppliers with significant remittance addresses often include those operating in the areas of telecom, waste management, industrial parts, post offices, and technology.

Many companies have been successful in persuading suppliers to accept all payments to one remittance address (regardless of division). The savings can be fairly significant for both parties, as the supplier realizes administrative savings by having fewer people handling incoming remittances. An additional benefit is the ability to more easily capture all payment activity through one supplier number for use in negotiating company-wide purchasing agreements. This is an initiative best pursued with procurement, as they can potentially make the one remit-to address a condition of doing business with your company.

4. Pursue Strategic Sourcing

With few exceptions, Fortune 1000 organizations are burdened with an over-sized base of suppliers. Given that the average Fortune 1000 company buys approximately 400–500 commodities and maintains a global supplier base of over 50,000 suppliers, this means that there is an average of over 100 suppliers per commodity. This is clearly not optimal from the procurement or accounts payable standpoint. Those organizations that have been successfully optimized their supply base have addressed the following challenges:

- Senior management understands and supports the quantified impact that an aggressive strategic sourcing program has on earnings per share;

- The procurement organization has created the necessary systems to capture global spending, and routinely quantifies the financial savings from sourcing projects;
- Preferred supplier agreements are in place for 80% or more of the organization's common purchases; and
- The proper structure and/or incentives have been implemented to ensure employees buy only from preferred suppliers, and that negotiated prices are fully complied with.

Until all four areas are addressed, accounts payable and procurement will be fighting a difficult battle in maintaining a streamlined supplier base.

Supplier Master File Screening Best Practices

In the document "Corporate Compliance Principles," developed by the National Center for Preventive Law, a compliance program encompasses the set of operational methods that a company uses to ensure its activities adhere to legal requirements and broader company values. Designing effective compliance programs is an important corporate concern for two reasons.

1. First, public harm and corporate injuries potentially resulting from corporate offenses and deviations from company values justify careful management of offense and misconduct risks. Second, under a number of recently developed legal standards – most notably the Federal Sentencing Guidelines for Organizations – firms with generally effective compliance programs can often significantly reduce or eliminate penalties for offenses that occur despite these programs.
2. In recent years, both federal and state governments have increased enforcement activities as they relate to corporate conduct and compliance. Publicly traded companies and businesses that operate pursuant to a license, permit, statutory scheme, or government regulatory approval find themselves subject to higher governmental expectations. And corporations that compete in industries of high government interest, such as health care and financial services, are particularly at risk and are increasingly targeted in both civil and criminal proceedings.

Today, globalization and strategic outsourcing have increased the importance of third-party partners. At the same time increased regulation is forcing companies to take a much more comprehensive look at screening processes for new and current suppliers.

Key Point: Now mission-critical suppliers can be anywhere in the world and this dramatically increases supplier-related risk. The evolving regulatory environment also forces companies to assess and address their internal and external risks in an effort to maintain stability and to avoid significant fines. In this environment, suppliers are often considered an extension of your company and should be managed with due diligence, applying the regulatory compliance requirements that pertain to your specific industry.

Minimum Requirements

The minimum requirements of an effective compliance program are summarized below. These include:

1. High-level management must be designated as responsible for compliance;
2. The development of written policies and procedures;
3. The institution of training programs;
4. A consistent internal auditing system to detect illegal conduct;
5. Reasonable steps by management to prevent further occurrences after illegal conduct is detected;
6. Consistent enforcement and sanctions against wrongdoers; and
7. The exercise of due care to avoid delegation of authority to those with a propensity to engage in illegal conduct.

Supplier Compliance Impact and Application to Specific Industries and Best Practices

The top five compliance areas that an AP professional should be aware of along with the specific industries that the compliance areas pertain to are included in the following table and are the focus of this toolkit.

Compliance Area	Industries
1. Office of Foreign Assets Control (OFAC)	All
2. Bureau of Industry and Security (BIS)	Global Companies
3. Office of Inspector General (OIG)	Health Care
4. System for Award Management (SAM)	US Federal Government Contractors
5. Foreign Corrupt Practices Act (FCPA)	All

1. Office of Foreign Assets Control (OFAC)

In the broadest sense, OFAC regulations apply to all US citizens and permanent resident aliens, companies located in the United States as well as overseas branches of US companies, and some overseas subsidiaries of US companies.

OFAC regulations apply to all types of US companies and organizations. Practically speaking, any business that is involved in commerce is subject to OFAC regulations. Each business must assess their individual risk and determine their proper course in regard to OFAC compliance.

There are certain industries, in particular, that the United States became more concerned with after 9/11. These are industries that, by the very nature of their business, could unwittingly be used by terrorists as fronts for money laundering or could provide the means for countries unfriendly to the United States to raise funds and create financial networks within the United States.

OFAC regulations prohibit any US business or financial institution from doing business with sanctioned or blocked persons or entities otherwise known as Specially Designated Nationals. While there is no specific law that requires businesses to compare their customer(s) name against OFAC's SDN List, doing just that is the only way for businesses to identify transactions involving a SDN and maintain compliance with any currently imposed sanctions.

What is the Specially Designated Nationals (SDN) List?

The Specially Designated Nationals list is updated as new individuals and entities are identified as enemies of the United States. In theory the list could change on a daily basis. Checking the latest edition of the SDN List as well as updated information and current restrictions that affect the countries and parties with which you plan to do business is central to any business or financial institution's OFAC compliance program.

OFAC Compliance Program Best Practices

1. A designated employee – or in the case of larger businesses, a team of employees – who is responsible for the overall administration and implementation of your OFAC compliance program.
2. All new suppliers should be screened before they are established on the supplier master file. Additionally, current suppliers should be monitored on a periodic basis.

3. An effective monitoring program developed and maintained by that designated employee which screens your business transactions and stays current on the ever-changing OFAC lists and sanctions.

4. Internal procedures that ensure when a positive match occurs that OFAC is notified within the 10-day requirement and the appropriate blocking of assets takes place.

5. Appropriate training for all impacted persons within the organization to ensure they understand the goals of the program and any procedures related to their jobs that assist in maintaining the program.

6. An annual internal audit of the program and its procedures to double-check their effectiveness and make adjustments as needed.

7. An OFAC Specially Designated Nationals Update Service which alerts businesses that an update or change has been made to the SDN List.

8. OFAC Recent Actions Notification Service also alerts businesses to updates to the SDN List but in addition it makes them aware of any significant changes to the OFAC website.

9. Treasury E-mail Notification Services provide alerts to changes on individual sanctions pages.

2. The Bureau of Industry and Security (BIS)

The United States Department of Commerce's Bureau of Industry and Security (BIS), formerly known as the Bureau of Export Administration, is responsible for administering and enforcing export controls on US commercial products, software, and technology.

Key Point: BIS is also responsible for overseeing export controls on "dual-use" items that can be used in weapons of mass destruction applications, terrorist activities, or human rights abuses.

In addition to enforcing the Export Administration Regulations (EAR), BIS is responsible for issuing and administering several restricted party lists that apply to export and reexport transactions for which the agency has jurisdiction as provided below.

1. **Denied Persons List:** Includes the names of individuals and companies that have been denied export privileges by BIS, usually due to a violation of US export control laws. US persons and companies are generally prohibited from engaging in export transactions with parties named on the Denied Persons List.

2. **Entity List:** Identifies the names of companies, individuals, government agencies, and research institutions that trigger export and reexport license requirements. US companies need to ensure that the appropriate export

licenses are in place before proceeding with transactions with parties on the Entity List.

3. **Unverified List:** Includes the names of foreign parties that BIS have been unable to conduct a pre-license check or post-shipment verification. Potential transactions with parties on the Unverified List are a "red flag" that must be addressed and resolved before proceeding with the export.

BIS Compliance Program Best Practices

1. Determine the risk and applicability to your company's P2P process. Ideally, your company may not want to take the risk of dealing with a supplier who has been on the Denied Persons List as this could be an indication of other possible sanctions that could put your company at risk.

2. Determine who will be held accountable for maintaining the procedures and updating the information in the written policy as changes in the Federal Register are published related to the relevant sections.

3. Determine who should perform these checks based on what their current role is and whether vulnerabilities could be eliminated through evaluation of this information at each person's role and step in the customer and transaction evaluation process. Your written procedures should also clearly define which management position has oversight for ensuring the performance of the checks, and who is responsible for verifying the completion of the documentation.

4. Determine when the checks will be performed within your P2P process to eliminate the risk points of vulnerability. Carry this information over to other sections of your compliance program.

5. Create double checks throughout the P2P process. Consider whether there are areas of particular risk to your company that management should emphasize from the corporate perspective. Determine how management will be informed of effectiveness or ineffectiveness of internal controls implemented.

6. Determine how management will actively participate in various due diligence strategies.

3. The Office of Inspector General (OIG)

Office of Inspector General's (OIG) mission is to protect the integrity of Department of Health & Human Services (HHS) programs as well as the health and welfare of program beneficiaries.

Since its 1976 establishment, OIG has been at the forefront of the nation's efforts to fight waste, fraud, and abuse in Medicare, Medicaid, and more than 300 other HHS programs. OIG screening is important to hospitals, health care systems, and health care insurance companies. HHS OIG is the largest inspector general's office in the federal government, with more than 1,700 employees dedicated to combating fraud, waste, and abuse and to improving the efficiency of HHS programs.

Key Point: A majority of OIG's resources goes toward the oversight of Medicare and Medicaid – programs that represent a significant part of the federal budget and that affect this country's most vulnerable citizens. OIG's oversight extends to programs under other HHS institutions, including the Centers for Disease Control and Prevention, National Institutes of Health, and the Food and Drug Administration.

OIG Compliance Program Best Practices

1. Policies and Procedures
   - Regularly review and update with department managers and Compliance Committee.
   - Assess whether they are tailored to the intended audience and their job functions.
   - Ensure policies and procedures are written clearly and include real-life examples.
2. Measuring Effectiveness
   - Develop compliance program with benchmarks and measurable goals.
   - Set up a system to measure how well you are meeting those goals.
   - Involve the Board in creating the program and regularly update the Board regarding compliance risks, audits, and investigations.
   - If one or more goals are not met, investigate why and how to improve in the future.
   - Assess whether the compliance program has sufficient funding and support.
3. Training
   - Regularly review and update training programs. Try different approaches.
   - Make training completion a job requirement.
   - Test employees' understanding of training topics.
   - Maintain documentation to show which employees received training.
4. Supplier Screening
   - Health care organizations should screen new suppliers to ensure that they are not on the "List of Excluded Individuals/Entities" (http://exclusions.oig.hhs.gov/).
   - Current suppliers should also be screened on a periodic basis (monthly to quarterly).

4. System for Award Management (SAM) (Formerly the Excluded Parties List Systems (EPLS)

SAM is a federal government-owned and operated free website that consolidates the capabilities in CCR/FedReg, ORCA, and EPLS. Future phases of SAM will add the capabilities of other systems used in federal procurement and awards processes. The EPLS Search Web service is now available on SAM.gov. It is in the same format as it was in EPLS. The following is access and description information.

SAM is combining federal procurement systems and the Catalog of Federal Domestic Assistance into one new system. This consolidation is being done in phases. The first phase of SAM includes the functionality from the following systems:

- Central Contractor Registry (CCR)
- Federal Agency Registration (FedReg)
- Online Representations and Certifications Application
- Excluded Parties List System (EPLS)

SAM Compliance Best Practices
1. Enter a DUNS number, CAGE code, or Business Name to search for the entities that you are interested in reviewing.
2. The top search bar allows you to enter any search term. You can also enter exclusion search terms to search for exclusion records.
3. If you want to search for only a CAGE code or a DUNS number you can use the bottom two search bars. Once a search has returned results, use the filters provided to narrow results.
4. Government employees must create a SAM user account with their government e-mail address. Log in before searching in order to see FOUO information and those registrants who selected to opt out of the public search.

5. The Foreign Corrupt Practices Act (FCPA)

When passed in 1977, the FCPA was characterized by the American Bar Association as the most extensive application of federal law to the regulation of business since the passage of the 1933 and 1934 Securities Acts. American corporations to government officials in a number of countries had reported improper payments.

Congress acted decisively to restore the reputation of American business and eliminate improper payments to foreign governments, politicians, and political parties. In fact, the FCPA is actually an amendment to the 1934

Securities Exchange Act and is generally administered by the Securities Exchange Commission.

The FCPA contains both provisions against bribery and rules establishing accounting standards. The accounting rules apply only to companies that are required to report financial information under the securities laws. These accounting and recordkeeping rules are broad. Your accounting adviser or securities lawyer can advise you if you think that you may be subject to these requirements. Summaries of the two fundamental objectives of the FCPA, which are still legal requirements, are included here.

The Foreign Corrupt Practices Act ("FCPA") generally applies to all US corporations, partnerships and other business organization (generically, a "company"), as well as all persons acting on behalf of those entities. For purposes of this discussion, suffice it to say that the FCPA applies to a US company and its corporate subsidiaries, as well as their officers, directors, agents and shareholders.

The FCPA prohibits any payment or offer of payment to a "foreign official" for the purpose of influencing that official to assist in obtaining or retaining business for a company. The Act applies to any act or event that is "in further-ance of" a payment to a foreign official. Further, the "payment" clause of the FCPA is broadly phrased. It covers not only the actual payment of money but also an offer, promise, or authorization of the payment of money and an offer, gift, promise, or authorization of the giving of "anything of value." The Act also applies to payments to foreign officials, foreign political parties, officials of foreign political parties, and candidates for foreign political office.

In addition to its anti-bribery provisions, the FCPA also imposes certain accounting requirements on companies. Specifically, the FCPA requires that a company maintain books, records, and accounts that, in reasonable detail, accurately reflect the transactions and dispositions of that company. In order to comply with these requirements, it is imperative that company employees, agents, and others acting on its behalf to maintain complete and accurate records with respect to all transactions undertaken on behalf of the company.

Key Point: The consequences of failing to comply with the FCPA are potentially disastrous for a company and its employees. Violation of the FCPA and related laws by a company employee can result in millions of dollars in fines against the company and can subject the employee to pros-ecution, criminal fines, and imprisonment, as well as disciplinary action by the company, including dismissal. Note that the FCPA states that fines and penalties imposed on individuals may not be paid directly or indirectly by any corporation for which they may have acted.

FCPA Compliance Program Best Practices

An effective FCPA compliance program can be broken into two components: (1) Governance and Communication, and (2) Validation and Testing. The Validation and Testing component is particularly important to the P2P professional since one would need to ensure that any potential bribery transactions are not processed through the accounts payable process.

- **Governance and Communication**
    1. Top Level Commitment and "Tone at the Top"
    2. Recommended FCPA Roles and Responsibilities
    3. Comprehensive FCPA Internal Controls Program
    4. Corporate FCPA Policies and Procedures
    5. FCPA Education and Training Program
    6. Reporting Suspected Criminal Conduct (FPCA/Ethics Hotline)
    7. Right to Audit Clauses in Contracts
    8. Third Party Due Diligence
- **Validation and Testing**
    9. Global FCPA Self-Assessment Programs
    10. Corruption and Bribery Risk Assessment
    11. Remediation and Disciplinary Procedures
    12. Annual Testing of the FCPA Compliance Program
    13. Periodic FCPA Compliance Certifications (Employees, Business Partners, Contractors, Agents, Suppliers, Others)
    14. Leveraging Other Risk Mitigation Procedures
    15. Continuous FCPA Compliance Monitoring Programs (Governance and Transaction Based)

Additionally, the supplier master file should be reviewed to ensure that foreign officials are not set up as suppliers. We recommend reviewing your supplier master file to ensure that your organization has not established any foreign officials as suppliers. Foreign officials are also identified as Politically Exposed Persons (PEP). Resources that can assist with the identification process are included in the next sections.

TIN Matching

TIN Matching is part of a suite of Internet-based pre-filing e-services that allows "authorized payers" the opportunity to match 1099 payee information against IRS records prior to filing information returns.

An authorized payer is one who has filed forms 1099-B, 1099-DIV, 1099-INT, 1099-K, 1099-MISC, 1099-OID, or 1099-PATR with the IRS in at least one of the two past tax years. Interactive TIN Matching will accept up to 25 payee TIN/Name combinations onscreen while Bulk TIN Matching will allow up to 100,000 payee TIN/Name combinations to be matched via a text file submission.

Both programs will:

- Match the payee name and TIN with IRS records;
- Decrease backup withholding and penalty notices; and
- Reduce the error rate in TIN validation.

Individuals who are authorized to act for the federal, state, local, or tribal government must first register to use e-services and select a username, password, and PIN. Then they can register to use TIN Matching from the suite of e-service products available.

Initially, users must register online with e-services and will create a username, password, and PIN that will allow them to access the system electronically. Once the online registration is completed, users receive, at their home address, a confirmation token that they must validate online within 28 days of the initial registration.

All users within a firm must complete their own registration to have an e-services account established for their individual username and password. Once users are confirmed, the principal, (person at your firm responsible for completing the TIN Matching application and assigning user roles), will complete the application and all confirmed users may begin using Interactive or Bulk TIN Matching that same day.

E-services Registration Information Needed

- Legal name (verified with IRS & SSA records)
- Social ssecurity number (verified with SSA records)
- Date of birth (verified with SSA records)
- Telephone number
- E-mail address
- Adjusted gross income (AGI) from either your current year or prior year filed tax return (verified from IRS records).
- Username – Select your preferred username. Please read the rules for selecting your username.

- Password and PIN – Select your password and PIN. Please read the helpful hints on selecting a secure, unique password and PIN.
- Reminder question to recover a forgotten username.
- Home mailing address (verified from IRS records). If you have moved since you last transacted with the IRS, please update your information when registering.

Performing TIN Matching: Interactive Sessions and Bulk Uploading

Enrolled users may TIN match in one of two ways:

1. **Interactively:** A user can submit up to 25 name/TIN combinations at a time during a session, and receive a response within five seconds.
2. **Bulk Uploads:** Bulk upload users may download .txt files composed of up to 100,000 name/TIN combinations and receive a response from IRS within 24 hrs.
   - In Bulk TIN Matching, you may attach a .txt file with up to 100,000 TIN/Name combinations to be matched. The .txt file will be formatted as follows:
     - TIN Type – 1 = EIN, 2 = SSN, 3 = Unknown
     - TIN Number – 9 digit taxpayer identification number
     - Entity Name – Up to 40 characters
     - Account Number – Optional field with up to 20 alpha/numeric characters
   - A semi-colon (;) will be the delimiter between fields. Each line of input will signify a new record.
   - You must submit a TIN/Name combination.
   - Due to privacy issues, IRS will not divulge an entity's name or TIN.
   - If you submit a record without the required fields (TIN Type, TIN, Name), the response you will receive will be Indicator 4, Invalid Request.
   - If you do not know the TIN Type, enter "3" and the system will check both the SSN and EIN master files.
   - Within 24 hours, the response will be sent to a secure mailbox and an e-mail notification will be sent to you indicating a response is waiting.
   - You will have 30 days to access and download the results file.
   - Once accessed, the results are retained for three days before being purged.
   - The same information you sent in the .txt file will be returned with one additional field containing the results indicator.

- The TIN Matching system is accessible 24 hours a day, seven days a week. Support services include online tutorials to assist customers with the registration, application, and TIN Matching process.
- Please see Pub 2108-A, On-Line Taxpayer Identification Number (TIN) Matching Program for more information. It can also be downloaded at: http://www.irs.gov/pub/irs-pdf/p2108a.pdf

 ## AP TOOL 30: SUPPLIER MASTER FILE CODING STANDARDS

About This Tool: A supplier master file that lacks discipline and control can cause several inefficiencies in the accounts payable process. One of the common outcomes of an "out of control" supplier master file is duplicate suppliers which can create scenarios for duplicate payments to occur.

Here are examples of supplier coding standards to consider when setting up new suppliers in your supplier master file and when cleaning up your supplier master file on an annual basis. We are providing you with coding standards to use when coding your supplier name and when coding your supplier address. And as bonus material, we're adding the abbreviation tables for streets, US states and territories, and Canadian provinces.

Examples of Supplier Coding Standard: Supplier Name

	Standard	Valid	Invalid
Supplier Name	No periods (.), commas (,) or punctuation marks (!)(/) should be keyed into the supplier name.	IBM John T Smith Dr Harry S Smythe MD	I.B.M. John T. Smith Dr. Harry S. Smythe M.D.
	"The" is eliminated if it is the first word in supplier/payees name.	Coca-Cola Company	The Coca-Cola Company
	No spaces should be used before or after special characters or initials.	B&B Enterprises AT&T 100% Incorporated @Radical Medical 2+2 Productions	B & B Enterprises A T & T 100% Incorporated @ Radical Medical 2 + 2 Productions

Numeric values used in the name field will be entered as such.	3M Corporation	Three M Corporation
	9 West	Nine West
	Club 33	Club Thirty Three
Do not use abbreviations for North, South, East, and West if it is part of the supplier name.	East Coast Supply	E. Coast Supply
	North American Van Lines	No. American Van Lines
	South Florida Fence Co	S. Florida Fence Co
No space between last names with 2 words.	McBeth	Mc Beth
	MacDonald Hunter Corp	Mac Donald Hunter Corp
	DeYoung	De Young

Examples of Supplier Coding Standard: Supplier Address

	Standard	Valid	Invalid
Supplier Address	A North, South, East, West street address will be abbreviated without periods.	120 S Baker	120 S. Baker
	Use numbers in street abbreviation versus words:	1st St	First Street
		49th Ave	Forty-Ninth Avenue
		100th St	One-Hundredth Street
	North, South, East, and West used in the city name should be spelled out in full.	North Hollywood	N. Hollywood
		West Palm Beach	W. Palm Beach
	Words in the city name should be spelled out in full.	Fort Myers	Ft. Myers
		Saint Louis	St. Louis

Standard Abbreviations for Street Addresses

Avenue	Ave
Boulevard	Blvd
Court	Ct
Drive	Dr
Expressway	Expy
Freeway	Fwy
Highway	Hwy
Lake	Lk
Lane	Ln
Place	Pl
Route	Rt
Square	Sq
Street	St
Terrace	Ter
Turnpike	Tpke
Way	Way

Abbreviations for US States/Territories and Canadian Provinces

State or Territory	Two-Letter Abbreviation	State or Territory	Two-Letter Abbreviation
Alabama	AL	North Dakota	ND
Alaska	AL	Ohio	OH
Arizona	AZ	Oklahoma	OK
Arkansas	AR	Oregon	OR
California	CA	Pennsylvania	PA
Canal Zone	CZ	Puerto Rico	PR
Colorado	CO	Rhode Island	RI
Connecticut	CT	South Carolina	SC
Delaware	DE	South Dakota	SD

Abbreviations for US States/Territories and Canadian Provinces

State or Territory	Two-Letter Abbreviation	State or Territory	Two-Letter Abbreviation
District of Columbia	DC	Tennessee	TN
Florida	FL	Texas	TX
Georgia	GA	Utah	UT
Guam	GU	Vermont	VT
Hawaii	HI	Virgin Islands	VI
Idaho	ID	Virginia	VA
Illinois	IL	Washington	WA
Indiana	IN	West Virginia	WV
Iowa	IA	Wisconsin	WI
Kansas	KS	Wyoming	WY
Kentucky	KY		
Louisiana	LA		
Maine	ME		
Maryland	MD	**Canadian Province**	**Abbreviation**
Massachusetts	MA	Alberta	AB
Michigan	MI	British Columbia	BC
Minnesota	MN	Manitoba	MB
Mississippi	MS	New Brunswick	NB
Missouri	MO	Newfoundland	NF
Montana	MT	Northwest Territories	NT
Nebraska	NE	Nova Scotia	NS
Nevada	NV	Nunavut	NT
New Hampshire	NH	Ontario	ON
New Jersey	NJ	Prince Edward Island	PE
New Mexico	NM	Quebec	QC
New York	NY	Saskatchewan	SK
North Carolina	NC	Yukon Territory	YT

STANDARDS OF INTERNAL CONTROL: SUPPLIER MASTER

Internal Control	Type of Control	Risks Mitigated
11.A Implement SoD Controls. SoD Controls will ensure that responsibilities for the supplier master are separated from the invoice processing and payment processes. **Refer to risks: 11-1, 11-2, 11-3, 11-4, 11-5, 11-6**	**Preventive** **Organizational** **Policy** **Procedure**	**11-1 Unauthorized Access to Supplier Master Data.** This risk may enable an employee to set up a new supplier, pay that supplier, and cover their tracks with an accounting entry. **11-2 Incorrect Supplier Payments.** Inappropriate, unauthorized, inaccurate, or duplicate payments to unauthorized suppliers. **11-3 Unauthorized access to sensitive information.** Intentional or accidental update to supplier master file which could impact safeguarding of assets, data corruption, violations of privacy. **11-4 Supplier Master File Accuracy.** Unauthorized or inaccurate or non-compliant supplier information in database, which could result in unauthorized payment to the supplier and significant fines. **11-5 Inaccurate Supplier Information.** Input of inaccurate information in enterprise resource planning (ERP) system may result in untimely payment to the supplier. **11-6 Phony Suppliers.** Fictitious suppliers, scam suppliers, shell companies, or employees posing as suppliers.

Internal Control	Type of Control	Risks Mitigated
11.B Define Ownership and Accountability for the Supplier Master File Process. Defining a data owner helps ensure accountability and responsibility for the accuracy and integrity of the supplier master file. **Refer to risks: 11-1, 11-2, 11-3, 11-4, 11-5, 11-6**	Preventive Organizational Policy Procedure	**11-1 Unauthorized Access to Supplier Master Data.** This risk may enable an employee to set up a new supplier, pay that supplier, and cover their tracks with an accounting entry. **11-2 Incorrect Supplier Payments.** Inappropriate, unauthorized, inaccurate, or duplicate payments to unauthorized suppliers. **11-3 Unauthorized access to sensitive information.** Intentional or accidental update to supplier master file which could impact safeguarding of assets, data corruption, violations of privacy. **11-4 Supplier Master File Accuracy.** Unauthorized or inaccurate or non-compliant supplier information in database, which could result in unauthorized payment to the supplier and significant fines. **11-5 Inaccurate Supplier Information.** Input of inaccurate information in enterprise resource planning (ERP) system may result in untimely payment to the supplier. **11-6 Phony Suppliers.** Fictitious suppliers, scam suppliers, shell companies, or employees posing as suppliers.

(Continued)

Internal Control	Type of Control	Risks Mitigated
11.C Implement System Access Controls. Many AP software packages have the ability to limit access to the supplier master file based on user IDs, passwords, and other controls. Password standards can be defined on password length, complexity, frequency of required change, and other restrictions. Access can be granted to read only, or change and update supplier master file data. **Refer to risks: 11-1, 11-2, 11-3, 11-4, 11-5, 11-6**	**Preventive** **Organizational** **Policy** **Procedure**	**11-1 Unauthorized Access to Supplier Master Data.** This risk may enable an employee to set up a new supplier, pay that supplier, and cover their tracks with an accounting entry. **11-2 Incorrect Supplier Payments.** Inappropriate, unauthorized, inaccurate, or duplicate payments to unauthorized suppliers. **11-3 Unauthorized access to sensitive information.** Intentional or accidental update to supplier master file which could impact safeguarding of assets, data corruption, violations of privacy. **11-4 Supplier Master File Accuracy.** Unauthorized or inaccurate or non-compliant supplier information in database, which could result in unauthorized payment to the supplier and significant fines. **11-5 Inaccurate Supplier Information.** Input of inaccurate information in enterprise resource planning (ERP) system may result in untimely payment to the supplier. **11-6 Phony Suppliers.** Fictitious suppliers, scam suppliers, shell companies, or employees posing as suppliers.

Internal Control	Type of Control	Risks Mitigated
11.D Establish Clear Supplier Set-up Procedures. The policies and procedures for supplier setup should be clearly documented. The use of a standard form or format will help ensure consistency and compliance with policies and procedures and naming conventions. **Refer to risks: 11-1, 11-2, 11-3, 11-4, 11-5, 11-6**	**Preventive** **Organizational** **Policy** **Procedure**	**11-1 Unauthorized Access to Supplier Master Data.** This risk may enable an employee to set up a new supplier, pay that supplier, and cover their tracks with an accounting entry. **11-2 Incorrect Supplier Payments.** Inappropriate, unauthorized, inaccurate, or duplicate payments to unauthorized suppliers. **11-3 Unauthorized access to sensitive information.** Intentional or accidental update to supplier master file which could impact safeguarding of assets, data corruption, violations of privacy. **11-4 Supplier Master File Accuracy.** Unauthorized or inaccurate or non-compliant supplier information in database, which could result in unauthorized payment to the supplier and significant fines. **11-5 Inaccurate Supplier Information.** Input of inaccurate information in enterprise resource planning (ERP) system may result in untimely payment to the supplier. **11-6 Phony Suppliers.** Fictitious suppliers, scam suppliers, shell companies, or employees posing as suppliers.

(Continued)

Internal Control	Type of Control	Risks Mitigated
11.E Implement Supplier Payment Controls. Ensure that bank accounts for new suppliers are verified and are changed with proper authorization and additional verification. Establish an approval process for all payments which include wires, international payments, and large payments over a specific dollar amount. (Example: > $250,000) **Refer to risk: 11-2**	**Managerial Review** **Preventive** **Organizational** **Policy** **Procedure** **Supervisory**	**11-2 Incorrect Supplier Payments.** Inappropriate, unauthorized, inaccurate, or duplicate payments to unauthorized suppliers.
11.F Implement a Controls Self-Assessment Process to Check for Duplicate and Erroneous Payments. Review the effectiveness of internal controls for this sub-process and review system-generated audit trails. Ensure that all issues are remediated in a timely manner to properly mitigate risk within the sub-process. **Refer to risks: 11-1, 11-2, 11-3, 11-4, 11-5, 11-6**	**Corrective** **Managerial Review** **Preventive** **Organizational** **Policy** **Procedure** **Supervisory**	**11-1 Unauthorized Access to Supplier Master Data.** This risk may enable an employee to set up a new supplier, pay that supplier, and cover their tracks with an accounting entry. **11-2 Incorrect Supplier Payments.** Inappropriate, unauthorized, inaccurate, or duplicate payments to unauthorized suppliers. **11-3 Unauthorized access to sensitive information.** Intentional or accidental update to supplier master file which could impact safeguarding of assets, data corruption, violations of privacy.

Internal Control	Type of Control	Risks Mitigated
		11-4 Supplier Master File Accuracy. Unauthorized or inaccurate or non-compliant supplier information in database, which could result in unauthorized payment to the supplier and significant fines.
		11-5 Inaccurate Supplier Information. Input of inaccurate information in enterprise resource planning (ERP) system may result in untimely payment to the supplier.
		11-6 Phony Suppliers. Fictitious suppliers, scam suppliers, shell companies, or employees posing as suppliers.
11.G Enforce New Supplier Approval Practices. Sufficient due diligence procedures should be in place requiring review and evaluation of new supplier criteria (financial and operational) prior to accepting a new supplier. **Refer to risks: 11-1, 11-2, 11-3, 11-4, 11-5, 11-6**	Managerial Review Preventive Organizational Policy Procedure Supervisory	**11-1 Unauthorized Access to Supplier Master Data.** This risk may enable an employee to set up a new supplier, pay that supplier, and cover their tracks with an accounting entry. **11-2 Incorrect Supplier Payments.** Inappropriate, unauthorized, inaccurate, or duplicate payments to unauthorized suppliers. **11-3 Unauthorized access to sensitive information.** Intentional or accidental update to supplier master file which could impact safeguarding of assets, data corruption, and violations of privacy.

(Continued)

Internal Control	Type of Control	Risks Mitigated
		11-4 Supplier Master File Accuracy. Unauthorized or inaccurate or non-compliant supplier information in database, which could result in unauthorized payment to the supplier and significant fines.
		11-5 Inaccurate Supplier Information. Input of inaccurate information in enterprise resource planning (ERP) system may result in untimely payment to the supplier.
		11-6 Phony Suppliers. Fictitious suppliers, scam suppliers, shell companies, or employees posing as suppliers.
11.H Establish a Supplier Validation Process. Ensure that new suppliers are compliance checked with Office of Foreign Assets (OFAC), Bureau of Industry and Security (BIS), Office of Inspector General (OIG), and Foreign Corrupt Practices (FCPA) lists as defined by the corporation. Other validation processes include obtaining a W-9 and completing TIN matching. Also obtain a W-8 and perform Value-Added Tax (VAT) verification. Also verify the supplier's address, phone number, and website. **Refer to risks: 11-1, 11-2, 11-3, 11-4, 11-5, 11-6**	Managerial Review Preventive Organizational Policy Procedure Supervisory	**11-1 Unauthorized Access to Supplier Master Data.** This risk may enable an employee to set up a new supplier, pay that supplier, and cover their tracks with an accounting entry. **11-2 Incorrect Supplier Payments.** Inappropriate, unauthorized, inaccurate, or duplicate payments to unauthorized suppliers. **11-3 Unauthorized access to sensitive information.** Intentional or accidental update to supplier master file which could impact safeguarding of assets, data corruption, and violations of privacy.

Internal Control	Type of Control	Risks Mitigated
		11-4 Supplier Master File Accuracy. Unauthorized or inaccurate or non-compliant supplier information in database, which could result in unauthorized payment to the supplier and significant fines.
		11-5 Inaccurate Supplier Information. Input of inaccurate information in enterprise resource planning (ERP) system may result in untimely payment to the supplier.
		11-6 Phony Suppliers. Fictitious suppliers, scam suppliers, shell companies, or employees posing as suppliers.
11.I Apply Consistent Naming Conventions. One of the simplest way to help ensure accuracy and integrity of the supplier master file is to establish naming conventions and make sure that everyone responsible for data entry is adequately trained on entering and maintaining suppliers. **Refer to risks: 11-1, 11-2, 11-3, 11-4, 11-5, 11-6**	Preventive Organizational Policy Procedure Supervisory	**11-1 Unauthorized Access to Supplier Master Data.** This risk may enable an employee to set up a new supplier, pay that supplier, and cover their tracks with an accounting entry. **11-2 Incorrect Supplier Payments.** Inappropriate, unauthorized, inaccurate, or duplicate payments to unauthorized suppliers. **11-3 Unauthorized access to sensitive information.** Intentional or accidental update to supplier master file which could impact safeguarding of assets, data corruption, and violations of privacy.

(Continued)

Internal Control	Type of Control	Risks Mitigated
		11-4 Supplier Master File Accuracy. Unauthorized or inaccurate or non-compliant supplier information in database, which could result in unauthorized payment to the supplier and significant fines.
		11-5 Inaccurate Supplier Information. Input of inaccurate information in enterprise resource planning (ERP) system may result in untimely payment to the supplier.
		11-6 Phony Suppliers. Fictitious suppliers, scam suppliers, shell companies, or employees posing as suppliers.
11.J Enforce Data Validation. While many AP software packages contain data validation editing to help ensure the accuracy of data input to the system, a suggested best practice is to have a quality assurance function where someone separate from data entry reviews key data entry fields for accuracy prior to updating the supplier master file. **Refer to risks: 11-1, 11-2, 11-3, 11-4, 11-5, 11-6**	Managerial Review Preventive Organizational Policy Procedure Supervisory	**11-1 Unauthorized Access to Supplier Master Data.** This risk may enable an employee to set up a new supplier, pay that supplier, and cover their tracks with an accounting entry. **11-2 Incorrect Supplier Payments.** Inappropriate, unauthorized, inaccurate, or duplicate payments to unauthorized suppliers. **11-3 Unauthorized access to sensitive information.** Intentional or accidental update to supplier master file which could impact safeguarding of assets, data corruption, and violations of privacy.

Internal Control	Type of Control	Risks Mitigated
		11-4 Supplier Master Accuracy. Unauthorized or inaccurate or non-compliant supplier information in database, which could result in unauthorized payment to the supplier and significant fines.
		11-5 Inaccurate Supplier Information. Input of inaccurate information in enterprise resource planning (ERP) system may result in untimely payment to the supplier.
		11-6 Phony Suppliers. Fictitious suppliers, scam suppliers, shell companies, or employees posing as suppliers.
11.K Remove Old/Unused Suppliers from the System. It is considered a best practice to keep the supplier master file up to date. However, it is important to understand the limitations and requirements of the organization's AP system prior to deleting any suppliers, especially if the system links to archived transactional records. A best practice used by several Fortune 500 companies is to review and purge duplicate supplier records on an annual basis when there has been no activity for 18 months. **Refer to risks: 11-1, 11-2, 11-3, 11-4, 11-5, 11-6**	**Managerial Review** **Preventive** **Organizational** **Policy** **Procedure** **Supervisory**	**11-1 Unauthorized Access to Supplier Master Data.** This risk may enable an employee to set up a new supplier, pay that supplier, and cover their tracks with an accounting entry. **11-2 Incorrect Supplier Payments.** Inappropriate, unauthorized, inaccurate or duplicate payments to unauthorized, suppliers. **11-3 Unauthorized access to sensitive information.** Intentional or accidental update to supplier master file which could impact safeguarding of assets, data corruption, and violations of privacy.

(Continued)

Internal Control	Type of Control	Risks Mitigated
		11-4 Supplier Master File Accuracy. Unauthorized or inaccurate or non-compliant supplier information in database, which could result in unauthorized payment to the supplier and significant fines.
		11-5 Inaccurate Supplier Information. Input of inaccurate information in enterprise resource planning (ERP) system may result in untimely payment to the supplier.
		11-6 Phony Suppliers. Fictitious suppliers, scam suppliers, shell companies, or employees posing as suppliers.
11.L Retaining the Right Records. Develop a record retention policy that is in compliance with federal, state, and local legal and regulatory requirements. Ensure that the supplier master file is in compliance with this policy. **Refer to risks: 11-1, 11-2, 11-3, 11-4, 11-5, 11-6**	**Managerial Review** **Preventive** **Organizational** **Policy** **Procedure** **Supervisory**	**11-1 Unauthorized Access to Supplier Master Data.** This risk may enable an employee to set up a new supplier, pay that supplier, and cover their tracks with an accounting entry. **11-2 Incorrect Supplier Payments.** Inappropriate, unauthorized, inaccurate, or duplicate payments to unauthorized suppliers. **11-3 Unauthorized access to sensitive information.** Intentional or accidental update to supplier master file which could impact safeguarding of assets, data corruption, and violations of privacy.

Internal Control	Type of Control	Risks Mitigated
		11-4 Supplier Master File Accuracy. Unauthorized or inaccurate or non-compliant supplier information in database, which could result in unauthorized payment to the supplier and significant fines.
		11-5 Inaccurate Supplier Information. Input of inaccurate information in enterprise resource planning (ERP) system may result in untimely payment to the supplier.
		11-6 Phony Suppliers. Fictitious suppliers, scam suppliers, shell companies, or employees posing as suppliers.
11.M Perform an Employee and Supplier Master File Cross Check. To ensure that employees are not posing as suppliers, run a cross check on the employee and supplier master files. Check for name, address, TIN, EIN, and SSN, contact information, and bank account data every 6 months to 1 year. Check to see if the employee's bank account has been changed on a frequent basis. **Refer to risk: 11-6**	Corrective Managerial Review Preventive Organizational Policy Procedure Supervisory	**11-6 Phony Suppliers.** Fictitious suppliers, scam suppliers, shell companies, or employees posing as suppliers.

CHAPTER TWELVE

Invoice Processing

INTRODUCTION

Invoice processing is the process of handling incoming invoices – from the arrival of invoices to posting. Invoices can have many variations and types, but in general, invoices are grouped into two main types:

1. Invoices associated with a purchase order (PO).
2. Invoices that do not have an associated request and/or no PO or non-PO.

Most organizations have a clear invoice system in place with instructions regarding the processing of incoming invoices within their accounts payable (AP) department. Instructions will vary whether an invoice is a PO-based invoice or a non-PO invoice.

The invoice process begins when a supplier invoice arrives to an organization, regardless of the methods of arrival. There are many ways an invoice could arrive to an organization including e-mail, postal mail, facsimile, electronic, etc. Once an invoice arrives, organizations can either process the invoice manually or through the use of invoice automation technology.

Key Point: The advent of invoice automaton technology redefined AP invoice processing and enables the automation of invoice processing from arrival to post. AP automation is defined as the solutions and services which automate the people- and paper-based processing invoices for approval and posting into the accounting system.

Invoice Processing Process Flow

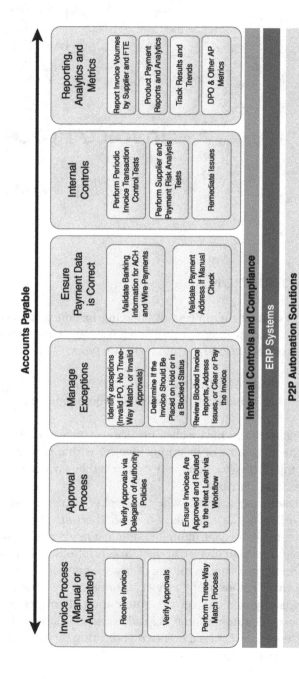

Accounts Payable

Invoice Process (Manual or Automated)
- Receive Invoice
- Verify Approvals
- Perform Three-Way Match Process

Approval Process
- Verify Approvals via Delegation of Authority Policies
- Ensure Invoices Are Approved and Routed to the Next Level via Workflow

Manage Exceptions
- Identify exceptions (Invalid PO, No Three-Way Match, or Invalid Approvals)
- Determine If the Invoice Should Be Placed on Hold or in a Blocked Status
- Review Blocked Invoice Reports, Address Issues, or Clear or Pay the Invoice

Ensure Payment Data is Correct
- Validate Banking Information for ACH and Wire Payments
- Validate Payment Address If Manual Check

Internal Controls
- Perform Periodic Invoice Transaction Control Tests
- Perform Supplier and Payment Risk Analysis Tests
- Remediate Issues

Reporting, Analytics and Metrics
- Report Invoice Volumes by Supplier and FTE
- Product Payment Reports and Analytics
- Track Results and Trends
- DPO & Other AP Metrics

Internal Controls and Compliance

ERP Systems

P2P Automation Solutions

INVOICE PROCESSING INSIGHTS

Invoice processing includes all the steps needed to process an invoice and is driven by the level of automation. As an example, a manual procedure is a hands-on process that is described in this section. Invoices have to be manually sorted, scanned, coded to the correct general ledger account, and approved. The amount of manual steps will increase the risk of manual manipulation and the cost to process a single invoice.

Defining the Invoice Processing Universe

From paper to payment, the invoice processing universe comprises six different functional components, including:

1. **Paper Invoice Receipt:** This is the hands-on process that is necessary to prepare paper invoices for scanning and electronic access. Steps may include sorting invoices into different batches (by cost center, business unit, supplier type, etc.), removing invoices from envelopes, removing staples, and making photocopies of smaller items, if required. Sometimes blank separator pages need to be inserted between invoices and their attachments. AP operators in the mailroom typically carry out the paper invoice receipt step.

2. **Document and Data Capture:** This is the process of converting paper invoices and other transaction-related documents into digital images and index data. Document scanning and data extraction could be centralized or remote, based on an organization's specific needs. Specific steps include scanning, image enhancement, indexing, validation, and data extraction, most of which are handled automatically by an invoice automation solution provider. In some cases, manual data entry or review of extracted data is required.

3. **Electronic Invoicing:** Most invoice automation solutions come bundled with a supplier portal or can be integrated with an electronic invoice network, which suppliers can utilize to submit invoices electronically. Suppliers have the option of selecting the method that best suits them from a range of electronic submission options: enter data manually in the portal; flip purchase orders into invoices; or browse and upload documents from accounting systems. The electronic invoice component is also configured with validation checks and buyer-defined tolerance levels to check invoices for missing information and exceptions. Suppliers are immedi-

ately notified about invoices that fail the validation criteria and are asked to correct the exceptions before the invoice is resubmitted and forwarded to the AP department.

4. **Content Management:** This refers to the delivery, storage, management, and disposition of electronic documents and index data. Some invoice processing automation solutions come bundled with a central repository that can store invoice images and data, while others rely on third-party content management solutions for this purpose. The content management system integrates closely with clients' existing ERP or back-end accounting systems to enable seamless retrieval of documents from within the client system to users with the appropriate access rights.

5. **Matching and Workflow:** This includes the matching of PO-based invoices as well as the electronic approval of non-PO invoices and the resolution of any exceptions related to PO invoices. Most solutions allow the creation and maintenance of workflows through a menu-driven, easy-to-use interface, which can be managed by business administrators without involvement of the IT department. Tasks and pending invoices can be routed to various individuals within the organization according to pre-defined business rules. Common features include automatic notifications to users when specific actions are required, reminder messages, and escalation procedures based on approval hierarchies.

6. **Reporting and Analysis:** Analyzing key invoice receipt-to-pay metrics and monitoring individual user's actions for quality control and load balancing are a key part of implementing a workflow automation solution. Typical reporting and analysis tools include the generation of standard and ad hoc reports detailing invoices pending approval, past due invoices, and average invoice processing time. Some solutions offer robust reporting functionality bundled with the solution, while others only allow for download of transactional data to third-party reporting tools.

The Matching Process

Matching is a process performed for goods and services ordered through a purchase order that takes place during the online invoice approval process. Invoices are matched to purchase orders (two-way matching), receiving information (three-way matching), and inspection information (four-way matching) as applicable. The invoices must meet matching tolerances or a hold is placed on the invoice and payment cannot be made until the hold is resolved or manually released.

The accounts payable process shares purchase order information from your organization's purchasing system or applicable ERP module to enable online matching with invoices. The visibility to this data allows the automated matching of invoice line items to the original purchase orders to ensure that your company issues payment only for the goods or services ordered and received. If your company is invoiced for an item over the amount and quantity tolerances you define in your tolerance policy, the invoice will be placed in a hold or blocked status until the issue is resolved.

In many cases, a single invoice can be matched to multiple purchase order shipments or multiple invoices can be matched to a single purchase order shipment. Internal controls within the accounts payable process ensure that you match only to valid purchase orders for the supplier on an open invoice and that the purchase order, date, and invoice currency match.

When an invoice is matched to a purchase order, the accounts payable process creates an invoice distribution using the purchase order distribution accounting information. An invoice distribution created through matching cannot be deleted. However, if accounts payable associate incorrectly matches an invoice to a purchase order, the individual distributions usually are voided with supervisory override to cancel the match.

TYPES OF MATCHING PROCESSES

1. **Two-Way Matching Process or Evaluated Receipt Settlement (ERS)**

   ERS is a business process between trading partners that conduct commerce without invoices. In an ERS transaction, the supplier ships goods based upon an advance shipping notice (ASN), and the purchaser, upon receipt, confirms the existence of a corresponding purchase order or contract, verifies the identity and quantity of the goods, and then pays the supplier. The purchaser matches the goods receipt (bill of lading, packing slip) to the ASN, purchase order, or contract to validate accuracy.

2. **Three-Way Matching Process**

   Three-way matching is a verification technique used by the accounts payable department and automated by most ERP systems. The use of automated three-way matching solutions includes the option to integrate to an ERP system, but even these solutions will kick out some transactions for which the automated solution fails, requiring manual investigation of discrepancies.

When accounts payable receives an invoice from a supplier, it matches the following information:

- The information on the invoice to a copy of the related purchase order that has been forwarded to it by the purchasing department. The purchase order states the quantity and price at which the company agrees to buy the goods or services stated on the supplier's invoice.
- The supplier invoice to receiving documentation forwarded to the accounting department by the receiving department, to ensure that the goods have been received, that they are in the correct quantity, and that they are in good condition.

Thus, the three-way match concept refers to matching three documents – the invoice, the purchase order, and the receiving report – to ensure that a payment should be made. The procedure is used to ensure that only authorized purchases are reimbursed, thereby preventing losses due to fraud and carelessness.

3. **The Four-Way Matching Process**

Many organizations define the four-way match concept that includes the verification of the acceptance documents and invoice information match within the quantity tolerances defined:

Quantity billed = Quantity accepted.

The acceptance is completed when after the goods are accepted. In summary, the components of the four-way match process include: the invoice, the purchase order, the receiving report, and the quality or inspection report. The four-way match process also refers to matching the purchase order, receipt, and invoice to the contracted terms and conditions.

AUTOMATING THE MATCHING PROCESS

If a company still has a fair number of purchases requiring three-way matching, it can consider doing so through an automated process. Doing so requires that the following system components be present:

- A document management system into which all supplier invoices are scanned as they are received.
- An automated matching system, as is found in some enterprise resource planning (ERP) systems.
- A data capture system that extracts information from scanned documents and stores this information in a database for use by the automated

matching system. Data capture requires that a number of rules be loaded in advance, detailing such issues as where information is located on a supplier invoice, for each supplier invoice template.

Ideally, this combination of systems should scan all incoming invoices, extract information from them, load it into the ERP system for matching purposes, and schedule the invoices for payment. A large amount of customization is required before these systems can be relied upon to consistently conduct three-way matching with minimal operator intervention. Typically, the system begins with a low success rate, which gradually increases as the data capture rules are improved to match the requirements of each supplier's invoice.

AP TOOL 31: ESTABLISHING TOLERANCES

About This Tool: According to Oracle, invoice tolerances determine whether matching holds are placed on invoices for variances between invoices and the documents you match them to, such as purchase orders. When you run the invoice validation process for a matched invoice, the process checks that matching occurs within the defined tolerances. For example, if the billed amount of an item exceeds a tolerance, a hold is placed on the invoice. You can't pay the invoice until the hold is released. You can define tolerances based on quantity or amount. For each type of tolerance, you can specify percentages or amounts.

Quantity-Based Tolerances

1. **Quantity-Based Tolerances:** Quantity-based tolerances apply to invoices with a match basis of quantity.
2. **Ordered Percentage:** The percentage difference more than the ordered quantity on a purchase order schedule line that you allow suppliers to invoice. Validation checks the billed quantity against the ordered quantity without considering price.
3. **Maximum Ordered:** The quantity difference more than the ordered quantity on a purchase order schedule line that you allow suppliers to invoice. Validation checks the billed quantity against the ordered quantity without considering price. You can use this tolerance if most of your purchase orders have the same relative value.
4. **Received Percentage:** The percentage difference more than the received quantity on a purchase order schedule line that you allow suppliers to

invoice. Validation checks the billed quantity against the received quantity without considering price.

5. **Maximum Received:** The quantity difference more than the received quantity on a purchase order schedule line that you allow suppliers to invoice. Validation checks the billed quantity against the received quantity without considering price. You can use this tolerance if most of your purchase orders have the same relative value.

6. **Price Percentage:** The percentage difference more than the unit price on a purchase order schedule line that you allow suppliers to invoice.

7. **Conversion Rate Amount:** The variance that you allow between an invoice amount and the amount of a purchase order schedule. Validation compares the ledger currency amounts, using the invoice and purchase order conversion rates, respectively. You can use this tolerance if you create foreign currency invoices.

8. **Schedule Amount:** The variance that you allow between all invoice amounts in the entered currency and the purchase order schedule amount.

9. **Total Amount:** The total variance that you allow for both the conversion rate amount and schedule amount tolerances combined. You can use this tolerance if you create foreign currency invoices.

10. **Consumed Percentage:** The percentage difference more than the consumed quantity on a consumption advice that you allow suppliers to invoice. Validation checks the billed quantity against the consumed quantity without considering price.

11. **Maximum Consumed:** The quantity difference more than the consumed quantity on a consumption advice that you allow suppliers to invoice. Validation checks the billed quantity against the consumed quantity without considering price.

Amount-Based Tolerances

1. **Amount-Based Tolerances:** Amount-based tolerances apply to invoices that have a match basis of amount.

2. **Ordered Percentage:** The percentage difference more than the ordered amount on a purchase order schedule line that you allow suppliers to invoice. Validation checks the billed amount against the ordered amount.

3. **Maximum Ordered:** The amount difference more than the ordered amount on a purchase order schedule line that you allow suppliers to invoice. Validation checks the billed amount against the ordered amount.

4. **Received Percentage:** The percentage difference more than the received amount on a purchase order schedule line that you allow suppliers to invoice. Validation checks the billed amount against the received amount.
5. **Maximum Received:** The amount difference more than the received amount on a purchase order schedule line that you allow suppliers to invoice. Validation checks the billed amount against the received amount.
6. **Conversion Rate Amount:** The variance that you allow between the invoice amount and the amount on a purchase order schedule. Validation compares the ledger currency amounts, using the invoice and purchase order conversion rates, respectively. You can use this tolerance if you create foreign currency invoices.
7. **Total Amount:** The total variance that you allow for both the conversion rate amount and schedule amount tolerances combined. You can use this tolerance if you create foreign currency invoices.

AP TOOL 32: FIVE FACTORS DRIVING THE AUTOMATION OF INVOICE PROCESSING

About This Tool: Over time, the drivers leading to invoice automation adoption have evolved from an efficiency standpoint to more strategic and tactical benefits that include spend visibility for accurate forecasting, cash management, increased control of the entire invoice process through workflows and business rules, and improved supplier relationships.

1. **Cash Management/Working Capital.** Invoice automation pays dividends to both buyers and suppliers in the form of liquidity and control. Through automation, buyers can manage their free cash and invest it for big returns in the form of early-payment discounts to suppliers. Suppliers benefit by the accelerated collection of receivables.

2. **Data Analytics.** Automated invoice processing solutions bring increased visibility into all invoices, which allows for greater control of cash flow and working capital management. Powerful reports can be quickly generated and used to make highly data-driven business decisions. Companies that harness this data are able to quickly drill down into report details with increasing granularity and accuracy for fast, effective decision making.

3. **Software-as-a-Service.** SaaS solutions have worked to significantly lower the cost of implementing an e-invoice and workflow solution. SaaS solutions are supplier maintained and updated, which provides users with the latest functionality with minimal commitment of IT resources.

4. Ease-of-Use. Today's turnkey purchase-to-pay solutions eliminate disparate legacy solutions, simplifying the approval process and moving documents along with clear rules, permissions, and escalations to ensure that invoices get to the right people, arrive on schedule, and get paid on time. The powerful functionality and usability of today's automation solutions allow for widespread adoption in companies of all sizes. Mobile functionality enables managers who travel to use their mobile device to approve an invoice for payment. This enhanced workflow functionality keeps invoices moving seamlessly through the system.

5. Results. It's hard to argue with results. The benefits of invoice processing via electronic invoicing and automated workflow have been well documented for both buyers and suppliers.

THE BENEFITS OF SENDING AND RECEIVING ELECTRONIC INVOICES

1. **Benefits of sending electronic invoices:**
   - Get paid faster with invoices going straight to processing
   - Cut costs and increase efficiency
   - Track the status and increase visibility of every invoice for improved cash flow and working capital management
   - Trade anywhere in the world with the correct sales tax automatically applied
   - Easily add digital signatures to comply with policies and regulations
   - Quickly resolve disputes and queries with collaboration features
   - Boost your green credentials by eliminating paper immediately
2. **Benefits of receiving electronic invoices:**
   - Save on every invoice – slash invoicing costs from day one
   - Eliminate paper and save time with invoice automation
   - Integrate automatically with any invoice processing or back-end system
   - Qualify for early payment discounts by paying suppliers faster
   - Bring new suppliers on board faster and get the relationship off to a flying start
   - Free up office space with easy-to-use electronic invoice archiving

AP TOOL 33: THE MOST COMMON FORMS OF INVOICE AUTOMATION

About This Tool: The common goal that all invoice automation solutions share is improving process management. Not every solution follows the same approach or provides the same functionality at each step of the invoice automation cycle. It's important for accounts payable professionals to fully understand the various forms that invoice automation solutions assume in order to decide which methods would work best in their specific workflow.

1. **Back-End Document Capture and Archival:** The simplest form of invoice automation is the usage of scanning technologies for back-end imaging and archival. This method does not impact the invoice approval process, since scanning and imaging occur after the fact. For this reason, back-end document capture and archival are not favored, as it is primarily a storage and retrieval solution that fails to yield any improvement or efficiency in workflow.

   In back-end document capture and archival, operators batch and scan paper documents at the end of the invoice receipt-to-pay process. AP staff then indexes the invoices manually by using a split screen view to keep information from invoice images into electronic forms. Once indexing is complete, the document images are stored in an electronic repository for retrieval, based on the searchable fields created.

   Historically, AP departments have used imaging in this manner to eliminate physical storage requirements, facilitate document retrieval for discrepancy resolution and audits, and improve responsiveness to supplier inquiries. Since scanning and indexing occur after approval processing, the invoice approval process continues to follow its current manual and paper-intensive course.

2. **Front-End Document and Data Capture:** In an imaging solution at the front end of the invoice processing cycle, invoices are scanned remotely or at a central processing facility upon receipt. Once invoices have been scanned and images enhanced to optimize recognition, data is extracted from the documents using automated image recognition technologies. Front-end document and data capture represents a quantum leap over back-end imaging because it sets up genuine improvements to the invoice receipt-to-pay cycle. This is truly the starting place for workflow automation.

Validation rules ensure that the data extracted is valid and accurate by directing the solution to compare specific fields against the information held in the appropriate back-end system (e.g. purchase order numbers against the purchasing system). The accuracy of such rules-based matching has reached the point that many companies now opt to automatically pay invoices that meet all validation rules, freeing AP staff to focus only on exceptions. Most current generation systems put the onus of exception and discrepancy correction back on suppliers, facilitating the evolution of AP departments into profit centers focused on spend analytics and working capital management.

3. **Data Extraction:** Tools and technologies that facilitate the extraction of information from scanned invoice images have had an interesting lifecycle beginning with template-based optical character recognition (OCR) to free-form recognition and, more recently, intelligent document recognition (IDR).

IDR systems enable end users to extract content from invoices without the system having to learn the layout of the invoice. Some intelligent engines are able to correctly sort batches on the fly, locate data fields such as invoice and PO number, as well as line item information, and then extract the desired content from those data fields. Intelligent solutions do not require the coding of rules or design form templates. Rather, the systems learn by reviewing a relatively small number of invoice samples. This helps the system scale to large invoice volumes and widely varying document layouts without requiring a human operator to specify a template for each one, or to explicitly create and tune an extensive library of keywords.

Embedded fuzzy search methods improve the extraction results by using other known data sources to automatically validate the information before exporting it to the ERP and document management systems. The benefit of this is that more invoices can be processed straight through, whereby documents can automatically flow from scan to post in the least amount of time and with minimal amount of manual intervention. Fuzzy logic can also make the IDR solution language-agnostic, allowing global organizations to process high volumes of invoices in multiple languages.

4. **Front-End Capture with Matching and Workflow:** In a more advanced form, invoice automation solutions combine front-end document and data capture with matching and workflow capabilities to streamline and automate invoice receipt and approval processing. Workflow solutions enable

AP departments to define how different types of invoices are processed. PO-based invoices can be matched against the purchase order and receipt documents automatically, while non-PO invoices can be routed to the person or people who are required to approve them. All tasks are routed based on pre-defined business rules and user roles, and access rights can be set to match the organization's existing approval hierarchy.

Approvers are typically notified via e-mail when invoices require their review and approval. Users click on the hyperlink contained in the e-mail message and log onto the system to view, code, and approve invoices online. Many solutions on the market today have mobile functionality that keeps invoices moving through the system when approvers are on the go. Mobile applications are becoming increasingly popular and allow users to approve or deny invoices for payment. Most invoice processing solutions available today come bundled with alerts and reminders, out-of-office delegation rules. and escalation procedures to ensure that invoices are processed in a timely manner.

Workflow-enabled invoice automation solutions automate more of the invoice receipt-to-pay cycle than stand along document and data capture solutions. They also deliver auditing, reporting, and management benefits that document and data capture solutions alone cannot provide. Workflow solutions track every action taken by each user on every invoice, providing a complete audit trail for all users and transactions. Users can respond quickly and effectively to supplier inquiries, while supervisors gain the ability to track the status of individual invoices, view the work of individual approvers, and monitor the entire approval process.

5. **Combining E-invoicing with Imaging and Workflow Automation:** The most sophisticated invoice automation solutions combine front-end document imaging and data capture with electronic invoicing and automated workflow. This enables organizations to process all the invoices – irrespective of whether they are submitted in paper or electronic format – through a single, common process.

Under this scenario, accounts payable staff members work with the technology solution provider to transition suppliers from paper to electronic means of invoice submission, usually a stand-alone portal or a shared supplier network. Most solutions offer suppliers multiple options when it comes to submitting electronic invoices including: direct integration with ERP and billing applications to transmit invoices in a hands-free manner without manual intervention; flipping purchase orders into invoices; and Web forms and templates that can be used to generate electronic invoices. Most solutions also provide supplier onboarding programs that aids in transitioning suppliers to electronic.

Once invoices have been submitted, they can be subjected to a range of validation criteria based on buyer-defined rules, check for mathematical integrity and duplicates, ensure completeness and accurately of information provided on invoices, and apply business rules and tolerances, etc. Invoices that do not meet any of the specified criteria are flagged as exceptions and suppliers are asked to correct the errors before resubmitting the invoice. Clean invoices are then forwarded for further processing.

For suppliers that continue to send paper invoices, organizations can use front-end imaging and data capture to extract information from the invoices. After the data extraction step, these invoices are also processed using the same matching and workflow rules as the electronic invoices.

Another practice that continues to gain in popularity is the outsourcing of the scanning and data capture function, in conjunction with electronic invoicing. In this case, a third-party service provider takes on the responsibility of receiving invoices, scanning them, and extracting the requisite data. These advanced invoice automation solutions enable organizations to process and approve all invoices from a common, integrated platform, irrespective of the channel of entry.

AP TOOL 34: SIX BEST PRACTICES FOR INVOICE PROCESSING

About This Tool: Companies often try to automate their existing accounts payable process, despite the fact that their existing process is broken. Implementing technology to a flawed process simply automates a bad process. The key to successful workflow automation lies in the redesign of invoice and payment management processes and a strong strategy to leverage the available technology to meet each organization's specific business requirements. Organizations should employ invoice processing best practices to leverage technology to maximize accuracy, speed, efficiency, control, cash management, and visibility of spend.

1. Invoice Receipt

Paper invoices are the enemy of efficiency. Often invoices are sent to the wrong department, or sit on an approver's desk for weeks on end before being entered into the accounting system.

Centralize. A formal policy mandating that all invoices be sent to the AP department is the first step in addressing this issue. Suppliers should be contacted and directed where to send invoices. Once invoices are received, they can be entered into the accounting system, with visibility to all relevant parties.

Leverage Automation Technology. Front-end imaging ensures that invoices enter the system quickly and are available to all parties immediately, irrespective of where they are located. Combining imaging with automated data capture adds further benefits in terms of quicker data extraction and fewer errors. An electronic invoicing solution goes a step further in streamlining the invoice receipt process. All invoices are submitted via a central solution and suppliers receive immediate confirmation that their invoices have been received.

2. **Invoice Validation**

In many cases, invoices are sent to the AP department for approval having missing or inaccurate information, which can take days or even weeks to resolve before the invoice can be processed and paid. The exception resolution process can involve a number of calls and/or e-mails between AP staff, field approvers, and suppliers. This arduous process of exception handling is compounded by the number of exceptions that AP staff must contend with.

Business Rules and Tolerances. Invoice automation solutions apply multiple validation checks to ensure that invoices have all the required and correct information. Is the PO number valid? Is the invoice number a duplicate? Does the invoice have the approver name on it? If the invoice fails to satisfy any of the validation criteria, the supplier is notified immediately and asked to correct the error, without any intervention from AP staff. This not only ensures that only clean invoices come into the AP department for processing, but that the clock on discounts doesn't start ticking until the supplier corrects all of the exceptions to the invoice.

3. **Approval Workflow**

The AP department typically deals with two types of invoices:

1. Purchase order (PO) based invoices – undergo a two- or three-way match before they can be paid.
2. Non-PO invoices – require approval from an authorized person within the buyer organization. Sometimes PO invoices need to be reviewed by an approver as well, if they fail the match process.

Formalizing the Process. Identify all people in the organization who can approve invoices. Approvers can be classified by the types of invoices they can approve, for example invoices from a specific supplier or certain spend types, up to a dollar limit. All AP employees who will route invoices for approval should have a copy of the list and be familiar with who should review what type of invoices. A similar list should be made identifying the appropriate persons who would be responsible for collaborating with the suppliers or buyers to resolve exception invoices. These lists should be updated periodically or when employees leave the organization; also ensure that old lists are collected and destroyed when new lists are created.

Going a Step Further. Organizations can further streamline the process by leveraging an automated workflow solution. In this case, the approver list is maintained and updated in the automated workflow solution itself. Invoices, once entered in to the solution, will be automatically routed to the required approver, based on pre-defined business rules. The business logic is typically configured at the time of solution implementation and can be updated as needed.

Employees who have invoices pending their approval receive e-mail notifications with links to specific invoices. Users have the option of either approving the invoice directly from the e-mail itself or they can log into the system to view more details about the invoice. Workflow solutions also come bundled with reminder and escalation features. If no action is taken on an invoice within a certain period of time, either a reminder can be sent to the employee or a message can be sent to the employee's manager. This ensures timely processing of invoices.

4. **Supplier Management**

To date, one of the biggest barriers to accounts payable automation initiatives, especially when it comes to electronic invoicing, has traditionally been supplier adoption. Persuading suppliers to change the way they do business to align with buyer's requirements can be a costly and time-consuming process. Success depends on the ability to present a compelling value proposition to suppliers, in addition to the advent of an aggressive supplier onboarding program provided by most solution providers.

In order to ensure the success of accounts payable automation efforts, buyer organizations need to be proactive in demonstrating the benefits of AP automation to their supplier base.

Involve Suppliers from the Start. When implementing any automation technology that will involve a change to the supplier process, whether it is around invoice receipt or payment, communicate this initiative to your suppliers as early as possible. If it is not possible to keep all of your suppliers involved, at least notify strategic suppliers about imminent changes. Keep suppliers in the loop as much as possible about any changes that are expected on their part. Supplier conversion and management should be a key component of any AP automation strategy and not an afterthought to the technology implementation process.

Supplier Onboarding Initiatives. Given that supplier adoption is a critical component to an electronic invoicing solution; many technology providers deliver strong value-added services around supplier recruitment and enablement. This includes segmenting suppliers based on different criteria to identify those most likely to adopt, developing mail/e-mail/phone activation campaigns for different supplier types, and actually contacting suppliers to bring them on board the automation solution. Organizations that do not have the in-house resources to tackle these tasks should leverage the expertise and experience of their technology provider for supplier onboarding.

In addition to aggressive supplier onboarding programs, many solution providers offer free supplier portals to help entice supplier adoption. The free supplier portals in addition to supplier onboarding initiatives are certainly paying off, as witnessed by the increase in supplier adoption.

5. **Discount Management**

One of the key drivers of AP automation has been senior management's emphasis on improving visibility to payment liabilities. This has come to bear along with a strong push toward increasing discount capture from suppliers. In today's economy with low-interest rates, an early payment discount term of 2% 10 net 30 translates to an APR of almost 36%, which is very appealing to buyer organizations. However, the biggest hindrance to discount capture is paper invoice receipt and processing.

Here are six drivers to improve your discount management and capture process.

1. Communication and integration between procurement and AP ensures that AP processors are aware of available discounts.
2. Front-end imaging, combined with automated workflow, makes invoices available to the approvers quickly and helps shrink the approval cycle.
3. Electronic invoicing can further compress the invoice receipt-to-pay cycle by as much as 10 days, by eliminating mail and desk float.

4. Validation capabilities that are provided in conjunction with e-invoicing place the burden of submitting a clean invoice on the supplier, instead of tying up valuable AP resources.
5. Prioritization capabilities available as part of approval workflow solutions allow organizations to move invoices with discounts to the top of the processing queue, ensuring that they are approved in a timely manner.
6. Alerts, reminders, out-of-office delegation, and escalation procedures keep the invoice approval process moving smoothly.

6. **Payment Processing**

There is no question that the lack of proper procedures around invoice receipt and approval lead to profit leakage through duplicate and erroneous payments. This is one reason third-party payment audits has grown into a billion-dollar industry. These firms are brought in by companies to comb through historical transactions and identify erroneous payments to suppliers, which they then try to recover.

Check Before You Pay. Prior to payment, all invoices should be checked against previous payments to ensure no duplicate payments are made. This means not just checking invoice numbers, but checking against a combination of criteria. For example, if the amount and date on two invoices are the same, it may be a duplicate even if the invoice numbers are different. If it's not possible to check every single payment, the AP department should at least spot-check a certain percentage of transactions each time payments are made.

Proactive Audits. Sophisticated invoice and payment audit technologies are now available as part of invoice automation solutions. Alternatively, a number of best-of-breed payment audit solutions that integrate seamlessly with numerous accounting applications are also available. These solutions run a variety of algorithms on the transactions to flag potential duplicates. Clients have the option of configuring the business logic, which will be applied to identify erroneous payments. On a periodic basis, a report is generated with potential payment errors, which need to be resolved before payments are made.

AP TOOL 35: THREE COMPONENTS OF IMAGING AND WORKFLOW

About This Tool: Imaging and workflow automation (IWA) solutions streamline the invoice receipt-to-pay cycle by enabling organizations to convert paper invoices into digital images, store them in a Web-enabled repository for rapid retrieval, and extract data from them to enhance approval processing.

1. **Document and Data Capture:** The process of converting paper invoices and transaction-related documents, such as proofs of receipt, into digital images and index data. Document scanning and data extraction could be centralized or remote based on the organization's needs. Specific steps include scanning, image enhancement, indexing, validation, and data extraction based on bar codes, optical character recognition (OCR), optical mark recognition (OMR), intelligent character recognition (ICR), or manual data entry.

2. **Content Storage and Management:** Refers to the delivery, storage, management, and disposition of electronic documents and data. Depending on the complexity of the solution, this may include enterprise content management (ECM) or business process management (BPM) capabilities for managing the transactional content across its entire life-cycle. This stage also addresses the archival and retrieval as well as backup and recovery options offered as part of IWA solutions.

3. **Workflow and Dispute Management:** This is the process that buyers follow to sort, route, review, dispute, and approve invoices for payment, including workflow. Web invoicing solutions support multiple levels of approval and include the ability to configure reminders and escalation procedures, if no action is taken on pending tasks in a specified period of time. The systems also allow buyers and suppliers to investigate and collaboratively resolve disputes and exceptions. Comments, attachments, and other supporting documents can be added to transactions to provide further visibility into the approval and dispute resolution process.

AP TOOL 36: NINE PERFORMANCE INDICATORS FOR INVOICE PROCESSING

About This Tool: The accounts payable invoice processing practice has many moving people and parts, and unless certain metrics are identified and performance is measured against these indicators, something is bound to fall through the cracks.

To ensure the smooth functioning of an AP department, key performance indicators (KPIs) should be measured at least once every quarter. These metrics become even more critical when a company is undergoing a merger or acquisition, new technology implementation, or organizational restricting.

Measuring and comparing KPIs before and after any of these initiatives is a good indication of the impact it had on the AP process.

Below are nine key KPIs every accounts payable department should track on a regular basis.

1. **Number of Invoices Processed per Day, per Operator.** This metric helps an organization understand the invoice efficiency of each AP operator. If some operators are way ahead of the curve, they may be able to share tips and train others that are lagging behind. Invoice efficiency also enables you to try different ways of allocating invoices to specialists – PO vs. non-PO invoices, by spend type or by geographic location/business unit, and determine the one that works best.

2. **Average Cost to Process an Invoice by Type.** Calculating processing costs can provide valuable insights into the factors driving the costs and ideas on reducing total costs. Include salaries and benefits, facilities and hardware, software and IT support, and managerial overhead in cost calculations. Also calculate processing cost by different types of invoices, for example clean vs. exception, and by steps involved in each process such as data entry vs. exception resolution, to address any expensive invoice types and processes.

3. **Exception Invoices as a Percentage of Total Invoices.** It is a well-known fact that exception invoices cost way more to process than clean invoices and drive up the overall processing costs for the AP department. Track the number of dollar value invoices that end up in an exception queue and log details such as expense type, supplier information, and type of exception. Understanding the source of exceptions and addressing them is critical to reduce the occurrence of exceptions.

4. **Average Time to Approve an Invoice from Receipt to Payment.** Knowing how long it takes an invoice from the time it gets to the AP department to the time it is ready to pay can help AP managers identify where the invoice spends the most time – data entry, approval, or exception management, and take the appropriate steps to compress the invoice receipt-to-pay cycle. Accelerating the processing cycle can help reduce late payment penalties and increase the capture of discounts offered by suppliers.

5. **Electronic Invoices as a Percentage of Total Invoices.** Electronic invoices are quicker and cheaper to process as there is no mail float, desk float, or data entry involved in the process. Track the percentage of electronic invoices as well as the percentage of suppliers sending them. Increasing the percentage of invoices that come into the AP department in electronic format will have a beneficial impact on the other two metrics you are tracking – average processing times and costs.

6. **Suppliers Onboarding E-invoicing as a Percentage of Total Suppliers.** The best electronic invoicing solution will not deliver a payback, unless a critical mass of suppliers have been successfully on boarded. Develop a supplier recruitment and enablement plan along with solution implementation itself and periodically track the percentage of targeted suppliers that have been migrated from paper to electronic invoicing. If the percentages are too low, then it is time to change the activation campaigns and supplier communication methods.

7. **Discounts Captured as a Percentage of Discounts Offered.** While a lot of suppliers may offer a discount for paying early, most companies are unable to capture all the discounts that are offered to them, due to a lack of visibility into the existence of discounts or lengthy approval cycles. Track the invoices where discounts are missed with reason codes as to why the discount was missed, so that invoices with associated discounts can be prioritized and processed as quickly as possible.

8. **Erroneous Payments as a Percentage of Total Payments.** Duplicate payments, missed discounts, reconciled returns, and other errors in payments are a huge drain on the bottom line. Tracking dollars lost to payment errors promptly can help recoup the monies from suppliers quickly. Keeping a log of error codes can help understand the source of errors and address the problem at the root itself, instead of trying to recover the funds after the fact.

AP TOOL 37: THE TWENTY-FIVE TOP REASONS FOR PROBLEM INVOICES

About This Tool: Many accounts payable organizations would love to focus on just the exceptions within the process. But many are faced with problem invoices. As any accounts payable professional knows, problem invoices bog down the process and create several "pain points." But these "pain points" can be levers for process improvement and automation initiatives if tracked and acted upon. The following table identifies the twenty-five top reasons for problem invoices and groups them into seven key categories which are:

1. Purchase Orders (POs)
2. The Approval Process
3. Pricing and Quantity
4. Invoice Process Discrepancies
5. Tax Calculation Errors
6. Supplier and Shipment Issues
7. Supplier Master File Issues

Purchase Orders (POs)

1. PO Not Approved
2. New PO Required
3. Blanket PO Limited Exceeded
4. Purchase Order Line Discrepancy
5. Invalid or Stale PO

The Approval Process

6. PO Approval Pending
7. Invoice Approval Pending
8. Approval Levels Incorrect – Additional Approvals Needed

Pricing and Quantity

9. Contract Pricing Discrepancy
10. Quantity Discrepancy

Invoice Process Discrepancies

11. Outstanding Credit Balance
12. Invoice Is Missing Information
13. Invoice Already Paid on a P-Card
14. Incorrect Freight Calculations
15. Invoice Keyed with Incorrect Date
16. Invoice Coded Incorrectly

Tax Calculation Errors

17. VAT Error
18. Sales and Use Tax Error
19. Incorrect Tax Calculations (Others)

Supplier and Shipment Issues

20. Invoice Sent for Goods or Services Not Received
21. Short or Shipment Errors
22. Supplier Referenced Wrong PO

Supplier Master File Issues

23. Duplicate Supplier in Master File
24. Remit Address Doesn't Match Supplier Master Record
25. Fraudulent Supplier

Tracking and Addressing Problem Invoices

Now how do we track and address these problem invoices? Here are some suggestions.

1. Today's ERP systems have the capability to block or park an invoice and assign a reason code to the specific issue. A blocked invoiced report can then be reviewed to determine the most common reason for the bottleneck.
2. Use the "problem" categories suggested in the previous section to develop analytics and tracking procedures for your biggest "pain points." You may identify other types of errors that are more specific to your company or industry.
3. Many accounts payable teams have established common procure-to-pay (P2P) metrics with procurement to ensure a level of accountability for the accuracy and timeliness of contract, purchase orders, pricing, and quantity discounts. Many organizations refer to this team effort as the P2P transformation process. The 20 metrics used to help track the results of the transformation include:

---

20 Metrics to Track the P2P Transformation Process

1. Percentage of E-invoices
2. Percentage of P-Card Invoices Paid
3. Percentage of Invoices Requiring Correction
4. Percentage of Invoices Requiring Manual Processing
5. Purchase Order Processing Cycle Time
6. Invoice Processing Cycle Time
7. Number of Invoices per P2P Full Time Equivalent (FTE) Employee
8. Number of Purchase Orders per P2P FTE Employee
9. Percentage of Invoices Paid on Time
10. Discount Dollars Taken
11. Discount Dollars Missed
12. Percentage of Payments on Contract
13. Percentage of Payments on Purchase Order
14. Percentage of Erroneous/Duplicate Payments
15. Percentage of Spend on Preferred/Strategic Suppliers
16. Percentage of Spend Through Catalogs
17. Requisition Conversion Cycle Time

(Continued)

20 Metrics to Track the P2P Transformation Process

18. Average Response to a Supplier/Customer Query
19. Clearing Account Dollar Variances
20. Percentage of E-payments vs. Manual Checks

STANDARDS OF INTERNAL CONTROLS: INVOICE PROCESSING

Internal Control	Type of Control	Risks Mitigated

12.A Segregation of Duties.
 	
The accounts payable function must be segregated from the following functions:
  a. Receiving;
  b. Purchasing;
  c. Disbursing cash or its equivalent.
Refer to risks: 12-1, 12-2
	Preventive	**12-1 Purchases may be stolen, lost, destroyed, or temporarily diverted.** The potential for errors and irregularities is substantially increased.
		
		12-2 Purchases may be received but never reported, or reported inaccurately.

12.B Invoice Accuracy.
 	
Prior to payment, supplier's invoices must be reviewed for receipt of material or services, checked for accuracy (price, quantity, mathematical extension, currency, proper freight charges, sales tax, etc.), account classification and distribution, and agreed to the PO/contract terms. Invoices with a discrepancy exceeding the tolerance limits or lacking reference information (PO/quantity/amount) must be resolved before payment is made. Business rules should be established for electronic invoices and automated processes.
	Preventive	**12-2 Purchases may be received but never reported, or reported inaccurately.**
		
		12-4 Incorrect Payments. Rather than being returned or refused, the following goods or services may be received and ultimately paid for:
		  a. Unordered goods or services.
		  b. Inventory that does not meet quality standards.
		  c. Excessive quantities or incorrect items.

Internal Control	Type of Control	Risks Mitigated
Refer to risks: 12-2, 12-4, 12-5, 12-6, 12-7, 12-8		**12-5 Materials may be received too early or too late for production.** Business interruption or excessive levels (quantity and/or dollar amount) or inventory may occur. **12-6 Payment may be made for goods or services not received and/or in advance of receipt.** **12-7 Payments to suppliers may be duplicated, incorrect, or fraudulent.** **12-8 Records may be lost or destroyed.**

12.C Alternative Processes. If alternative processes are used, such as pay on receipt, consignment inventories, or e-invoicing, the procedures in place to ensure correct pricing and received quantities must be documented and approved by local operating and financial management.
 	
Refer to risks: 12-1, 12-3, 12-4, 12-5, 12-7, 12-8
	Preventive	**12-1 Purchases may be stolen, lost, destroyed, or temporarily diverted.** The potential for errors and irregularities is substantially increased.
		
		12-3 Purchases or services may be ordered and received by an unauthorized individual.
		
		12-4 Incorrect Supplier Payments. Rather than being returned or refused, the following goods or services may be received and ultimately paid for:
		  a. Unordered goods or services.
		  b. Inventory that does not meet quality standards.
		  c. Excessive quantities or incorrect items.
		
		12-7 Payments to suppliers may be duplicated, incorrect, or fraudulent.
		
		12-8 Records may be lost or destroyed.

(Continued)

Internal Control	Type of Control	Risks Mitigated
12.D Invoice Approval. Invoices without a purchase order or receiving report (e.g. non-production services, lease payments, check requests, one-time purchases, etc.) must be approved by authorized personnel in accordance with their approval limits before payment using an automated workflow approval process if applicable. **Refer to risks: 12-2, 12-3, 12-7, 12-9**	Preventive	**12-2 Purchases may be received but never reported, or reported inaccurately.** **12-3 Purchases or services may be ordered and received by an unauthorized individual.** **12-7 Payments to suppliers may be duplicated, incorrect, or fraudulent.** **12-9 Records may be misused or altered to the detriment of the company or its suppliers.**
12.E Duplicate Payments. A process must be in place to detect and prevent duplicate payments. Supporting documents for the payments must be originals and must be effectively canceled after payment to prevent accidental or intentional reuse. No payments should be based upon a statement unless the supplier has been pre-approved for such. **Refer to risks: 12-7, 12-9**	Preventive	**12-7 Payments to suppliers may be duplicated, incorrect, or fraudulent.** **12-9 Records may be misused or altered to the detriment of the company or its suppliers.**
12.F Goods Receipt – Invoice Receipt (GR/IR in SAP). Aged, unmatched purchase orders, receiving transactions, and invoices must be periodically reviewed, investigated, and resolved. **Refer to risks: 12-2, 12-4**	Preventive and Detective	**12-2 Purchases may be received but never reported, or reported inaccurately.** **12-4 Incorrect Supplier Payments.** Rather than being returned or refused, the following goods or services may be received and ultimately paid for: a. Unordered goods or services.

Internal Control	Type of Control	Risks Mitigated
		b. Inventory that does not meet quality standards. c. Excessive quantities or incorrect items.
12.G Supplier Statements. Supplier statements must be regularly reviewed for past due items and open credits, to be resolved in a timely manner. The currency used for statements and invoices should be consistent. **Refer to risks: 12-2, 12-4, 12-7, 12-8, 12-9**	**Preventive and Detective**	**12-2 Purchases may be received but never reported, or reported inaccurately.** **12-4 Incorrect Supplier Payments.** Rather than being returned or refused, the following goods or services may be received and ultimately paid for: a. Unordered goods or services. b. Inventory that does not meet quality standards. c. Excessive quantities or incorrect items. **12-7 Payments to suppliers may be duplicated, incorrect, or fraudulent.** **12-8 Records may be lost or destroyed.** **12-9 Records may be misused or altered to the detriment of the company or its suppliers.**
12.H Reconciliations. Items forwarded to payments should be reconciled (contents are known and status is current) monthly with payments actually made and recorded in the general ledger. The accounts payable trial balance should also be reconciled (contents are known and status is current) with the general ledger each month. All differences must be resolved on a timely basis. **Refer to risks: 12-8, 12-9**	**Preventive and Detective**	**12-8 Records may be lost or destroyed.** **12-9 Records may be misused or altered to the detriment of the company or its suppliers.**

(Continued)

Internal Control	Type of Control	Risks Mitigated
12.I Debit Balance Accounts. Accounts payable should review debit balance accounts at least quarterly and request remittance on debit amounts outstanding for over 90 days. Any significant debit balance should be classified as an accounts receivable. **Refer to risks: 12-6, 12-7**	Preventive and Detective	**12-6 Payment may be made for goods or services not received and/or in advance of receipt.** **12-7 Payments to suppliers may be duplicated, incorrect, or fraudulent.**
12.J Debit and Credit Memos. Debit and credit memos issued to supplier accounts must be documented, recorded, controlled, and approved by authorized personnel in accordance with their approval limits. **Refer to risks: 12-6, 12-7, 12-9**	Preventive and Detective	**12-6 Payment may be made for goods or services not received and/or in advance of receipt.** **12-7 Payments to suppliers may be duplicated, incorrect, or fraudulent.** **12-9 Records may be misused or altered to the detriment of the company or its suppliers.**
12.K Debit and Credit Memo Audit Trails. Debit and credit memos must be uniquely identifiable and traceable. Company-generated documents must be pre-numbered for security control. **Refer to risk: 12-9**	Preventive	**12-9 Records may be misused or altered to the detriment of the company or its suppliers.**

12.L Established Suppliers. Prior to payment accounts payable must ensure the supplier is established on the approved supplier list/database. Suppliers not on the approved supplier list/database must be validated independent of the originating source.
 	
Refer to risks: 12-4, 12-7, 12-9
	Preventive	**12-4 Incorrect Supplier Payments.** Rather than being returned or refused, the following goods or services may be received and ultimately paid for:
		  a. Unordered goods or services.
		  b. Inventory that does not meet quality standards.
		  c. Excessive quantities or incorrect items.

Internal Control	Type of Control	Risks Mitigated
		12-7 Payments to suppliers may be duplicated, incorrect, or fraudulent.
		12-9 Records may be misused or altered to the detriment of the company or its suppliers.
12.M Liability Accruals. Procedures and controls must be in place to identify and capture all items and services that have been billed but not yet received and received but not yet billed. These items must receive proper treatment in the accounting records.	Preventive	**12-1 Purchases may be stolen, lost, destroyed, or temporarily diverted. The potential for errors and irregularities is substantially increased.**
Refer to risks: 12-1, 12-2, 12-6		**12-2 Purchases may be received but never reported, or reported inaccurately.**
		12-6 Payment may be made for goods or services not received and/or in advance of receipt.

CHAPTER THIRTEEN

P-Cards

 INTRODUCTION

A purchasing card (also abbreviated as PCard or P-Card) is a form of company charge card that allows goods and services to be procured without using a traditional purchasing process. In the United Kingdom, purchasing cards are usually referred to as procurement cards. Purchasing cards are usually issued to employees who are expected to follow their organization's policies and procedures related to P-Card use, including reviewing and approving transactions according to a set schedule (at least once per month).

The organization can implement a variety of controls for each P-Card; for example, a single-purchase dollar limit, a monthly limit, merchant category code (MCC) restrictions, and so on. In addition, a cardholder's P-Card activity should be reviewed periodically by someone independent of the cardholder.

P-Cards are a payment tool designed to make the business purchasing process more efficient by reducing paperwork, providing greater control over spending, and visibility into spending patterns. P-Cards can reduce the workload for both accounts payable and purchasing departments at essentially no cost to an organization. In addition, P-Card purchases simplify the reconciliation process, eliminate out-of-pocket expenses, and improve supplier negotiations.

TYPES OF PAYMENT CARDS

P-Cards are not limited to plastic cards; they can also utilize non-plastic account numbers. The term "card" is used when describing any type of commercial card product, regardless of whether or not a plastic card is issued. Other types of P-Cards include corporate/travel cards, One Card, fleet card, ghost cards, virtual cards, and single-use card – each card is used to handle different types of purchases and/or spend categories. Following are four types of different cards to consider.

Corporate Card/Travel Card

The corporate card or travel card is generally used by organizations for employee travel and entertainment related expenses. The card allows employees to use the card for payment of travel expenses and provides essential data to the employer. Employees are provided the corporate card for payment of approved, business-related expenses that are most often travel-related as designated by the employer. The card is issued in the company's name with the name of the individual employee displayed on the card.

Few companies issue corporate cards, which are issued based upon an established banking relationship or an offer that was organized directly with the card holder. The company's credit is considered when applying for the card.

Corporate credit cards are divided into two groups, individual payment cards and company payment cards. If an employee is given an individual payment card, the employee is responsible for submitting their own expense reports. Company policies must be followed and the card issuer is paid directly for charges incurred. If an employee utilizes a company payment card, the employer pays all company charges. If there are unapproved or personal charges, the employee pays the card issuer directly.

1. **One Card**

   The One Card is a type of commercial card that simplifies card administration and reporting without compromising control or convenience from payment to supplier negotiations. Processes are streamlined through eliminating steps such as supplier setup and purchase order data entry.

   The card leads to increased productivity and employee convenience because it is a single payment solution. The One Card offers better management of expenditures, such as business supplies, maintenance, repair, operational and travel expenses through spending controls, and point-of-sale (POS) restrictions. The single payment solution integrates data with a company's general ledger, ERP, and other existing systems to reduce manual data entry and create a single monthly payment for all transactions. The result is a complete view of the corporation's spending patterns.

The One Card provides flexibility and convenience through managing procurement and travel expenses. The One Card is the payment tool of choice for many organizations based on the card's versatile controls and online approval process for transactions.

2. **Fleet Card**

A fleet card or fuel card is a product used by organizations to pay for fuel and related expenses on company vehicles. The card is used as a payment card that is commonly utilized for fuel purchases such as gasoline, diesel, and other fuels at gas stations. The fleet cards may be used to pay for vehicle expenses and maintenance if allowed by a fleet owner or manager. The benefit of a fleet card is increased security for cardholders, and for fleet drivers that no longer need to carry money.

With the use of fleet cards, the fleet owners or managers receive real-time reports that reveal transactions. The fleet owners or managers can set purchase controls that provide detailed use of business-related expenses. The fleet card provides convenient and comprehensive reports of business transactions.

3. **Ghost Cards/Virtual Cards/Single Use**

Ghost cards, virtual cards, or single-use cards are card accounts issued to a specific supplier to process all the organization's transactions. Companies can use virtual cards as another payment option instead of providing a credit card to each employee. The ghost card provides a single account for organizations to pay employee charges.

Ghost cards reduce fraud and overspending. Unless the company, which owns the ghost card, approves the charges to the account, the employee cannot spend the funds. Approval is required. Purchases are only finalized after the employer authorizes the charges to the account. The employer budgets expenses such as business trips, and expenses above the budgeted amount will not be permitted.

P-Card Process Flow

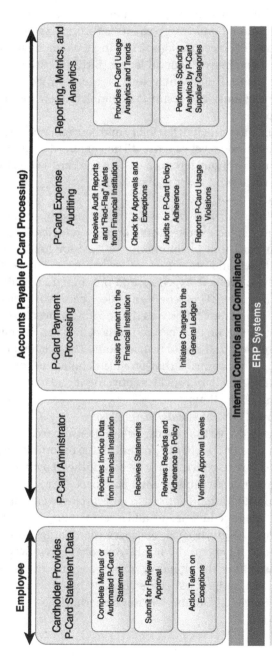

P-Card Process Insights

According to the Professional Association for the Commercial Card and Payment Industry (NAPCP), P-Cards provide a means for streamlining the procure-to-pay process, allowing organizations to procure goods and services in a timely manner, reduce transaction costs, track expenses, take advantage of supplier discounts, reduce or redirect staff in the purchasing and/or AP departments, reduce or eliminate petty cash, and more. Originally, P-Cards were targeted for such low-value transactions as supplies and maintenance or repair and operations (MRO), where their use eliminated purchase orders and invoicing. Over the years, their use has expanded to higher-value transactions as the industry has grown and greater controls have been introduced.

Purchasing cards (P-Cards) or non-plastic account numbers are issued to employees (i.e. cardholders) responsible for making purchases or payments on behalf of their employer; for example, cardholders can order and pay for office supplies via a supplier's website. Suppliers accept P-Cards for payment, utilizing the existing credit card infrastructure for payment processing. Transaction data is captured by a supplier's POS system and transmitted through the card network. The level of transmitted data depends on the supplier's process and technology systems; data levels include the following:

	Date	Supplier	Transaction Amount	Sales Tax	Customer-Defined Code	Line-Item Detail
Level 1 Standard	X	X	X			
Level 2 Variable Data	X	X	X	X	X	
Level 3 Detailed Data	X	X	X	X	X	X

Beyond replacing the purchase order and invoice processes that frequently cost more than the low-value items being bought, P-Cards—including virtual cards, ghost cards, and single-use cards—are used for paying invoices if agreed between the purchasing company and the supplier.

P-CARD DEFINITIONS

The NAPCP states that in addition to cardholders and suppliers, other parties involved with the P-Card payment are defined below.

Issuers work directly with end users to implement and grow programs, issue cards, and invoice posted P-Card transactions. The issuer uses the services of the networks and processors to facilitate card issuance, authorize transactions, and provide data. Many financial institutions are issuers. Issuers are sometimes referred to as card "providers."

Merchant acquirers enroll suppliers in the card acceptance process and implement equipment and software solutions related to this purpose. In addition, they facilitate payment flow, including payment to suppliers. A merchant acquirer is sometimes referred to as a supplier's "bank."

Networks facilitate the movement of transactional data between the issuer and merchant acquirer and set the rules pertaining to card acceptance by suppliers. Organizations in this role include Visa, Master-Card, and American Express. (Note: American Express also assumes the roles of issuer and merchant acquirer.) Networks are sometimes referred to as "associations" (an outdated term) or the card brand.

Processors provide various services to card issuers and merchant acquirers, which may include card production, statement printing, authorization, and data delivery.

With P-Cards, the end-user organization assumes liability for payment – the cardholder neither owes the card issuer nor makes payments. However, cardholders are expected to follow their organization's policies and procedures related to P-Card use, including reviewing and approving transactions according to a set schedule (at least once per month). The organization can implement a variety of controls for each P-Card; for example, single-purchase dollar limit, a monthly limit, merchant category code (MCC) restrictions and so on. In addition, a cardholder's P-Card activity should be reviewed periodically by someone independent of the cardholder.

Drivers for the Use of P-Cards

The attraction of a P-Card program is the automation and process efficiency it brings to both the buyer and supplier. On the buyer side, the convenience of a P-Card program for small items, where it is difficult to justify the high overhead of using requisitions, purchase orders, approvals, matching, and settlement by check through the AP process, is the number one benefit. By simply using a P-Card for small items, companies can shave a lot of overhead from the process and provide the convenience of simply swiping a card. Further increasing the attraction of P-Cards is the rebates that buyers can obtain from the P-Card provider. Rebates are based on the dollar amount spent on the card, and can add up to significant savings. Additional buyer benefits of P-Card programs include:

1. Convenience of purchasing without a PO – reduce cycle time of purchasing transactions.
2. Increased efficiency through automated payments is a result of utilizing P-Cards as a strategic form of payment in AP on high-priced items and B2B services.
3. Increased employee satisfaction and reduced manual labor hours – payment requests, petty cash, and personal funds are eliminated.
4. Simplified purchasing and payment process.
5. Lower overall transaction processing costs per purchase.
6. Increased visibility into spending patterns.
7. Ability to set and control purchasing dollar limits – restrict maverick spend.
8. Ability to control purchases to specific merchant categories and suppliers.
9. Receipt of rebates from the purchasing card provider based on dollar volume of total purchases.
10. Expedited delivery of goods.
11. Better pricing on goods.
12. Reduction in paperwork.
13. Improved supplier relations – suppliers receive payment within 2–5 days.
    Other drivers include:

1. **Lower Processing Costs.** Organizations want to automate and reduce overhead in the purchasing process and P-Cards provide an effective way of realizing significant cost savings. Whether a company is purchasing a million-dollar piece of equipment or a five-dollar tape dispenser, most companies use identical processes for these transactions. Cost studies have shown that the typical cost to process a single transaction can be over $15. Obviously, cost-conscious purchasing operations don't want to send over $15 to purchase something that is worth about $10. By utilizing purchasing cards, most of the overhead can be eliminated by cutting out requisitions, approvals, purchase orders, purchasing channels, receipts, and follow-up to be sure the item is charged to the correct department. Such an elaborate, carefully controlled process may be justified for large purchases; however, fewer stewards think such an expensive process is justified for small purchases.

Typically low-risk and low-value purchasing transactions represent an excellent target for purchasing cards which can remove the bureaucracy and administration cost while empowering employees. By eliminating the typical purchasing route, the purchasing process is streamlined by removing the traditional purchase order steps and approvals. Predetermined spending controls and requirements such as spending limits are able to be channeled via more cost effective routes.

2. **Transaction Control.** Companies want to control where purchases are made. Most companies make an effort to consolidate the number of suppliers they use, in an effort to channel more business to fewer providers to increase purchasing volume and negotiate price discounts. The more often employees are permitted to engage in "rogue buying" – going anywhere they want to purchase company goods – the more the buying company's negotiating leverage is diluted. On the opposite side, the more employees purchase through preferred providers, the greater the price discounts the company can negotiate. Thus, a successful P-Card program is the key to reduced overhead and discounted or lower prices for items purchased.

In an effort to rein in rogue buying, a company can issue P-Cards to employees, instruct them to purchase what they need and charge it to the card, and block usage of the card at any merchant in a merchant category that does not have preferred status. For example, a company can contract to purchase office supplies at Staples for a 3% discount and block P-Cards transactions with all suppliers in the office supply category except Staples. Such a policy provides better control over letting employees purchase needed items with their own funds or cash advances and then turn in expense reports for such purchases.

In an effort to help control transactions, card providers have identified three levels of data capture and reporting for card transactions. Level-3 is the highest level of processing and defines what is being purchased and combines that information with the payment transaction and delivers it electronically to customers. Level-3 line-item detail provides specific purchase information, detailed merchant establishment information, and cardholder information. Level-3 information is useful to P-Card customers to help streamline accounting, merge purchase data with e-procurement systems, and accurately manage transactions with the least amount of costly manual intervention.

3. **Attractive Rebates.** Organizations want to collect rebates based on their purchasing volume. P-Cards are a lucrative product of the banks that issue them; therefore, the marketplace has become very competitive. Large volume programs can earn a significant amount in rebates. With the right P-Card provider, a company can save money on overhead, obtain lower prices for goods and services purchased, and get cash back from the card

issuer. It's no surprise why P-Card usage is on the rise and why small and medium-size companies want to get in on the savings.

 ## AP TOOL 38: P-CARD PROGRAM BEST PRACTICES

About This Tool: MasterCard suggests the following twenty best practices in their "MasterCard Corporate Purchasing Card Best Practices Guide" The recommended best practices are grouped into these categories and expanded in the following table.

- Planning and Implementation
- Program Management
- Compliance, Auditing, and Reporting
- Program Expansion[1]

Planning and Implementation

1. Perform a Purchase Transaction Analysis
2. Quantify Purchasing Card Expansion ROI
3. Form a Cross-Functional Program Enhancement Team
4. Set Performance Goals
5. Track Performance

Program Management

6. Rationalize Expense Policies and Procedures
7. Provide Comprehensive Training and Communications
8. Optimize Purchasing Card Deployment
9. Identify Ghost Card Opportunities (P-Card for Supplier Settlement)
10. Manage Supplier Relationships
11. Leverage Data Integration Opportunities
12. Utilize a Best Practice Scorecard

Compliance, Audit, and Reporting

13. Establish a Sales Tax Strategy
14. Use and Report on 1099 and MWBE (Diversity) Suppliers
15. Manage by Exception

Program Expansion

16. Mandate the Use of P-Cards
17. Expand Supplier Acceptance
18. Extend P-Card Usage within the P2P Environment
19. Use a Single Card for Multiple Expense Categories
20. Continuously Review for Program Opportunities

---

[1]Mastercard Corporate Purchasing Card Best Practices Guide, accessed on September 12, 2020, https://cdn.ymaws.com/www.napcp.org/resource/resmgr/resource_center/mastercard_corporate_purchas.pdf.

The Functional Map for a P-Card Program

P-Card solutions streamline the purchasing process for small items by giving end users a highly automated self-service option. They can also be structured to steer buyers to preferred suppliers that are under contract to provide price discounts and earn the buying company attractive rebate checks. A successful P-Card program can be broken down into six specific parts, as outlined here.

Six Components of the P-Card Management Functional Map

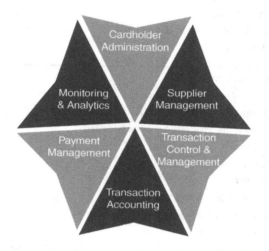

1. **Cardholder Administration.** P-Card programs require a person to oversee the operation; issue new cards, terminate cards when an employee leaves or is reassigned; monitor activity, including times when a transaction is refused; generate reports to management and communicate with the issuer. Typically, one person does this as a full-time job, but a small program might have a part-time administrator and a large one might have a staff of two. Most of the features in issuers' reporting and management software have been designed with the program administrator in mind, including tools to turn cards off and on, adjust credit limits, and receive a host of reports.

2. **Supplier Management.** Card acceptance is critical to the success of a P-Card program. If most of a company's suppliers do not accept card payments, the program will stall. Therefore, enrollment of suppliers is a

key component to any good program. Much of that effort consists of notifying suppliers that do not accept card payments that the buying company would like them to start accepting. Many P-Card providers have supplier onboarding programs to help with this step in the process. Such programs should be taken into consideration when evaluating the right P-Card solution for your company. Beyond enrolling suppliers, supplier management involves tracking spending with particular suppliers and using this data to show the supplier how much business you bring them. This documented volume can be used to try to negotiate supplier discounts. P-Card providers are able to differentiate card spend by merchant, which is a useful tool for negotiating supplier discounts.

3. **Transaction Control and Integration.** Restrictions such as transaction limits whether they are daily, weekly, or monthly limits can quickly and easily be put into place and work to prohibit unsanctioned card usage. In addition, unauthorized merchants can be blocked by Merchant Category Code (MCC). This forces buyers to purchase from preferred suppliers that are under contract to provide discounts and earn the buying corporation attractive rebate checks. Different limits and restrictions can be built into company card programs for different card holder accounts – e.g. a CFO may have fewer restrictions on his/her account than a new hire middle manager. The customized controls or restrictions placed on the card protect the buying company against fraud and misuse.

4. **Transaction Accounting.** P-Card programs seamlessly integrate with accounting systems and provide accuracy and efficiency. Card purchases are matched to transaction statements and card transactions are allocated to the appropriate general ledger (GL) and cost center codes. Purchases can easily be split and administrators have the ability to override default codes and redirect purchase to other accounts based on the GL codes. This automated process reduces errors and processing time, allowing for timely payment and control.

5. **Payment Management.** Paper checks are waning as more efficient payment processes gain in popularity – such as purchasing card programs. Suppliers are happy because they get paid promptly with the bank's money and with no action required on the part of the buying company. The bank provides credit to the buyer and the bank pays the buyer. As a result, the supplier takes a discount due to the early payment. Since there is a benefit to early payment, the bank and buyer negotiate a payment date. Most often payments are paid monthly but there can be additional rebates or lower program fees when payments are made bi-monthly, weekly, or daily. Payment schedules can be negotiated by the buyer and bank.

6. **Program Monitoring and Analytics.** P-Card programs have powerful reporting functionality that allows program administrators and procurement, financial, and accounting executives to precisely track how the cards are being utilized. The high-level reporting capabilities provide detailed data for spend analysis and financial decision making. Visibility into spend patterns and spend activity is another added benefit of P-card programs. P-Card solution providers offer a wide range of standard and ad hoc reporting capabilities. Reports can be scheduled for certain days each week or month, to meet a company's specific needs.

MCC Codes

A Merchant Category Code (MCC) is a four-digit number used by the bankcard industry to classify suppliers into market segments. There are approximately 600 MCCs that denote various types of business (e.g. 5111 Office Supplies, 7299 Dog Grooming Services, 5722 Household Appliance Stores).

The MCC is assigned by the acquiring financial institution when a supplier first begins accepting payment cards. The MCC is assigned based on the supplier's primary line of business. For example, if a supplier primarily sells computers, it may be assigned MCC 5732 Computer Hardware. If a supplier primarily repairs computers, it may be assigned MCC 7379 Computer Maintenance, Repair, and Services.

Key Point: Although use of the MCC list is optional, it provides a convenient and reliable way to identify reportable transactions and greatly simplifies the annual task of 1099 reporting.

What Are the Eight Success Factors for a Good P-Card Program?

The advantages to streamlining the P2P process through P-Card programs far outweigh the disadvantages to such programs. A variety of factors contribute to the success of a P-Card program or its stagnation.

1. **Implementation of a good program administrator.** An effective purchasing card administrator who knows the P-Card industry and best practices is the key to the success of a company's program.
2. **Solid partnership with card issuer.** Be sure to choose a program that best fits your company's needs and expectations. Discuss roles and responsibilities with your card issuer to be sure both sides are clear about set expectations.

3. **Strong internal communication and supplier communication.** A good communication plan is the key to getting internal employees to embrace the P-Card implementation. In addition, purchasing card requirements will need to be conveyed to suppliers. Early supplier education and onboarding are key factors to the success of the program.
4. **Set program goals and benchmarking.** Goals need to be clearly defined for policies and procedures to be developed. Benchmarking needs to be completed to measure progress and success against goals. Benchmarking can also be used to identify improvement opportunities.
5. **Proper training.** Be sure the card issuer you choose to partner with provides a mandated training program.
6. **Policies and procedures.** Documented policies and procedures need to be aligned with program goals and be updated as the program evolves and grows.
7. **Strike a control balance.** Companies don't want to under-control or over-control a P-Card program. Striking the right balance of controls is more important that the sheer number of controls. Auditing each and every transaction for every cardholder in every period reduces the process savings inherent to P-Cards. A long-term approach is for companies to review the cost versus benefit and consider its level of risk tolerance.
8. **Effective card distribution.** Put cards in the right hands by determining which employees initiate purchases or requisitions.

P-Card Purchases

Most companies make a large number of small purchases or low dollar value purchases, and these purchases are a logical starting place for P-Card purchases. Some companies draw a line between small purchases from suppliers used often and small purchases from suppliers used only occasionally. Adopting a policy of using the P-Card to charge all small dollar purchases from infrequently used suppliers is a quick way to cut overhead with minimal financial risk. The small purchases from suppliers used frequently justify more planning. The usual strategy is to start with small purchases and then work up to higher value transactions.

Issuing P-Cards

The usual complaint is that companies are too suspicious and security conscious, resulting in the restriction of cards to only a handful of trusted employees. This undercuts the premise and value of the program. Each company will have to make its own choices on exactly who gets cards.

Some companies issue cards to procurement professionals and continue to channel small purchases through them, but the consensus among companies with successful purchasing card programs is that the greatest gains in process efficiency come from putting the cards in the hands of end users and letting them buy what they need, when they need it – with predetermined restrictions and controls set to prevent misuse.

How to Grow Your P-Card Program

1. As organizations realize the benefits of using P-Cards is to reduce costs and control expenses, many forward-thinking companies are exploring ways to expand their program's reach. The advent of robust controls and security measures that card issuers have implemented to prevent unauthorized charges or employee misuse provides companies with the comfort to convert higher dollar, low-volume payments to cards.
2. Utilizing virtual cards allows companies to lock down purchase controls as they see fit. Each virtual card is tied to an underlying billing account that is not shared with suppliers, which prevents the chances of unauthorized spending or fraudulent activity. When virtual cards are combined with a successful purchasing card program, it can help organizations derive greater financial benefits and process improvements.
3. Issuers of P-Cards can help companies grow their programs through supplier onboarding initiatives. Ongoing support and communications programs to targeted suppliers can help educate suppliers on the benefits of purchasing card acceptance.

P-Card Rebates

More and more companies are cashing in on P-Card rebates to drive savings. Rebates which provide cash back to an organization are based on annual purchase volume; therefore, companies with large volumes reap the most rewards from rebates. With a rebate program, the card issuer pays back to your organization a negotiated portion of the volume of purchases made with the cards. Rebates typically are paid annually and generally are made available to organizations that meet an established card volume threshold.

Key Point: Rebates can be ideal for situations in which corporate card use can be mandated. If a company can develop and enforce a policy that all employees participate in the card program, companies will capture more spend and maximize rebates. The more a company spends, and the faster the card issuer is paid, the greater the rebate is likely to be.

AP TOOL 39: P-CARD PROGRAM IMPLEMENTATION BEST PRACTICES

About This Tool: Here are a series of best practices to consider when implementing or improving your P-Card program.

1. **Policies and Procedures**
   1. Policies and procedures for the P-Card program are in place and updated regularly.
   2. Establish criteria to determine who should be issued a P-Card.
   3. A well-defined and communicated P-Card cardholder agreement is implemented.
   4. Involve senior management and HR up front to ensure that the organization takes the appropriate action if there is an incident of non-compliance.
   5. The cardholder understands the consequences of non-compliance to the company's policies and procedures and there are training sessions for new cardholders.
2. **The Role of the P-Card Administrator**
   6. Ensure there is proper segregation of duties between the P-Card program owner and the P-Card administrator.
   7. The P-Card administrator has well-defined roles and responsibilities.
   8. The P-Card administrator participates in ongoing training with the issuer to ensure that all the system functionality and reporting is being fully utilized.
   9. The P-Card administrator keeps an index of available reports and the data provided and the P-Card administrator reports usage trends.
   10. The role of the P-Card administrator is rotated on a two-year basis to ensure there is no collusion with other employees or suppliers.
3. **Internal Controls Program**
   11. Use proactive controls like Merchant Category Codes (MCC).
   12. Ensure there is a specific escalation process if a fraud is suspected by the company's management team, an internal controls review, an internal audit review, or by the P-Card administrator.
   13. A well-defined internal controls program has been created by the management team and approved by the company's internal audit team.
   14. The internal controls program is updated at least annually.
   15. P-Card cardholders are aware of their company's commitment to internal controls.
4. **Auditing Techniques**
   16. Review transactions that take place on weekends or for shipments made to the cardholder's home address.

17. Watch for split purchases to avoid the signature authority needed for a purchase order.
18. Keep a separate supplier master file for P-Card supplier and audit quarterly against the main file to check for duplicates. Also, do a check against the employee master file.
19. Conduct random audits on a monthly basis of 15–20% of all cardholder statements.
20. Conduct an annual payment review and comparison of P-Card, AP, and T&E transactions to check for potential duplicates.

AP TOOL 40: THE P-CARD HOLDER AGREEMENT

About This Tool: The P-Card holder agreement is a critical control for any P-Card program and should be signed by the holder when presented with the card. If the cardholder does not sign the agreement, your organization should not issue the card. As an additional "check and balance" the P-Card administrator should ensure that the cardholder is aware of the requirements and consequences of the agreements and that the individual is not just signing the agreement to obtain a P-Card. This template can be modified to fit the needs of your organization and should be included with your P-Card policy and procedures. Lastly, all new P-Card holders and their managers should attend training sessions to make sure all program requirements are fully understood.

P-Card Holder Agreement Template

[Insert Name of Organization/Company] is pleased to present you with this P-Card. It represents trust in you and your empowerment as a responsible agent to safeguard and protect the assets of our organization. Please ensure that you will use this P-Card responsively.

I, [Name of Employee], Employee ID # [Number], hereby acknowledge receipt of a Card Number XXXX-XXXX-XXXX-[Last four digits], a P-Card issued by [Insert Name of Issuing Bank], that will only be used to acquire materials and supplies for [Name of Organization/Company]. I agree to comply with the following terms and conditions relating to my use of the P-Card.

1. As an authorized cardholder, I agree to comply with the terms and conditions of this Agreement and with the provisions of the P-Card Policy and Procedures. I have received a copy of the P-Card Policy and confirm that I have read and understand its terms and conditions. In addition, I have completed the required P-Card Training.

2. I understand that [Insert Name of Organization/Company] is liable to the [Issuing Bank] for all charges I make on the P-Card.

3. I agree to use the P-Card for authorized official business purchases only and agree not to charge personal purchases. I authorize [Name of Organization/Company] to take whatever steps are necessary to collect an amount equal to the total of the improper purchases, including but not limited to declaring such purchases an advance on my wages to the extent allowed by law.

4. I agree to notify [Name of Organization/Company] P-Card Administrator at [Insert Phone Number] or [Insert E-mail Address] if my name or contact information changes. I further acknowledge that name changes will require proof of change, i.e. copy of marriage license and/or decree of legal change.

5. If the P-Card is lost or stolen, I will **immediately** notify the [Issuing Bank]. I will also notify [Name of Organization/Company] P-Card administrator in writing, at the first opportunity during normal business hours.

6. I understand that improper or fraudulent use of the P-Card may result in disciplinary action, up to and including termination of my employment. I further understand that [Name of Organization/Company] may terminate my right to use the P-Card at any time for any reason.

7. I agree to surrender the P-Card immediately upon request or upon termination of employment for any reason.

Signature Section

Agreed and accepted this [Date] day of [Month], 20[XX].

Procurement Card (P-Card) Holder:

Signature: _____   Date:

Print Name: Phone:

Entity/Department:

Organization/Company P-Card Administrator:

Signature: _____   Date:

Print Name: Phone:

AP TOOL 41: THE P-CARD SCORECARD

About This Tool: Have you ever wondered if your company is achieving all the expected benefits from your P-Card program? And have you thought about implementing the current best practices for your P-Card program? This scorecard allows you to take a look at your entire P-Card program and determine how well things are working. The scorecard suggests several best practices within the following six categories.

1. P-Card Program Planning and Implementation
2. Policies and Procedures
3. The Role of the P-Card Administrator
4. Internal Controls Program
5. Auditing Techniques
6. Program Expansion

Depending on the maturity of your P-Card program, you can modify the scorecard to best fit your needs. You can use one or two of the categories or you can you utilize the entire scorecard. Your overall score can be calculated by one of the following methodologies: (1) Assign a numerical ranking to the scorecard component (1–5), (2) Assign a percentage (1–100%), (3) Assign a grade (A–F), (4) Assign a pass/fail (P or F), or (5) Assign a "stoplight" ranking (red, yellow, green, blue). Then determine the average performance for each section of the scorecard. We have even provided a summary page that allows you to summarize your results.

1. P-Card Program Planning and Implementation

Suggested Best Practice	Date	Complete (Y/N)	Status	Next Steps	Overall Score
Assign a P-Card program sponsor.					
Implement a cross functional P-Card implementation and enhancement team.					
■ Select P-Card Provider					
■ Develop Policies and Procedures					
■ Define P-Card Program Roles and Responsibilities					
Assign a P-Card program manager.					

Assign a P-Card administrator

Perform Cost Benefit and ROI for P-Card program implementation.

Establish and track performance goals and metrics.

- Reductions in Payments Processed
- Reductions in Errors/ Discrepancies
- Number of Manual Checks Requested
- Cycle Time Improvements
- Improvements in Payment Stratification Trends

Identify strategic sourcing opportunities.

- Diversity Suppliers

Average Score

2. Policies and Procedures					
Suggested Best Practice	**Date**	**Complete (Y/N)**	**Status**	**Next Steps**	**Overall Score**
Policies and procedures include:					

- Expense Authorization
- Delegation of Authority Limits
- Expense Types
- Capitalization Limits
- PO and P-Card Purchases
- Internal Controls and Audit Requirements
- The Consequences of P-Card Abuse

The policies and procedures are updated on a monthly/ quarterly/annual basis.

The P-Card cardholder agreement is implemented and utilized.

The P-Card training program is in place for cardholders and their managers.

Average Score

3. The Role of the P-Card Administrator

Suggested Best Practice	Date	Complete (Y/N)	Status	Next Steps	Overall Score
There is a well-defined job description for both the P-Card program Manager and the P-Card administrator.					
Segregation of duties is in place between the program manager and administrator.					
Policies and procedures are updated on a monthly/quarterly/ annual basis.					
P-Card cardholder agreement is implemented and utilized					
P-Card training program is in place for cardholders and their managers.					
The P-Card administrator utilizes all reporting provided by the provider to track exceptions, report trends, and to highlight issues in a timely manner.					
The P-Card administrator makes recommendations to management regarding spending issues, limits, or the need to revoke or cancel a card.					
Average Score					

4. Internal Controls Program

Suggested Best Practice	Date	Complete (Y/N)	Status	Next Steps	Overall Score
A well-defined internal controls program is in place that has been approved by the company's internal audit team.					
The internal controls program is updated annually.					
MCC Codes are utilized.					
An escalation process is in place for significant internal controls issues.					
There is a remediation process and action plan for all internal control issues identified.					
P-Card cardholders are aware of their company's commitment to internal controls.					
A P-Card training program is in place for cardholders and their managers.					
Average Score					

5. Auditing Techniques

Suggested Best Practice	Date	Complete (Y/N)	Status	Next Steps	Overall Score
Audit suspicious transactions that take place on weekends or for shipments made to a cardholder's home address.					
Audit PO policy transactions for avoidance of creating a purchase order and obtaining approvals.					
A P-Card designation is indicated on the Supplier Master File.					
Conduct random audits on a monthly basis for 15–20% of all cardholder statements.					
Review all individual transactions over a specified amount for proper approvals and documentation ($5,000, $10,000, or $15,000 depending on the company).					
Conduct an annual review of the payment files for P-Cards, T&E, and AP to check for duplicate or erroneous payments.					
Average Score					

Program Expansion

Suggested Best Practice	Date	Complete (Y/N)	Status	Next Steps	Overall Score
Implement a PO and P-Card policy mandating the use of P-Cards for all purchases over a specified dollar limit.					
Establish thresholds for the sizes and types of purchases that a P-Card can be used for.					
Prioritize suppliers that will accept the P-Card.					
Work with suppliers that currently do not accept the P-Card.					
Extend P-Card usage within the purchase to pay environment.					
■ Integration of Electronic Invoicing Presentation and Payment (EIPP) Systems and Processes ■ Expand Invoice Payment via P-Cards					
Utilize a single card for multiple expense categories.					
Look for ways to improve all the components of your P-Card program.					
■ Policies and Procedures ■ Training ■ Communication ■ Internal Controls					
Average Score					

Program Component	Component Score
1. P-Card Program Planning and Implementation	
2. Policies and Procedures	
3. The Role of the P-Card Administrator	
4. International Controls Program	
5. Auditing Techniques	
6. Program Extension	
Total Score	

 STANDARDS OF INTERNAL CONTROLS: P-CARD PROCESS

Internal Control	Type of Control	Risks Mitigated
13.A Delegation of Authority (DOA) Approval and Review. Management with delegation of authority (DOA) is responsible for 100% audit of cardholder's statement and supporting documentation/receipts. Additionally, management's DOA signature approval required on cardholder's statement (DOA applies to each transaction on the statement, not the statement total). **Refer to risks: 13-I, 13-2, 13-3, 13-4, 13-5, 13-6, 13-7**	Detective Management Review Supervisory Policy Preventive Procedure	**13-1** Controls may be bypassed, allowing the potential for theft or error. **13-2** Expenditures or services may be ordered and received by an unauthorized individual. **13-3 Duplicate Payments.** Duplicate payments may occur, or payments may be made for the wrong amount or to unauthorized or nonexistent suppliers. **13-4 Unauthorized Purchases or Services.** Purchases or services may be unauthorized, recorded for the wrong amount or in the wrong period, and/or payment made to the wrong entity. **13-5 Items may be recorded and payment made for goods or services not received.** **13-6** Operations may be adversely affected as suppliers may refuse future business with the company. **13-7 Cash utilization may not be optimized.**

Internal Control	Type of Control	Risks Mitigated

13.B P-Card Statement Submission and Tracking.
1. The cardholder submits statement with supporting documentation for each transaction.
2. The P-Card administrator reviews spending activity in credit card online recording and reporting system.
3. The P-Card Administrator reviews every statement upon receipt to ensure that it is:
  ■ Date stamped with date received in AP.
  ■ Verified for appropriate management delegation of authority (DOA).
4. The P-Card administrator tracks each statements on P-Card audit log:
  ■ Used to monitor submission of statements.
  ■ Follow-up on outstanding statements.
  ■ Document audit activity.
Refer to risks: 13-I, 13-2, 13-3, 13-4, 13-5, 13-6, 13-7
	Detective
	
	Management Review
	
	Supervisory
	
	Policy
	
	Preventive
	
	Procedure
		13-1 Controls may be bypassed, allowing the potential for theft or error.
		
		13-2 Expenditures or services may be ordered and received by an unauthorized individual.
		
		13-3 Duplicate Payments. Duplicate payments may occur, or payments may be made for the wrong amount or to unauthorized or nonexistent suppliers.
		
		13-4 Unauthorized Purchases or Services. Purchases or services may be unauthorized, recorded for the wrong amount or in the wrong period, and/or payment made to the wrong entity.
		
		13-5 Items may be recorded and payment made for goods or services not received.
		
		13-6 Operations may be adversely affected as suppliers may refuse future business with the company.
		
		13-7 Cash utilization may not be optimized.

13.C Random Audits. Conduct a minimum of 10% of the total cardholder population; however, on average audit 20–30% of all statements. The random audit process should include the following components.
 	
  ■ **Supplier Review** – Appropriateness of purchase.
  ■ **Misuse of Card** – Personal purchases.
  ■ **Justification** – Documentation/explanation for unusual purchases and pre-approvals if applicable.
Refer to risks: 13-I, 13-2, 13-3, 13-4, 13-5
	Detective	**13-1 Controls may be bypassed, allowing the potential for theft or error.**
		
		13-2 Expenditures or services may be ordered and received by an unauthorized individual.
		
		13-3 Duplicate Payments. Duplicate payments may occur, or payments may be made for the wrong amount or to unauthorized or nonexistent suppliers.
		
		13-4 Unauthorized Purchases or Services. Purchases or services may be unauthorized, recorded for the wrong amount or in the wrong period, and/or payment made to the wrong entity.
		
		13-5 Items may be recorded and payment made for goods or services not received.

(Continued)

Internal Control	Type of Control	Risks Mitigated
13.C Random Audits. Conduct a minimum of 10% of the total cardholder population; however, on average audit 20–30% of all statements. The random audit process should include the following components. ■ **Supplier Review** – Appropriateness of purchase. ■ **Misuse of Card** – Personal purchases. ■ **Justification** – Documentation/explanation for unusual purchases and pre-approvals if applicable. **Refer to risks: 13-I, 13-2, 13-3, 13-4, 13-5**	Detective	**13-1 Controls may be bypassed, allowing the potential for theft or error.** **13-2 Expenditures or services may be ordered and received by an unauthorized individual.** **13-3 Duplicate Payments.** Duplicate payments may occur, or payments may be made for the wrong amount or to unauthorized or nonexistent suppliers. **13-4 Unauthorized Purchases or Services.** Purchases or services may be unauthorized, recorded for the wrong amount or in the wrong period, and/or payment made to the wrong entity. **13-5 Items may be recorded and payment made for goods or services not received.**
13.D Targeted Audits: Targeted audits should be conducted in addition to random audits and are specific to cardholder, general ledger account, and supplier spend. The following components should be addressed, ■ Review all charges over a designated dollar amount. Examples are $10,000.00, $15,000.00, or $20,000.00 **Note:** This amount is usually determined by your company's PO policy. ■ Preferred supplier spending on office supplies. ■ Look for any charitable contributions. ■ Review 100% of statements for retail or restaurant spending to identify misuse or unusual purchases.	Detective	**13-1 Controls may be bypassed, allowing the potential for theft or error.** **13-2 Expenditures or services may be ordered and received by an unauthorized individual.** **13-3 Duplicate Payments.** Duplicate payments may occur, or payments may be made for the wrong amount or to unauthorized or nonexistent suppliers **13-4 Unauthorized Purchases or Services.** Purchases or services may be unauthorized, recorded for the wrong amount or in the wrong period, and/or payment made to the wrong entity. **13-5 Items may be recorded and payment made for goods or services not received.**

Internal Control	Type of Control	Risks Mitigated
▪ Use credit card online reporting tools and reports to assist with audit and review spend activity. ▪ Review all payments to foreign suppliers. ▪ Review payments to employees. **Refer to risks: 13-l, 13-2, 13-3, 13-4, 13-5**		
13.E P-Card Policy and Training. The policy should state clearly what the P-Card can and cannot be used to purchase. The policy also should identify the disciplinary action for accidental misuse versus intentional misuse. The policy contains a P-Card cardholder agreement and specifics the training requirements for the cardholder and their manager. **Refer to risks: 13-l, 13-2, 13-3, 13-4, 13-5**	Policy Preventive Procedure	**13-1 Controls may be bypassed, allowing the potential for theft or error.** **13-2 Expenditures or services may be ordered and received by an unauthorized individual.** **13-3 Duplicate Payments.** Duplicate payments may occur, or payments may be made for the wrong amount or to unauthorized or nonexistent suppliers **13-4 Unauthorized Purchases or Services.** Purchases or services may be unauthorized, recorded for the wrong amount or in the wrong period, and/or payment made to the wrong entity. **13-5 Items may be recorded and payment made for goods or services not received.**
13.F Segregation of Duties. The P-Card administrator should be allowed to make decisions on the company's P-Card program. Additionally, the P-Card administrator should not be granted physical or system access to accounts payable suppliers or purchasing information. **Refer to risks: 13-l, 13-2, 13-3, 13-4, 13-5, 13-6, 13-7**	Policy Preventive Procedure Management Review Supervisory	**13-1 Controls may be bypassed, allowing the potential for theft or error.** **13-2 Expenditures or services may be ordered and received by an unauthorized individual.** **13-3 Duplicate Payments.** Duplicate payments may occur, or payments may be made for the wrong amount or to unauthorized or nonexistent suppliers.

(Continued)

Internal Control	Type of Control	Risks Mitigated
		13-4 Unauthorized Purchases or Services. Purchases or services may be unauthorized, recorded for the wrong amount or in the wrong period, and/or payment made to the wrong entity.
		13-5 Items may be recorded and payment made for goods or services not received.
		13-6 Operations may be adversely affected as suppliers may refuse future business with the company.
		13-7 Cash utilization may not be optimized.

CHAPTER FOURTEEN

Travel and Entertainment

 INTRODUCTION

The term "T&E" means either "Travel & Expense" or "Travel & Entertainment Expenses." These phrases (T&E, T and E, travel and expense, and travel and entertainment) are often used when talking about the second largest operational cost, after salaries. According to Aberdeen, "business expenses related to travel and entertainment encompass 8 Percent to 12 Percent of the average organization's total budget." So T&E is an important focus if you're concerned about both saving money and improving controls for your company.

According to the Aberdeen Group's "State of Travel and Entertainment Expense Management Guide for 2014" report, over 53% of the companies surveyed place a high priority on expense management. It makes sense, when you think about it, because your company's travel and expenses budget is one of the key places where you could be looking to reduce costs.[1]

---

[1]"State of Travel and Entertainment Expense Management Guide for 2014," accessed September 12, 2020, https://www.aberdeen.com/cfo-essentials/the-travel-and-expense-management-guide-for-2014-trends-for-the-future/.

T&E Process Flow

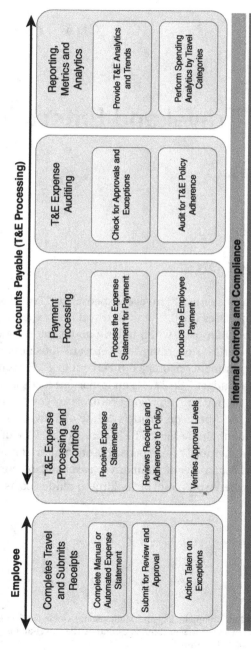

T&E Process Insights

Concur offers many case studies and suggestions on detecting and preventing T&E Fraud. One of the biggest challenges cam be writing a policy that is well defined and in line with the organization's corporate culture. Concur offers the following suggestions for developing a T&E policy.

- Divide up your policy into sections: air travel, hotel lodging, dining, entertainment expenses, and car rental.
- Provide a section that clearly states what is not reimbursable.
- Let employees know what enforcement measures will be taken to ensure policy compliance.
- Include a guideline around traveling with spouses or significant others. What if an employee chooses to stay over extra days? Or over a weekend?
- Who is responsible for travel charges if the employee cancels a reservation or is a "no show"?
- What is your policy about home offices? Can employees be reimbursed for internet and/or phone charges? What about office supplies or office furniture?
- What's your company's policy about consuming alcohol at meals with clients? If alcohol is permitted, what is your policy about paying for an alternative ride back home or to a hotel if the employee can't drive?
- If a receipt is missing, let employees know all is not lost. Ask for an explanation of the expense, business need, date of the expense, supplier, location, and dollar amount. You might also consider calling the supplier for a duplicate receipt if possible.
- Update your mileage reimbursement rate. Should employees start the mileage count from your company's headquarters? Or from home? (One company automatically deducts 20 miles when an employee submits a mileage expense form – even when the employee works from home.)
- Are credit card statements an acceptable form of receipt? Or do you require itemization and a store receipt along with a credit card slip?
- Also, be sure to fit the current mode of your company growth. Are you in growth mode or cost-cutting mode? Are you a smaller company or larger? How high in the management structure do expenses need to be approved?[2]

---

[2]Lara Edwards, "Need a Travel and Expense Policy? Create One in Three Minutes," April 7, 2020, accessed September 12, 2020, https://www.concur.com/newsroom/article/need-travel-expense-policy-create-one-three-minutes#:~:text=What%20will%20a%20T%26E%20policy,your%20first%20port%20of%20call.&text=The%20maximum%20amount%20you%20can,what%20cabin%20employees%20may%20book.

Other T&E Policy Considerations

According to American Express, the three guiding principles for any T&E policy are:

(1) Maximizing savings to the organization, while simultaneously improving (or at least maintaining) both traveler (2) Satisfaction, and (3) Productivity.

Key Point: Organizations must determine the appropriate mix to satisfy their business requirements and corporate culture, as changes in any one of these areas will have an immediate impact on the others.

The six elements of a T&E policy are:

1. Culture
2. Content
3. Comprehensiveness
4. Communication
5. Control
6. Compliance

1. Culture

An organization's culture is reflected in all of its operating policies and procedures, including its business T&E policy. Corporate culture is a critical link to each of the other five key elements. Decision makers in travel management are required to have an intuitive grasp of their company's culture. Travel management requires a deliberate balancing act between potential savings and a company's status quo. Issues that may impact corporate culture are those that can affect an employee's comfort and/or convenience level while travelling. Any changes to corporate culture require strong and visible support from senior management.

2. Content

The success of a T&E policy hinges on the topics addressed. Critical topics need to be included in order to maximize the effectiveness of the policy. Travelers need to know what management's expectations are. A T&E policy should cover information on each component of T&E spending as this will ensure that travelers understand management's expectations on all components of business travel.

3. Comprehensiveness

The success of your organization's T&E policy hinges not only on the actual topics included, but also on the level of comprehensiveness within each topic. If all details are not clearly defined in the T&E policy, travelers will not understand the company's expectations.

4. Communication

Improve communication methods and obtain senior management support. Even a meticulously crafted policy cannot deliver savings if travelers are not familiar with it or its contents.

5. Control

A good T&E policy supports the internal control requirements of the company. The strength and effectiveness of the specific policy language enforces strategies and defines the process for dealing with non-compliance. The policy also defines the methods that will be used to monitor compliance.

6. Compliance

Once a company has developed and communicated its T&E policy, a key question still remains: are travelers complying with it? All imposed restrictions must be monitored for traveler compliance as non-compliance results in higher than necessary costs.[3]

 ## AP TOOL 42: RED FLAGS FOR THE T&E PROCESS

About This Tool: There are certain red flags that indicate possible trouble with T&E. Understanding what they are – and what to do if they exist – will help you strengthen internal controls in this area.

---

[3]"Drive Savings Through Smart T&E Expense Management," American Express, accessed September 12, 2020, https://corporate.americanexpress.com/content/InControlQ2Direct.

1. Out-of-Policy Spending

There are two primary causes of out-of-policy spending. First, different units of a business interpret policies and enforce reporting procedures differently. Second, certain managers, often those who run a company or division, act as if T&E policy and procedures don't apply to them.

Out-of-policy spending by managers can also create morale problems. Other employees will wonder why they have to fly coach while their bosses are in first class. Plus, spending disparities and selective enforcement of the policy can push employees who are predisposed to travel fraud over the edge. That is, they will rationalize the submission of padded expense reports because "the boss does it."

What to do: The most important control tool for T&E is a comprehensive policy and procedures manual. Be sure that the policies are fair and that they are communicated to all employees. If warranted, set up special T&E standards for senior managers or special groups. If this is necessary, communicate the reasons for such special treatment. Explain, don't ignore, special travel status. Also:

- Implement an automated T&E system with built-in parameters that polices departures from your travel policy;
- Use e-booking software, which identifies the cheapest trip and requires explanations for traveler negation (available directly from travel websites or from suppliers of T&E software);
- Hold the traveler financially responsible for unauthorized purchases; and
- Punish persistent non-compliance with disciplinary action, up to and including dismissal.

2. No Cost Standards

An organization should have cost standards for T&E spending. Otherwise, the T&E policy is weakened and enforcement becomes difficult.

What to do: Employ a database system that tracks individuals, departments, and business reasons for spending according to such things as: dollars spent, exceptions approved and disapproved, destination, length of stay, and accomplishments and objectives reached.

Another cost standard some organizations use are T&E per diems for meals, auto rental, and hotel overnights. Some firms come up with their own amounts or use those issued by the General Services Administration (www.gsa.gov). These amounts establish uniform expenditure levels for your corporate travelers as well as help you spot non-compliance with T&E policy. Be aware that most travelers consider the government-issued per diems to be unrealistically low. Thus, companies concerned with T&E fraud might consider using different and higher norms, such as those published annually by Business Travel News (www.btnonline.com).

3. Use of Personal Credit Cards

Transactions on private credit cards lack the visibility that they would otherwise have if run through corporate cards. For instance, a traveler may pay for an airline ticket, hotel room, meeting room, or entertainment venue on his or her private card, receive a genuine receipt, and then get reimbursed. However, he or she may also receive a personal credit or adjustment that never gets reported to the company.

Airline tickets are especially vulnerable in this situation. For example, an unscrupulous employee could buy a ticket in business class, obtain a refund, and rebook in coach. Then, he or she submits the receipt for the more expensive fare for reimbursement.

What to do: Scrutinize personal credit card charges. While checking every such charge is unnecessary, select and review a percentage of these charges each month. Make sure your travelers know you have undertaken these reviews. To avoid this, you can require employees to use company-issued credit cards and review card statements for adjustments or credits that belong to the company. Also:

- Implement a user-reward system for travelers switching from personal to corporate credit cards (this will compensate for the loss of personal credit card premiums and rebates); and
- If company credit cards are used, have the card data fed automatically into the expense reporting system.

4. Under-the-Radar Spending

The threshold for requiring receipts is $75. That is, the Internal Revenue Service may disallow deductions for T&E transactions that are more than $75 if the taxpayer cannot substantiate the deduction with receipts. But if an organization requires receipts only for transactions exceeding $75, a traveler may exploit this threshold by recording bogus or inflated expenses below that amount.

What to do: Some companies still use the old IRS threshold for requiring T&E receipts, which was $25. Also, you can use the government per diems for travelers. There are per diems by city and metro area. Companies that restrict traveler spending to these per diems do not have to substantiate T&E deductions with receipts. At the same time, they help to cap traveler spending.

5. Canceled Trips

There could be a problem if the system for monitoring travel spending does not show whether travelers actually used the airline ticket for which they submitted a receipt.

To take advantage of advance purchase discounts, a traveler may buy an airline ticket several months before the trip. If the traveler charges that expense on his or her credit card, most companies reimburse the employee prior to his or her having to pay the card charge. But what if the trip is canceled? How can you be sure the company gets any credit?

What to do: Record airline advance purchases in a prepaid account. Then, debit travel expense when the trip is both completed and accounted for, thus clearing the original charge. Check regularly with employees who are frequent flyers about the existence of open canceled tickets. (While airlines carry this information for 12 months, they will not notify you about cancellations.) Other ideas:

- Use a travel agency that can track and compare purchased flights to flights actually taken; and
- Require travelers to verify the flight and cost of ticket in a post-trip T&E report, if the company or travel agent pays directly for the ticket.

6. Late Expense Reports

Travelers may claim they are too busy to file their expense reports on time. But as T&E data age, the traveler may say he or she can't remember the details of a trip. This enables unscrupulous employees to claim they made honest mistakes when, for instance, they submit duplicate expenses. In one case, a director of a prestigious US university used the excuse of late filing to explain how he double-billed for $150,000 in business travel expenses.

Another problem is that a traveler may receive advances in excess of travel monies spent and thus owes the employer the remaining money. But if the employee has financial difficulties, he or she may use the excess to pay personal bills. Then, this traveler delays the expense report. The point here is that many companies are unaware that employees have not accounted for trips until they actually submit their travel expense report.

What to do: Institute and enforce a deadline – so many days after the completion of a trip – to receive timely reimbursement. Also, eliminate or minimize travel advances. This way, travelers are out-of-pocket for incidental travel spending. But they never owe unspent advance money to the employer. Other ideas:

- Prepopulate expense reports with credit card data – these both facilitate T&E report preparation and red-flags the existence of outstanding expenses;
- Link directly with preferred suppliers that report charged expenses to corporate partners to bring spending details to AP more rapidly; and
- Connect travelers using automated T&E systems to database systems that flag duplicate dates and items on expense reports.

STANDARDS OF INTERNAL CONTROL: T&E PROCESS

Internal Control	Type of Control	Risks Mitigated
14.A Establishment and Communication of Company Policy. Managers and employees are aware of the policy and are aware of the repercussions when the policy is violated. **Refer to risks: 14-1, 14-2, 14-3, 14-4, 14-5**	**Management Review** **Policy** **Procedure** **Preventive** **Supervisory**	**14-1 Improper SoD and System Access.** The lack of good segregation of duties and system access controls may result in incorrect payments and accounting data. Incorrect payments may be undetected for a lengthy period, and payments that are too high may be unrecoverable. **14-2 Violation of Corporate T&E Policies.** Policies may be violated, leading to duplicate, erroneous, or fraudulent payments being issued to employees. **14-3 Poor visibility or errors during the review process.** The lack of a timely review process may cause errors to be undetected and incorrect payments to be made.

(Continued)

Internal Control	Type of Control	Risks Mitigated
		14-4 Unclear and undefined roles and responsibilities. Unclear responsibilities for the cardholder and management may result in corporate card abuse and inappropriate payments.
		14-5 Misstatement of Financial Results. Financial statements, records, and operating reports may be misstated. Critical decisions may be based upon erroneous information resulting in the misstatement of financial results.
14.B Validation and Approval of T&E Expenses. Reimbursement requests are approved and there are appropriate approval controls in placed to prevent unauthorized T&E transactions. T&E reimbursement requests are independently validated for compliance with company policy and accuracy. Approvers have the option of adding comments to their approval. Each approver must execute specific approvals, unless he/she has delegated this to another approver. If delegation has been made, then the delegated approver must accompany the approval process. **Refer to risks: 14-2, 14-5**	Detective Management Review Policy Procedure Preventive Supervisory	**14-2 Violation of Corporate T&E Policies.** Policies may be violated, leading to duplicate, erroneous, or fraudulent payments being issued to employees. **14-5 Misstatement of Financial Results.** Financial statements, records, and operating reports may be misstated. Critical decisions may be based upon erroneous information resulting in the misstatement of financial results.

Internal Control	Type of Control	Risks Mitigated
1.C Delegation of Authority. Approval of T&E requests is based on the organizational hierarchy defined by the DOA policy. The employee's designated approver receives a notification of the pending approval. If an approver will be out of the office on leave or vacation, he/she must delegate their authority enabling the request to smoothly continue through the system. **Refer to risks: 14-2, 14-3, 14-5**	**Management Review** **Policy** **Procedure** **Preventive** **Supervisory**	**14-2 Violation of Corporate T&E Policies.** Policies may be violated, leading to duplicate, erroneous, or fraudulent payments being issued to employees. **14-3 Poor visibility or errors during the review process.** The lack of a timely review process may cause errors to be undetected and incorrect payments to be made. **14-5 Misstatement of Financial Results.** Financial statements, records, and operating reports may be misstated. Critical decisions may be based upon erroneous information resulting in the misstatement of financial results.
14.D Avoiding Duplicate T&E Transactions. T&E transactions are reviewed to ensure there are no duplicate transactions. **Refer to risks: 14-2, 14-3, 14-5**	**Detective** **Management Review** **Policy** **Procedure** **Preventive** **Supervisory**	**14-2 Violation of Corporate T&E Policies.** Policies may be violated, leading to duplicate, erroneous, or fraudulent payments being issued to employees. **14-3 Poor visibility or errors during the review process.** The lack of a timely review process may cause errors to be undetected and incorrect payments to be made. **14-5 Misstatement of Financial Results.** Financial statements, records, and operating reports may be misstated. Critical decisions may be based upon erroneous information resulting in the misstatement of financial results.

(Continued)

Internal Control	Type of Control	Risks Mitigated
14.E T&E Transaction Audits. Audited T&E reimbursement requests go through a field validation checks before posting. The key fields include the following: Cost Center, Project Number, and Employee Number. **Refer to risks: 14-2, 14-3, 14-5**	Detective	**14-2 Violation of Corporate T&E Policies.** Policies may be violated, leading to duplicate, erroneous, or fraudulent payments being issued to employees. **14-3 Poor visibility or errors during the review process.** The lack of a timely review process may cause errors to be undetected and incorrect payments to be made. **14-5 Misstatement of Financial Results.** Financial statements, records, and operating reports may be misstated. Critical decisions may be based upon erroneous information resulting in the misstatement of financial results.
14.F T&E Transaction Reviews. T&E processing personnel reviews and corrects any errors and contacts the requestor's supervisor or supplier management, as necessary, to resolve the error. Additionally, the T&E processing supervisor reviews the transactions in the Error Status to ensure timely resolution. The errors are generally resolved by the follow day. **Refer to risks: 14-2, 14-3, 14-5**	Detective	**14-2 Violation of Corporate T&E Policies.** Policies may be violated, leading to duplicate, erroneous, or fraudulent payments being issued to employees. **14-3 Poor visibility or errors during the review process.** The lack of a timely review process may cause errors to be undetected and incorrect payments to be made. **14-5 Misstatement of Financial Results.** Financial statements, records, and operating reports may be misstated. Critical decisions may be based upon erroneous information resulting in the misstatement of financial results.

Internal Control	Type of Control	Risks Mitigated
14.G T&E System Access. On a quarterly basis, the T&E system access table is reviewed. The access table is reviewed to ensure that recent system access changes resulting from changes in job responsibility are properly reflected, and for appropriate level of access based on the job function and appropriate segregation of duties within the organization. **Refer to risks; 14-1, 14-2**	Detective Preventive	**14-1 Improper SoD and System Access.** The lack of good segregation of duties and system access controls may result in incorrect payments and accounting data. Incorrect payments may be undetected for a lengthy period, and payments that are too high may be unrecoverable. **14-2 Violation of Corporate T&E Policies.** Policies may be violated, leading to duplicate, erroneous, or fraudulent payments being issued to employees.
14.H High Value T&E Transaction Approval. If the value of the T&E reimbursement request exceeds $1,500 for new T&E processors or $9,000 for second-level T&E processors, the request must be approved by the supervisor or manager. The supervisor can approve up to $10,000 and the manager up to $99,999. **Refer to risks: 14-2, 14-3, 14-5**	Management Review Policy Procedure Preventive Supervisory	**14-2 Violation of Corporate T&E Policies.** Policies may be violated, leading to duplicate, erroneous, or fraudulent payments being issued to employees. **14-3 Poor visibility or errors during the review process.** The lack of a timely review process may cause errors to be undetected and incorrect payments to be made. **14-5 Misstatement of Financial Results.** Financial statements, records, and operating reports may be misstated. Critical decisions may be based upon erroneous information resulting in the misstatement of financial results.

CHAPTER FIFTEEN

The Payment Process

INTRODUCTION

Payments are defined as the act of paying out or disbursing money. The accounts payable department is responsible for the oversight of all payments issued. The disbursement process is the last step in the purchase order (PO) process. Organizations need to plan disbursement of company funds in a systematic manner in order to capture discounts and reduce the costs associated with late payment penalties. While paper checks still dominate as the number one method of payments, electronic payments are gaining momentum due to reduced transaction costs and increased accountability.

Payment Process Definitions

1. **Checks:** Paper checks can be used to pay money from one company to another. Two parties involved in check transactions are the payee and the drawer. The drawer is the person/company who issues or writes the check, and the payee is the company getting the check as payment. The payee deposits the check into the bank and if the drawer has enough funds in his account, the money will be credited to the payee's account, usually within 2–3 business days.

2. **ACH:** Automated clearing house is a secure payment transfer system that connects all US financial institutions. The ACH network acts as the central clearing facility for all electronic fund transfer (EFT) transactions that

occur nationwide. ACH payments are frequently used by end-user organizations as the payment method by which to pay their issuer.

3. **Wire Transfers:** Bank wire transfers are immediate transfers of funds from one bank to another. Wire transfers are fast and provide real-time processing.

4. **P-Cards:** P-Cards are a form of company charge card that allows goods and services to be procured without using a traditional process. Please refer to Chapter 13 for more detailed information on purchasing cards.

Payment Process Flow

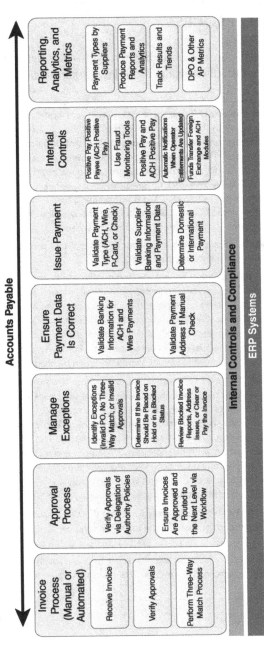

AP TOOL 43: EFFECTIVELY MANAGING YOUR PAYMENT PROCESS

About This Tool: There are a number of ways to effectively manage payments. A P2P professional should consider the following six ways to effectively manage the disbursement process.

1. **Controlled Disbursement:** A method employed in corporate cash management which is used to regulate the flow of checks through the banking system on a daily basis. Controlled payments mandate a once-daily distribution of checks, which usually occurs early in the day. Through controlled disbursement, organizations can keep only the funds required to clear the checks presented for the day in the account, and the rest can be efficiently invested. Organizations simply need to fund the account with the exact amount needed, pooling the remaining funds for investment or debt reduction; this eliminates balances and overdraft charges. Invested funds earn interest up to the time they are needed to fund payments.

2. **Positive Payee:** Delivers an additional layer of positive pay protection against alteration of only the payee name on the check.

3. **Positive Pay:** A cash management service deployed to deter check fraud. Banks utilize Positive pay to match the checks a company issues with those it presents for payment. Any check that is considered to be potentially fraudulent is sent back to the issuer for examination. Positive pay identifies the mismatches in check numbers and amount between what was sent across by the bank in terms of details of checks that have been issued by them, and the actual checks presented. The company is immediately notified of any suspicion of fraud, in which event transactions can be stopped.

4. **Reverse Pay:** This method of disbursement management is similar to positive pay but in reverse. With reverse pay, banks provide details of the checks presented – serial number, account number, amount, etc. – and the company compares the information with its internal records. The company then lets the bank know which checks match their internal information, and the bank pays those checks. The bank verifies the checks that do not match, with the company's records, and will correct any misreads or encoding errors that may have occurred and will then determine if the cause is due to fraudulent behavior or is an error. The bank pays only some exceptions, those that can be reconciled with the company's internal records.

5. **Teller Positive Pay:** Enables bank tellers to access the client issue information to determine if a check presented for cashing at a branch is valid.

6. **Pooling:** This technique is used to offset the cash deficit in one business unit with the cash surplus in another, which reduces the short-term borrowing cost and increases the short-term refunds from investments. This makes the best use of the company's net cash position.

AP TOOL 44: FIVE ACH CONTROLS

About This Tool: Here are five critical ACH controls that should be implemented for your electronic payment process.

Control	Description
1. ACH Block	■ The ACH debit block is also a powerful tool in the prevention of fraud. ■ By completing an ACH Debit Block Agreement, you direct your bank to permit NO ACH transactions to your business account(s) or you provide a list of the company identification numbers that are permitted to complete ACH transactions, thereby blocking all others.
2. ACH Block	■ This service automatically returns all ACH debits and/or credits that are directed to a particular bank account. No client intervention is required once the service is established with your financial institution.
3. ACH Debit Filter	■ Automatically returns all ACH items for designated accounts, except those that are pre-authorized. ■ Authorized ACH originators are identified by providing the bank with specific identifier information such as the originating company ID, or individual ID number. Some banks offer the flexibility of allowing customers to further fine-tune their payment criteria based on maximum dollar amounts, exact dollar amounts, and maximum number of occurrences.
4. Post No Checks Block	■ Blocks checks from a depository account or an account used for electronic debits only.
5. ACH Transaction Review	■ Use this fraud mitigation service to review and confirm ACH debit and credit transactions that post to your account on a case-by case basis. Use ACH transaction review as a complement to our ACH debit blocking service to review ACH transactions not blocked via that service. Simply determine if the transaction in question is authorized and return any transactions that are not. Filter transactions that you wish to review by any combination of: ■ Debits and credits ■ Company IDs ■ Dollar amount/range ■ Transaction types

AP TOOL 45: PREVENTING DUPLICATE PAYMENTS

About This Tool: Duplicated payments are typically prevented by ERP systems if all the data elements in an invoice are an exact match. While these "perfect matches" are identified and prevented, management often does not know, in the absence of an external third-party audit, whether other duplicate payments have been made. The critical issue is to understand that there are many causes of potentially duplicated payments within the accounts payable process.

Understanding which transactions are critical to review for potential risk makes monitoring the accounts payable process even more difficult. Many controllers, chief financial officers (CFOs), and accounts payable professionals face these challenges with limited staff resources. Ongoing changes to compliance regulations have further increased organizational workloads. I often see these scarce resources prioritized for ERP implementations and automation implementations other than used for internal controls, testing, and reporting solutions.

Following our theme of internal controls best practices, we'll look at the top ten causes of duplicate payments that I've identified as a result of several years of experience as a controller and working in the procure-to-pay (P2P) field. We'll look at the accounts payable process impacted, the risk and what your staff can do to mitigate the risk. Here's how the table works.

The table below provides an internal controls matrix in which I identify the:

> **1st Column: Accounts Payable Process Impacted.** This is the specific accounts payable process in which a duplicate payment error can occur. The three main process areas are: (1) The Supplier Master File, (2) Invoice Processing, and (3) P-Cards.
>
> **2nd Column: The Risk.** Here are my "Top Ten Reasons for Duplicate Payments" organized by the accounts payable process impacted.
>
> **3rd Column: What Your Staff Can Do.** Here are examples of the controls and suggested processes your staff can implement to prevent duplicate payments and errors from recurring.

Accounts Payable Process Impacted	The Risk: Cause of the Duplicate Payment	What Your Staff Can Do: Examples of the Controls and Suggest Processes
Supplier Master File	**1. Duplicate Suppliers.** Supplier name and address is duplicated for the same company, increasing the risk for a duplicate payment or a supplier coding error.	**1.1 Implement Supplier Coding Standards.** A lack of supplier coding standards may be one of the main reasons for duplicate suppliers. Coding standards include naming and field conventions for the supplier name, address, state, phone, contact name, and e-mail address.

1.2 Identify Inactive Suppliers. The identification and periodic blocking or segregation of inactive suppliers increases processor keying speed, reduces errors, and will likely enhance system response time. The recommended timeframe is to focus on suppliers with no invoice activity within the prior 18 months. This covers seasonality and retains those supplier that invoice once-a-year.

1.3 Remove Duplicate Suppliers. Duplicate suppliers are an exposure for any accounts payable organization, but represent an increased risk for an organization that has absorbed multiple locations and/or systems into a centralized operation. Duplicate suppliers increase the likelihood of duplicate payments, and intensify the difficulty in compiling a comprehensive spend profile for supplier negotiations (i.e. "IBM," "I.B.M.," "International Business Machines," etc.).

1.4 Consolidate Multiple Remittance Addresses. Many of larger suppliers will have multiple remittance locations. These addresses are often geographically placed to expedite the flow of funds into the supplier's operation, or can be a function of the supplier's ownership structure. Suppliers with significant remittance addresses often include those operating in the areas of telecom, waste management, industrial parts, post offices, and technology. |

(Continued)

Accounts Payable Process Impacted	The Risk: Cause of the Duplicate Payment	What Your Staff Can Do: Examples of the Controls and Suggest Processes
	2. Poor Segregation of Duties Controls. Without good controls and segregation of duties controls, employees could set themselves up as suppliers. This means that either supplier or phony invoices could be diverted to employees.	**2.1 Perform an Employee Master Comparison Against your Supplier Master.** This analysis is often performed by internal audit departments on an annual basis. The employee master is obtained from the human resources department and compared with the supplier master file. The following fields are analyzed: name, address, TIN, EIN, SSN, and bank account. Any matches are investigated.
Invoice Processing	**3. Invoice Paid in Wrong Currencies.** The invoice was paid to a company subsidiary in a currency other than USD, creating a duplicate payment situation.	**3.1 Currency and Intercompany Rules.** Ensure that accounting rules for intercompany and trade payables are enforced.
	4. Invoice Paid in Multiple Systems. Due to multiple ERP systems or AP locations, an invoice was processed and paid twice.	**4.1 Duplicate Check Across Multiple Systems.** Perform a duplicate check across if your company has multiple ERP systems and AP departments.
	5. Supplier Invoice Error. Supplier does business under multiple names and sent duplicate invoices under both names. Both invoices were paid.	**5.1 Updates to Supplier Master File.** Alert your procurement department to ensure that any changes to supplier names or "DBA" impacts are noted and reviewed for potential contact and purchase order impact.
	6. Invoice Coding. Keying an additional letter or number after/before on an invoice (e.g. 103207, 103207A). Also, keying a 0 as a O, or a 1 as an I, or a simple accidental transposition, can potentially lead to a duplicate payment, as the ERP system will not recognize this as the same.	**6.1 Invoice Coding Rules.** Establish and enforce a set of standardized coding rules for invoice numbers. These rules should address the handling of leading zeros, spaces, dashes, special characters, invoices without true invoice numbers, etc. Additionally, specific examples of overpayments should be shared with the invoice processing staff to demonstrate how critical their contribution is and the resultant cost impact of inconsistencies.

Accounts Payable Process Impacted	The Risk: Cause of the Duplicate Payment	What Your Staff Can Do: Examples of the Controls and Suggest Processes
	7. Coding the Invoice to an Incorrect Supplier. The same invoice number and invoice amount was paid to a different supplier.	**7.1 Invoice Coding Rules.** Ensure that the accounts payable team is trained on the importance of coding invoices to the correct supplier. Specific examples of these supplier coding errors should be shared with the processing team and can be tracked as performance metrics for the overall team and as a means for continuous improvement.
	8. Inconsistent Invoice Amounts. This is difference in the invoice amount that was entered for payment vs. the amount of the actual invoice.	**8.1 No Manual Adjustments.** Review the current procedures for making manual adjustments to invoices. The typical reason for the differing invoice amounts is manually excluding additional charges (e.g. freight/sales tax) on one submitted invoice but not on the other.
	9. Offsetting Credit with the Same Numeric Amount. A credit memo is paid as an invoice.	**9.1 Review Open Debit and Credit Balances.** A credit memo may be issued because the client returned goods to the supplier, there was an over shipment of goods, there was a pricing dispute, a marketing allowance was issued, a duplicate payment occurred, the supplier was unable to apply the payment to the correct invoice resulting in a situation of unapplied cash, or an invoice was overpaid. These balances should be reviewed on a monthly to quarterly basis. Many companies perform an internal statement mailing process in which statements are requested from their top suppliers. Others use a third-party audit firm to assist with the process.
P-Cards	**10. P-Card Payment Invoice.** Even though a supplier has been paid with a payment or procurement card, they may still provide an invoice for the transaction that is promptly paid, resulting in a duplicate payment.	**10.1 Annual P-Card and AP Payment Review.** Conduct an annual comparison of accounts payable disbursements against P-Card payments to ensure that no duplicate payments have been made. Your P-Card provider can deliver the payment data to you and many third parties can assist with the review. Some third-party firms have developed subscription fee plans to aid in the identification of duplicates between paid invoices and P-Card disbursements.

In summary, the dilemma of duplicate payments can be challenging. Managing duplicate payments includes a variety of internal control standards, tests, and reviews to determine the best detective and preventive methodologies.

Self-audit software solutions can support a continuous controls monitoring (CCM) environment. This approach creates the foundation for an excellent self-assessment process for your accounts payable process in which the "root cause" for duplicate payments can be identified and remediation actions can be implemented quickly to avoid any future errors.

The Drivers for Implementing an Electronic Payment Process

Key drivers of this trend are the reduction of transaction costs and acceleration of payments to avoid late payment penalties and consistently capture early-payment discounts. Companies are actively investigating electronic payment options to reduce procure-to-pay costs and ACH payments are gaining momentum.

There are a number of factors that are driving organizations to focus on electronic payments. Reducing payment costs, removing paper from the AP department, and better cash management rank are usually the top three drivers.

Key Internal Controls for the Payment Process

Reconcile all bank account statements within 30 days of receipt. Any discrepancies should be investigated and reconciled immediately. This is a task that sometimes gets overlooked when work piles up. Bank reconciliation keeps bank records and general ledger cash account records in balance. It is a good control procedure for identifying:

- Inaccuracies introduced by the bank's accounting of checks and deposits.
- Payments, possibly unauthorized, that have not been accounted for through cash payments records.
- Old outstanding checks that may never be cashed.
- Adjustments generated by the bank.

All well-controlled P2P organizations have certain controls that are exercised during period end. These controls are designed to help identify errors or irregularities that might have occurred during the period. They serve as key internal controls over the accuracy of automated accounts payable records. Generally, period-end balancing includes four types of balancing and reconciliation:

1. **Balancing the accounts payable master file to a manual log of control totals.**
2. **Reconciling the accounts payable master file to the general ledger.**
3. **Balancing the Accounts Payable Master File.** To help verify that the accounts payable master file was correctly carried forward from the beginning of the period and that activity was correctly posted during the period, a simple reconciliation should be performed at the end of each period.
   - An error in the arithmetic of the balancing calculation.
   - An unposted batch recorded in the log but not the open voucher report.
   - Invoices that were posted to the accounts payable master file, but not written in the log.
   - Adjustments, discounts, or recurring vouchers not properly accounted for either in the log or the system.
   - A system error during the period such as an incorrect file version being used or a double posting occurring during the period.
4. **Reconciling to the General Ledger.** As part of the period-end process, an accountant will also reconcile the total open vouchers from the open voucher report to the general ledger accounts payable liability account. Essentially this balances the subsidiary ledger (the accounts payable master file) to the corresponding general ledger account(s). Completing this procedure helps ensure that the interface to the general ledger is working properly and that the journal entries shown in the general ledger distribution have been properly posted to general ledger accounts.

An out-of-balance condition usually occurs only because of special circumstances and warrants intervention by information resources personnel. A flaw in the system's logic for updating these account balances can cause this condition. Alternatively, someone who has compromised the built-in system controls that coordinate and limit access to these two files can also cause such an out-of-balance condition.

 ## AP TOOL 46: EIGHT BEST PAYMENT PRACTICES

About This Tool: In today's difficult economic times, fraud is and will continue to be more of a problem, particularly in the payments area. To help tighten up your disbursement controls, we recommend the following eight best practices.

We find that many organizations use positive pay but do not use the positive payee service.

Best Practice	Description
1. Positive Pay Warning	Positive pay is an automated check-matching service that will identify any check that was not legitimately issued or has an altered dollar amount. The check issuer sends the bank disbursement information (check amount and check number) immediately after each check run. The information allows the bank to validate check numbers and payment amounts before a check is paid. Positive pay is one of the most effective fraud-fighting tools available today.
2. Positive Payee Warning	Positive payee identifies potential alterations to a check's payee line by comparing a payee name from the image of the check with payee information gathered from the issue file sent in by your business customers. Suspect items are automatically flagged for review in making pay or return decisions.
3. Examine Bank Statements Promptly (Within 30 Days)	It is essential to exercise reasonable promptness in examining bank statements. Consider the situation where a company's checks are used illegally because of a forged signature. An important related rule is commonly known as the repeater rule. If a bank customer does not report a forged signature, and the same thief forges a signature on additional checks that are paid more than 30 days after the first forged check or bank statement was made available, the repeater rule becomes effective. In such a case, the bank has no liability on the additional forged checks so long as it acted in good faith and was not negligent.
4. Report Losses Promptly	Just as it is important to promptly examine bank statements, it is equally important to quickly report to the bank any unauthorized payments due to forgeries or alterations.
5. Maintain Tight Security Over Checks	One of the most important steps any business owner or executive can take is to ensure that all checks are stored safely and securely. Implement the following steps. 1. Checks should be kept in an area that is locked and secure. Restrict access to only those persons with responsibility for issuing checks. To strengthen security, it is recommended that the keys or combination locks that safeguard checks be changed annually. 2. Perform an inventory of the check supply quarterly. Keep check boxes sealed until they are actually required for use. Turn the sealed boxes over monthly to ensure that the bottom has not been sliced open and checks removed. 3. Keep the check reorder form under lock and key. A stolen check reorder notice has a street value of $100. A forger changes the SHIP TO address and mails it in. In two weeks, he has your original checks.

6. Separate Financial Responsibilities for Checks (Segregation of Duties)	To minimize the likelihood of embezzlement, it is important that you assign separate check-issuing and reconciliation responsibilities within your organization. For example, the persons responsible for check stock custody and preparing checks for signature should not reconcile the monthly bank statements.
7. Conduct Periodic Audits or Control Self-Assessments (CSAs)	It is important to conduct periodic surprise audits/assessments of the various check control functions. Audits/assessments should test the overall system to ensure it is functioning as it should. Independent, experienced persons trained in systems and theft detection should conduct such audits.
8. Use Secure Check Stock	Legal experts agree that check security features could well become an important element of the legal definition of ordinary care. Brent Gorey, an attorney who specializes in the banking industry and the legal aspects of checks, says, "In appropriate cases, a strong argument can be made that the failure by a business to use security features to protect its checks constitutes negligence."[1]

Automating the Payment Process

Invoice automation tends to get more attention than automating the payments process. Both are equally critical to the successful acceleration of cash flow and the optimization of working capital management.

Obstacles to Automation

So what's holding up the automation of business-to-business (B2B) payment receipt processes? Achieving full electronic payment processing capability is challenging due to the sheer number of payment types, which include: paper checks, wire transfers, automated clearing house (ACH), credit and debit card, mobile, and corporate trade exchange (CTX). As if that weren't enough, there's the wide range of payment capture points, from internal mailrooms to bank lockboxes.

Changing Solutions Landscape

Fortunately, there exist today numerous electronic payment processing solutions to choose from, including in the form of software-as-a-service (SaaS) models that minimize up-front implementation costs as well as total cost of ownership.

[1] Larry La Hue, "Who's Liable? As a Victim of Check Fraud, It Could Be You!" Writeguard.com, accessed on September 12, 2020, https://www.writeguard.com/catalog/check_security.php.

Eight Benefits of Payment Automation

1. **Customer Service.** Such solutions can flexibly incorporate ACH and credit card payments, set up recurring payments, and schedule future payments to better accommodate your customers.

2. **Cash Capability.** Automated payment solutions can include remittance files with enough data capacity to allow automated cash application and invoice-to-payment matching.

3. **Automated Early Pay Discount.** Early pay discounts can be an effective cash acceleration tool, however the potential pitfalls are well known to AR pros. Customers may take the discount out of compliance with terms, causing AR to spend time researching before either charging back the amount or letting it go.

4. **Automation of Deductions.** Improved deduction and exceptions management is another bonus, since the solution can automatically highlight deductions and exceptions and send them to the AR staff for handling.

5. **Enhanced Collection Activity.** Greater visibility into cash flow allows for more strategic targeting of collection efforts and eliminates unnecessary calls.

6. **Lockbox Integration.** Your bank lockbox can be transformed into an electronic lockbox service that processes not only paper but electronic payments as well, with imaging technology to allow viewing of all payment and remittance data at a single location. From the electronic lockbox, all payment data is merged into a consolidated file for posting into the AR system.

7. **Single Receivables Processing Hub.** This "hub," which aggregates payments and remittance detail from any source, replaces the multiple processes previously needed to deal with all the payment types and capture points.

8. **Analysis and Reporting Functionality.** A final benefit is consolidated reporting, based on the solution's ability to extract and export data to enable trend analysis and provide an accurate view of the company's cash position. Payment information is transformed into payment analytics in the form of reports for use by the CFO and top management.

AP TOOL 47: TACKLING PAYMENTS FRAUD

About This Tool: As we continue to face economic challenges and fraudsters become more technology savvy, payments fraud will continue to be more of a problem. Fraudsters are always looking for any way possible to generate "quick cash."

According to the 2020 AFP Payments Fraud and Control Survey Report, 81% of companies were targets of payments fraud last year, once again proving that no industry is immune.

- 75% of organizations experienced Business E-mail Compromise (BEC).
- 54% of organizations reported financial losses as a result of BEC.
- 42% of BEC scams targeted wires, followed by ACH credits at 37%.
- 74% of organizations experienced check fraud in 2019 – up from 70% in 2018.
- Nearly one-third of organizations indicated that they have not received advice from their banking partners about mitigating potential risks associated with same-day ACH credit and debit transactions. (Refer to Chapter 2 for additional statistics on the impact of fraud.)

We'll set the stage by defining three types of fraud that can occur and we'll focus on the common disbursement controls that can be applied to accounts payable, payroll, and T&E.

1. **Internal Fraud:** One or more employees facilitate the activity. Employee has access to assets that are easily converted to cash such as currency, bank accounts, or inventory. Often these frauds are concealed for a time in that the perpetrator also has access to accounting systems and can make false entries to cover the fraudulent activities.
2. **External Fraud:** Someone outside the company is able to gain access to assets through fraudulent means for the purpose of misappropriating or extorting those assets.
3. **Conspiracy Fraud or Collusion:** This is a combination of both internal and external fraud where an employee conspires and colludes with someone outside the company such as a supplier, or third party.

Positive Pay and Positive Payee

"Positive pay" is an industry term for the check matching service banks offer as a means of reconciling accounts and reducing exposure to fraud. It is actually a match of checks being presented for payment against those issued.

Payee positive pay enhances the positive pay validation process by allowing the client to include the Payee as an additional point of comparison between checks presented and the issue data file. Match the payee name that should appear on the check with the actual name on the item presented for payment. As with the standard positive pay program, online flagging of exception item images speeds the decision-making process and helps reduce the risk of fraud within the shared services organization.

Check Controls

Common payment controls for accounts payable consists of both built-in system features and manual procedures that help ensure the accuracy and integrity of cash payments. Much of these controls relate to the printing and distribution of checks, including important procedures for restricting physical access to unprinted check stock.

Physical Controls. Ideally, we would love to alleviate physical checks, but unfortunately checks are still needed for the payments process. Because checks are negotiable documents, restricting their physical access is important. Often the safest way to accomplish this is by storing unprinted check stock in a locked filing cabinet under dual control. This means that two locks are on the cabinet and two different people hold one of the keys. Smaller businesses often choose not to use dual-control procedures because of the overhead involved. At a minimum, any organization should lock the check stock in a cabinet under the custody of a responsible accounts payable supervisor.

Check signature plates may be similarly controlled. Large organizations separate the custody of signature plates from custody of the check stock creating dual control over the items required to produce a completed check. The idea here is that the checks are not valid without the signature plates and that keeping the plates under separate custody constitutes dual control. But, of course, locked signature plates do not justify keeping the check stock unlocked.

Check Limits. The enterprise resource planning (ERP) system's limitation over the maximum amount of the check can be considered a stop loss control over cash disbursement.

ACH Blocks and Filters

- Debit block keeps all ACH debits from posting to bank accounts
- Debit filters allow ACH debits from only known trading partners
- Advance authorization – transmit expected transactions to your bank, and only transactions that match all criteria would post to your account

STANDARDS OF INTERNAL CONTROL: PAYMENT PROCESS

Internal Control	Type of Control	Risks Mitigated
15.A Segregation of Duties. The function of disbursing cash or its equivalent must be segregated from the following functions: a. Receiving b. Purchasing c. Invoice processing d. Accounts payable e. General ledger reconciliation f. Supplier master setup and changes **Refer to risks: 15-1, 15-2, 15-3, 15-7**	Organizational Preventive	**15-1 Controls may be bypassed, allowing the potential for theft or error.** **15-2 Purchases or services may be ordered and received by an unauthorized individual.** **15-3 Items or services may be received but not reported, or reported inaccurately.** Unrecorded liabilities, misstated inventories, and over/under payments to suppliers may result. **15-7 Items may be recorded and payment made for goods or services not received.**
15.B Payment Reconciliations. All payments and other disbursement activities must be traceable, uniquely identifiable, and reconciled (contents are known and status is current) with general ledger and bank statements on a monthly basis. **Refer to risks: 15-l, 15-4**	Management Reviews Organizational Preventive Procedure	**15-1 Controls may be bypassed, allowing the potential for theft or error.** **15-4 Duplicate payments may occur, or payments may be made for the wrong amount or to unauthorized or nonexistent suppliers.**

(Continued)

Internal Control	Type of Control	Risks Mitigated
15.C Supporting Documentation. Requests for checks, electronic funds transfers, and bank transfers must be supported by approved purchase orders, receiving transactions, or original invoices. This documentation will be provided to the signers for their review as part of the approval process. **Refer to risks: 15-2, 15-3, 15-4, 15-7**	**Management Reviews** **Organizational** **Preventive** **Procedure**	**15-3 Items or services may be received but not reported, or reported inaccurately.** Unrecorded liabilities, misstated inventories, and over/under payments to suppliers may result. **15-4 Duplicate payments may occur, or payments may be made for the wrong amount or to unauthorized or nonexistent suppliers.** **15-6 Purchases or services may be unauthorized, recorded for the wrong amount or in the wrong period, and/or payment made to the wrong person.** **15-7 Items may be recorded and payment made for goods or services not received.**
15.D Payment Approval. Approved payments must be aged and made in accordance with corporate policy or within the agreed terms and conditions. **Refer to risk: 15-8**	**Management Reviews** **Organizational** **Preventive** **Procedure** **Supervisory**	**15-8 Operations may be adversely affected as suppliers may refuse future business with the company.**
15.E Supplier Discounts. All eligible supplier discounts should be taken whenever favorable to the company. **Refer to risks: 15-5, 15-9**	**Preventive**	**15-5 Financial statements, records, and operating reports may be misstated.** Critical decisions may be based upon erroneous information. **15-9 Cash utilization may not be optimized or may be misappropriated.**

Internal Control	Type of Control	Risks Mitigated
15.F Recording in Accounting Records. All payments must be recorded in the period payment was made. Expenses must be properly and accurately recorded in the accounting period in which the liability was incurred. **Refer to risks: 15-3, 15-5, 15-6, 15-9**	**Management Reviews** **Organizational** **Preventive** **Procedure** **Supervisory**	**15-3 Items or services may be received but not reported, or reported inaccurately.** Unrecorded liabilities, misstated inventories, and over/under payments to suppliers may result. **15-5 Financial statements, records, and operating reports may be misstated.** Critical decisions may be based upon erroneous information. **15-9 Cash utilization may not be optimized or may be misappropriated.**
15.G Bearer Checks. If manual checks are issued, they must not be made payable to cash or bearer. **Refer to risks: 15-1, 15-3, 15-7**	**Management Reviews** **Organizational** **Preventive** **Procedure** **Supervisory**	**15-1 Controls may be bypassed, allowing the potential for theft or error.** **15-3 Items or services may be received but not reported, or reported inaccurately.** Unrecorded liabilities, misstated inventories, and over/under payments to suppliers may result. **15-7 Items may be recorded and payment made for goods or services not received.**
15.H Blank Check Storage. Blank checks must be safeguarded from destruction or unauthorized use. The supply of blank checks must be numerically controlled and regularly accounted for as issued, voided, or unused. Employees that have access to unissued checks must be independent of the check signing and voucher preparation functions.	**Management Reviews** **Organizational** **Preventive** **Procedure** **Supervisory**	**15-1 Controls may be bypassed, allowing the potential for theft or error.** **15-3 Items or services may be received but not reported, or reported inaccurately.** Unrecorded liabilities, misstated inventories, and over/under payments to suppliers may result.

(Continued)

Internal Control	Type of Control	Risks Mitigated
Refer to risks: 15-I, 15-3, 15-4, 15-7		15-4 Duplicate payments may occur, or payments may be made for the wrong amount or to unauthorized or nonexistent suppliers.
		15-7 Items may be recorded and payment made for goods or services not received.
15.I Voided and Canceled Checks. Spoiled, voided, and canceled checks must be altered or voided immediately. These checks must be accounted for and protected. They may be destroyed, provided the destruction is witnessed, and documented by an additional individual. **Refer to risks: 15-1, 15-7**	Management Reviews Organizational Preventive Procedure Supervisory	15-1 Controls may be bypassed, allowing the potential for theft or error. 15-7 Items may be recorded and payment made for goods or services not received.
15.J Bank Account Limits. Specific limits of signing authority for checks, promissory notes, and bank transfers must be established and approved according to an appropriate board of director's banking resolution and communicated to the disbursing entity and the appropriate bank(s). **Refer to risks: 15-1, 15-3, 15-7**	Management Reviews Organizational Preventive Procedure Supervisory	15-1 Controls may be bypassed, allowing the potential for theft or error. 15-3 Items or services may be received but not reported, or reported inaccurately. Unrecorded liabilities, misstated inventories, and over/under payments to suppliers may result. 15-7 Items may be recorded and payment made for goods or services not received.

Internal Control	Type of Control	Risks Mitigated
15.K Positive Pay/Payee Controls. Checking accounts must be provided with "match pay" or "positive pay or payee" controls that permit a preview of checks presented to the bank for payment. If such controls are not practical, bank accounts must be subject to activity limits and dual signatory controls. **Refer to risks: 15-1, 15-4, 15-7**	Preventive	**15-1 Controls may be bypassed, allowing the potential for theft or error.** **15-4 Duplicate payments may occur, or payments may be made for the wrong amount or to unauthorized or nonexistent suppliers.** **15-7 Items may be recorded and payment made for goods or services not received.**
15.L Records Management. Documents or electronic data supporting expenditures must be safeguarded from loss or destruction and must be in a retrievable format. Such records must be retained and maintained in accordance within the company's records management policy. **Refer to risks: 15-5, 15-10**	Preventive	**15-5 Financial statements, records, and operating reports may be misstated.** Critical decisions may be based upon erroneous information. **15-10 Fines or penalties may be imposed if required supporting documents are not available.**
15.M Wire Transfers. Where practical, payments by wire transfer must be made only to pre-established bank accounts. Where practical, recurring wire payments should be established as repetitive payments within the wire transfer system. Non-repetitive wires require independent review and approval. **Refer to risks: 15-1, 15-4, 15-6, 15-7, 15-8**	Management Reviews Organizational Preventive Procedure Supervisory	**15-1 Controls may be bypassed, allowing the potential for theft or error.** **15-4 Duplicate payments may occur, or payments may be made for the wrong amount or to unauthorized or nonexistent suppliers.** **15-6 Purchases or services may be unauthorized, recorded for the wrong amount or in the wrong period, and/or payment made to the wrong person.**

(Continued)

Internal Control	Type of Control	Risks Mitigated
		15-7 Items may be recorded and payment made for goods or services not received.
		15-8 Operations may be adversely affected as suppliers may refuse future business with the company.

CHAPTER SIXTEEN

Accounting, Reconciliation Processes, Self-Audit Tools, and Internal Controls

 INTRODUCTION

This chapter focuses on the accounting, reconciliation, self-audit tools, and internal controls that are integral to the AP process. AP can impact the financial close if payments and accruals are incorrect. Reconciliations and self-audit tools indicate how well the accounts payable process is working. Lastly, internal control programs validate that the AP process is well controlled and risk is well managed.

AP and the Financial Close

Accounts payable plays a critical role with the month-end accrual process. The complexity of the process will be driven by how your finance organization is structured. Some large companies have separate groups that focus only on calculating and tracking accrued expense amounts in the general ledger. In smaller companies, accounts payable will often take the lead role in determining the value of the accruals, reversing the prior period accruals, and entering the current month-end accruals. In this case, any journal entries that are done by accounts payables are reviewed and approved by the controller before they can be entered into the general ledger.

Roles and Responsibilities

Accrual accounts should be assigned to individuals who are held accountable for reconciling the accrual account (and what is contained in it) at the end of each month-end. The controller or an equivalent manager in the finance/accounting organization should review each balance sheet account and clearly understand how the ending value in the account was derived as part of a the monthly closing process to ensure that all expenses are captured to the greatest degree possible in the month that they are incurred.

Additionally, the controller has the ultimate responsibility of ensuring that proper internal controls are in place to make sure that only valid and authorized payables are recorded in financial statements and paid to the correct supplier. This is critical control to ensure segregation of duties and proper delegation of authority are in place for the accrual process.

Accounting and Reconciliation Process Flow

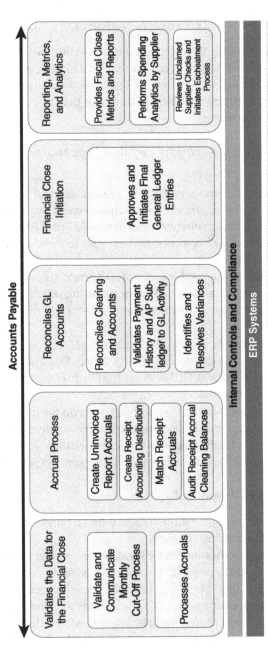

Accounting and Reconciliation, Internal Controls, and Self-Audit Tools Process Insights

Since AP is responsible for the accurate processing of a company's supplier expenditures, it has a large impact on the fiscal closing process. As noted, the AP process needs to be validated by sound accounting, reconciliation, and internal controls processes. Self-audit tools can help to ensure that the end-to-end AP process is working.

Sample Month-End Accounts Payable Procedure

Documentation

1. Upon receipt of a supplier invoice, the invoice will be date stamped and forwarded to the appropriate accounts payable processor. A match between the supplier invoice, original purchase order (PO), and packing slip/receiving report will be performed in order to form a voucher package. If a match is unable to be processed, the invoice will be placed on hold until matching issues are resolved with the appropriate process owners.

    Note: Most enterprise resource planning (ERP) systems perform the matching process automatically and will "block" the invoice if a match does not occur.

2. All invoices must be reviewed to ensure:
    a. Proper authorization of the PO. **Note:** The authorization is usually included in most ERP systems that link to the company's delegation of authority table.
    b. Quantities shown shipped or delivered on the invoice are the same as those found on the packing slip and/or receiving report.
    c. Pricing is in alignment with the PO pricing.
    d. Any discrepancy will be investigated prior to payment.

Recording and Payment

1. The voucher package will be coded with the appropriate general ledger accounts and supplier number.
2. The voucher will then be batched with other voucher packages and entered into the accounts payable system weekly and posted to the accounts payable sub-ledger. The voucher packages will be temporarily filed alphabetically by supplier name, in the unpaid invoice files, to await payment.
3. On a weekly basis, invoices will be selected within the system for payment according to their payment terms. All discounts offered by suppliers should be taken advantage of during this process.

4. A listing of all invoices to be paid (insert report name here) will be printed and reviewed by the accounts payable manager and/or controller. Upon approval, checks will be printed. The checks will subsequently be matched to the voucher package. Checks over $X, will be submitted to the controller (or other designated individual) for signing.

   Note: The approval limit of specific checks will depend on the size of a company and their risk management approach. Many companies also include specific approval limits for all wire transfers.

Manual Checks

1. Manual checks for the purchase of goods and services will not be processed. All purchases requiring an advance of funds should be paid through the use of the company's P-Card.

   Note: In this policy and procedural example, this company has alleviated the use of manual checks and has moved to the P-Card process as a best practice.

Accrued Expenses

1. At the close of each month, accrual procedures are needed to ensure that all expenses related to that month are properly included in the company's financial statements. Accrued expenses represent amounts due for services or benefits that the company has received but have not yet been paid. Accrual process shall be accomplished in a timely and accurate manner and must be in compliance with all applicable financial and accounting standards.
2. In determining what accruals should be made, the following should be considered:
   a. The expense must have been incurred during the month being closed; that is, the product or service must have been received on or before the last day of the month in order to qualify as an expense.
   b. Only expenses >$X will be accrued.
   c. Types of expense to be accrued can include:
      - Advertising
      - Commissions
      - Interest
      - Payroll and Payroll Taxes
      - Rent
      - Utilities

Property and Business Taxes

1. Payables and accrued liabilities shall be recorded at face value plus or minus any interest premium or discount and other appropriate adjustments. The payable amount can be determined from the billing received and should be verified against purchase orders/requisitions, contract terms, or any other appropriate documents prior to recording liability.
2. When actual values are not available, recorded value should be based on best available estimates. Estimates should be based on current market price, past history, and a comparison of prior periods.

Four Best Practices to Streamline your Month-End Accrual Process

Here are four best practices that can help streamline the month-end accrual process and facilitate a smoother closing process.

1. Using corporate credit and debit cards to view and download statements allows cardholders to view activity in advance of the month-end closing period.
2. Requiring a PO to be issued on every purchase over a specified dollar amount and mandating the use of a P-Card for lower dollar purchases provides additional visibility into the month-end accrual process. Many companies have instituted a PO policy in which suppliers are not paid without a PO.
3. Utilizing e-invoicing or requiring supplier invoices to be mailed to a common lockbox or location prevents invoices from be mailed to procurement or business partner locations.
4. For the T&E process, require any employee with out-of-pocket expenses to make for their expenses within a specified deadline. This can be easily accomplished by utilizing an automated T&E system.

Organizations that have ERP systems should be leveraging their software to its fullest. For ERP systems that include purchasing modules, be sure to use system-generated purchase orders and follow up by receiving all goods into the system. Purchases made in this way will be properly classified and in many systems, automatically accrued. Most ERP systems include "received not vouchered" functionality that will alert you to any goods received but not yet invoiced by the supplier.

However, for goods or services purchased without a purchase order, almost any accounts payable system or accounts payable module in an ERP system will allow you to "log" invoices into the system when received, even if they aren't being paid immediately. As an example, a future due date still requires management approval.

If your organization does not have an ERP system, a simple log of unpaid invoices can be created and maintained using a spreadsheet or simple database. Information about what to accrue for can be gleaned from previous months. Remember that when you accrue manually, you'll still need to relieve those accruals either manually, or as system-generated reversing entries.

Key Point: If the right combination of disciplined and automated processes is established, the collection of data to establish a month-end accruals process will be largely automated. This allows the accounts payable professional to focus on the analysis of the data to prevent over- or under-accruals from occurring.

AP TOOL 48: THE FINANCIAL CLOSE CHECKLIST FOR ACCOUNTS PAYABLE

About This Tool: Even if you are a seasoned veteran and are familiar with all the steps required for the fiscal close, this checklist will serve as an excellent roadmap to ensure you and your team cover all the bases from establishing schedules, to fine-tuning your supplier information, ensuring your company's accruals are correct, and completing AP account reconciliations. This practical tool is a step-by-step checklist that can be shared with your controller, accounting team, procurement team, and business partners.

---

1. Establish a calendar or schedule that contains all the deadlines and cutoffs. Provide all appropriate team members with a copy of the schedule.
2. Remember that those who file T&E reimbursement requests need this fiscal year-end cutoff information, too.
3. Review your 1099 supplier information to make sure it is complete. Review your supplier master file for missing TINs and try to obtain as many as possible. We suggest an annual tax identification number (TIN) matching process prior to completing your 1099 process.
4. Consider scheduling calls to business units and/or departments in mid-December to ensure they are aware of the requirements for the fiscal year-end closing process.
5. Coordinate with accounting to ensure that their schedule and to-do lists coordinate with AP's. Consider publishing a joint calendar or schedule.
6. Review year-end policy and procedures and update the documentation if required.
7. Assign specific year-end related tasks to appropriate team members.
8. Review vacation schedules to ensure adequate staffing – particularly in the week between Christmas and New Year's Day.

(Continued)

9. Determine what routine tasks (if any) can be delayed in order to comply with year-end closing requirements.

10. Make sure that all invoices that have been received are entered into the system.

11. Review recurring payments to ensure that they will fall into the correct accounting period.

12. Ensure all routine journal entries are completed in a timely manner.

13. Establish the proper procedures for accruing amounts due for invoices that are not received by the end of the year. Consider closing schedules of your key suppliers during the holiday period.

14. Adjust any prepaid items, such as insurance, that should be expensed.

15. Journalize any other accruals for year-end that won't be paid until the following calendar year.

16. Review all invoices received shortly after the new year has begun to determine when the goods were received or services performed to ensure that the accrual is made for the correct amount.

17. Complete intercompany transfers.

18. Research and properly account for voided and outstanding checks.

19. Review and reconcile AP clearing and other AP accounts.

20. Schedule the production, review, and archival of year-end reports.

AP Self-Audit Tools

Today's AP self-audit tools provide powerful data analysis and reporting to detect a wide range of transaction errors such as duplicate payments, pricing and discount anomalies, fraudulent trends/patterns, and data quality issues. Most tools contain claim workflow management to ensure that once a recovery has been identified it can be tracked until final resolution.

In a continuous controls monitoring (CCM) environment, a self-audit tool for the accounts payable process can provide both detective and preventive controls. When properly used, the tool can prevent a duplicate or erroneous payment from being made. The tool can also detect a process issue by combining additional analytics with audit results and by reviewing supplier payment trends.

Implementing Your Automated AP Self-Audit Process

Most self-audit tools are implemented by establishing a historical database of at least two years of payment data. This data usually contains supplier master file details, invoice details (header and line item), general ledger information, ERP document information, and payment information.

A production process is then established in which a current payment file is sent to the solution provider to apply against the historical database. In a CCM environment, the payment file is sent daily or whenever there is a payment run within the accounts payable process.

Key Point: Some companies prefer to use the self-audit tool as in a payment recovery mode. This means they'll review payments already made to suppliers and will only send payment files on weekly, monthly, quarterly, or annual basis for review.

Your Automated Self-Audit Solution

With an automated AP self-audit solution, there are usually five steps as recommended below. Depending on the solution and the user approach to implementation, the steps may change.

1. **Identify Duplicates.** Duplicates are identified by reviewing payment data to determine if there is a high likelihood of a duplicate payment being made. Many accounts payment departments utilize filters and may select certain suppliers and higher dollar amounts to conduct this review before the payment run is initiated.

2. **Review Duplicate Reports.** Reports are reviewed by supplier and invoice to determine the status in the workflow process.

3. **Manage a Supplier Claim.** If a duplicate payment is identified after a payment has been made to a supplier, this potential claim is money due to your company. Your self-audit tool should have a built-in claims management process so that you can initiate and track the status of a claim.

4. **Review Workflow Reports.** AP management may want to determine how well the self-audit process is working. Workflow reports are typically designed to give an insight into volume and value of duplicate payments, root cause errors, as well as the suppliers the duplicate payments are being made to.

5. **Review Additional Analytics.** AP management and associates may want to perform additional analytics to fully "close the loop." If a supplier has a significant amount of duplicate payments, there may be other concerns to review. A self-audit tool that provides supplier risk and compliance analytics can help you determine if there is a supplier fraud situation that requires additional action.

STANDARDS OF INTERNAL CONTROLS: ACCOUNTING, RECONCILIATION PROCESSES, SELF-AUDITS, AND INTERNAL CONTROLS

Internal Control	Type of Control	Risks Mitigated
16.A Utilize the Trial Balance Report. Start the closing cycle with a trial balance report. Review the balances to identify any anomalies from what is expected. Review the transaction details for any accounts you are uncertain of and note any adjustments that need to be made and that accruals are correct. **Refer to risks: 16-1, 16-2, 16-3, 16-4, 16-5**	Detective Management Review Organizational Policy Preventive Procedure	**16-1 Unreconciled General Ledger Accounts.** Unreconciled GL Accounts can cause delays and accuracy issues with the financial close, and fraudulent payment transactions can be undetected. **16-2 Poor visibility or errors during the review process.** The lack of financial close policies and procedures may cause errors to be undetected. **16-3 Accruals.** Accruals may be processed late, which leads to incorrect financial data. **16-4 Unclear and undefined roles and responsibilities.** Roles and responsibilities and expected results during the financial close are undefined causing errors, duplication of efforts, and uncompleted tasks impacting the accurate creation of financial statements. **16-5 Misstatement of Financial Results.** Financial statements, records, and operating reports may be misstated. Critical decisions may be based upon erroneous information resulting in the misstatement of financial results.

Internal Control	Type of Control	Risks Mitigated
16.B Adjusted Trial Balance. Generate an adjusted trial balance report to review the final balances in the ledger. Verify that the trial balance matches on the debit and credit side. Verify that the balances are accurate, checking the account activity if needed. Trial balances will vary from the initial report due to the adjusting entries. This helps you identify any entries that posted incorrectly and need to be corrected prior to your approval process. **Refer to risks: 16-1, 16-2, 16-3, 16-4, 16-5**	**Detective** **Management Review** **Organizational** **Policy** **Preventive** **Procedure**	**16-1 Unreconciled General Ledger Accounts.** Unreconciled GL accounts can cause delays and accuracy issues with the financial close, and fraudulent payment transactions can be undetected. **16-2 Poor visibility or errors during the review process.** The lack of financial close policies and procedures may cause errors to be undetected. **16-3 Accruals.** Accruals may be processed late, which leads to incorrect financial data. **16-4 Unclear and undefined roles and responsibilities.** Roles and responsibilities and expected results during the financial close are undefined, causing errors, duplication of efforts, and uncompleted tasks impacting the accurate creation of financial statements. **16-5 Misstatement of Financial Results.** Financial statements, records, and operating reports may be misstated. Critical decisions may be based upon erroneous information resulting in the misstatement of financial results.

(Continued)

Internal Control	Type of Control	Risks Mitigated
16.C Establish a Financial Closing Calendar with Defined Cutoffs. Establish a closing date by which all expenses and revenue must be posted. Communicate the closing date to everyone who has access to modify the ledger. **Refer to risks: 16-1, 16-2, 16-3, 16-4, 16-5**	Detective Management Review Organizational Policy Preventive Procedure	**16-1 Unreconciled General Ledger Accounts.** Unreconciled GL accounts can cause delays and accuracy issues with the financial close, and fraudulent payment transactions can be undetected. **16-2 Poor visibility or errors during the review process.** The lack of financial close policies and procedures may cause errors to be undetected. **16-3 Accruals.** Accruals may be processed late, which leads to incorrect financial data. **16-4 Unclear and undefined roles and responsibilities.** Roles and responsibilities and expected results during the financial close are undefined, causing errors, duplication of efforts, and uncompleted tasks impacting the accurate creation of financial statements. **16-5 Misstatement of Financial Results.** Financial statements, records, and operating reports may be misstated. Critical decisions may be based upon erroneous information resulting in the misstatement of financial results.

Internal Control	Type of Control	Risks Mitigated
16.D Establish a Financial Closing Checklist and Communication Process. The checklist should define the roles and responsibilities of all AP staff along with the business process owners that can impact the integrity of the process. **Refer to risks: 16-1, 16-2, 16-3, 16-4, 16-5**	Detective Management Review Organizational Policy Preventive Procedure	**16-1 Unreconciled General Ledger Accounts.** Unreconciled GL accounts can cause delays and accuracy issues with the financial close, and fraudulent payment transactions can be undetected. **16-2 Poor visibility or errors during the review process.** The lack of financial close policies and procedures may cause errors to be undetected. **16-3 Accruals.** Accruals may be processed late, which leads to incorrect financial data. **16-4 Unclear and undefined roles and responsibilities.** Roles and responsibilities and expected results during the financial close are undefined, causing errors, duplication of efforts, and uncompleted tasks impacting the accurate creation of financial statements. **16-5 Misstatement of Financial Results.** Financial statements, records, and operating reports may be misstated. Critical decisions may be based upon erroneous information resulting in the misstatement of financial results.

(*Continued*)

Internal Control	Type of Control	Risks Mitigated
16.E Adjusting Entries. Create the adjusting entries to recognize prepaid expenses, accrue outstanding invoices, relieve accruals that have been paid, and recognize depreciation and other amortizations. Post adjusting entries to correct the current balance of any ledger account that reflects expense postings in error. **Refer to risks: 16-1, 16-2, 16-3, 16-4, 16-5**	Detective Management Review Organizational Policy Preventive Procedure	**16-1 Unreconciled General Ledger Accounts.** Unreconciled GL accounts can cause delays and accuracy issues with the financial close, and fraudulent payment transactions can be undetected. **16-2 Poor visibility or errors during the review process.** The lack of financial close policies and procedures may cause errors to be undetected. **16-3 Accruals.** Accruals may be processed late, which leads to incorrect financial data. **16-4 Unclear and undefined roles and responsibilities.** Roles and responsibilities and expected results during the financial close are undefined, causing errors, duplication of efforts, and uncompleted tasks impacting the accurate creation of financial statements. **16-5 Misstatement of Financial Results.** Financial statements, records, and operating reports may be misstated. Critical decisions may be based upon erroneous information resulting in the misstatement of financial results.

Internal Control	Type of Control	Risks Mitigated
16.F Complete Reconciliations. Reconcile the AP ledger to the sub-ledger and any Goods Receipt/Invoice Receipt (GI/IR) clearing accounts on a monthly basis. **Refer to risks: 16-1, 16-2, 16-3, 16-4, 16-5**	Detective Management Review Organizational Policy Preventive Procedure Supervisory	**16-1 Unreconciled General Ledger Accounts.** Unreconciled GL accounts can cause delays and accuracy issues with the financial close, and fraudulent payment transactions can be undetected. **16-2 Poor visibility or errors during the review process. The** lack of financial close policies and procedures may cause errors to be undetected. **16-3 Accruals.** Accruals may be processed late, which leads to incorrect financial data. **16-4 Unclear and undefined roles and responsibilities.** Roles and responsibilities and expected results during the financial close are undefined, causing errors, duplication of efforts, and uncompleted tasks impacting the accurate creation of financial statements. **16-5 Misstatement of Financial Results.** Financial statements, records, and operating reports may be misstated. Critical decisions may be based upon erroneous information resulting in the misstatement of financial results.

(Continued)

Internal Control	Type of Control	Risks Mitigated
16.G Period End Reporting. Create reporting to show the final expense and payment activity for the period and year-to-date. **Refer to risks: 16-1, 16-2, 16-3, 16-4, 16-5**	Detective **Management Review** Organizational Policy Preventive Procedure	**16-1 Unreconciled General Ledger Accounts.** Unreconciled GL accounts can cause delays and accuracy issues with the financial close, and fraudulent payment transactions can be undetected. **16-2 Poor visibility or errors during the review process. The** lack of financial close policies and procedures may cause errors to be undetected. **16-3 Accruals.** Accruals may be processed late, which leads to incorrect financial data. **16-4 Unclear and undefined roles and responsibilities.** Roles and responsibilities and expected results during the financial close are undefined, causing errors, duplication of efforts, and uncompleted tasks impacting the accurate creation of financial statements. **16-5 Misstatement of Financial Results.** Financial statements, records, and operating reports may be misstated. Critical decisions may be based upon erroneous information, resulting in the misstatement of financial results.

Internal Control	Type of Control	Risks Mitigated
16.H Establish an AP Self-Assessment Process. Validate the effectiveness of the internal controls for your AP process and ensure that payments are made correctly to suppliers. Ensure that risks are properly and timely mitigated. Ensure that internal control weaknesses are properly reported and remediated. **Refer to risk: 16-7**	Detective Management Review Organizational Policy Preventive Procedure	**16-7 Control Weaknesses are not Identified.** Control issues are not identified or remediated in a timely manner, increasing the risk of fraud and process challenges.
16.I Escheatment Process. Escheatment is the process of identifying a check payment to a supplier that is considered abandoned and remitting the funds to the appropriate state if the supplier cannot be located or contacted. Once the check payment is deemed "abandoned" it becomes reportable to the state of the owner's last known address and is subject to be escheated. **Refer to risk: 16-6**	Detective Management Review Organizational Policy Preventive Procedure	**16-6 Escheatment and Unclaimed Supplier Checks.** Unclaimed supplier checks may not be properly identified and state escheatment rules may not be applied in a timely manner, leading to penalties or fees.

17

Customer Service

 INTRODUCTION

A well-defined customer service process includes the prompt attention and response to supplier-related questions. The response and resolution time to customer service issues should be tracked against established goals. The data from customer service issues should be used to identify the root cause of potential process issues. Customer service data can also be used to drive AP process improvements and automation opportunities. This data can also highlight process disconnects between receiving, procurement, and AP.

Customer Service Process Flow

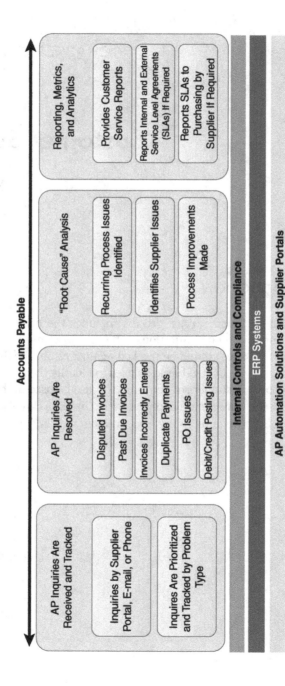

Accounts Payable

AP Inquiries Are Received and Tracked
- Inquiries by Supplier Portal, E-mail, or Phone
- Inquires Are Prioritized and Tracked by Problem Type

AP Inquiries Are Resolved
- Disputed Invoices
- Past Due Invoices
- Invoices Incorrectly Entered
- Duplicate Payments
- PO Issues
- Debit/Credit Posting Issues

"Root Cause" Analysis
- Recurring Process Issues Identified
- Identifies Supplier Issues
- Process Improvements Made

Reporting, Metrics, and Analytics
- Provides Customer Service Reports
- Reports Internal and External Service Level Agreements (SLAs) If Required
- Reports SLAs to Purchasing by Supplier If Required

Internal Controls and Compliance

ERP Systems

AP Automation Solutions and Supplier Portals

Customer Service Process Insights

Customer service is defined as the assistance and advice provided by a company to those people who buy or use its products or services. Since AP provides customer service internally (within the company) and externally (to suppliers and customers), the level of service and standards should be the same. The customer service process is always driven by questions related to the financial status of a transaction. Many questions focus on payment status, issuing a credit, and the status of a product shipment or return.

Customer service can also be defined as the relationship between the customer and the company or service provider. It is the act of taking care of the customer's needs by providing and delivering professional, helpful, high-quality service and assistance before, during, and after the customer's requirements are met.

Outstanding customer service leads to both customer satisfaction and loyalty. Poor customer service can cause significant damage to the company's, the department's, and individual's reputation. In today's world of social media, one is able to communicate a personal experience with poor customer service immediately.

As previously noted, outstanding AP customer service should be consistent with adherence to the same level of standards – both internally and externally. This is very difficult to do with staff members since their interaction with a customer is influenced by the staff member's personality and behavioral traits. There is also a high level of subjectivity in the process. That's why many AP departments have established goals to provide an online site where the status of any type of AP payment can be verified by any customer. This helps ensure that correct and consistent answers are given.

Key Point: Many AP departments have goals of improving their internal and external website to not only provide payment status, but to also include frequently asked questions (FAQs), instructions, and closing calendars. Some AP departments find themselves in "fire drill" mode because a supplier has had a bad customer service experience. These departments are often faced with the need to develop a customer service team to provide a highly professional communication and damage control. This solution can be very expensive and is not a good long-term solution.

Implementing customer service metrics within your AP department can help avoid that "fire drill" mode and can prevent a customer service disaster like Comcast. We're providing a series of metrics for you to consider to determine the state of your customer service process and to see how things improve with an automated website. Developing a monthly customer service scorecard can help AP track the real issues and focus on root cause analysis. Your scorecard can be incorporated into a set of operating metrics. This approach will help communicate and track all the services that AP provides.

AP Customer Service Metrics

1. **General Customer Service**
   - Number of AP Staff Supporting Customer Service
   - Number of Calls (Call Volume)
     - Cost per Resolved Call
     - Calls Answered
     - Calls Abandoned
     - Average Wait Time
   - Number of Queries (E-mail, via Website)
     - Cost per Resolved Query
   - Percentage of Suppliers Using Customer Service Website
2. **Customer Service Query Analysis**
   - Percentage of External Supplier Payment Status
     - Payment Information Provided
     - Invoice Not Received
     - Duplicate Invoice
     - Credit Memo Problem
   - Percentage of Internal Company Payment Status
     - Queries by Business Unit
     - Emergency Payment Requests
3. **Supplier Master Maintenance Issues**
   - W-8 and W-9
   - Compliance Screening
   - Incorrect Tax Information
   - Invalid Address
   - Invalid Phone Number
   - Invalid E-mail Address
   - Duplicate Supplier

High volumes of transactions, increased levels of operational complexity, and an often diverse range of AP processes and systems make managing the AP process challenging. AP executives and professionals are often focused on internal controls and regulatory compliance with scarce resources. This means that AP customer service can be overlooked until there is a crisis. Defining customer service as a core competency for the AP process can provide unlimited benefits for cost savings and process improvements with the proper tools, approach, and metrics.

STANDARDS OF INTERNAL CONTROLS: CUSTOMER SERVICE PROCESS

Internal Control	Type of Control	Risks Mitigated
17.A Establish a Customer Service Process for AP. Prioritize, research, and resolve customer service inquires for the AP process. Highlight and escalate significant process, supplier, and payment issues immediately. **Refer to risks: 17-1, 17-2, 17-3, 17-4, 17-5, 17-6, 17-7**	Detective Management Reviews Organizational Procedure	**17-1 Lack of Customer Service and the Untimely Resolution of Invoice and Payment Issues.** Without a customer service process, AP process and supplier payment issues may be undetected for a significant period of time. **17-2 AP payment process issues are not identified nor resolved.** **17-3 Insufficient Customer Satisfaction.** Internal and external suppliers' expectations and requirements. **17-4 Expectations and contracted payment requirements are not achieved, causing supplier satisfaction concerns.** **17-5 Lack of Customer Service Metrics, Reporting, and Analytics.** Results of the customer service process are not reported or tracked. **17-6 AP Performance issues are not identified.** **17-7 AP Payment processes are not improved.** Problems with the AP process causing incorrect payments are not identified and addressed in a timely manner.

(Continued)

Internal Control	Type of Control	Risks Mitigated
17.B Establish a Process for Timely AP Inquiry Resolution. All inquiries should be resolved according to established metrics and internal and external SLAs with a focus on customer service and satisfaction. **Refer to risks: 17-1, 17-2, 17-3, 17-4, 17-5, 17-6, 17-7**	Detective Management Reviews Organizational Procedure	**17-1 Lack of Customer Service and the Untimely Resolution of Invoice and Payment Issues.** Without a customer service process, AP process and supplier payment issues may be undetected for a significant period of time. **17-2 AP payment process issues are not identified nor resolved.** **17-3 Insufficient Customer Satisfaction.** Internal and external suppliers' expectations and requirements. **17-4 Expectations and contracted payment requirements are not achieved, causing supplier satisfaction concerns.** **17-5 Lack of Customer Service Metrics, Reporting, and Analytics.** Results of the customer service process are not reported or tracked. **17-6 AP Performance issues are not identified.** **17-7 AP Payment processes are not improved.** Problems with the AP process causing incorrect payments are not identified and addressed in a timely manner.

Internal Control	Type of Control	Risks Mitigated
17.C "Root Cause" Analysis and Process Improvements. Track and analyze the "root causes" of inquiries; report and implement process improvements. **Refer to risks: 17-6, 17-7**	Detective **Management Reviews** Organizational **Procedure**	**17-6 AP Performance issues are not identified.** **17-7 AP Payment processes are not improved.** Problems with the AP process causing incorrect payments are not identified and addressed in a timely manner.
17.D Metrics, Reporting and Analytics. Ensure that all required SLAs are reported and customer service process reports are communicated monthly. **Refer to risk: 17-5**	Detective **Management Reviews** Organizational **Procedure**	**17-5 Lack of Customer Service Metrics, Reporting, and Analytics.** Results of the customer service process are not reported or tracked.
17.E Track AP Customer Service Performance. Establish a performance tracking process to ensure that AP customer service goals are met on a monthly basis and that all required internal and external SLAs' goals are archived. **Refer to risks: 17-4, 17-5**	Detective **Management Reviews** Organizational **Procedure**	**17-4 Expectations and contracted payment requirements are not achieved, causing supplier satisfaction concerns.** **17-5 Lack of Customer Service Metrics, Reporting, and Analytics.** Results of the customer service process are not reported or tracked

CHAPTER EIGHTEEN

Reporting, Analytics, and Benchmarking

 INTRODUCTION

Metrics are used to drive improvements and help businesses focus their people and resources on what's important. The range of metrics that companies can employ vary from those that are mandatory for legal, safety, or contractual purposes to those that track increases in efficiency, reductions in complaints, greater profits, and better savings across the company.

Overall, metrics should reflect and support the various strategies for all aspects of the organization, including finance, marketing, competition, standards, or customer requirements and expectations. Metrics indicate the priorities of the company and provide a window on performance. Ultimately, metrics will tell the organization:

- Where it has been
- Where it is heading
- Whether something is going wrong
- When the organization reaches its target

Metrics, Analytics, and Benchmarking Process Flow

Accounts Payable

Produce Metrics and Reporting by Categories
- Spending
- Process Efficiency
- Internal Controls
- Customer Service

Identify Payment Anomalies
- Determine Root Cause
- Address Invoice Processing and Payment Issues
- Identify Supplier Issues and Report to Purchasing

Internal Controls and Fraud Reviews
- Determine Payment Risks and Update Controls
- Conduct Supplier and Payment Risk Analysis

Reporting, Analytics, and Metrics
- Produce Spend Reports and Analytics
- Track Results and Trends
- Report
- Develop and Report AP Metrics

Internal Controls and Compliance

ERP Systems

P2P Automation Solutions

AP TOOL 49: HOW TO IMPLEMENT A SUCCESSFUL METRICS PROCESS

About This Tool: The following five steps establish the basics for implementing a successful metrics program.

1. **Define the metrics.** All metrics should be clearly defined so that an organization can benchmark its success. One way to keep metrics understandable is to use the SMART (specific, measurable, achievable, relevant, and time-based) model. The achievable step in this model is particularly important. There's no point setting targets that cannot be achieved, as people will feel defeated even before they begin.

2. **Key Point:** As noted, all metrics must be carefully defined within your metrics program. As an example, many organizations struggle with determining what cost components should be included in the cost-per-invoice metric. One of the biggest questions is: Should allocations from IT and other corporate functions be included in the calculation?

3. **Secure buy-in from senior management and employees.** The successful implementation of any new metric requires the approval and interest of senior managers. They have to lead the culture change from the top. Using a new set of metrics to measure performance is a change that may well attract resistance from across the company, so high-level endorsement and open communication is needed to get everyone on board.

4. **Understand what data is needed and how to collect it.** It's not unusual for companies to set a metric, only to discover that either their processes or tools (or both) cannot generate the data they need. It could mean some investment is required, but be clear about how much the business will benefit from having the metric before spending money. Metrics need to be reliable and give out the same answer no matter who calculates it. They also need to be standardized, with data being collected in exactly the same way across single or multiple departments, facilities and offices, nationally or internationally. Fudging metrics benefits no one. To deliver real progress, everyone involved with the metric needs to be completely honest and be prepared to answer questions about the calculation of the metric.

5. **Measure and share the results.** It may seem a little obvious, but a large number of companies go to the trouble of designing metrics and buying expensive tools, and then do not actually do very much with the results. Usually it is because too many metrics have been set. There's a difference between gathering large amounts of information vs. reporting metrics that provide an indication of how the team is performing.

6. **Do not forget the "continuous" part of improvement.** When implementing metrics, don't forget that the organization will need to revise its metrics from time to time based on process or system changes. If an e-invoicing process is introduced in accounts payable, the set of metrics will change since the team will want to report invoices set manually vs. electronically. Lastly, metrics should set the foundation for an environment of continuous improvement since there is more visibility to data, trends, and results.

Characteristics of Benchmarking

Benchmarking is an integral part of reporting and monitoring performance metrics. controllers compare the performance of their products or processes externally to those of competitors and best-in-class companies, as well as internally to other operations within their own firm that perform similar activities. Additionally, organizations track performance by comparing their own results over time (e.g. month-to-month, year-to-year).

The results are productivity and performance gains. The benchmark becomes the performance standard. It helps organizations identify the standard in other organizations and offers the opportunity to introduce and adapt it as their own. Benchmarking helps organizations determine where they stand when compared to similar entities, enabling them to resolve problems and identify opportunities that improve performance. Best practices can come from anywhere, but generally, the most practical sources are from organizations similar in size or industry.

Best-in-class organizations are particularly accomplished in both efficiency and effectiveness, or, in a more basic sense, cost and quality. The most effective benchmarking efforts do not simply copy the exemplary performance of others; they exceed it.

Benchmarking can answer the following questions:

- How are we doing compared to others?
- What lessons can be learned from others?
- Where should we concentrate our time?
- What are the best practices?
- What are areas for potential process improvements?
- What key performance indicators (KPIs) are important?

Benchmarking is a tool for comparing and assessing performance as a means of achieving continuous improvement. Benchmarking is part of the total quality management process, and includes the following key elements:

- Focuses on processes rather than outcomes.
- Encourages information sharing.
- Implies a willingness to change and a desire to implement best practices within the accounts payable process.
- Benchmarking is a dynamic process that should drive continuous improvement initiatives. Organizations that use benchmarking as a final product miss the opportunity to measure continuous process improvements.

Benchmarking Methodology

A benchmarking initiative may be led by a controller and his or her staff. The methodology does not merely look at internal performance measure. Benchmarking considers the total organizational impact by:

- Determining how leading organizations perform a specific process
- Comparing those methods with its own
- Using the information to improve or modify a process

When analyzing best-in-class organizations, the objective is to gain an understanding of the steps taken to achieve the best-in-class status. These organizations have faced and overcome significant process challenges, and have implemented techniques to prioritize and address a multitude of opportunities. One of the keys to successful benchmarking is to understand the challenges faced, and experiences learned by best-in-class firms.

It is also essential to determine why and how to collect data. However, perhaps more importantly, it is imperative to know how to analyze the collected data.

Planning for Implementation

The planning phase is comprised of three steps:

1. Determining Objectives
2. Understanding the Process
3. Selecting the Right Organizations to Benchmark

1. Determining objectives

The objective of benchmarking is to improve the bottom line by getting, adapting, and improving the successful ideas of others.

Find examples of superior performance and understand the processes and practices that drive that performance. Companies improve their performance by tailoring and incorporating those best practices. Imitation does not work. Adaptation of and innovation on those best practice principles are keys to long-term success.

2. Understanding the process

An individual can perform benchmarking, but using a team approach leverages differing perspectives and skill sets, as well as allowing for distribution of the process improvement activities for faster implementation. Team members profit from group dynamics by learning from and brainstorming with others. Frequently, a consultant facilitates these groups. It is important to understand the difference between a survey and a benchmark. A survey provides good general information. A benchmark process must provide good comparative information.

3. Selecting the right organizations to benchmark

There are two basic types of resources from which to obtain external benchmarking data. These are:

- Independent organization sponsors
- Ad hoc collaborative groups

Independent organization sponsors keep individual results confidential, but usually provide the mean, median, and range of performances. Sponsors are effective catalysts for compiling standardized data; however, there are no strong consistency or accuracy assurances. If the instructions become too detailed in an effort to achieve accuracy and consistency, participation diminishes. The sponsors generally do not have the ability to audit results. In addition to concerns about the quality of the data, the benchmarking sponsor must keep the data up-to-date. Nonetheless, the benchmarking studies emanating from independent organization sponsors are exceedingly useful.

Relevant questions for the data user to ask about a sponsor include:

- Who are the benchmarking candidates/participants?
- Are they germane to our business/process?
- Do the participants have a good understanding of the benchmarking questions asked?

An ad hoc collaborative benchmarking group consists of two or more organizations that share their own results and exchange detailed information as to how those results were obtained. Usually, this approach includes reciprocal visits to the groups' facilities. By thoroughly grasping the process being reviewed, a reliable baseline of comparison is established.

An evaluation of potential groups should include the following questions:

- Are they similar in their business/process?
- Will they share information readily?
- Is their data reasonably standard and reliable?
- Are they above-average performers?

A company must be reasonably assured that another organization with which it collaborates will be candid about their performance and will freely exchange information. Sometimes, taking the lead and "opening up" will elicit a reciprocal response, as frequently happens in personal relationships.

Types of Benchmarking

There are three common types of benchmarking initiatives. These include:

1. Internal
2. Industry/Volume
3. World Class

1. Internal Benchmarking

Benchmarking works best within an organization because the accounting and other measurement principles are similar. The measurement criteria are standardized and well understood. These benefits are magnified if the units being measured are homogeneous. The organization has the resources to drill down to details in analyzing differences.

In such an environment, the starting point is reasonably even/level. From there, the company can observe differences in performance. Organizations have been very effective in benchmarking internally.

Internal benchmarking can be used as strong incentives, as well as a basis for knowledge. However, sole reliance on internal benchmarking can lead to problems. For example, based upon their top revenue position in the 1980s, Sears Roebuck & Co. spent considerable effort analyzing internal data, while neglecting to benchmark their performance against Walmart and Target. Internal benchmarking can involve the following:

- Homogeneous units: Unit A vs. Units B, C, and D
- Individuals: Key entry associates Mary, John, and Kate vs. budget; standard, last month, and each other
- Overall progress or tracking trends: This month vs. budget; last month, last year

2. Industry/Volume Benchmarking

Staying within your industry increases the likelihood of finding similar processes, thus providing more relevant and compelling comparisons.

Additionally, an entity gets the most value when it compares itself to organizations similar to itself in volume, as well as process. High-volume transaction business processes generally have lower per-transaction costs. As a result, higher volume units should be benchmarked.

Lower transaction costs are attributable to economies of scale and more advanced technology. The smaller business processes cannot replicate the economies of scale but can consider the technology as a possibility, as automation continues to become more affordable.

3. World-Class Benchmarking

In world-class benchmarking, a company compares a business process to the best in class. This may mean crossing industry lines in order to obtain new ideas. For example, Motorola wanted to improve its order entry/fulfillment and sought out Lands' End, a best-in-class company, whose core business relied upon that process. Many companies have studied process leaders like Walmart for supply chain and FedEx for tracking excellence, in spite of differences in industry and scale.

Data Collection

It's important to identify the data components that are pertinent to the business process area. Some cost considerations are included below.

- Salaries – differences based upon scale, experience, and skill mix required.
- Indirect Salaries – remote processors and related costs.
- Managerial Salaries – this may or may not include part or all of a department manager such as a controller.
- Benefit Costs – social security taxes, unemployment taxes, pension, medical and other perks differing based upon benefit plans.
- IT Software and Hardware – The business process owner may be considered to be the client for systems supporting the process.
- Equipment – equipment depreciation and interest on the undepreciated portion within the department, including furniture and fixtures.
- Occupancy – geographical differences influence real estate, property taxes, construction, and utilities, while company standards influence the work environment.
- Travel
- Training

- Telecommunications – inbound and outbound.
- Delivery – postage, express mail.

Due to the variability of the use and nature of the above elements, a simple salary and benefit cost is most often preferred. In an effort to level the playing field on varying costs and systems, many organizations use cost per full time employee (FTE) equivalent.

Analyzing Benchmark Results

The benefit of a benchmarking initiative is the results. This information can be used to establish goals and identify areas for process improvements and cost reductions. It's useful to see how other organizations are doing things.

1. Evaluating Improvement Opportunities

In order to make recommendations for change suitable to its environment and increase the likelihood for success, the participants should ask the following questions about the study:

- Who are the best-in-class process leaders?
- How did they do it?
- How are the leaders organized?
- How are we unique?
- Are our differences necessary?
- Can we apply the approach?
- What is most revealing?
- Which programs close the gaps?
- What are our priorities?
- What are the barriers to change?
- How can we gain advantage?

2. Factors Affecting Metrics

Benchmarking and metrics are considered to be similar processes. As in benchmarking, there are several considerations to address when developing a metrics program.

- Controlled environment – necessity for controls, based upon risks internally and externally

- Controlled culture – willingness of management to take risks or spend money to exercise control
- Departmental (non-finance) administration – "quasi" accounting functions performed at the operating level
- Degree/quality of automation – system development and integration
- Training associates
- Experience of associates
- Time in business
- Industry practices
- Management's access to data/information
- Nature and differentiation of inquiries
- Expected response/service level
- Retention/retrieval system
- Error tolerance
- Level of standardization/complexity

3. Pitfalls in Benchmarking and Metrics

Do not focus too narrowly on one metric or key performance metric (KPI). As an example, a one-dimensional reduction in AP cost per invoice will have tradeoffs, such as sacrificing quality aspects, as well as affecting control, internal service, and supplier relations. Unfortunately, some of these components of success are difficult to measure. Consider total cost when considering process improvement because some improvements could add expense in other areas, such as IT, software, hardware, and other various services, including outsourcing.

Process improvements should be carefully prioritized. It is also critical to understand the impacts on internal controls. The organization needs to consider the feasibility of a process improvement and determine if a similar company or organization has benefited. Lastly, a process improvement that works well in a SAP environment may not work well in an Oracle or legacy environment.

Summary of Benchmarking Benefits

There are several important benefits to implementing a benchmarking project which include the following results.

- Forces an external view
- Broadens perspective to "see" beyond the barriers
- Nurtures thinking "outside the box"
- Identifies innovation, breakthroughs, and trends

- Identifies competitive position
- Assists in goal setting and decision making
- Supports process development
- Provides organizations with an accelerated change methodology
- Builds confidence that objectives can be reached
- Eliminates non-value-adding activities

 ## STANDARDS OF INTERNAL CONTROL: REPORTING, ANALYTICS, AND BENCHMARKING PROCESS

Internal Control	Type of Control	Risks Mitigated
18.A Ensure there is ongoing visibility to company spending. Spending results are tracked, analyzed, and reported to business stakeholders. **Refer to risks: 18-1, 18-2, 18-3, 18-4, 18-5**	Detective Organizational Preventive Procedure	**18-1 Spending Anomalies and Trends.** Opportunities to address a spending issue for a specific supplier or commodity are not visible to the company, causing potential payment problems. **18-2 Strategic Sourcing.** Opportunities for strategic sourcing are not identified nor acted upon. **18-3 Lack of Visibility to AP Process Results.** The results and impact of the AP process and resulting payments are not reported nor acted upon, and risks to the process are not identified nor acted upon. **18-4 Action on Payment Anomalies.** Opportunities are lost to address or implement additional controls for payment anomalies. **18-5 AP Reporting Process.** Visibility to analytics and metrics is lost.

(Continued)

Internal Control	Type of Control	Risks Mitigated
18.B Implement AP Process Metrics. Implement metrics to report procurement process results, identify process improvements, and address payment issues in a timely manner. Metrics should focus on: Cost, Process Efficiency, Internal Controls and Customer Service impacts to the payments process. Metrics should be organized by: Cost, Process Efficiency, Internal Customers, and Customer Service. **Refer to risks: 18-3, 18-.4, 18-5**	Detective Organizational Preventive Procedure	**18-3 Lack of Visibility to AP Process Results.** The results and impact of the AP process and resulting payments are not reported nor acted upon, and risks to the process are not identified nor acted upon. **18-4 Action on Payment Anomalies.** Opportunities are lost to address or implement additional controls for payment anomalies. **18-5 AP Reporting Process.** Visibility to analytics and metrics is lost.
18.C Develop a Reporting Process for AP Metrics Develop a reporting process so that the results of metrics and analytics are reported and acted upon in a predictable manner – at least monthly. **Refer to risks: 18-3, 18-4, 18-5**	Detective Organizational Preventive Procedure	**18-3 Lack of Visibility to AP Process Results.** The results and impact of the AP process and resulting payments are not reported nor acted upon, and risks to the process are not identified nor acted upon. **18-4 Action on Payment Anomalies.** Opportunities are lost to address or implement additional controls for payment anomalies. **18-5 AP Reporting Process.** Visibility to analytics and metrics is lost.

Internal Control	Type of Control	Risks Mitigated
18.D "Root Cause Analysis" and Process Improvement Procedures. Identify opportunities to improve the process based on "root analysis" of results, trends, and benchmarks. **Refer to risks: 18-3, 18-4, 18-5**	Detective Organizational Preventive Procedure	**18-3 Lack of Visibility to AP Process Results.** The results and impact of the AP process and resulting payments are not reported nor acted upon, and risks to the process are not identified nor acted upon. **18-4 Action on Payment Anomalies.** Opportunities are lost to address or implement additional controls for payment anomalies. **18-5 AP Reporting Process.** Visibility to analytics and metrics is lost.

Other AP Business Processes

This section explores the other business process components that impact the AP department. All accounts payable professionals should be aware of the basics of supply chain financing (SCF), escheatment, sales and use tax, the 1099 process, and business continuity planning. The following chapters explain how these processes are integral to the AP process.

19

Supply Chain Financing (SCF)

 INTRODUCTION

According to PricewaterhouseCoopers, today's executives are actively looking at SCF options in terms of lowering their overall financial supply chain costs. PWC believes that they are attracted by the promise of supply chain financial savings, increased supply chain stability, and the efficiencies that SCF offers to both buyer and supplier.[1]

Key Point: SCF can include different types of financing and payment arrangements between the supply chain partners. This chapter explores one of the prominent types of SCF in which a third-party financier provides liquidity to suppliers by leveraging their buyer's higher credit rating – an arrangement that often involves the use of a technology platform to automate transactions and provide visibility into the invoice approval status to all parties involved.

---

[1]Understanding Supply Chain Finance (SCF), PwC, accessed on September 12, 2020, https://www.pwc.com/vn/en/deals/assets/supply-chain-finance-jul17.pdf.

UNLOCKING SUPPLY CHAIN VALUE

1. Extends buyer's accounts payables terms
2. Accelerates seller's access to lower-cost capital
3. Reduces risks imbedded in the supply chain
4. Enhances cash forecasting capabilities
5. Supports advanced treasury and working capital business strategies
6. Strengthens buyer-seller relationships

Defining the SCF Solution

From PricewaterhouseCoopers' perspective, SCF boils down to a balanced approach for enhancing working capital for both buyers and sellers in a transaction, using an intermediary tool to link buyers, sellers, and third-party financing entities, thereby reducing supply chain risks/costs and strengthening business relationships.

Presented another way, the SCF solution combines a set of technology solutions and services that link all the parties in the supply chain – the buyers, sellers, and providers of financing – in order to enable end-to-end visibility, lower financing costs, increase availability, and expedite the delivery of cash.

SCF solutions can help combat the inherent problems created by more traditional supply chain working capital enhancement approaches such as factoring, early payment discounts, accelerated terms, and deferred payment strategies.

These traditional solutions tend to view working capital enhancement from a single perspective, either the buyer's attempt to defer payment/reduce payment size or the seller's attempt to accelerate cash collection – often pitting one side of the buy/sell transaction against the other. Simply shifting the burden from one party to the other can add significant risk to the supply chain, including customer loss, business continuity risk, supplier viability risk, material cost inflation, deteriorating support, and a host of other issues. Supply chain finance provides an opportunity to collaborate and create benefits for each side of the transaction.

While reducing the amount of capital tied up in accounts receivable and minimizing investments in inventories are fairly straightforward, the keys that will unlock the value in your supply chain, extending accounts payable terms carries the potential for significant risks. These risks include: supplier instability, impact to business continuity, and eroded service among them.

To manage and minimize the overall risk inherent in extended payable approaches, leading companies are turning to SCF. SCF is a powerful tool that offers the following benefits:

1. Allows companies to extend the payables cycle in a manner that adds value to both parties in a trade agreement.
2. Buyers maintain cash liquidity longer and achieve a more stable supply chain, while sellers gain faster access to lower-cost cash and enjoy improved business continuity.
3. Cash forecasting effectiveness is enhanced and buyer-seller relationships are strengthened.

 ## AP TOOL 50: DEFINING WHO BENEFITS FROM AN SCF SOLUTION

About This Tool: As you can see, there are four primary players in this model, each with a key role in driving the SCF solution. When implemented properly, each party should realize multiple benefits.

1. **Buyer Benefits.** Because the buyer is using SCF to mitigate the costs for a seller, it will be well positioned to negotiate better terms and conditions with sellers. As a result of these negotiated terms/conditions, the buyer will realize a significant working capital benefit from an extension in payment terms and will free up cash for use in other critical areas.

2. **Seller Benefits.** The seller is obtaining access to capital at a lower cost through leveraging the buyer's credit rating. Additionally, the seller will see a reduction in Days Sales Outstanding (DSO) and an improvement in cash forecasting, two key drivers to effectively navigate through the current credit crunch.

3. **Funding Bank Benefits.** Even in today's credit-constrained environment, when banks are not doing much lending, the funding bank will typically earn a higher return on this type of product than other more common financing vehicles. Banks are proponents of this model because it's a limited credit risk; the lending periods are short, it provides an alternative revenue stream, and it opens the door to potential new business.

4. **Technology Platform Provider Benefits.** Typically, the system provider earns revenue when suppliers sell their invoices early. Additionally, depending on the provider, there are opportunities for cross-selling other products and services.

How to Implement SCF

1. Establish a cross-department committee (accounting, procurement, treasury) to guide the project, address opportunities, and implement solutions.
2. Perform a thorough upfront analysis to identify potential benefits and to target appropriate suppliers.
3. Use enabling technology to enhance efficiency and drive process improvements.
4. Communicate and collaborate with trade partners throughout implementation.
5. Discuss alternatives with multiple players and evaluate each solution carefully – getting buy-in so that change will stick and will deliver your expected ROI.
6. Leverage existing banking partners to capitalize on a current overall bank relationship and management strategies.

CHAPTER TWENTY

Escheatment

 INTRODUCTION

The origins of modern unclaimed property laws lie in British common law where in feudal times land reverted to the appropriate medieval lord or the king in a process known as "escheat." In contrast to early escheats, contemporary state unclaimed property laws generally do not involve a permanent taking of property and in most cases applies only to intangible personal property rather than tangible or real property. Thus, modern unclaimed property laws are considered "custodial" in nature.

This means that the property remitted or transferred to a state, as required under its unclaimed property laws, is held by the state only until such time as the owner claims it. The state as custodian holds the property in perpetuity on behalf of the rightful owner.

Today, "escheat" is a term of art referring to the transfer or delivery of property to state authorities as required by statute or regulation. All fifty states, Guam, Puerto Rico, the Virgin Islands, and the Canadian provinces of Alberta, British Columbia, Ontario, and Quebec have unclaimed property laws on their books.

UNIFORM UNCLAIMED PROPERTY ACT (THE 2016 ACT)

The 2016 revision of the Uniform Unclaimed Property Act represents an extraordinary four-year effort to improve unclaimed property laws conducted in consultation with more than 150 public and private groups and organizations that submitted more than 100 sets of detailed comments and recommendations, all of which are available for public review and were subject to vigorous and thorough public evaluation.

In the summer of 2016, the Uniform Law Commission (ULC) adopted a revised Uniform Unclaimed Property Act (the 2016 Act). The 2016 Act is, in a number of respects, a better product than both the 1981 and 1995 versions; unfortunately, the 2016 Act left intact and expanded a number of highly controversial – and likely unconstitutional – provisions from the prior Acts. In particular, the 2016 Act expands states' jurisdiction to escheat unclaimed property inconsistent with federal common law.[1]

TRENDS IN UNCLAIMED PROPERTY AUDIT AND COMPLIANCE ISSUES

Unclaimed property audits and compliance issues will continue to be a challenge for companies in a wide range of industries. States view escheat as an important source of revenue, and contingent fee auditors will do their part to broaden the scope of escheat laws. State legislatures have been especially active in this area in the past few years, and 2020 promises to be another year of changes in state laws. Companies under audit confront difficult choices, while those companies not (yet) under audit face an uncertain risk and compliance landscape. Here are five key trends to watch in 2020.

---

[1]Ethan D. Millar, Scott J. Heyman, and Charlotte F. Noel, "The Revised Uniform Unclaimed Property Act Is an Improvement, But Constitutional Defects Should Be Addressed before Approval," American Bar Association – Business Law Section, February 2, 2018, (accessed July 30, 2020), https://businesslawtoday.org/2018/02/revised-uniform-unclaimed-property-act-improvement-constitutional-defects-addressed-approval/#:~:text=InPercent20thePercent20summerPercent 20ofPercent202016, ActPercent20(thePercent202016Percent20Act).&text=InPercent20parti cularPercent2CPercent20thePercent202016Percent20Act,inconsistentPercent20withPercent-20federalPercent20commonPercent20law.

1. **Rapidly Evolving State Unclaimed Property Laws.**

   State legislatures have been extremely active on unclaimed property issues over the past few years, and this trend is expected to continue in 2020. Following the promulgation of a new model law for unclaimed property in 2016 (the 2016 Uniform Act), more than half a dozen states have enacted wholesale replacements to their unclaimed property statutes, and other states are considering similar legislation.

2. **Audit Estimation Methods Again Under Assault.**

   The long-running dispute over the use of controversial estimation techniques has heated up again with a new round of litigation against Delaware filed by four companies in late 2019. Delaware's estimation techniques, pioneered by its lead auditor Kelmar Associates, are controversial because they can result in a disproportionate assessment due to Delaware. Because the lookback period for an audit often exceeds typical record retention periods, auditors will use estimation techniques to estimate a liability for periods where records are not available. And most significantly, for companies incorporated in Delaware, the state continues to take the aggressive position that it has the authority to review all of the company's data, regardless of jurisdiction, and to issue an estimated assessment for a 50-state liability, due to Delaware, for the periods where complete records are no longer available.

3. **The Enforcement Push and Compliance "Invitations."**

   States and third-party auditors are also continuing to target new companies for audits and enforcement, with increased expectations that all companies should be in compliance. A number of states are now using internal data to identify companies that they believe may be out of compliance, by looking for gaps in filing history, property types, and/or non-filers.

4. **False Claims Act Litigation Raises the Stakes for Compliance.**

   Another concerning development for holders is the emerging trend of state false claims act lawsuits involving unclaimed property. These lawsuits typically allege that a company has knowingly and willfully underreported amounts owed to the state. Because the false claims acts are quasi-fraud statutes and provide for treble damages, the potential for false claims act litigation raises the stakes for unclaimed property compliance and risk management. Holders not only need to be prepared to defend their escheatment and reporting decisions against state revenue departments and third-party auditors, but they now may also face lawsuits by private parties. The false claims acts invite a new class of potential opponents – state attorneys general and the plaintiffs' bar – who may be driven by incentives that do not necessarily align with the purpose of unclaimed property laws.

5. **The Impact of Changes to Federal Law for Retirement Accounts.**

In 2020, changes to federal law will continue to have ripple effects on state unclaimed property reporting for retirement accounts, including both individual retirement accounts (IRAs) and employer plans (such as 401(k) and 403(b) accounts governed by ERISA). In late 2019, Congress passed the Secure Act, which among other provisions, raises the age for required minimum distributions (RMD) from 70½ to age 72. For IRAs, this creates an immediate tension with unclaimed property laws in states that have codified a dormancy trigger based on age 70½, which was the RMD date under prior law.

THE THREE OBJECTIVES OF UNCLAIMED PROPERTY LAWS

1. While the purpose of these laws is to return unclaimed property to the rightful owner, only a small portion is actually returned. Consider that in 2006, $1.754 billion dollars was returned to rightful owners by state unclaimed property authorities while they safeguarded approximately $33 billion dollars in unclaimed property. This equates to about 5% of the property being returned to the rightful owners.

2. Another objective of unclaimed property laws is to relieve businesses of liability and minimize the burden associated with holding unclaimed property. The 1995 Uniform Act §10(b) states: "Upon payment or delivery of property to the administrator, the state assumes custody and responsibility for the safekeeping of the property. A holder who pays or delivers property to the administrator in good faith is relieved of all liability arising thereafter with respect to the property."[2]

3. Finally, a third objective of state unclaimed property laws is to give the state, rather than a holder, the benefit of any economic windfall resulting from the property owner or their heirs being truly lost. State unclaimed property laws are designed to ensure that the benefits of such property are shared by the public at large and not by the entity that is holding the unclaimed property.

---

[2]The American Bar Association, accessed September 12, 2020, https://www.americanbar.org/groups/business_law/publications/blt/2014/10/03_kasner/#:~:text=Section%2010(b)%20makes%20it,%5D%20may%20prescribe."%2015%20U.S.C.

Two Basic Types of Unclaimed Property

There are two basic types of unclaimed property: tangible and intangible. Almost entirely, state unclaimed property laws apply to intangible property even though some statutes apply to the contents of safe deposit boxes (i.e. jewelry, official papers, or valuable collections) and in some states the law applies to property confiscated by law enforcement authorities (i.e. automobiles).

There are two general categories of intangible property under the jurisdiction of state unclaimed property laws that relate to corporations:

1. General Ledger Related
2. Securities Related Property

Common Types of Unclaimed Property

The most common types of unclaimed property held by corporations are:

1. Accounts payable – uncashed supplier and other checks or payments
2. Payroll – uncashed wage and expense checks
3. Third-party administrator payments
4. Accounts receivable – unused customer/client credits, refunds, unapplied cash
5. Aged amounts in suspense accounts
6. Equity – uncashed dividend or redemption checks, underlying shares, stock certificates
7. Non-qualified retirement plans
8. IRA distributions – uncashed/unused mandatory distributions

Update: Unclaimed property holders should take notice of IRS rules concerning the escheatment of individual retirement accounts effective Jan. 1, 2020. In Revenue Ruling 2018-17, the IRS ruled that the escheatment of an IRA or annuity to a state unclaimed property fund will be subject to federal tax withholding and reporting. In other words, escheatment will be treated as a designated distribution to the IRA owner subject to withholding at a 10% rate. This assumes there is no withholding election by the IRA owner.

Many states provide that retirement accounts are eligible forms of property subject to a state's unclaimed property law. Like other property types, IRA distributions that remain unclaimed for a certain period of time (i.e. the dormancy period), are presumed abandoned and are

required to be escheated to the state. A number of state laws and procedures must be followed before the property is ultimately escheated.[3]

9. Insurance – claims payments, refunds
10. Bonds – uncashed interest checks and bond proceeds

AP TOOL 51: ACTION PLAN FOR THE HOLDER OF UNCLAIMED PROPERTY

About This Tool: Once the practitioner has retrieved a list of outstanding
items that are potentially unclaimed property and determined which state's
unclaimed property provisions may apply, the next step is to consider what
actions these laws require in order for the business to be compliant. While state
laws vary as to the when and how these requirements and obligations are to be
met, the basic unclaimed property obligations are generally the same:

1. **Record Review:** States require that businesses annually review their
   records to determine if they hold reportable property. This is the obligation that can and should be modified by businesses as a risk management
   strategy to minimize liability and risk. Creating and implementing record
   review and outstanding item resolution procedures not only minimizes
   liability but can pinpoint areas where specific controls need modification.
   These policies and procedures are the key component in effective escheatment management.
2. **Statutory Owner Notification:** The requirement to notify owners is
   commonly referred to as the "due diligence" requirement. Businesses
   are required to make a final effort to notify owners of the property they
   hold. Most states require that this notification be by letter sent to the last
   known address of the owner in the business's records prior to preparing
   state reports. For specific industries, some states require that the owner be
   notified by publication in a newspaper prior to the report being submitted
   to the state. State laws assign time periods within which the due diligence
   must be performed, the method, content of the notification, and what
   circumstances may waive the due diligence requirement.

---

[3]RSM, IRA unclaimed property escheat rules effective in 2020, Posted on June 21, 2020,
(accessed on July 22, 2020), https://rsmus.com/what-we-do/services/tax/state-and-local-tax/
unclaimed-property/ira-unclaimed-property-escheat-rules-effective-in-2020.html#:~:
text=UnclaimedPercent20propertyPercent20holdersPercent20shouldPercent20take,federal
Percent20taxPercent20withholdingPercent20andPercent20reporting.

3. **Timely Reporting and Remitting of Unclaimed Property:** All states require reporting and remitting of property on or before a specific deadline. The deadline varies among states by industry. November 1st is the most common deadline for corporations to report and remit property in most states. There are a few states that require reporting in late winter or early spring. Note, however, that many states have a spring reporting deadline for life insurance companies and a few states have special deadlines for financial institutions. Unlike most other states' deadlines, Michigan changed the reporting deadline to July 1st beginning in 2011. State laws and regulations also dictate the format and media for the reports and the media for the remittance. Note that remitting unclaimed property in the manner required by states can prevent late filing or other non-compliance penalties. For this reason, attention must be paid to the state remittance directives.

4. **Record Retention:** The 1995 Uniform Disposition of Unclaimed Property Act states that a holder required to file a report must maintain the records containing the information required to be included in the report for ten years after the report is filed. The drafter's notes to the Act state that records are to be kept for ten years from the date the property was first reportable. Most states require that proof of required due diligence, copies of filed reports, and substantiation for the reports be maintained for at least ten years from the date the property was reported or remitted or was otherwise reportable.

AP TOOL 52: BASIC PROCEDURES FOR MANAGING YOUR COMPANY'S ESCHEATMENT OBLIGATIONS

About This Tool: The key factor in successfully managing a business's escheatment obligations is the establishment of appropriate policies, procedures, and timelines. Below is an outline that serves as a rough framework for building and customizing the procedure and adding timelines, defined tasks, responsibilities and policies to fit within a business's existing staffing, technology, and policies and procedures. **Note:** This outline is very broad and high level.

I. **Compile Outstanding Item Information**
   1. Schedule specific months to generate or retrieve outstanding item lists.
   2. Review all outstanding items. Consider whether items were voided or reversed that should have been considered as potentially unclaimed property.
   3. Determine the type of the outstanding items (i.e. stale-dated, RPO, duplicate).

II. **Perform Research and Resolve Items with Owner**
1. Research items that are over one hundred and eighty (180) days old and valued at more than the appropriate materiality limit to identify accounting errors, search for a new address, or review for possible exemption. Take appropriate action based on status.
2. Create and maintain notations supporting and explaining any reversals due to accounting errors or any exemptions applied. Move unresolved items to an unclaimed property liability account.
3. For items unresolved after steps 1 and 2, within one year after issuance, either send a notification letter to the apparent owner at the last known address after the property identified is unclaimed, or if appropriate contact the payee by phone or Internet and follow-up the contact with written correspondence (i.e. fax, printed, e-mail) acknowledged by return/signature of the payee. Maintain a written record of this contact. If there is no record of an owner address, identify the amount for possible escheatment. Move the item to unclaimed property liability account.
4. Take appropriate action based upon contact with owner or owner letter response (i.e. void, reissue, update account info, reinstate).
   a. For items that are unresolved, hold the items for statutory owner notification (due diligence letter or publication).

III. **Statutory Owner Notification**
1. Create or select appropriate templates and generate necessary due diligence letters or publications.
2. Mail appropriate due diligence letters in a timely manner and effect any necessary publication.
3. Retain proof of due diligence mailings and/or publication.
4. Record responses to mailings and/or publication.
5. Take appropriate action based upon responses to the due diligence letters and/or publication (i.e. void, reissue, update account info, reinstate, flag for escheat).
   a. For items that are unresolved, move items to the unclaimed property liability account and, as required by state law, hold the items for statutory owner notification (due diligence letter or publication).

IV. **Report and Pay the Property to the Appropriate State**
1. Determine the specific reporting periods and formats for each state, depending on the addresses of the owners of the outstanding property.
2. Prepare and mail report and remittance before each applicable state's deadline.

V. **Maintain Records**

1. Retain documentation showing reason code or ultimate disposition of item
2. Items that have been mitigated through research should be documented or noted. All unresolved items should be easily identified.
3. Retain copies of the following:
   a. State unclaimed property reports
   b. Notes, memorandum, faxes, e-mails from payees acknowledging the item, or that the payments are not owed, or that they are aware of the account and choose for it to remain open, etc.
   c. Due diligence letters mailed
   d. A listing of due diligence responses received
   e. A list of those due diligence letters returned by the post office

 ## AP TOOL 53: UNCLAIMED PROPERTY CHECKLIST

About This Tool: This tool can be used to review and validate your current process to identify and track unclaimed property.

1. **Assess the current status of compliance**
   - ☐ Determine if the company has ever reported unclaimed property;
   - ☐ Review what property was reported and to which states; and
   - ☐ Make sure all subsidiaries or recently acquired companies are included in the process.
2. **Check for prior audits**
   - ☐ Find out if the company has ever been audited by any state over unclaimed property; and
   - ☐ If an audit took place, review the results.
3. **Identify the types of unclaimed property (Note: This list is not exhaustive.)**
   - ☐ Outstanding checks issued to suppliers;
   - ☐ Employee expense reimbursements;
   - ☐ Credit checks and memos;
   - ☐ Payroll checks;
   - ☐ Payments for commissions;
   - ☐ Refunds due customers;
   - ☐ Rebates;
   - ☐ Royalties;
   - ☐ Unredeemed gift certificates;
   - ☐ Remittance and suspense accounts;

☐ Deposits;

☐ Cash or stock dividends;

☐ Common or preferred stock;

☐ Long-term debt;

☐ Uncashed bond interest checks;

☐ For banks: demand deposit and savings accounts, travelers checks, holiday club accounts, credit balances arising from loans; and

☐ For insurance companies: death claims payments, refunds due under policy terms, annuity payments, agent commissions.

4. **Determine due diligence needed**

☐ Check for changes in state laws, such as dormancy periods;

☐ An attempt to contact the owner must be made prior to reporting the unclaimed property and turning it over to the state;

☐ Review the rules for due diligence for the states involved, such as the minimum dollar amount, timing, and content of the notice;

☐ Determine if the notice can be via letter or other method, such as publication in a newspaper; and

☐ Prepare a due diligence letter that addresses key elements, such as the response deadline, property type, and claiming instructions.

5. **Prepare reporting and remittance**

☐ Check the reporting due dates for the states involved;

☐ File for extensions if needed (request must be made at least two weeks before filing deadline);

☐ Determine the correct reporting medium (paper, diskette, CD, or magnetic tape);

☐ Use the correct cover sheet (prescribed by the state) and have it signed (and notarized, if required);

☐ Remit payment; and

☐ Make sure amounts match (amount on report and amount remitted).

6. **Reconcile accounts**

☐ Reconcile the general ledger to the report and remittance amounts; and

☐ Reconcile items that were paid to the appropriate account, department, or division.

7. **Retain records**

☐ Retain copies of filed reports, list items for which due diligence was performed, and backup documentation for reversals;

☐ Check federal retention period, which is currently ten years (from date report was filed or property was first reportable) under the Uniform Unclaimed Property Act of 1995; and

☐ Check state statutes for relevant retention periods

CHAPTER TWENTY ONE

Sales and Use Tax

INTRODUCTION

Sales and use taxes are a complex issue that every controller should be aware of, and regarding which they should be able to evaluate the requirements for their operations. Sales and use taxes touch virtually every area of a company from procuring goods to managing inventory, making sales, marketing, investing in assets, and business structure. Sales and use taxes impact the bottom line and if not handled correctly could result in significant reductions in a business's profits. Due to the complexity of these taxes, controllers should discuss these issues with their tax or financial adviser.

Sales taxes were first enacted following the Depression as a taxing scheme to replace revenue losses from declining property taxes. Mississippi was the first state to enact a general sales tax in 1930. By 1938, 27 states had implemented a sales tax.

Today, sales and use taxes are a significant revenue source for governmental authorities. In 2010, the average combined state and local sales and use tax rate was 9.6420%, the highest rate recorded since the study began in 1981.

Sales and gross receipts taxes averaged approximately 48% of the total taxes collected in 2009. This is by far the leading state government tax, with personal income tax coming in second at approximately 34.4%. In 2009, state and local governments collected $342.2 billion from all types of sales, use, and gross receipts taxes. This is compared with state and local corporate income taxes, which amounted to $40.4 billion dollars, or about 6% of total state and local tax revenue.[1] But states are missing out on significant additional amounts of sales and use taxes due to the increase in business occurring online. Many online businesses are not required to collect tax in states other than their own. Although consumers owe the use tax, compliance, particularly by individuals, is not high.

When the states first enacted their sales taxes, the tax was imposed only on in-state sales. There was no use tax. As businesses began to offer delivery services and customers realized they could avoid sales taxes by ordering products from businesses in a different state, the complementary use tax was enacted. Currently, every state that imposes a general sales tax also imposes a use tax.

 ## WHAT THE WAYFAIR DECISION MEANS FOR OUT-OF-STATE SELLERS

Not only has the Wayfair decision on nexus directly empowered the states to impose sales and use tax collection and remittance obligations on businesses that had been beyond their reach, but it has also indirectly inspired other changes in state taxation rules across the country.

The Supreme Court of the United States made headlines this summer when it announced a decision that would dramatically affect how states impose sales tax collection responsibilities. The court's ruling in South Dakota v. Wayfair allowed states to require that sellers collect and remit sales tax based on the establishment of an "economic nexus," doing away with the previous "physical presence" test. The ruling has significantly expanded the states' authority in the sales tax arena, and businesses in every state will likely be impacted.

What Is Nexus and Why Does It Matter?

In its simplest form, nexus is a link or a connector. For tax purposes, nexus is the connection to a jurisdiction that gives that jurisdiction the right to regulate businesses and individuals. Within certain limits, each state gets to define what type of activities within its borders will create nexus that will require a taxpayer

---

[1]Federation of Tax Administrators, accessed September 12, 2020, https://www.taxadmin.org/revenues-and-burdens

to comply with its regulations. It's important that businesses with activities in multiple jurisdictions be aware of the obligations that may arise as a result.

How Wayfair Changes Things

The ability of any state to regulate an out-of-state business is limited by the commerce clause of the US Constitution. Before Wayfair, the Supreme Court held that states could only require a seller to collect and remit sales tax on transactions if the seller had a "physical presence" within the jurisdiction. That rule made it harder for a state to impose sales tax collection obligations on sellers who merely ship goods to customers within the state's borders.[2]

The following states have adopted Wayfair: Colorado (notice-and-reporting only), Hawaii, Maine, Oklahoma, Tennessee, and Vermont. September 1, 2018: Mississippi. October 1, 2018: Alabama, Illinois, Indiana, Kentucky, Michigan, Minnesota, New Jersey, North Dakota, Washington, Wisconsin. November 1, 2018: North Carolina.

Sales and Use Tax Definitions

As each state, and in some cases, localities, administers its own tax, definitions differ by jurisdiction. It is imperative to review the particular jurisdiction's definitions and exemptions as they relate to your business, as incorrect interpretation may result in liability to your business. This discussion defines terms generally and should not be used as a basis for a definition within a particular jurisdiction.

Sales tax is defined as a tax on the sale, transfer, or exchange of a taxable item or service. The sales tax generally applies on the sale to the end user or ultimate consumer. The sales tax is generally added to the sales price and is charged to the purchaser. Sales tax in its truest definition applies only to intrastate sales where the seller and the customer are located in the same state. Sales taxes are considered "trust taxes" where the seller collects the tax from the customer and remits the collected tax to the appropriate taxing jurisdiction.

In **consumer tax** states, the tax is imposed on the buyer, with responsibility for collection by the seller. The seller is still required to remit the tax even if it is not collected from the buyer, but it is usually easier to recover the tax from the buyer. The tax is generally imposed on the privilege of using or

---

[2]Donna Niesen and April Meade, "What the Wayfair Decision Means for Out-of-State Sellers," KSM Blog, Posted on October 5, 2018, (accessed July 30, 2020), https://www.ksmcpa.com/blog/what-the-wayfair-decision-means-for-out-of-state-sellers.

consuming the products or services purchased. Under audit, the state can collect the tax from either the seller or the purchaser. New York and Ohio are two of the consumer tax states.

Gross receipts taxes are a type of sales tax. The tax is a percentage of the total dollar amount of the transaction. This includes gross receipts from sideline operations such as occasional sales or sales outside the regular course of business. As a general rule there are very few deductions allowed under a gross receipts tax structure. In most gross receipts tax states, many services are subject to tax that are not taxed in states that impose a sales tax. Hawaii and New Mexico are two of the gross receipts tax states.

Complementary to the sales tax is the **use tax**. Use tax is defined as a tax on the storage, use, or consumption of a taxable item or service on which no sales tax has been paid. The use tax does not apply if the sales tax was charged. The use tax applies to purchases made outside the taxing jurisdiction but used within the state. The use tax also applies to items purchased exempt from tax that are subsequently used in a taxable manner. There are two types of use taxes: consumer use tax and supplier/retailer use tax.

Consumer use tax is a tax on the purchaser and is self-assessed by the purchaser on taxable items purchased where the supplier did not collect either a sales or supplier use tax. The purchaser remits this tax directly to the taxing jurisdiction. This is what most people think of when they talk about "use tax."

Supplier or retailer use tax applies to sales made by a supplier to a customer located outside the supplier's state or sales in interstate commerce if the supplier is registered in the state of delivery. Many people also consider this as sales tax. However, it is important to make the distinction, as differences can exist between the sales tax and the retailer use tax in relation to who has the liability for the tax, the sourcing of the tax, and the tax rate. For example, in Illinois the sales tax is an origin tax and can include local taxes. However, the use tax is sourced to the customer delivery location and there is no local use tax that is required to be collected by the seller. Only in the city of Chicago is there a local use tax.

A "sale" is defined as any transfer of title or possession, exchange or barter, conditional or otherwise, in any manner by any means whatsoever of tangible personal property for consideration. The imposition of tax is determined upon the passage of ultimate ownership or title or possession of tangible personal property or a taxable service. A transfer of title is an indication that ownership has been transferred. A transfer of title does not require that possession has also occurred. Thus, a sale has occurred when the "right to use" the property has changed hands. An actual change in possession need not occur. A transfer of possession is a transfer of control over a piece of property. A transfer of possession, temporary or permanent, may result in a sale. A lease involves a transfer of possession but not of title. Most states include both transfers of title and possession in its definition of sale. Illinois does not. Illinois only includes transfer of title in its definition. Therefore, true leases are not subject to Illinois sales or use tax.

Barter transactions are included in the definition of sale. Therefore, it is important to determine if a non-cash transaction has a sales tax implication. If either side of the barter transaction would be taxable if it had been a cash transaction, a value of the item must be determined. Generally, the person obtaining the taxable item owes consumer's use tax on the taxable value. Before the item is deemed taxable, all possible exemptions should be evaluated, including occasional sale.

Use is defined as the storage, use, or consumption of taxable property or services and includes the exercise of any right or power incident to the ownership of the property. Louisiana defines use as "the exercise of any right or power over such property incident to ownership, including distribution." The US Supreme Court found that because the Louisiana statute includes distribution in its definition of use, the use tax applied to the cost of catalogs mailed by an out-of-state printer to residents of Louisiana. The owner of the catalogs had a presence in the state.[3]

Some states do not include storage in their definition of use. This generally will exclude from taxation property temporarily stored within the jurisdiction for shipment to and use in another state. This is commonly referred to as "temporary storage exclusion."

Use includes the conversion of property purchased exempt from sales tax that is used in a taxable manner. This includes samples, donations, and converted inventory. Most states impose the tax on the cost of property. Therefore, for items removed from inventory that are self-manufactured, the material cost is generally the basis subject to tax. Some states define the tax basis on these items as manufactured costs, and a few states impose tax on the retail selling price. Before assuming the tax is due, verify that no other exemption would apply.

---

[3]D.H. Holmes Co., LTD v. Shirley McNamara, Secretary of Revenue & Taxation, US Supreme Court, No. 87-267, May 16, 1988, accessed September 12, 2020, http://supremecourtopinions.wustl.edu/files/William_Brennan_Finding_Aid.pdf.

Tangible personal property is often defined as personal property that can be seen, weighed, measured, felt, and touched or anything that is perceptible to the senses. Some states define tangible personal property as anything that is not real property. Some states have added to their definition of tangible personal property items which they would like included, but that otherwise may not be considered tangible personal property. Illinois used this method to include canned computer software in its definition.

Intangible property generally includes stocks, bonds, contracts, mineral rights, mortgages, patents, copyrights, and other similar items. Intangible property may be considered tangible property if it is transferred in a tangible means. Some states have considered copies of otherwise intangible assets to be converted to tangible personal property.

Real property is defined as land, buildings, fixtures, and structures affixed or attached to the land and buildings. Most states require permanent affixation to the real property for an item of tangible personal property to be considered real property. How this is determined varies by state. For example, in some states carpet that is glued to the floor becomes an item of real property. However, if the same carpet is tacked to the floor, it remains tangible personal property.

Services are generally defined as the occupation or function of serving, repairing, or providing an activity to satisfy a public demand. As most services include the transfer of some items of tangible personal property with the provision of the service, the true object of the transaction must be determined.

Did the customer pay for a service with the transfer of property incidental to the service? Or did the customer pay for the property, with the service being incidental? States vary in their determination as to what is incidental. Illinois generally uses a 35% rule while Texas considers 5% to be incidental. Other states use 10% or 50%. If property is transferred incidental to the sale of a service, the service provider owes tax on the cost of the materials transferred since there is no sales tax on the transaction.

Nexus

"Nexus" is a term of art that defines a level of connection between a taxing jurisdiction and an entity. Nexus is required before a taxing jurisdiction can impose its taxes on an entity. Nexus determination is controlled by the US Constitution under the due process clause and the commerce clause. The due process clause requires a definite link or minimum connection between the state and the person, property, or transaction it seeks to tax. However, the commerce clause requires a higher level or connection. The commerce clause requires a substantial presence in a taxing state by the entity the state desires to tax. Other federal provisions play a part in the determination of whether a state tax is constitutional.

The United States Supreme Court along with various state level courts has shaped the interpretation of nexus over the history of the sales tax. The most recent case which defined nexus for sales and use tax is Quill Corporation v. North Dakota, 112 S.Ct. 1904 (1992).

Today, most states define nexus under their definition of a retailer engaged in business as "maintaining, occupying, or using permanently or temporarily, directly or indirectly or through a subsidiary, an office, place of distribution, sales or sample room or place, warehouse or storage place or other place of business."[4]

Procurement Processes and Transaction Taxes

Although most people think sales taxes apply to retailers only, sales and use taxes are a significant issue for procurement professionals to understand. The structure of a contract, the format of a purchase order, the supplier location, and how an accounts payable invoice is coded and entered into the general ledger all can impact not only whether the transaction is subject to tax, but also the tax rate and who is liable for the tax. Sales and use taxes are evaluated traditionally on the "form" of the transaction rather than the "substance" of the transaction.

The beginning of the procurement process starts with an individual or department preparing a requisition. This is the individual who has the most knowledge of the use of the item. However, this person probably has the least knowledge of sales and use tax rules. Therefore, it is not likely they will or should have tax responsibility. Since this person knows how and where the product will be used, it is recommended that the requisition form include information about the item that can assist other departments in making the tax determination.

The purchasing department has responsibility for preparing the purchase order or placing the order with the supplier. The purchasing department has the greatest opportunity to influence the taxability of the transaction and should be well educated on the rules related to their industry and states where they do business. Many companies include a taxability decision box on the purchase order or process fully loaded purchase orders, including sales tax. This can assist the supplier with understanding the use of the item and

---

[4]Quill Corporation v. North Dakota, 112 S.Ct. 1904 (1992), LexisNexus Law School Brief, accessed September 12, 2020, https://www.lexisnexis.com/community/casebrief/p/casebrief-quill-corp-v-north-dakota.

help them more accurately calculate the tax on their invoices. In some businesses, this is a manual process. Tax department personnel should provide guidance and training to the purchasing department. It may be advisable on major purchases for the purchasing department to consult with the tax department in order to ensure correct tax determination.

The receiving department has responsibility for receipt of the goods. In some cases, the receiving department knows where the goods will be used. In this case, they may be able to indicate this information on the receiving report. In some businesses, the receiving department may also have responsibility for a "central stores" department. In this instance, the receiving department must provide appropriate information about the use of the goods to the tax department for tax reporting.

The accounts payable department has responsibility for payment of the procurement invoices. Since they review each payables invoice, they generally have responsibility for use tax review and determination. In some businesses, this is a completely manual process dependent on accounts payable clerks understanding tax rules and knowing the use of the items purchased. If tax determinations are indicated on the purchase order or requisition form, this can assist the accounts payable clerk in making the tax determination. Many common enterprise resource planning (ERP) systems provide interfaces to major tax calculation engines that automate the tax determination not only within the accounts payable process but also during the procurement process.

Tax Validation

Many businesses don't spend much time reviewing taxes charged by their suppliers and therefore may be overpaying the tax. Since most accounts payable systems don't require the tax charged on the invoice to be separately entered into either voucher entry or the general ledger, it is difficult to track the actual tax payments. Making this minor change can facilitate the ability to manually review taxes that have been paid, assist in use tax audits, and also provide the opportunity to automate the use tax determination, validation, and accrual. This is discussed later in the chapter.

Procurement Cards and E-procurement

Many businesses have embraced the movement to procurement cards (P-Cards). They can offer many benefits including reporting, pricing, and rebates. However, they also can result in significant risks and costs related to sales and use tax. The determination of the taxability of items purchased depends on understanding what was purchased, the quantity of items purchased as well as whether the supplier charged sales tax on the transaction. If the only documentation that is retained is the credit card statement, this critical data is lost. Without the detailed invoices, under audit by a state revenue department for sales and use tax, there is a risk that the auditor will assess use tax on total P-Card purchases.

Key Point: In developing a P-Card program, as well as during the enforcement of the program rules once it is functioning, it is important to ensure transaction level detail is maintained and accessible when needed. Level 3 suppliers should be providing more details that are helpful in supporting the use tax determination; however, many states still demand to see the detailed invoice from the supplier. If the P-Card program can be used for all types of purchases, including services, travel, and fixed assets, as well as general operating expenses, it is imperative to incorporate a use tax process into the program.

Some recommendations for a P-Card use tax process include incorporating a supplier charged tax field on the electronic reconciliation system for the users to populate during their monthly approval process, performing a test audit and determining a use tax due average percent of purchases for use in making a monthly accrual, or incorporating a full automated use tax accrual process against each detailed P-Card transaction. Whichever method is selected, maintenance of the backup detail and coordination of training for new users as well as enforcement of the process impact the minimization of use tax risk to ensure all the benefits of moving to a P-Card system are actualized.

Government Contracting

A number of states have passed or introduced legislation setting guidelines on who is allowed to enter into contracts with state agencies. These states have made it clear that their agencies are not allowed to do business with suppliers who are not registered to collect and remit sales and use tax in their state even if they do not have nexus with the state. A new trend is emerging in which states are not allowing suppliers to do business with their agencies if an affiliate of the supplier should, but has not registered to collect and remit sales and use tax in their state. Legislation has been passed in many states, including: Alabama (2006), California (2003), Connecticut (2003), Georgia (2004), Illinois (2003), Indiana (2003) Kentucky (2008), Missouri (2003), New Jersey (2004), New York (2004), North Carolina (1999), and Virginia (2004).

With these requirements, it is important for procurement professionals to realize the registration requirements and implications to the company if there is an interest in bidding on a government contract. Once the company is registered, it is required to collect sales tax on all taxable sales into that state, file period sales and use tax returns, and be subject to audits. If an RFP has this requirement, the company's tax department should be consulted before proceeding.

Streamlined Sales Tax Project

The Streamlined Sales and Use Tax Project (the "Project") was initiated in September of 1999 in order to develop a sales and use tax system that eases the burden of tax compliance for all retailers. The Project has worked to improve administrative procedures, provide uniform definitions within the tax laws, and provide technology systems for the tax collections that are in line with current technology.

Click-Through Nexus Legislation ("Amazon" Laws)

Amazon.com, Overstock.com, and other Internet retailers became subject to tax in New York under the Commission-Agreement Provision enacted effective June 1, 2008. This provision presumes that out-of-state retailers without physical presence in the state are soliciting business in the state (creating nexus) if any New York residents are compensated for directly or indirectly referring potential customers, including by link on an Internet website, and the receipts from these referrals exceed $10,000. If this is met, the out-of-state entity must register, collect, and remit New York sales tax.

The Amazon law is so named because the New York legislature made no secret that the law was intended to target large online retailers, Amazon.com in particular. As a result of the law, Amazon.com and Overstock.com brought actions challenging the statute on constitutional grounds. Amazon had implemented an "associates program," whereby it engaged New York residents (i.e. associates) to advertise its website on the associate's website through a direct-access link in exchange for a referral fee. While Amazon conceded it met the statutory requirements of the presumption, it argued that the law was both unconstitutional on its face and in its application. The trial court found that the statute was carefully crafted to provide the state with sufficient basis to tax Amazon and that the application of the law met constitutional safeguards.

Amnesty and Voluntary Disclosure

There are a number of enforcement methods used by states. States will periodically send out routine mass-mailing letters indicating that the company may be subject to tax in the state. They will include a nexus questionnaire for the company to complete and return by mail. These questionnaires typically include many activities that a business may engage in that would result in further inquiry by the state. Extreme care should be taken when responding to these questionnaires. In some states like Texas, the mere receipt of a questionnaire may preclude an entity from entering into a voluntary disclosure agreement with the state.

CHAPTER TWENTY TWO

Independent Contractors and the 1099 Process

 ## TIN MATCHING AND 1099 FILERS

TIN matching is a service implemented by the IRS that allows a 1099 filer to check the TIN (taxpayer identification number) and a specific name to ensure that there is a match for it in the IRS database. This process helps filers avoid IRS penalties and B-Notices for missing TINs or incorrect Name/TIN combinations.

The IRS created TIN matching to increase compliance and to reduce the costs associated with sending notices and the additional processing. TIN matching is not consistent with W-2 or 1095 filing results.

Using the social security number as a TIN is standard practice for freelancers and independent contractors that are not incorporated. Payers are required by the IRS to annually file a 1099 tax form for each payee; the form reports the annual income and tax withheld. TIN matching verifies that the tax identification of a business or individual matches the IRS database.

- 1099-A, Acquisition or Abandonment of Secured Property
- 1099-B, Proceeds from Broker and Barter Exchange Transactions
- 1099-C, Cancellation of Debt
- 1099-CAP, Changes in Corporate Control and Capital Structure
- 1099-DIV, Dividends and Distributions
- 1099-G, Certain Government Payments

- 1099-H, Health Coverage Tax Credit (HCTC) Advance Payments
- 1099-INT, Interest Income
- 1099-K, Merchant Card and Third Party Network Payments
- 1099-LTC, Long-Term Care and Accelerated Death Benefits
- 1099-MISC, Miscellaneous Income
- Form 1099-NEC – The PATH Act, P.L. 114-113, Div. Q, sec. 201, accelerated the due date for filing Form 1099 that includes nonemployee compensation (NEC) from February 28 to January 31 and eliminated the automatic 30-day extension for forms that include NEC. Beginning with tax year 2020, use Form 1099-NEC to report nonemployee compensation.[1]
- 1099-OID, Original Issue Discount
- 1099-PATR, Taxable Distributions Received from Cooperatives
- 1099-Q, Payments from Qualified Education Programs (Under Sections 529 and 530)
- 1099-R, Distributions from Pensions, Annuities, Retirement or Profit-Sharing Plans, IRAs, Insurance Contracts, etc.
- 1099-SA, Distributions from an HSA, Archer MSA, or Medicare Advantage MSA
- Form 1099-INT

1099 Miscellaneous Reporting Changes

As closing the tax gap continues to occupy both Congress and the IRS, we can expect to see continued IRS enforcement efforts designed to increase reporting by payers, increase the withholding of federal tax where required, and produce more accurate reporting of income by taxpayers.

Proposed Mandatory Withholding

The National Taxpayer Advocate has for years recommended mandatory withholding on all Form 1099 reportable payments to individuals and sole proprietors, including disregarded-entity Limited Liability Companies (LLCs). The proposed rate is usually around 3–6% (not 28%). In recent years, the legislative withholding focus has been on service payments reported in box 7 of the 1099-MISC, but most any form of legislation addressing withholding on any reportable payment is possible.

---

[1]Instructions for Forms 1099-MISC and 1099-NEC (2020), IRS, accessed July 22, 2020, https://www.irs.gov/instructions/i1099msc.

Voluntary Withholding Upon Request of a Contractor

Proposals continue to circulate that would permit payees/suppliers to request that a payer withhold taxes from a Form 1099 reportable payment. In February 2012, it was included among the legislative proposals of the Obama administration to Congress in connection with the President's fiscal 2013 budget. Any reportable contractor could require a payer to withhold a designated percentage (15, 25, 30, or 35% as selected by the contractor) of gross payments and deposit it with the IRS. This would make withholding from AP payments, periodic deposit of federal withholding, and Form 945 reconciliation reporting all routine in payables operations, instead of being the exception that currently arises only if backup withholding must be applied due to not having the payee TIN or as a result of an unanswered B-Notice.

Mandatory TIN Certification

The National Taxpayer Advocate has also recommended that all payees, including those receiving payments reportable on Form 1099-MISC, be required to certify their TINs (i.e. through use of Forms W-9 signed under penalty of perjury). In February of 2012, a legislative recommendation to this effect was issued by the Obama administration as part of the president's fiscal 2013 budget.

FATCA: New Regime of Documentation and Withholding on Payments to Foreign Entities

The Foreign Account Tax Compliance Act (FATCA), which was passed as part of the HIRE Act, generally requires that foreign financial Institutions and certain other non-financial foreign entities report on the foreign assets held by their US account holders or be subject to withholding on withholdable payments.

The Foreign Account Tax Compliance Act (FATCA) established a new regime under Chapter 4 of the Internal Revenue Code for documentation of foreign entity payees and withholding from payments in the absence of certain documentation. These requirements are in addition to the documentation, withholding and reporting required under Chapter 3 of the Code. FATCA compliance. Some FATCA requirements will affect payers that make the types of payments reportable on Form 1099-MISC and Form 1042-S. Payers will need to update their procedures to ensure compliance with both sets of documentation and withholding requirements: the new rules for FATCA, and the previously existing rules for withholding at source on certain payments to non-resident alien individuals, foreign corporations, and other foreign entities. New tax regulations for FATCA were proposed by the IRS in February, 2012.

In connection with the publication of FATCA regulations, the Treasury department released a joint statement with France, Germany, Italy, Spain, and the United Kingdom in which these governments announce an agreement to explore a common approach to FATCA implementation and the facilitation of enforcement through domestic reporting and reciprocal automatic exchanges of tax information.

FACTA Compliance Rules

FATCA compliance rules will be separated according to whether the foreign entity receiving a payment is a foreign financial institution, or a non-financial foreign entity. The proposed FATCA regulations would expand the categories of foreign financial institutions (FFIs) that would be deemed to comply with US FATCA requirements without the need to enter into an agreement with the IRS, and reduce the administrative burdens on FFIs. Relief in several other areas of FFI FATCA compliance is also proposed under these regulations. Examples of such payments to FFIs are: interest; bank fees; loan guarantee payments; and even payments on notional principal contracts (swaps) and other hedges or derivatives. To avoid the withholding of 30% on these payments, the FFI payee will need to either qualify for exemption as a "deemed compliant" FFI, or to "register" with the IRS: to enter into an agreement with the IRS to identify in their records and disclose to the IRS their US depositors, investors, and shareholders.

In regard to non-financial foreign entities (NFFEs), the proposed regulations would create an exception from withholding on payments to an NFFE which certifies to being an "active NFFE" defined as: less than 50% of its gross income for the previous calendar year was passive income, and less than 50% of its assets are assets that produce or are held for the production of dividends, interest, rents, and royalties (other than those derived in the active conduct of a trade or business), annuities, or other passive income. A group of payment types identified as "ordinary course of business payments" will be exempt from FATCA 30% withholding; this is relief which was not spelled out in the tax law but is offered under the proposed new FATCA regulations. Under this relief provision, the following will not be treated as FATCA withholdable payments: nonfinancial services, office and equipment leases, software licenses, transportation, freight, gambling winnings, awards, prizes, scholarships, and interest on outstanding accounts payable arising from the acquisition of nonfinancial services, goods, and other tangible property. Payers should be alert to how FATCA will affect their internal operations, and watch for the final FATCA regulations which will probably be issued before the end of 2012.

New Forms W-8 Will Be Issued for Payee Certification of Status

In conjunction with the implementation of the FATCA law under new tax regulations, the IRS will revise several of the existing Forms W-8 (used for non-US persons to certify their status to the US payer), and very likely will issue some additional Forms W-8. The effects on W-8 documentation are broad because the forms will change not only for everyone who has to obtain W-8s for FATCA purposes, but also all those who obtain W-8s under the longstanding rules which support Form 1042-S tax reporting of payments to non-US persons.

A new Form W-8BEN just for foreign individuals: The IRS has already said in public meetings that a new type of "individual" W-8BEN will be created for documentation of individual non-US persons. This will set it apart from the W-8BEN which will be used for foreign entities (FATCA rules apply to foreign entities, but not to foreign individuals).

New Forms W-8 for foreign entities: We also anticipate several new W-8s for entities, but the number of new forms is not publicly known. There may be separate new W-8s for certifications from foreign financial institutions (known as FFIs) that enter into an agreement with the IRS to identify and report US owners to the IRS ("participating FFIs"); for certifications from foreign financial institutions that fail to enter into an agreement; and for certifications from non-financial foreign entities.

According to the IRS, use Form W-8 BEN to the withholding agent or payer if you are a foreign person and you are the beneficial owner of an amount subject to withholding and submit Form W-8 BEN when requested by the withholding agent or payer whether or not you are claiming a reduced rate of, or exemption from, withholding.[2]

Gross Reporting of Credit Card Receipts

As of January 1, 2011, tax regulations relating to the new Form 1099-K reporting by payment settlement entities have provided Form 1099-MISC relief for many payments made through payment cards and third-party electronic settlement organizations.

New section 6050W of the tax code requires Form 1099-K reporting of gross payment amounts settled for the payee that accepted a card or a third-party electronic transaction for a purchase. Form 1099-K must be filed by "payment settlement entities," which are the banks or other organizations

---

[2]Internal Revenue Service (IRS), accessed September 12, 2020, https://www.irs.gov/forms-pubs/about-form-w-8-ben.

that initiate the instructions to transfer funds into the accounts of payees to settle reportable transactions in which the payee accepted payment through a card or a third-party payment network. These payment settlement entities report the gross amount paid for the year, and also a breakdown of the gross amount paid each month. With the intent of preventing the reporting of the same transaction more than once, the final tax regulations for section 6050W provide that if a payment is reportable under the Form 1099-K requirements, it is not reportable under the Form 1099-MISC requirements. Payers that can take advantage of this relief can code payments they make through cards and third-party networks as not requiring Form 1099-MISC reporting.

Form 1099 Penalties Have Increased

Large Businesses with Gross Receipts of More Than $5 Million (*Average annual gross receipts for the most recent 3 taxable years) and Government Entities (Other than Federal entities) IRC 6721 & IRC 6722[3]

Time returns filed/furnished	Not more than 30 days late	31 days late – August 1	After August 1 or Not at All	Intentional Disregard
Due 01-01-2020 thru 12-31-2020	$50 per return or statement – $556,500* maximum	$110* per return or statement – $1,669,500* maximum	$270* per return or statement – $3,339,000* maximum	$550 per return or statement – No limitation
Due 01-01-2019 thru 12-31-2019	$50 per return or statement – $545,500* maximum	$100 per return or statement – $1,637,500* maximum	$270* per return or statement – $3,275,500* maximum	$540* per return or statement – No limitation
Due 01-01-2018 thru 12-31-2018	$50 per return or statement – $536,000* maximum	$100 per return or statement – $1,609,000* maximum	$260* per return or statement – $3,218,500* maximum	$530* per return or statement – No limitation

---

[3]Internal Revenue Service (IRS), Increase in Information Return Penalties, accessed on September 12, 2020, https://www.irs.gov/government-entities/federal-state-local-governments/increase-in-information-return-penalties.

Time returns filed/furnished	Not more than 30 days late	31 days late – August 1	After August 1 or Not at All	Intentional Disregard
Due 01-01-2017 thru 12-31-2017	$50 per return or statement – $532,000* maximum	$100 per return or statement – $1,596,500* maximum	$260* per return or statement – $3,193,000* maximum	$530* per return or statement – No limitation
Due 01-01-2016 thru 12-31-2016	$50 per return or statement – $529,500* maximum	$100 per return or statement – $1,589,000* maximum	$260* per return or statement – $3,178,500* maximum	$520* per return or statement – No limitation
Due 01-01-2011 thru 12-31-2015	$30 per return or statement – $250,000 maximum	$60 per return or statement – $500,000 maximum	$100 per return or statement – $1,500,000 maximum	$250 per return or statement – No limitation

Note: Increased penalty amounts may apply for certain failures in the case of intentional disregard. See IRC 6721(e)(2) and IRC 6722(e)(2).

Small Businesses with Gross Receipts $5 Million or Less (*Average annual gross receipts for the most recent 3 taxable years) IRC 6721 & IRC 6722[4]

Time returns filed/furnished	Not more than 30 days late	31 days late – August 1	After August 1 or Not at All	Intentional Disregard
Due 01-01-2020 thru 12-31-2020	$50 per return or statement – $194,500* maximum	$110 *per return or statement – $556,500* maximum	$270* per return or statement – $1,113,000* maximum	$550* per return or statement – No limitation
Due 01-01-2019 thru 12-31-2019	$50 per return or statement – $191,000* maximum	$100 per return or statement – $545,500* maximum	$270* per return or statement – $1,091,500* maximum	$540* per return or statement – No limitation

(Continued)

---

[4]Internal Revenue Service (IRS), Increase in Information Return Penalties, accessed on September 12, 2020, https://www.irs.gov/government-entities/federal-state-local-governments/increase-in-information-return-penalties.

Time returns filed/furnished	Not more than 30 days late	31 days late – August 1	After August 1 or Not at All	Intentional Disregard
Due 01-01-2018 thru 12-31-2018	$50 per return or statement – $187,500* maximum	$100 per return or statement – $536,000* maximum	$260* per return or statement – $1,072,500* maximum	$530* per return or statement – No limitation
Due 01-01-2017 thru 12-31-2017	$50 per return or statement – $186,000* maximum	$100 per return or statement – $532,000* maximum	$260* per return or statement – $1,064,000* maximum	$530* per return or statement – No limitation
Due 01-01-2016 thru 12-31-2016	$50 per return or statement – $185,000* maximum	$100 per return or statement – $529,500* maximum	$260* per return or statement – $1,059,500* maximum	$520* per return or statement – No limitation
Due 01-01-2011 thru 12-31-2015	$30 per return or statement – $75,000 maximum	$60 per return or statement – $200,000 maximum	$100 per return or statement – $500,000 maximum	$250 per return or statement – No limitation

Backup Withholding Audits

The IRS includes examination of backup withholding in its audit routine for payers, and uses "B-Notice" lists (lists of name-TIN combinations filed on Forms 1099 that did not match a name-TIN combination in federal government files) to target companies for review of B-Notice processing procedures.

Worker Classification Audits

The issue of misclassified workers continues to be a prime focus of federal and state tax agencies, and there is increased data sharing between federal and state agencies in the search for payers that are improperly treating workers as independent contractors, when they should be classified as employees. Federal legislation has been introduced in Congress that would require companies to notify workers of their classification, and permit the IRS to prospectively require reclassification of workers who are presently misclassified.

Beginning in September, 2011, and continuing in 2012, the IRS is offering a Voluntary Classification Settlement Program (VCSP) under which taxpayers that have been improperly treating workers as non-employees may voluntarily disclose the facts to the IRS, reclassify the workers as employees for future tax periods, settle federal employment tax liability for the most recently closed tax year at just 10% of what is due, pay no interest or penalties on the tax liability, and not be subject to employment tax audit for prior years. Participating employers will, for the first three years after they enter into the VCSP closing agreement with the IRS, be subject to a special six-year statute of limitations rather than the usual three years that generally applies to payroll taxes.

1042-S Audits Continue to Be a Tier I IRS Issue

Payments of US-source income to non-US persons are subject to reporting on Form 1042-S and 30% federal income tax withholding. IRS audits of tax compliance in this area continue to be emphasized.

Payment Cards

It has become common practice to use payment cards (corporate credit cards; P-Cards; procurement cards, etc.) to make payments in the course of a trade or business.

The use of payment cards is efficient and convenient for many reasons; however, for many years the use of the cards also created tax reporting and withholding problems for the payer organization that used the card, because Form 1099 (and 1042-S) tax reporting obligations, and liability for withholding tax when required, arise without regard to the form in which payments are made.

That is, the obligations that apply to payments made by cash, check, wire transfer, etc., are the same obligations that apply to payments made by payment card. The payment is made at the time the card is "swiped," and the payer is the person who has agreed to make the payments on the card (e.g. the employer of the employee who uses the corporate card).

An employee's or contractor's use of her personal card generally will not generate tax reporting and withholding obligations on the part of the employer. However, use of a card on which the employer has assumed any liability for payment, including jointly with the employee or contractor, will trigger these obligations.

For payments made through the use of a card up to December 31, 2010, the responsibility for Form 1099 reporting was solely on the payer (the company or organization that used the card). Fulfilling these tax reporting and withholding obligations meant payers had to solicit the names/TINs, addresses, tax status information, etc. from suppliers paid with the payment card, identify payments as reportable or not reportable, enter the data into their reporting systems, generate and mail the statements to the supplier/payee, and file the returns with the IRS.

Effective at the beginning of 2011, new tax regulations generally shifted the burden of Form 1099 reporting of payments made through payment cards from the organization that used the card to the payment settlement entity that moved the funds to the account of the "merchant" that accepted the card for payment. The payment settlement entity is now required to report the gross proceeds paid to the merchant, using the new IRS Form 1099-K. The organization that used the card does not report the payments on Form 1099-MISC if they are being reported by the payment settlement entity on Form 1099-K.

The same new rule applies to payments made through a third-party electronic network other than a card account. The third-party electronic settlement entity must report payments on Form 1099-K, and where payments are reported on Form 1099-K, the organization that made the purchase is relieved of the requirement to report on Form 1099-MISC.

However, this new shifting of the tax information reporting burden does not extend to payments in which cards or electronic networks are used to pay foreign entities. The 30% federal income tax withholding and Form 1042-S reporting rules apply to payments of US-source income paid to non-US persons, even if the payment is made with a payment card. As with the Forms 1099, a payer's failure to withhold tax when required exposes the payer to liability for the amount of tax that should have been withheld, as well as interest and penalties.

Identifying Your Payee

US or Non-US Person

Unless specifically exempted, payments made in the course of a trade or business are reportable to the IRS, and to the payee on an information return. Non-wage payments are reported on Forms 1099 or 1042-S.[5] Consequently, payers must be able to identify their payees as US or non-US from initial contact with them, as well as determine whether payments made to them throughout the course of the year will be reportable. Payers must also obtain appropriate withholding certificates – Forms W-9, W-8, or 8233 – and determine their income tax withholding obligations.

---

[5]Wages paid to a non-US individual may also be reportable on Form 1042-S. See IRS Publication 515 for more information on reporting wages to non-US individuals.

AP TOOL 54: IDENTIFYING YOUR PAYEE

About This Tool: Identifying your payee as US or non-US is crucial for your accounts payable processes, as all documentation, reporting, and withholding decisions will follow from your categorization of your payee as US or non-US.

Below is a summary chart outlining the basic non-payroll reporting and withholding obligations for US and non-US persons.

US Persons	Non-US Persons
Worldwide Income	**US Source Income**
Entity Payees	**Entity Payees**
Organized under the laws of the United States, including the 50 states and the District of Columbia	Organized under the laws of a country other than the United States, including US territories, protectorates, and possessions, such as Puerto Rico, Guam, American Samoa, US Virgin Islands, and the Northern Mariana Islands
Individuals	**Individuals**
■ US Citizens, including Puerto Rican nationals US residents "green card" holders ■ Individuals who pass the substantial presence test (SPT)[1]	■ Non-US citizens ■ Non-US residents, including individuals present in the United States who are exempt from counting days toward passage of the SPT
Form W-9	**Form W-8** BEN, CE, ECI, IMY, or EXP or Form 8233
Form 1099 **28% backup withholding, if required**	**Form 1042-S** **30% withholding, unless exception** Income tax treaty may apply to reduce or eliminate 30% income tax withholding requirement.
Exceptions to reporting ■ Goods purchases ■ Payments to government, tax-exempt, and most corporate payees[2] ■ Payments aggregating less than $600 over the course of the year[3]	**Exceptions to reporting** ■ Goods purchases ■ Non-US source income ■ No corporate exemption or minimum dollar threshold applies

(Continued)

US Persons	Non-US Persons
Form 945/945-A	**Form 1042**
Due Dates	**Due Dates**
◼ Form 1099 Statements due to payees January 31st	◼ Form 1042-S Statements due to payees by March 15th
◼ Form 1099 Returns due to IRS between February 28th and April 30th, depending on method of filing and whether filing extension was requested	◼ Form 1042-S Returns due to IRS between March 15th and April 15th, depending upon whether filing extension was requested

[1]The substantial presence test is a yearly test that works as follows: The payee must:
◼ Be physically present in the US for 31 days in the current year, and
◼ Be physically present in the US for a total of 183 days during a 3-year period counting:
  ◼ All the days present in the current year,
  ◼ 1/3 of days present in the immediately previous year, and
  ◼ 1/6 of days present in the next previous year.
See IRS Pub. 515 for more information on the SPT.

[2]No Form 1099 reporting corporate exemption exists for payments for medical or legal services.

[3]Not all payments are subject to the $600 threshold. Some payments are subject to a $10 threshold, such as payments of royalties, bank-deposit interest, dividends, distributions from IRAs, etc.

Responding to an IRS Audit

Audits come in many forms, so you must know the type of audit the IRS wishes to conduct as well as the scope of the review to be undertaken. For example, the IRS B-Notice list is actually a type of audit, as is the penalty notice. Regardless of the type of notice you receive from the IRS, make sure your response is timely and professional. Evidence of good-faith attempts to comply with reporting and withholding requirements can go a long way toward successful completion of an examination. In contrast, behaving unprofessionally or failing to respond at all can quickly lead to disastrous results with the IRS.

A bad start with the IRS is very hard to turn around. The agency keeps track of your company's responses, the types of notices and assessments your company receives, and when you pay penalties. It even keeps a list of "bad payers." You do not want your department to create a bad history with the IRS, to pay penalties, or to ever get on the "bad payer" list, so you will need to fix what is broken and show the IRS that you are doing all that is possible to keep the error from happening again.

Scope

The first step is to determine for what the IRS is actually asking. Generally, IRS examiners are looking to establish that you have systems and procedures in place to meet your tax obligations. In the context of an AP audit, this generally will include your Form 1099 and 1042-S processes.

The IRS will review your systems and policies to determine whether they work; whether you know your payees; whether you are appropriately identifying your payments; and whether you are reporting and withholding correctly.

The IRS will look to see what has gone through your accounts payable transaction process. Typically you will be asked to furnish your entire supplier list, and after it has been reviewed by the agent you will be asked to furnish the documentation supporting a sample of payments to selected suppliers. This would include invoices, purchase orders, contracts, documentation of the payee's status for tax purposes such as a Form W-9 or one of the Forms W-8, and tax information returns. The agent's review of this detailed payment documentation may stop at that point if all is in good order, but if questions arise there will be further requests for documentation, and the scope of the examination may be extended and additional payments may be examined.

The IRS typically will also ask to see data on payments that have been made by your organization outside of accounts payable. IRS requests for documents for examination are now routinely specifying backup copies of electronic accounting software records, instead of paper books and records. The IRS SB/SE division (Small Business/Self Employed division, which is heavily involved in Form 1099 tax reporting and withholding, among other issues) published a set of FAQs to provide information for payers that receive Information Document Requests (IDRs) requesting electronic accounting records. You may want to know:

- The IRS will want your backup files on a CD, DVD, or flash/jump drive.
- The IRS will also want the administrator's username and password
- Reconstructed, new, or modified files will not meet the requirement of the IRS IDR.
- The IRS wants a copy of the backup of the books and records of original entry.
- Data converted to Excel spreadsheets will not meet the requirement of the IRS IDR. The IRS wants the backup file because it is an exact copy of the original books of entry and allows the IRS to review and test the integrity of the original electronic records using the software program. It per-

mits the IRS examiner to view transactions to see the date the transaction was originally created, the dates of subsequent changes, what changes were made, and the username of the person who entered or changed the transaction.

- If the backup file given to the IRS contains data for years not under examination, the IRS will not utilize that data during the examination of the specified year, except for transactions in the month immediately prior to the tax period being examined, and the month immediately after the end of the tax period being examined, if the transactions in those timeframes are relevant to the examination.

Auditors will also look to:

- assess the knowledge of your key employees,
- make sure you are not skipping over payees you should be reporting,
- determine that you have all appropriate withholding certificates (Forms W-9 and W-8) on your payees,
- determine that your B-Notices are properly processed, and
- make sure that withholding taxes are deposited in a timely manner and returns (e.g. Forms 945; 1042) are accurate.

Additionally, the IRS will ask for samples of your documentation for the particular types of payments under audit. An information document request (IDR) will ask for such things as copies of your Forms W-9, W-8, 1042, and 1042-S, for example, as well as copies of your policies and procedures manuals and system descriptions.

The IRS will review all payments and systems to determine how you set up suppliers, how you identify payments as requiring or not requiring tax information reporting, how you obtain documentation of your payees' identity and status for tax purposes, and how you identify payments on which tax must be withheld.

You are expected to be able to furnish documentation to the IRS regardless of any changes in systems or programs that may have been implemented within your organization since the time when the requested documentation entered or was created in your records. This includes the ability to print paper copies and furnish them to the IRS agent. Your organization should be familiar with the requirements of IRS Revenue Procedure 97-22, "Electronic Storage System for Books and Records" and IRS Revenue Procedure 98-25, "Record Maintenance in Electronic Systems."

Audit Process Steps

1. Withholding tax adjustment will come from the documentation provided in response to the IDR (extrapolated).
2. The IRS will provide you with a Notice of Proposed Adjustment (Form 5701). You have a right to respond to this, including explaining, when appropriate, why the amounts proposed should be decreased. Following your response, the IRS will provide you with a Final Adjustment.
3. Penalty and interest charges will also be included.
4. Consider remediation, if available (but getting W-9s and W-8s after the fact is up to auditor, and you will need to get them from all payees on whom they are missing but required, not just those missing in the sample).
5. Note that there will be a follow-up compliance check to make sure that the agreed-upon plan was followed.

How the IRS Finds Foreign Suppliers

Review of Supplier Files – expect IRS Computer Audit Specialist (CAS):

- Supplier's EIN Starting with 98-xxxxxxx
- Supplier's ITIN Starting with 999-7/8x-xxxx
- Address Fields:
  - COUNTRY = Not US
  - COUNTRY = BLANK
  - ZIP CODE = NOT US FORMAT (xxxxx-xxxx)
  - STATE = NOT A US STATE
  - STATE = BLANK
  - CITY = FOREIGN CITY
- Supplier number or system codes
- Anything else they find along the way

How the IRS Finds and Sorts Payments

- Looks at all expenses which might be 1099 or 1042 reportable/withholdable
- Interest
- Royalties
- Personal Service Fees, Wages
- Annuities and Pensions

- Rents
- Transactional sampling to determine sourcing practices (including sampling and interpretation of contracts)

Pointers

- Quickly assess your state of compliance and determine where the potential trouble spots are;
- Determine if you will use internal staff or outside advisers;
- Know your potential exposure, what caused it, and what you are doing to fix it;
- Consider voluntary disclosure if problems are found;
- Know your rights to appeal or litigation (dollars may warrant it and you will need to make sure as the audit progresses that you are preserving your defenses);
- Stay on top of the terms of any closing agreement – may require you to file new 1042, 1042-S, 945, 1099, etc.

Avoiding an Audit

This section provides insight on how to avoid an audit of your 1099 process. These suggestions can be integrated into your 1099 process as additional internal controls.

Following up on Questionable Information and Tips for Increasing Supplier Compliance

Due to the complexity of the reporting requirements, it often occurs that payees provide incorrect or questionable information to payers. Remember that payers are entitled to rely on information obtained from payees unless they have reason to know or suspect it is incorrect. Reasons to know or suspect information is incorrect include, but are not limited to:

- An LLC that indicates it is incorporated;
- Foreign addresses, ITINs, EINs beginning with "98," or indicators of foreign corporate status on the Form W-9;
- A payee's appearance on a B-Notice list;
- Name/TIN mismatch from the IRS TIN Matching Program;
- The provision of TINs such as 999-99-9999 or 12-3456789, etc.;
- A claim to be exempt from tax because of religious reasons or because the payee has relinquished its US citizenship or US status, etc., as a result of which it is no longer subject to the US tax law.

While some of these claims are obviously false, others are made because of misunderstandings of the tax law or the requirements.

When following up, it is always a good idea to explain to payees that payers are asking for this information not because of their own policies, but because IRS requirements compel them to.

In addition, remember that a payee's appearance on a B-Notice list or a mismatch revealed through use of the TIN matching program is not evidence that the payee has provided an incorrect TIN. Rather, it indicates that information in the TIN, when combined with information in the payee's name, does not match IRS files.

The name/TIN mismatch could easily occur as result of using an incorrect name, which could easily arise because of a merger or acquisition, marriage, use of a d/b/a, etc. When following up, it is always a good idea to explain that it is the name/TIN combination that does not match, rather than to declare that the payee provided an incorrect TIN.

AP TOOL 55: COMPLIANCE CHECKLIST AND YEAR-END REVIEW

About This Tool: As for obviously specious claims, a payer's only real recourse, when dealing with payees who refuse to provide accurate information, despite a payer's best attempts to obtain it, is to effect backup withholding on reportable payments and appropriately report the payments. Remember that failure to backup withhold when required renders a payer potentially liable for the amount, which, in effect, means that the payer becomes responsible for paying the payee's taxes.

---

1. Identify payees as US or non-US at the time of initial account opening or contact.
2. Request TINs from all suppliers at initial account opening or setup.
3. Obtain appropriate Form W-8 from non-US persons.
4. Withhold 30% on payments of US-source income to non-US persons, unless a documented exception applies.
5. Ensure that non-US persons are present in the appropriate immigration status prior to engaging them for the performance of services.
6. Use IRS TIN Matching Program to verify payees' name/TIN combinations.
7. Assume all payees and all payments are reportable unless you can find a specific exemption.

(Continued)

8. Be alert to payments to employees that should be reported as wages rather than on Form 1099-MISC.

9. Ensure that all workers are appropriately classified as employees or independent contractors.

10. Obtain necessary information from in-house counsel, attorneys, risk management departments, etc., regarding the reportability of legal damages payments.

11. Review state filing requirements, particularly those of the state in which the business is located and states in which business is transacted.

12. File returns with the IRS using the IRS FIRE system and avoid filing paper forms; complete Form 4419 to obtain a transmitter control code (TCC) for electronic filing of Forms 1099 if your organization has not already done so; complete Form 4419 to obtain a transmitter control code (TCC) for electronic filing of Forms 1042-S (note that the TCC for electronic 1099 filing is different from the TCC for electronic 1042-S filing).

13. Register for and use the Combined Fed/State Filing Program to meet many state filing requirements.

14. Request the automatic 30-day extension of time to file Forms 1099 to the IRS every year by completing Form 8809.

15. Review file data prior to filing returns with the IRS and sending statements to payees.

16. Ensure that B-Notices are processed in a timely fashion and institute backup withholding when required; contact Martinsburg-IRS ECC at 1-866-455-7438 each spring and fall to determine whether IRS sent a B-Notice list to your organization.

17. Respond to any proposed penalty notice with a waiver request letter and not with a payment.

CHAPTER TWENTY THREE

Business Continuity Planning

 INTRODUCTION

The global outbreak of COVID-19 has significantly changed the way we live and do business. According to CNN, the food industry is struggling to cope with the impact of the COVID-19 pandemic.[1] The restrictions on transportation links that move food around the globe are now at risk. We can no longer go to the grocery store and purchase everything on our list. We're currently dependent on the delivery of our food and other critical item to our homes. Now what about COVID-19's impact on the business world?

COVID-19 is considered to be a "black swan" event which is an extremely rare, unpredicted, and unprecedented event that is dramatically changing our global economy, society, and history. However, a black swan event initially creates significant chaos but can be considered to be a driver of change for the longer term. Many companies are focused on the future by developing, revising, and updating their business continuity plans (BCPs).

---

[1]Jessie Yeung, "The Coronavirus Pandemic Could Threaten Global Food Supply, UN Warns," CNN, June 10, 2020, accessed September 12, 2020, https://www.cnn.com/2020/04/10/asia/coronavirus-food-supply-asia-intl-hnk/index.html.

HOW COVID-19 IS IMPACTING TODAY'S BUSINESS ENVIRONMENT

Ernest and Young (E&Y) recommends the following points to help focus on business continuity during these unprecedented times.[2]

1. Prioritize people safety and continuous engagement.
2. Reshape strategy for business continuity.
3. Communicate with relevant stakeholders including customers, employees, suppliers, creditors and investors, government and regulators.
4. Build resilience in preparation for the new normal.

E&Y suggests that companies will want to review and revise their current BCPs once COVID-19 is no longer a crisis. Companies are taking a hard look at their current BCPs to determine if the plans worked and if current plans need to be improved. But as we navigate through this crisis, many firms are already developing and enhancing their BCPs in real time and are identifying ways to tighten up business continuity process to get a jump-start on the future.

BCPs could have serious deficiencies that are due to not defining and prioritizing risk, not understanding the nuances of current business processes, the lack of BCP governance, poor communication, and unclear roles and responsibilities. During this pandemic, companies are hindered by too many manual processes and outdated business process solutions.

Suppliers and employees need to be paid in order to keep going. Automated business processes such as accounts receivable, procurement, and accounts payable are enabling many companies to function as usual. Additionally, automated solutions for procure to pay (P2P) provide accurate spending data to enable accurate cash management. Automated order-to-cash (O2C) systems facilitate the customer billing and accounts receivable process to allow timely and accurate revenue recognition.

 ## BUSINESS CONTINUITY BASICS

The business continuity plan (BCP) is used by organizations of all sizes to detail how business will continue if a disaster or emergency occurs. The business continuity plan documents all business operational functions by department,

---

[2]COVID-19 Enterprise Resilience, E&Y, accessed September 12, 2020, https://www.ey.com/en_us/covid-19.

company, employee, supplier information, inventory, emergency procedures, and post-disaster plans.

What Is a Business Continuity Plan (BCP)?

Your BCP should focus on the people, processes, and solutions that will keep your company running during a time of crisis. A comprehensive plan also identifies the manual processes that still need to be supported during the crisis.

Many BCPs may be outdated, which jeopardizes the company's ability to continue as a viable entity. As many companies are finding, during this black swan event the following risks are created due to the lack of a solid BCP.

1. The company may incur a severe disruption in business operations if a function is not able to recover in the event of an unanticipated processing disruption.
2. Critical financial systems may not be recovered first. As a result, the company could sustain substantial financial loss and incur regulatory fines.

 ## THE DIFFERENCE BETWEEN DISASTER RECOVERY AND BUSINESS CONTINUITY

There is a specific difference between business continuity and disaster recovery. Business continuity planning is a strategy. A BCP can ensure the continuity of operations with minimal disruption. Some companies have just a disaster recovery plan. In these situations, a recovery plan should be defined for your primary business functions, information systems, and corporate support functions.

Balancing your planning strategies is a matter of priorities. If the majority of your business transactions are automated, you'll need to make data protection your number one concern. You could not bill customers, pay suppliers, access your spending information, or close the books without accurate data.

In summary, business continuity requires you to keep operations functioning during and immediately after the event. Disaster recovery focuses on how you respond after the event has completed and how you return to normal.

 ## OTHER DEFINITIONS AND TERMS

Business Continuity Plan (BCP): These are the prearranged plans and procedures that critical business functions will execute to ensure business continuity during a disaster or unprecedented event.

Critical Application: These applications are integral to the company because they support major revenue activities, movement of goods to customers, a strategic manufacturing process, or to fulfill contractual or regulatory obligations. Depending on your industry, examples of critical applications are: procurement, accounts payable, financial and general ledger systems, payroll, employee, customer and supplier support, order entry, inventory control, manufacturing resource planning, purchasing, warehouse control, and quality assurance.

Disaster: A disaster causes a loss of resources to the extent that routine recovery measures cannot restore your company's business operations within 24 hours.

Disaster Recovery: This is the restoration of services following a disruption resulting from a disaster. Global companies reacted to the "shelter in place orders" during the COVID-19 pandemic by supporting the current "work from home" environment.

Vital Business Assessment: This is a process required to determine what business functions and supporting applications are critical for the company to continue to conduct business in the event of a disaster. This assessment will identify the types of critical applications noted in the definition above.

 MANAGING A CRISIS

A BCP is an essential part of a company's risk management strategy. It should be updated as solutions, people, and processes change. Every risk that can affect a company's operations is identified within the BCP. We can't prevent a crisis from happening, but a solid BCP can help companies be prepared.

A typical BCP includes:

- The identification of all potential risks to the company and understanding how these risks will interfere or affect business operations;
- The determination of the effect of the risk on the company's normal operations;
- Establishing procedures and safeguards that mitigate risks and offer rapid solutions;
- Testing these procedures to ensure they are current;
- Developing a methodology to test your BCP; and
- Constantly reviewing the BCP for effectiveness.

ASSESSING THE RISK AND DEVELOPING A STRATEGY

Business continuity management refers to the processes and procedures in place to ensure the continuation of regular business operations during a disaster. The accurate identification of such procedures is dependent on an accurate and timely risk assessment. Here are some tips on how to perform a business continuity risk assessment.

1. **Identify the risks to your company.** List all factors that could put your company at risk and ask the question, "What can go wrong?"
2. **Analyze the impact to your company.** Once you've identified the risks that your company may face, determine the types of risk by business process. Could there be a financial impact? Are you able to pay suppliers and employees? Can you produce invoices to customers? Will your supply chain be impacted?
3. **Update your current risk management plan.** Update your risk management plan with the risks that you've identified and map the risks to business processes.
4. **Prepare a BCP.** Think of your critical business process and how you should prioritize the risks that can be mitigated. Are there financial processes that can be automated today – not only to mitigate risk but to add efficiency and reduce cost?

 ## TAKING BUSINESS CONTINUITY TO THE CLOUD

Because cloud computing relies heavily on hardware-independent technology, it enables enterprises to quickly back up data, applications, and even operating systems to a remote data center (or cloud). Many automated business process such as procurement and accounts payable are supported by cloud-based solutions, so business continuity is not an issue.

When developing your BCP, identify the critical business processes that are supported by cloud-based solutions to ensure that the data needed to run your company is available in the cloud.

When selecting your cloud-based provider, determine the following.

1. **The provider must stratify the services provided into different categories.** Some services are so mission critical that they require

redundancy. Other applications are mission critical but require recovery rather than redundancy.

2. **The cloud provider must have the ability to test recovery from a disaster.** Even if the corporation chooses not to do such tests internally, there should be evidence that a provider has done it for others. This evidence should be available.

3. **The cloud provider must demonstrate no single points of failure.** The provider should have a recovery process which is the equivalent of backing up onto the same server. And as a recommended best practice, the provider should follow the same checklists used for the corporation.

HOW TO ENSURE CONTINUOUS BUSINESS CONTINUITY

When initiating your business continuity planning process, consider the potential impacts of a disaster or catastrophic event on your people, processes, and solutions. How can you properly plan for a disaster if you have little idea of the likely impacts on the company for different scenarios? What happens if you haven't identified critical business processes?

The business continuity process should have management support, such as the controller, chief procurement officer (CPO), and chief information officer (CIO), and defined stakeholders. Stakeholders are usually business process owners such as procurement managers, accounts payable management, and accounts receivable manager. Ensure that management knows that a total effort is needed to develop and maintain an effective plan that includes the following actions:

- Define your business continuity efforts in terms of business processes;
- Document the impact of an extended loss of operations and key business functions;
- Select teams that provide the details for a proper plan;
- Develop a BCP that is and easy to maintain;
- Define how to integrate continuity planning issues into ongoing business planning and system development processes to ensure the plan is viable over time; and
- Consider integrating the testing of the BCP into internal controls programs. Determine that your BCP is working.

Having developed the business continuity plan, it is sensible to perform an audit or test. This evaluation should occur not just initially, but at regular intervals. That's why we suggest, including the testing process with current internal control programs. (See the Addendum for recommended BCP internal controls.) This helps ensure that the BCP remains current, and that it stands up to rigorous examination. The following types of tests are recommended.

- Walkthrough Testing;
- Simulation Testing;
- Checklist Testing;
- Full Interruption Testing; and
- Parallel Testing.

AP TOOL 56: SIX BCP BEST PRACTICES

About This Tool: Companies can't anticipate every possible situation, but they can be prepared by automating manual processes, protecting company assets and data, and by analyzing possible business risks. Going forward, companies need to always ask, "What can go wrong?" and "Will I be prepared for the next 'black swan' event?" Here are six best practices that should help.

Six BCP Best Practices

1. **Dedicate and Empower Staff.** Be sure to include all business process owners in the development and testing of the BCP.

2. **Divide and Conquer.** In order to ensure business involvement in the development and maintenance of the business continuity plan, Martin Gomberg, CTO of A&E Television Networks, has separated business continuity planning and disaster recovery into two initiatives, each with its own governance and goals.

3. **The BCP Should Stand Alone.** The BCP should be well written so that it can be understood by other stakeholders and business process owners in your company. Use a template when developing your plan and use titles (not names) when defining roles and responsibilities.

4. **Align BCP with Every Automated Solution.** When an automated solution is implemented, be sure to validate and test its BCP.

5. **Tabletop Tests Don't Work.** In addition to tabletop tests, some companies implement mock disasters for a defined crisis management team, which is made up of stakeholder, business process owners, and even board members.

6. **Hold Post Mortems and Make Revisions.** What you do with the results of the test is a critical part of disaster recovery planning. Be sure to communicate and retest any revisions to your BCP.

AP TOOL 57: A ROADMAP FOR DEVELOPING YOUR BCP

About This Tool: The business continuity planning process should encompass the steps that are needed if a disruption in business occurs. The following steps provide a roadmap to consider when developing a plan for your company.

A Roadmap for Developing Your BCP

1. **Document key internal employee and backups.** These are key employees that are integral to the function of your business processes. A controller should identify the key employees by each business process. It's important to consider backups.
   - Consider which job functions are critically necessary on a daily basis.
   - Make a list of all those individuals with all contact information including business phone, home phone, cell phone, business e-mail, personal e-mail, and any other possible way of contacting them in an emergency situation where normal communications might be impacted.

2. **Identify people that can work from home.**

3. **Document external contacts.** If you have critical suppliers or contractors, build a special contact list that includes a description of the company (or individual) and any other absolutely critical information about them including key personnel contact information. Include in your list people like attorneys, bankers, and consultants. This list should include anyone that you might need to call to assist with various operational issues.

4. **Identify processes that have been outsourced.** Identify your outsourced processes and how your business partners will be impacted if everyone needs to work from home. Ideally, your business partner provided a BCP when the outsourcing agreement was initiated.

5. **Document all manual processes and determine applicable contingencies.** How can manual supplier invoices be processed? How can new suppliers be screened and validated manually?

6. **Document all automated processes.** Ensure that segregation of duties (SoD) and access controls are in place.

7. **Determine critical data needs. Identify the data needed for decision making, analysis, and cash management in a time of crisis.**

8. **Identify critical files and documents.** These include articles of incorporation, financial key supplier contracts, utility bills, banking information, critical HR documents, building lease papers, and tax returns.

9. **Define a "How-to List" based on specific scenarios.** It should include step-by-step instructions on what to do, who should do it, and how. (Remember: people, process, and solutions). Your business process documentation, policies, procedures, and internal control processes are critical. Public companies can use Sarbanes-Oxley documentation for this purpose. Ensure that business processes are assigned to a "lead" person as suggested in step 1. Processes with a high risk factor and significant financial impact should be prioritized.

10. **Consolidate the components of your BCP.** A BCP is useless if all the components are scattered all over the company or within their silos.

11. **Communicate.** Make sure everyone in your company is familiar with the BCP. Hold mandatory training classes for all employees. Ensure that employees are familiar with video communication solutions and can use these solutions to communicate on a daily basis.

10. **Test the plan.** All business continuity plans should be tested to make sure all the key components have been identified and the plan can be executed.

11. **Plan to change the plan.** No matter how good your plan is, and no matter how smoothly your test runs, there will be opportunities for improvement.

12. **Review and revise.** Every time something changes, update all copies of your business continuity plan. With all the changes in technology, it important to ensure that the plan is never outdated.

13. **Consider next steps.** Consider the next steps for recovery and identify what needs to happen to bring the organization, region, country, or division back online.

AP TOOL 58: FIVE RECOMMENDED BCP INTERNAL CONTROLS

About This Tool: Like any critical business process, there should be a series of internal controls for your BCP process. Here are five recommendations.

Five Recommended BCP Internal Controls

1. **Recovery Priority.** Business process owners must classify their recovery priority. The priority assessment should include the following:
   a. Conduct a vital business assessment to quantify the risk in terms of dollars, production volume, or other measurable terms due to partial or total loss of processing the application;
   b. Assess the lead time between loss of application processing and adverse impact on operations as part of determining acceptable downtime.

2. **Alternative Processes and Facilities.** A BCP should provide the most effective alternative methods for processing both critical and non-critical applications. Such alternatives include:
   a. Processing at a third-party location;
   b. Processing at a conditioned site maintained by a recovery site supplier; not processing applications until company operations are restored;
   c. Detailing technical and business process owner requirements and special skills needed in the event of an unanticipated processing disruption; and
   d. Storaging critical records, replacement forms, supplies, and documentation at another location such as a home office or in the cloud.

(Continued)

3. **Documentation and Testing.** Detailed business continuity plans must be documented and tested at least annually to ensure recovery can be accomplished. Where tests of the full plan are found to be impractical due to business conditions or the cost of testing, test plans must be developed and implemented to test portions of the plan. Business process owners must participate in the test to certify business recovery capability.

4. **Annual Review of Disaster Recovery Plans.** Business process owners must review and update their BCPs at least annually or more frequently when significant changes are made to the applications or business process.

5. **Recovery Time Targets.** Owners/service providers responsible for developing business continuity plan arrangements must specify and publish to users the target times for recovery of:
   a. Mission-critical functions
   b. Normal business operations

7

Addendum

This final section of *The New AP Toolkit* includes (1) an Accounts Payable: Quarterly Controls Self-Assessment Questionnaire and (2) a Glossary.

1. Accounts Payable: Quarterly Controls Self-Assessment Questionnaire
   The questionnaire can be used to validate the effectiveness of internal controls for your AP process and can be used to identify areas of risk. This checklist is at a summary level and can highlight where an additional review of controls is necessary.
2. Glossary
   The glossary provides the key terms pertinent to the AP process with their definitions. This glossary is a good desk reference in case there is a question on specific terminology.

Accounts Payable: Quarterly Controls Self-Assessment Questionnaire

Business Process Area: Accounts Payable	Date:
	Page: Page 1 of 3
	Revision:
	Prepared By:
	Approved By:

Purpose: To establish a quarterly process that monitors the effectiveness of internal controls for the accounts payable process using a self-assessment questionnaire.

Example Scope: This responsibility should be accomplished by following a formal process outlined in this policy per functional area and a complete understanding of the respective functional accounting area the staff member is accountable for within the business unit accounting department. Preparation and completion of the questionnaire is a joint requirement shared amongst business unit accounting managers and their respective staff members. Submittal of completed questionnaires is due to the business unit controller on the seventh day of the month immediately following the completion of a fiscal quarter (e.g. first quarter ends March 31st, due April 7th).

Record Management: All documentation referenced in this procedure must reside in a file labeled "Accounts Payable Quarterly Controls Self-Assessment" for the given fiscal quarter located within the business unit accounting department electronic filing system.

ACCOUNTS PAYABLE CONTROLS QUESTIONNAIRE

Questionnaire Instructions: The following questionnaire has been prepared by the technology corporation business unit controller to facilitate an assessment of whether the controls within the Business unit are operating effectively. Please respond to these questions as accurately as possible and feel free to insert comments and further explanations, as you deem necessary.

 ## PROCESS BACKGROUND INFORMATION

1. Manager responsible for process
2. Number of FTEs in accounts payable process
3. Average number of invoices processed per month
4. Average number of disbursements/checks per month
5. Days Payable Outstanding (DPO)
6. Number of information system(s) and/or applications used in the accounts payable process
7. Is the accounts payable system directly linked to the general ledger?

 ## INTERNAL CONTROL ASSESSMENT

How would you evaluate the effectiveness of the current process in achieving the following control objectives? Use a scale of 1 to 5, with 1=Not effective and 5=Highly effective.

Control Objective	Evaluation				
	1	2	3	4	5
1. Accounts payable and cash disbursements/electronic fund transfer disbursements are properly authorized.					
2. All liabilities are recorded on a timely basis.					
3. Accounts payable are accurately and completely recorded on a timely basis.					
4. Cash disbursements/electronic fund transfer disbursements are accurately and completely made and recorded on a timely basis.					

5. Accounts payable and cash disbursements/electronic fund transfer disbursements are reliably processed and reported.

6. Recorded accounts payable balances are substantiated.

7. Recorded accounts payable balances are evaluated.

8. Performance measures used to control and improve the process are reliable.

9. Employees and management are provided with the information they need to control the accounts payable process.

10. Costs are reduced as much as possible.

11. Processing time is minimized.

12. Management develops alliances with key suppliers.

 ## REMEDIATION PLAN

Remediation Required	Owner	Manager/ Supervisor	Completion Date	Requires Escalation (Y/N)

Overall Ranking

How would you rate the overall quality of this process? Use a scale of 1 to 5, with 1=Poor and 5=Best Practice or Best in Class.

1	2	3	4	5

Glossary

Access Controls   These are the procedures and controls that limit or detect access to critical network assets to guard against loss of integrity, confidentiality, accountability, or availability. Access controls provide reasonable assurance that critical resources are protected against unauthorized modification, disclosure, loss, or impairment.

Account Number   Defines the accounting transaction type for the transaction and includes a system generated number tied to a corporate's chart of accounts.

Accounting Policy   Basic concepts, assumptions, policies, methods, and practices used by a company for maintaining accounting principles and summarization into financial statements as prescribed by GAAP. A policy can be described as "what" needs to happen to ensure that accounting cycles are working within boundaries of internal control.

Accounting Procedure   The routine steps in processing accounting data during an accounting period. In sequence, (1) occurrence of the transaction, (2) classification of each transaction in chronological order (journalizing), (3) recording the classified data in ledger accounts (posting), (4) preparation of financial statements, and (5) closing of nominal accounts. A procedure ensures that a policy is properly executed and explains "how." Other procedures or policies will be referenced if applicable.

Accounts Payable   AP is as "an entity's short-term obligation to pay suppliers for products and services, which the entity purchased on credit." If accounts payable are not paid within the payment terms agreed to with the supplier, the payables are considered to be in default, which may trigger a penalty or interest

   We define the AP process as a strategic, value-added accounting function that performs the primary non-payroll disbursement functions in an organization. As such, the AP operation plays a critical role in the financial cycle of the organization. AP enables an organization to accomplish its objectives by bringing a systematic, disciplined approach to evaluate and improve the effectiveness of the entire payables process. In addition to the traditional AP activities whereby liabilities to third-party entities (suppliers, suppliers, tax authorities, etc.) are recognized and paid based on the credit policies agreed to between the company and its suppliers, today's AP departments have taken on much wider roles including fraud prevention, cost reduction, workflow system solutions, cash-flow management, internal controls, and supplier (supply chain) financing.

Accounts Payable Automation AP automation refers to the technology that is used to streamline and automate accounts payable processes, which includes removing manual tasks and providing better visibility and control over important financial data.

Accruals Accruals are adjustments for (1) revenues that have been earned but are not yet recorded in the accounts, and (2) expenses that have been incurred but are not yet recorded in the accounts. The accruals need to be added via adjusting entries so that the financial statements report these amounts.[1]

Artificial Intelligence (AI) AI textbooks define the field as the study of "intelligent agents": any device that perceives its environment and takes actions that maximize its chance of successfully achieving its goals. Colloquially, the term "artificial intelligence" is often used to describe machines (or computers) that mimic "cognitive" functions that humans associate with the human mind, such as "learning" and "problem solving."

Assertions Financial statement assertions are claims made by an organization's management regarding its financial statements. The assertions form a theoretical basis from which external auditors develop a set of audit procedures and all of the information contained within the financial statements has been accurately recorded.

Audit Committee The audit committee's role includes: the oversight of financial reporting; the monitoring of accounting policies; the oversight of any external auditors; regulatory compliance; and discussion of risk management policies with management. The audit committee may approve and review the status of the company's internal annual internal audit plan and is usually apprised of any suspicions of fraud reported via the ethics hotline process.

Benford's Law Benford's Law is a well-known audit technique used to flag questionable patterns of activity. Intuitively, one would expect a range of numbers to begin with each digit 10% of the time (10% for 0, 10% for 1, 10% for 2, etc.). Benford discovered that when testing groups of transactions from various unrelated sources, a mathematical phenomenon confirms that about 30% of the numbers have 1 as the first digit, 18% have 2, and only 5% have 9. If the numbers for an individual supplier do not conform to this established pattern (+/- a certain percentage), it may indicate that the non-conforming transactions are fraudulent

Benchmarking According to Wikipedia, benchmarking is the practice of comparing business processes and performance metrics to industry bests and best practices from other companies. Dimensions typically measured are quality, time, and cost.[2]

---

[1] Accounting Coach, "What Are Accruals," accessed January 1, 2019, https://www.accounting-coach.com/blog/what-are-accruals.

[2] Wikipedia, "Benchmarking," accessed March 2, 2019, https://en.wikipedia.org/wiki/Benchmarking.

Best Practices Implementation of the highest quality, most advantageous, repeatable processes achieved by applying the experiences of those with the acquired skill or proficiency. Best practices are achieved by implementing processes, templates, and checklists that will improve cycle time, reduce cost, and provide the foundation for continuous improvement.

Blockchain Blockchain is an open ledger in which every transaction on the network is recorded and available for allowed participants to see and verify. It can be thought of as a "secured spreadsheet" that sits in the cloud that multiple parties can review but no one can change. Bitcoin popularized the blockchain technology and was proposed in 2008 in a whitepaper by Satoshi Nakamoto (pseudonym).

Budget Process A budget process refers to the process by which companies create and approve an annual budget. Most companies track results on a monthly basis through internal reporting processes where actual expenses are compared with the approved budget for a cost center or operating unit. This monthly review will identify excessive spending that could reflect a control issue.

Business Continuity Planning This is the process of developing advance arrangements and procedures that enable an organization to respond to an event in such a manner that critical business functions continue with planned levels of interruption or essential change.

Business Continuity Program This is an ongoing program supported and funded by executive staff to ensure business continuity requirements are assessed, resources are allocated; recovery strategies and procedures are completed and tested.

Business Unit A logical element or segment of a company (such as accounting, production, marketing) representing a specific business function, and a definite place on the organizational chart, under the domain of a manager. A business unit is also called a department, division, or a functional area.

Cash Pooling The primary target of cash pooling is the optimization and use of surplus funds of all companies in a group in order to reduce external debt and increase the available liquidity. Furthermore, especially, interest benefits in multiple ways can be achieved for the pool participants on the payable and on the receivable side.

Change in Accounting Principle When a company adopts an alternative generally accepted accounting principle from a previously used principle to account for the same type of transaction or event, that action is called a change in accounting principle. The term "accounting principle" includes not only accounting principles and practices but also the methods of applying them.

The initial adoption of an accounting principle in recognition of events or transactions occurring for the first time or that were previously immaterial in their effect is not considered a change in accounting principle. A change in accounting principle differs from a change in accounting estimate in that a change in accounting estimate results when new events occur, more experience is acquired, or additional information is obtained that affects the previously determined estimate.

Common Chart of Accounts   In accounting, a common chart of accounts is a numbered list of the accounts that comprise a company's general ledger. A company should establish accounting policies and rules for the use of specific account numbers. As a best practice, a simplified chart of accounts will enable a faster close. The accounting department should monitor the use of accounts, and identify and correct any anomalies.

Company Code   The business transactions relevant for financial accounting are entered, saved, and evaluated at company code level. You usually create a legally independent company in ERP systems (e.g. the applicable ERP system) with one company code.

Compensating Controls   In some cases, an employee will perform all activities within a process. In this scenario, segregation of duties does not exist and risk cannot be identified nor mitigated in a timely manner. As a result, the implementation of additional compensating controls should be considered. A compensating control reduces the vulnerabilities in ineffectively segregated functions. A compensating control can reduce the risk of errors, omissions, irregularities, and deficiencies, which can improve the overall business process.

However, it should be noted that many companies include compensating controls in their internal controls programs as additional measures to reduce risk. These controls can be embedded in continuous controls monitoring (CCM) and controls self-assessment (CSA) processes. Continuous controls monitoring (CCM) refers to the use of automated tools and various technologies to ensure the continuous monitoring of fiscal transactions and other types of transactional applications to reduce and mitigate risk. A CCM process includes the validation of authorizations, systems access, system configurations, and business process settings.

Contingency Plan   Contingency plans are defined as a set of measures to deal with emergencies caused by failures due to human action or natural disasters that impact the operation of a company. Contingency planning includes the prearranged plans and procedures that critical business functions will execute to ensure business continuity until computer and telecommunications facilities are reestablished following a disaster.

Continuous Auditing (CA)   CA is an automatic method used to perform auditing activities, such as control and risk assessments, on a more frequent basis. Technology plays a key role in continuous audit activities by helping to automate the identification of exceptions or anomalies, analyze patterns within the digits of key numeric fields, review trends, and test controls, among other activities.

The "continuous" aspect of continuous auditing and reporting refers to the real-time or near real-time capability for fiscal information to be checked and shared. Not only does it indicate that the integrity of information can be evaluated at any given point of time, it also means that the information is able to be verified constantly for errors, fraud, and inefficiencies. It is the most detailed audit.[3]

---

[3] Wikipedia, "Continuous Auditing," accessed March 2, 2019, https://en.wikipedia.org/wiki/Continuous_auditing.

Continuous Controls Monitoring (CCM)   According to Gartner, continuous controls monitoring (CCM) is a set of technologies to reduce business losses through continuous monitoring and reducing the cost of audits through continuous auditing of the controls in fiscal and other transactional applications.[4]

Controller   According to TechTarget, "a financial controller is a senior-level executive who acts as the head of accounting, and oversees the preparation of financial reports, such as balance sheets and income statements A financial controller, who may also be referred to as a financial comptroller, usually reports to an organization's chief financial officer (CFO). In smaller organizations that do not have CFOs, the controller might be the top financial officer. In addition to preparing reports, the controller's responsibilities may also include compliance audits, monitoring internal controls, participating in the budgeting process and analyzing financial data to varying degrees. At some companies, financial controllers are involved in evaluating and selecting technology for use within the finance department or other related departments within the organization."[5]

Corporate Card/Travel Card   The corporate card or travel card is generally used by organizations for employee travel and entertainment related expenses. The card allows employees to use the card for payment of travel expenses and provides essential data to the employer. Employees are provided the Corporate Card for payment of approved, business-related expenses that are most often travel-related as designated by the employer. The card is issued in the company's name with the name of the individual employee displayed on the card.

Cost Center   The designated accounting location, in which costs are incurred, defined as a sub-unit of a legal entity and in some cases the business unit depending on how the business unit code is utilized. All cost centers are assigned to a company's legal entity. However, only some cost centers may be assigned to business or operating units. The assignment of a cost center is distinguished by an area of responsibility, location, or accounting method.

Cost Management   Cost management is comprised of the fiscal processes, reporting, and analytics that support cost accounting, inventory accounting, and cost analysis.

Counterparty   A counterparty is the other party that participates in a financial transaction, and every transaction must have a counterparty in order for the transaction to go through. More specifically, every buyer of an asset must be paired up with a seller who is willing to sell and vice versa.

Countertrade   "Countertrade is a reciprocal form of international trade in which goods or services are exchanged for other goods or services rather than for hard currency. This type of international trade is more common in developing countries

---

[4] "Continuous Controls Monitoring (CCM)," IT Glossary, Gartner, accessed March 2, 2019, https://www.gartner.com/it-glossary/continuous-controls-monitoring-ccm.

[5] Margaret Rouse, TechTarget, "Definition Financial Controller," Updated July 2013, accessed May 4, 2020, https://searcherp.techtarget.com/definition/financial-controller.

with limited foreign exchange or credit facilities. Countertrade can be classified into three broad categories: barter, counterpurchase and offset."[6]

Corrective Control A control designed to correct errors or irregularities that have been detected.

Corporate Trade Exchange (CTX) A corporate trade exchange is an electronic fund transfer system used by companies and government agencies to make recurring payments to a number of parties with a single funds transfer.

Consumer Tax In consumer tax states, the tax is imposed on the buyer, with responsibility for collection by the seller. The seller is still required to remit the tax even if it is not collected from the buyer, but it is usually easier to recover the tax from the buyer. The tax is generally imposed on the privilege of using or consuming the products or services purchased. Under audit, the state can collect the tax from either the seller or the purchaser. New York and Ohio are two of the consumer tax states.

Critical Application A critical business application is one that a company must have to support major revenue activities, movement of goods to customers, a strategic manufacturing process, or to fulfill contractual or regulatory obligations. In addition, the application's availability is deemed by management to be vital to the continued functioning of company business. Examples of critical applications are: customer service support, order entry, inventory control, manufacturing resource planning, purchasing, warehouse control, quality assurance, and finance.

Critical Processes A critical business processes is one that if disrupted or made unavailable for any length of time will have a significant negative impact on the success of the business.

Customer Relationship Management (CRM) Customer relationship management (CRM) is a technology for managing a company's relationships and interactions with customers and potential customers.

Cycle Time Cycle time is the total time from the beginning to the completion of a process.

Cycle time includes process time, during which a unit is acted upon to bring it closer to an output, and delay time, during which a unit of work is spent waiting to take the next action.

Data Model A data model establishes data definitions and processes for reference, ensures data rules are utilized, and provides a schematic view of the underlying components comprising the data that drives the fiscal function.

Days Payable Outstanding (DPO) According to CFI, "DPO refers to the average number of days it takes a company to pay back its accounts payable. Therefore, DPO measures how well a company is managing its accounts payable. A DPO of 20 means that on average, it takes a company 20 days to pay back its suppliers."[7]

---

[6] Will Kenton, "Countertrade," Investopedia, Updated March 28, 2020, accessed April 13, 2020, https://www.investopedia.com/terms/c/countertrade.asp.

[7] Corporate Finance Institute (CFI), "What Is Days Payable Outstanding?," accessed on May 4, 2020, https://corporatefinanceinstitute.com/resources/knowledge/accounting/days-payable-outstanding/.

Debt Covenant Debt covenants are agreements between a company and a creditor usually stating limits or thresholds for certain financial ratios that the company may not breach.

Delegation of Authority (DoA) As one of the critical corporate controls for a company, the Delegation of Authority policy is confused with a segregation of duties policy. Although, the two provide the foundation of good internal controls and corporate governance, the delegation of authority policy focuses on the establishment of approval levels for specific business transactions to specific individuals within the company. Additionally, the policy communicates the delegation of those approval levels to others when the approval owner is away from the office. Delegation of authority is usually a corporate policy that is administrated by the corporate secretary and is approved by the board of directors.

Detective Control Designed to detect errors or irregularities that may have occurred. Examples are reconciliations, authorized signatures, and credit checks and approvals.

Disaster A disaster is defined as a loss of computing or telecommunication resources to the extent that routine recovery measures cannot restore normal service levels within 24 hours, which impacts the company's business significantly.

Due Diligence Due diligence is the investigation or exercise of care that a reasonable business or person is expected to take before entering into an agreement or contract with another party, or an act with a certain standard of care. It can be a legal obligation, but the term will more commonly apply to voluntary investigations.

Dynamic Discounting Dynamic discounting solutions provide suppliers the flexibility to discount their approved invoices at any point up to the maturity date and pass on a portion of the finance charges to buyers. This functionality has gained acceptance and popularity as it offers financing to suppliers at attractive rates while delivering an additional income stream to buyers. Solution providers and banks facilitate the transactions through a simple, intuitive Web interface that provides visibility to all parties, including the ability to change rates and terms in real time, thus the term dynamic.

Dynamic discounting serves the cash management needs of buyers and suppliers alike. Solution providers create the technological framework to facilitate this process. The transaction can be self-funded by the buyer or a bank can stand in as a short-term lender. Through Web-based buyer-supplier networks, buyers are able to project compressed settlement terms through supplier discounts. Suppliers are able to pick and choose among an array of payment options for each outstanding invoice. Banks pay the bill and collect from the buyer the full original price minus a percentage of the discount savings; an arrangement often referred to as "revenue sharing."

Electronic Invoicing Electronic invoicing solutions streamline the invoice receipt-to-pay cycle by enabling organizations to electronically exchange purchase orders and invoices, use sophisticated workflow tools for approval processing, and make electronic settlement against approved invoices. The various solutions featured in this report offer electronic invoicing, payments automation, or both in order to create an end-to-end solution that integrates with enterprise and other legacy business applications.

Escheatment Escheat refers to the right of a government to take ownership of estate assets or unclaimed property. It most commonly occurs when an individual dies with no will and no heirs. (See Unclaimed Property)

Enterprise Resource Planning (ERP) System An ERP is business process management software that allows an organization to use a system of integrated applications to manage the business and automate many back office functions related to technology, services, and human resources. Examples of ERP systems are the applicable ERP system, Oracle, Microsoft Dynamics, and Sage.

Evaluated Receipt Settlement (ERS) This is an arrangement in which payments to suppliers are based on the quantities received, rather than a supplier invoice. The payment to the supplier is based on the number of units received and the price per unit stated in the authorizing purchase order. It is often referred to as a "two-way" matching process.

External Audit According to Wikipedia, "an external audit is a periodic audit conducted by an independent qualified auditor with the aim to determine whether the accounting records for a business are complete and accurate. According to Wikipedia, an external auditor performs an audit, in accordance with specific laws or rules, of the financial statements of a company, government entity, other legal entity, or organization, and is independent of the entity being audited. Users of these entities' fiscal information, such as investors, government agencies, and the general public, rely on the external auditor to present an unbiased and independent audit report. For public companies listed on stock exchanges in the United States, the Sarbanes-Oxley Act (SOX) has imposed stringent requirements on external auditors in their evaluation of internal controls and financial reporting.[8]

External Reporting Companies prepare external financial statements to report their business information to outside observers, including potential investors, stakeholders, shareholders, and the SEC.

FATCA According to the IRS, the Foreign Account Tax Compliance Act (FATCA), which was passed as part of the HIRE Act, generally requires that foreign financial institutions and certain other non-financial foreign entities report on the foreign assets held by their US account holders or be subject to withholding on withholdable payments. The HIRE Act also contained legislation requiring US persons to report, depending on the value, their foreign financial accounts and foreign assets.[9]

---

[8] Wikipedia, "External Audit," accessed March 2, 2019, https://en.wikipedia.org/wiki/External_auditor.

[9] Foreign Account Tax Compliance Act (FATCA), IRS, accessed August 6, 2020, https://www.irs.gov/businesses/corporations/foreign-account-tax-compliance-act-fatca

Financial Accounting Standards Board (FASB) This is a private, non-profit organization standard-setting body whose primary purpose is to establish and improve Generally Accepted Accounting Principles (GAAP) within the United States in the public's interest.

Financial Architecture Financial Architecture is the structure in which business processes and systems within a finance function are organized and integrated. This architecture is used to set the foundation for all finance and accounting processes and systems. It is also used to identify areas for automation and process and system improvement.

Financial Hierarchy A company's financial hierarchy is usually structured with retained earnings at the top, followed by debt financing and then external equity financing at the bottom and is supported by a structure of cost centers.

Fixed Assets A fixed asset is a long-term tangible piece of property that a firm owns and uses in its operations to generate income. Fixed assets are not expected to be consumed or converted into cash within 1–2 years. Fixed assets are known as property, plant, and equipment (PP&E). They are also referred to as capital assets.

Financial, Planning and Analysis (FP&A) Financial planning and analysis (FP&A) is a group within a company's finance organization that provides senior management with a forecast of the company's profit and loss (income statement) and operating performance for the upcoming quarter and year.

Fiscal Close The fiscal close or financial closing process establishes a "cut-off" of fiscal activity so a company can generate monthly, quarterly, and financial reports for stakeholders and shareholders. The steps within the fiscal close include: (1) Transaction Accumulation, Reconciliation, and Sub-Ledger Close, (2) Corporate Close and Consolidation, and (3) Reporting and Analysis or "The Final Mile."

Fleet Card A fleet card or fuel card is a product used by organizations to pay for fuel and related expenses on company vehicles. The card is used as a payment card that is commonly utilized for fuel purchases such as gasoline, diesel, and other fuels at gas stations. The fleet cards may be used to pay for vehicle expenses and maintenance if allowed by a fleet owner or manager. The benefit of a fleet card is increased security for cardholders, or the fleet drivers that no longer need to carry money. With the use of fleet cards, the fleet owners or managers receive real-time reports that reveal transactions. The fleet owners or managers can set purchase controls that provide detailed use of business related expenses. The fleet card provides convenient and comprehensive reports of business transactions.

Forecast Process A fiscal forecast is a financial management tool that presents estimated information based on past, current, and projected fiscal conditions. This will help identify future revenue and expenditure trends that may have an immediate or long-term influence on strategic goals.

Four-Way Matching Process The four-way matching process is used when an operating location is using online receiving and inspection. In four-way matching an invoice is matched to the corresponding purchase order for quantity and amount, receiving, and inspection information. The four-way matching process also refers to matching the invoice, purchase order, and receiving document to the terms and conditions of a contract.

Fraud Fraud occurs when a person or business intentionally deceives another with promises of goods, services, or financial benefits that do not exist, were never intended to be provided, or were misrepresented. Typically, victims give money but never receive what they paid for. Millions of people in the United States are victims of fraud crimes each year.

"Virtually anyone can fall prey to fraudulent crimes. Con artists do not pass over anyone due to such factors as a person's age, finances, educational level, gender, race, culture, ability, or geographic location. In fact, fraud perpetrators often target certain groups based on these factors."[10]

General Accounting Financial processes that support the close, general accounting, and intercompany processes.

General and Administrative (G&A) Expenses General and administrative (G&A) expenses are incurred in the day-to-day operations of a business and may not be directly tied to a specific function or department within the company. G&A expenses include rent, utilities, insurance, legal fees, and certain salaries.

General Data Protection Regulation (GDPR) The GDPR was approved and adopted by the European Union (EU) Parliament in April 2016. The regulation took effect after a two-year transition period and, unlike a directive, did not require any legislation to be passed by government. GDPR came into force on May 25, 2018. The GDPR not only applies to organizations located within the EU but also applies to organizations located outside of the EU if they offer goods or services to, or monitor the behavior of, EU data subjects. It applies to all companies processing and holding the personal data of data subjects residing in the EU, regardless of the company's location.

The GDPR applies to "personal data," meaning any information relating to an identifiable person who can be directly or indirectly identified in particular by reference to an identifier. This definition provides for a wide range of personal identifiers to constitute personal data, including name, identification number, location data or online identifier, reflecting changes in technology and the way organizations collect information about people.[11]

Ghost Cards/ Virtual Cards/ Single Use Ghost cards, virtual cards, or single use cards are card accounts issued to a specific supplier to process all the organization's transactions. Companies can use virtual cards as another payment option instead of providing a credit card to each employee. The ghost card provides a single account for organizations to pay employee charges. Ghost cards reduce

---

[10] United States Department of Justice, U.S. Attorneys, District of Alaska, "Financial Fraud Crimes," accessed May 4, 2020, https://www.justice.gov/usao-ak/financial-fraud-crimes.

[11] European Union (EU) General Data Protection Regulation (GDPR), "GDPR FAQs," accessed January 4, 2019, https://eugdpr.org/the-regulation/gdpr-faqs/.

fraud and overspending. Unless the company, which owns the ghost card, approves the charges to the account, the employee cannot spend the funds. Approval is required. Purchases are only finalized after the employer authorizes the charges to the account. The employer budgets expenses such as business trips and expenses above the budgeted amount will not be permitted.

Gross Receipts Tax   Gross receipts taxes are a type of sales tax. The tax is a percentage of the total dollar amount of the transaction. This includes gross receipts from sideline operations such as occasional sales or sales outside the regular course of business. As a general rule there are very few deductions allowed under a gross receipts tax structure. In most gross receipts tax states, many services are subject to tax that are not taxed in states that impose a sales tax. Hawaii and New Mexico are two of the gross receipts tax states.

Hire to Retire (H2R)   "Hire to retire (H2R) is a human resources process that includes everything that needs to be done over the course of an employee's career with a company. Human resources are the people who work in an organization. Human resources are the people who work for an organization in jobs that produce the products or services of the business or organization. The evolution of the human resources function gave credence to the fact that people are an organization's most important resources. The specific sub-processes included in the H2R process are payroll preparation and security; payroll payment controls; distribution of payroll; compensation and benefits; hiring and termination; education, training, and development; and contingent workforce. Distribution of payroll provides the standards required for the distribution of payroll, unclaimed wages, and non-wage payments. Human resources management must establish and maintain policies and guidelines for the hiring, promotion, compensation, transfer, relocation, and termination of employees"[12]

Highly Significant Transaction   A highly significant transaction is one that could reasonably result in a 10% or greater variance in revenues or would result in a 5% or greater variance in the net worth (assets minus liabilities).

Imaging and Workflow Automation (IWA)   These solutions streamline the invoice receipt-to-pay cycle by enabling organizations to convert paper invoices into digital images, store them in a Web-enabled repository for rapid retrieval, and extract data from them to enhance approval processing. IWA solutions may provide document and data capture, workflow, or both in order to create an end-to-end imaging and workflow solution that integrates with enterprise and line of business applications.

Imprest System   According to Wikipedia, "the imprest system is a form of financial accounting system. The most common imprest system is the petty cash system. The base characteristic of an imprest system is that a fixed amount is reserved, which

---

[12] Christine H. Doxey, 2019, *Internal Controls Toolkit*, "CHAPTER 5: Hire to Retire (H2R) Process," Wiley On-Line Library, accessed May 4, 2020, https://onlinelibrary.wiley.com/doi/abs/10.1002/9781119554424.ch5.

after a certain period of time or when circumstances require, because money was spent, it will be replenished."[13]

Intercompany Accounting Intercompany accounting is the process of recording financial transactions between different legal entities within the same parent company.

Internal Audit The internal audit department is an independent, objective assurance and consulting activity designed to add value and improve an organization's operations and to identify and mitigate risk.

Internal Controls The integrated framework approach defines internal control as a: process, effected by an entity's board of directors, management, and other personnel, designed to provide reasonable assurance regarding the achievement of objectives in the following categories: (A) reliability of financial reporting, (B) effectiveness and efficiency of operations, and compliant with applicable laws and regulations.

Internal Reporting Internal financial reporting traditionally means compiling and distributing generic reports that show a company's past, short-term fiscal performance with budget results. Internal reporting can also be generated by divisions, profit centers, and regions.

International Accounting Standards (IAS) International Accounting Standards (IAS) are older accounting standards that were replaced in 2001 by International Financial Reporting Standards (IFRS), issued by the International Accounting Standards Board (IASB).

International Financial Reporting Standards (IFRS) These standards issued by the IFRS Foundation and the International Accounting Standards Board (IASB) to provide a common global language for business affairs so that company accounts are understandable and comparable across international boundaries. IFRS is a set of accounting standards developed by an independent, not-for-profit organization called the International Accounting Standards Board (IASB).

International Financial Reporting Standards (IFRS) are accounting standards and interpretations adopted by the International Accounting Standards Board (IASB). They include IFRS issued by the IASB since its formation on July 1, 2000, and International Accounting Standards (IAS) previously issued by the International Accounting Standards Committee (IASC) and adopted by the IASB upon its formation.

These standards focus on establishing general principles derived from the IASB conceptual framework reflecting the recognition, measurement, and reporting requirements for the transactions covered by the standards. IFRS tends to limit additional guidance for applying the general principles to typical transactions, thus encouraging management to use professional judgment in applying the general principles to specific transactions of an entity or industry.

---

[13] Wikipedia, "Imprest System, accessed on May 4, 2020, https://en.wikipedia.org/wiki/Imprest_system.

The Internet of Things (IoT)   This is a system of interrelated computing devices, mechanical and digital machines provided with unique identifiers (UIDs) and the ability to transfer data over a network without requiring human-to-human or human-to-computer interaction.

The Information Technology Laboratory (ITL)   One of six research laboratories within the National Institute of Standards and Technology (NIST), ITL is a globally recognized and trusted source of high-quality, independent, and unbiased research and data. ITL's mission, to cultivate trust in information technology (IT) and metrology, is accomplished using its world-class measurement and testing facilities and encompassing a wide range of areas of computer science, mathematics, statistics, and systems engineering.

Key Performance Indicator (KPI)   A KPI is a measurable value or metric that demonstrates how effectively a process is working.

Management Review Controls   Requirements from the Public Company Accounting Oversight Board are causing auditors to require a level of precision and specificity for management review controls beyond prior years. Auditors are also reviewing far more documentation than they used to. At the same time, there is a lack of clarity on what exactly is sufficient in management review controls and how precise they need to be. This is troubling, since MRCs are crucial to the financial reporting process.

Management review controls (MRCs) are the reviews conducted by management of estimates and other kinds of financial information for reasonableness. They require significant judgment, knowledge, and experience. These reviews typically involve comparing recorded amounts with expectations of the reviewers based on their knowledge and experience. The reviewer's knowledge is, in part, based on history and, in part, may depend upon examining reports and underlying documents. MRCs are an essential aspect of effective internal control. Examples of MRCs include:

- Any review of analyses involving an estimate or judgment (examples: estimating a litigation reserve or estimating the percentage of completion for long-term construction projects);
- Reviews of financial results for components of a group;
- Comparisons of budget to actual; and
- Reviews of impairment analyses.

Manual Controls   Manual reconciliations, authorized signatures, and credit checks and approvals that are not executed systematically.

Merger and Acquisition (M&A)   In a merger, the boards of directors for two companies approve the combination and seek shareholders' approval. After the merger, the acquired company ceases to exist and becomes part of the acquiring company.

Net Value   A net (sometimes written "nett") value is the resultant amount after accounting for the sum or difference of two or more variables. In economics, it is frequently used to imply the remaining value after accounting for a specific, commonly understood deduction.

Net Income   Net income is equal to net earnings (profit) calculated as sales less cost of goods sold, selling, general and administrative expenses, operating expenses, depreciation, interest, taxes, and other expenses.

The National Institute of Standards and Technology (NIST)   This organization was founded in 1901 and is now part of the US Department of Commerce. NIST is one of the nation's oldest physical science laboratories. Congress established the agency to remove a major challenge to US industrial competitiveness at the time – a second-rate measurement infrastructure that lagged behind the capabilities of the United Kingdom, Germany, and other economic rivals.[14]

Nexus   "Nexus" is a term of art that defines a level of connection between a taxing jurisdiction and an entity. Nexus is required before a taxing jurisdiction can impose its taxes on an entity. Nexus determination is controlled by the US Constitution under the Due Process Clause and the Commerce Clause. The Due Process Clause requires a definite link or minimum connection between the state and the person, property, or transaction it seeks to tax. However, the Commerce Clause requires a higher level or connection. The Commerce Clause requires a substantial presence in a taxing state by the entity the state desires to tax. Other federal provisions play a part in the determination of whether a state tax is constitutional.

OCR and Data Capture   What is commonly called OCR is actually two processes. OCR converts an image file into machine-readable text. Data capture reads the text and converts it into useful information. An OCR engine will recognize the phrase "Purchase Order," but a data capture application will put those words into proper context to locate and extract the string of characters that represent the actual purchase order number on that document. Almost all of the invoice capture recognition solutions in the market today combine both OCR and data capture tools.

All scanning and OCR solutions share the goal of improving organizations' management of their invoice receipt-to-pay processes. To address the paper problem, many accounts payable departments are turning to optical character recognition (OCR) and data capture solutions, which use an optical-sensing device and special software to read machine print.

One Card   The One Card is a type of commercial card that simplifies card administration and reporting without compromising control or convenience from payment to supplier negotiations. Processes are streamlined through eliminating steps such as supplier setup and purchase order data entry. The card leads to increased productivity and employee convenience because it is a single payment solution. The One Card

---

[14] The National Institute of Standards and Technology (NIST), "About NIST," accessed April 13, 2020, https://www.nist.gov/about-nist.

offers better management of expenditures, such as business supplies, maintenance, repair, operational, and travel expenses through spending controls and point of sale restrictions.

Operational Change Management Organizational-development change management refers to a component of a major company overhaul designed to fix an ineffective workplace. Operational change management typically refers to more common changes in certain work processes, reporting structure or job roles. As an example, AP and P2P processes will be impacted by automation and process transformation and require change management processes to determine and address the specific changes on these processes.

Operational-Level Agreement (OLA) An operational-level agreement (OLA) defines the interdependent relationships in support of a service-level agreement (SLA). The agreement describes the responsibilities of each internal support group toward other support groups, including the process and timeframe for delivery of their services. OLA refers to the operational level of agreement, and SLA refers to the service level of agreement. SLA focuses on the service part of agreement, like the uptime of services and performance.

Order to Cash (O2C) Order to cash (OTC or O2C) is a set of business processes that involve receiving and fulfilling customer requests for goods or services. It is a top-level, or context-level, term used by management to describe the finance-related component of customer sales

Organizational Controls These controls should cover all aspects of a company's activity without overlap, and be clearly assigned and communicated.

- Responsibility should be delegated down to the level at which the necessary expertise and time exists.
- No single employee should have exclusive knowledge, authority, or control over any significant transaction or group of transactions.
- Agreeing on realistic qualitative and quantitative targets strengthens responsibility.
- The structure of accountability spends upon continuing levels of competence of employees in different positions and the development of competence so that responsibility and reporting relationships can be regrouped in more efficient ways.

Policy Controls Policy controls are the general principles and guides for action that influence decisions. They indicate the limits to choices and the parameters or rules to be followed by a company and its employees. Major policies should be reviewed, approved, and communicated by senior management. Policies are derived by:

- Considering the business environment and process objectives.
- Identifying the potential categories of risks that the environment poses toward achievement of the objectives.

Preventive Controls There is no difference between preventive and preventative controls. They are both adjectives that mean "used to stop something bad from happening." Both words are commonly used in contexts concerning internal controls as in "preventive/preventative controls." Preventive, however, is used much more frequently than preventative.

Procedure Controls Procedure controls prescribe how actions are to be performed consistent with policies. Procedures should be developed by those who understand the day-to-day actions.

Process A process is a systematic series of actions directed to some end; a continuous action or operation taking place in a definite manner.

Process Flow A process flow communicates the actual process currently in place. It is a picture of the flow and sequence of work steps, tasks, or activities and will include the flow or sequence of steps throughout the process; the person responsible for each task; and the decision points and their impact on the flow of work.

Procurement Card (P-Card) A Purchasing Card (P-Card) is a type of Commercial Card that allows organizations to take advantage of the existing credit card infrastructure to make electronic payments for a variety of business expenses (e.g. goods and services). In the simplest terms, a P-Card is a charge card, similar to a consumer credit card. However, the card-using organization must pay the card issuer in full each month, at a minimum. P-Cards are also known as Procurement Cards (ProCards), Payment Cards, Purchase Cards or similar terms.[15]

Procure to Pay (P2P) "Procure to pay" is a term used in the software industry to designate a specific subdivision of the procurement process. P2P systems enable the integration of the purchasing department with the accounts payable department and consider all the supporting processes.

Procure-to-Pay (P2P) Automation Also known as purchase-to-pay, the procure-to-pay process is the manner in which companies and other organizations identify potential suppliers, choose the best ones for their needs, electronically order goods and services, and issue automated payments to suppliers.

Profit Center A profit center is an area of responsibility for which an independent operating profit is calculated.

Project According to the Project Management Institute (PMI), a project is temporary in that it has a defined beginning and end in time, and therefore defined scope and resources. And a project is unique in that it is not a routine operation, but a specific set of operations designed to accomplish a singular goal.

Project Accounting Project accounting is a specific form of accounting that corresponds to a defined project. This accounting process helps to adequately track, report, and analyze fiscal results and implications.

The Public Accounting Oversight Board (The PCAOB) The PCAOB is a non-profit corporation established by Congress to oversee the audits of public companies in

---

[15] "What Are P-Cards," NACPC, accessed June 26, 2020, https://www.napcp.org/page/WhatArePCards.

order to protect investors and the public interest by promoting informative, accurate, and independent audit reports. The PCAOB also oversees the audits of brokers and dealers, including compliance reports filed pursuant to federal securities laws, to promote investor protection.

The Sarbanes-Oxley Act of 2002, which created the PCAOB, required that auditors of US public companies be subject to external and independent oversight for the first time in history. Previously, the profession was self-regulated.

The five members of the PCAOB Board, including the chairman, are appointed to staggered five-year terms by the Securities and Exchange Commission, after consultation with the chair of the Board of Governors of the Federal Reserve System and the secretary of the Treasury.[16]

Record to Report (R2R)   According to Wikipedia, "R2R is finance and accounting management process which involves collecting, processing and delivering relevant, timely and accurate information used for providing strategic, financial and operational feedback to understand how a business is performing."[17]

Related Parties   A related party is a person or an entity that is related to the reporting entity: A person or a close member of that person's family is related to a reporting entity if that person has control, joint control, or significant influence over the entity or is a member of its key management personnel.

Request for Information (RFI)   Some organizations may choose to initiate a request for information (RFI) which focuses on obtaining information from the solution providers. The RFI is not as formal as the RFP process but may require similar information.

Request for Proposal (RFP)   A request for proposals (RFP) is a document that reflects the detailed requirements by a prospective buyer in order to receive supplier offerings. Usually dedicated to automation solutions, an RFP is issued to select any kind of products (tangibles) and services (non-tangibles).

Review Controls   These controls include an ongoing self-assessment process as required by the Sarbanes-Oxley Act of 2002. A self-assessment is a series of questions that validate the effectiveness of the control environment. A self-assessment must be conducted every fiscal quarter; in some situations, the manager of the operating unit may elect to conduct a self-assessment test more frequently. It is imperative that all weaknesses found in the testing process are remediated through a corrective action and follow-up process.

Revenue   Revenue is the amount of money that a company actually receives during a specific fiscal period, including discounts and deductions for returned merchandise. It is the top line or gross income figure from which costs are subtracted to determine net income.

---

[16] PCAOB, "About the PCAOB," accessed February 14, 2019, https://pcaobus.org/About.

[17] Wikipedia, "Record to Report," accessed May 4, 2020, https://en.wikipedia.org/wiki/Record_to_report.

Revenue Recognition Revenue is one of the most important measures used by investors in assessing a company's performance and prospects. However, previous revenue recognition guidance differs in Generally Accepted Accounting Principles (GAAP) and International Financial Reporting Standards (IFRS) – and many believe both standards were in need of improvement.

On May 28, 2014, the FASB and the International Accounting Standards Board (IASB) issued converged guidance on recognizing revenue in contracts with customers. The new guidance is a major achievement in the Boards' joint efforts to improve this important area of financial reporting.

Presently, GAAP has complex, detailed, and disparate revenue recognition requirements for specific transactions and industries including, for example, software and real estate. As a result, different industries use different accounting for economically similar transactions.

"The objective of the new guidance is to establish principles to report useful information to users of financial statements about the nature, amount, timing, and uncertainty of revenue from contracts with customers. The new guidance:

- Removes inconsistencies and weaknesses in existing revenue requirements
- Provides a more robust framework for addressing revenue issues
- Improves comparability of revenue recognition practices across entities, industries, jurisdictions, and capital markets
- Provides more useful information to users of financial statements through improved disclosure requirements, and
- Simplifies the preparation of financial statements by reducing the number of requirements to which an organization must refer."[18]

Return on Investment (ROI) ROI is a performance measure used to evaluate the efficiency of an investment. ROIs are also used in the decision-making process when selecting an automated solution, new equipment, or other capital expenditures.

Robotic Process Automation (RPA) According to CIO, "RPA is an application of technology, governed by business logic and structured inputs, aimed at automating business processes. Using RPA tools, a company can configure software, or a "robot," to capture and interpret applications for processing a transaction, manipulating data, triggering responses and communicating with other digital systems. RPA scenarios range from something as simple as generating an automatic response to an email to deploying thousands of bots, each programmed to automate jobs in an ERP system."[19]

Roll Forward In accounting, this is the systematic establishment of new accounting period balances by using (rolling forward) prior accounting period data. There are

---

[18] Financial Accounting Standards Board (FASB), "Why Did the FASB Issue a New Standard on Revenue Recognition?," accessed January 1, 2019, https://www.fasb.org/jsp/FASB/Page/Image BridgePage&cid=1176169257359.

[19] Clint Boulton, "What Is RPA? A Revolution in Business Process Automation," CIO, posted on September 3, 2018, accessed on July 20, 2020, https://www.cio.com/article/3236451/what-is-rpa-robotic-process-automation-explained.html.

two approaches: (1) Roll forward both asset and liabilities on a consistent basis from a consistent earlier date (possibly the last annual review) or, (2) take the most up to date asset and liability figures as the starting point (which may be at different dates) to produce roll forward estimates of assets and liabilities; in securities, it is when an investor replaces an old options position with a new one having a later expiration date (and same strike price).[20]

Sales and Use Tax   Use tax is a complementary or compensating tax to the sales tax and does not apply if the sales tax was charged. Consumer use tax is a tax on the purchaser and is self-assessed by the purchaser on taxable items purchased where the supplier did not collect either a sales or supplier use tax.

Sarbanes-Oxley (SOX) Act 2002   The act can be divided into three main points:

1. The scope of an external audit firm has been restricted in which CPA's no longer have the right to set standards for their practice.
2. There are new duties for boards of directors in general and for audit committees in particular. Corporate governance provisions include a required code of ethics or standards of business conduct.
3. There are new requirements for the CEO and CFO. Each SEC filing (10K and 10Q) stating that:
   a. The report fairly represents in all material respects the company's operations and fiscal condition.
   b. The report does not contain any material misstatements or omit to state a material fact necessary in order to make the statements made, in light of the circumstances under which the statements were made, not misleading.
   c. The report containing financial statements complies with section 13(a) or 15(d) of the Securities and Exchange Act of 1934.
   d. The company's control system is in place and effective.

Securities and Exchange Commission (SEC)   The US Securities and Exchange Commission (SEC) is an independent federal government agency responsible for protecting investors, maintaining fair and orderly functioning of securities markets, and facilitating capital formation. The US Securities and Exchange Commission (SEC) has a three-part mission: protect investors; maintain fair, orderly, and efficient markets; facilitate capital formation.

Segregation of Duties (SoD)   A SoD control is one of the most important controls that your company can have. Adequate SoD reduces the likelihood that errors (intentional or unintentional) will remain undetected by providing for separate processing by different individuals at various stages of a transaction and for independent reviews of the work performed. The SoD control provides four primary benefits: (1) the risk of a deliberate fraud is mitigated as the collusion of two

---

[20] Venture Line, "Definition of Roll Forward," accessed April 2, 2019, https://www.ventureline.com/accounting-glossary/R/roll-forward-definition/.

or more persons would be required in order to circumvent controls; (2) the risk of legitimate errors is mitigated as the likelihood of detection is increased; (3) the cost of corrective actions is mitigated as errors are generally detected relatively earlier in their lifecycle; and (4) the organization's reputation for integrity and quality is enhanced through a system of checks and balances.

Service-Level Agreement (SLA) A service-level agreement (SLA) is a commitment between a service provider and a client. Particular aspects of the service include quality, availability, responsibilities and are agreed between the service provider and the service user. The SLA process is based upon established performance metrics which are usually included in supplier contracts.

Service-Level Management (SLM) SLM is a process that is established to ensure that responsibilities are defined for service management processes, operational level agreements, and underpinning contracts which are appropriate for the agreed-upon service-level targets.

Single-Factor Authentication Authentication methods based on "something you know" where the primary method of identifying the user is a password.

Significant Deficiency This is a single control deficiency, or combination of control deficiencies, that adversely affects the company's ability to initiate, authorize, record, process, or report external fiscal data reliably. There is more than a remote likelihood that a misstatement of the company's annual or interim financial statements that is more than inconsequential will not be prevented or detected.

Standard Operating Procedures Standard operating procedures, or SOPs, are formal written guidelines that denote daily operational procedures, assist in long-range planning and provide instructions for incident responses. While the exact layout and purpose of an SOP document varies somewhat from industry to industry, all SOPs share some traits in common. They have operational, system, and accounting standard components, and they are essential to a successful fiscal closing process. For the fiscal close process, SOPs should include roles and responsibilities, key stakeholders, procedures, flowcharts, templates, and checklists for every component of the fiscal close.

Standards of Internal Control The standards define a series of internal controls that address the risks associated with key business processes, sub-processes and entity-level processes. The standards are the product resulting from over thirty years of experience in the finance, accounting and internal controls field. The standards are a body of work that leverages experience at large technology companies. They were developed when implementing internal control programs for approximately eighty business processes and sub-processes that include payroll, the fiscal closing process, logistics, procurement, accounts payable, and accounts receivable.

"Super User" A "super user" is a user of an ERP with special privileges needed to administer and maintain the system or a system administrator. The special privileges may include the ability to process a fiscal transaction and may changes in the general ledger to modify the transaction. "Super user" privileges must be monitored to ensure that access rights are not used to incorrectly modify or falsify a transaction resulting in risk to the company.

Supervisory Controls Supervisory controls are situations in which managers ensure that all employees understand their responsibilities and authorities, and the assurance that procedures are being followed within the operating unit. They can also be considered as a compensating control in which a supervisory review is necessary to augment segregation of duties controls.

Supplier Master File The supplier master file is the repository of a considerable amount of information about a company's suppliers. This data is used for the supplier management, drives spend analysis, establishes the foundation for contracts and purchase orders, and the accurate and timely payment of supplier invoices. If the data in the supplier master file is accurate, all the components of the procure-to-pay (P2P) cycle will be correct.

Supplier or Retail Use Supplier or retailer use tax applies to sales made by a supplier to a customer located outside the supplier's state or sales in interstate commerce if the supplier is registered in the state of delivery. Many people also consider this as sales tax. However, it is important to make the distinction, as differences can exist between the sales tax and the retailer use tax in relation to who has the liability for the tax, the sourcing of the tax, and the tax rate. For example, in Illinois the sales tax is an origin tax and can include local taxes. However, the use tax is sourced to the customer delivery location and there is no local use tax that is required to be collected by the seller. Only in the city of Chicago is there a local use tax.

Supply Chain Financing (SCF) Supply chain finance is a set of tech-based business and financing processes that lower costs and improve efficiency for the parties involved in a transaction. Supply chain finance works best when the buyer has a better credit rating than the seller and can thus access capital at a lower cost. Unlike traditional factoring, where a supplier wants to finance its receivables, reverse factoring is a financing solution initiated by the ordering party in order to help its suppliers to finance its receivables more easily and at a lower interest rate than what would normally be offered.

Systems Access (SA) Policy The systems access (SA) policy applies to both domestic and international financial and operational systems and is an integral part of segregation of duties. The scope of the systems access policy is worldwide. The policy applies to the approval of new access requests and the establishment of an internal controls environment for general system access. The SA policy ensures that transactions cannot be systematically generated to create segregation of duties control issues. There are two types of segregation of duties controls that must be in place. They are (1) control of security object privileges, and (2) control of multiple security profiles.

System for Award Management (SAM) The System for Award Management (SAM) is an official website of the US government. There is no cost to use SAM. Controllers can use this site to:

- Register to do business with the US government
- Update or renew your entity registration
- Check status of an entity registration
- Search for entity registration and exclusion records [21]

System Controls These are system-generated controls which include the three-way match of invoices for payment, batch control totals, field level edits/validations, duplicate payment validation, and the identification of segregation of duties conflicts.

Three-Way Match Process The "three-way match" concept refers to matching three documents – the invoice, the purchase order, and the receiving report – to ensure that a payment should be made. The procedure is used to ensure that payments are issued for authorized payments, thereby preventing losses due to fraud and carelessness. Many ERP systems provide an automated three-way matching process. And several solutions provide automatic matching as part of an electronic invoice solution.

The goal of three-way matching is to highlight any discrepancies in three important documents in the purchasing process – purchase orders, order receipts/packing slips, and invoices – in order to save businesses from overspending or paying for an item that they did not receive.

TIN Match TIN match (Taxpayer Identification Number Matching) is a tool to confirm the name and taxpayer identification number for 1099 suppliers. The On-Line Taxpayer Identification Number (TIN) Matching Program is a free web-based tool offered by the IRS through e-services and was established for payers of reportable payments subject to the backup withholding provisions of section 3406 of the Internal Revenue Code.

Tolerance According to Oracle, invoice tolerances determine whether matching holds are placed on invoices for variances between invoices and the documents you match them to, such as purchase orders. When you run the invoice validation process for a matched invoice, the process checks that matching occurs within the defined tolerances. For example, if the billed amount of an item exceeds a tolerance, a hold is placed on the invoice. You can't pay the invoice until the hold is released. You can define tolerances based on quantity or amount. For each type of tolerance, you can specify percentages or amounts.

Travel and Entertainment (T&E) According to Concur, the term T&E is bandied about often in business and, as with most business acronyms, people assume that it's automatically understood. In case you have ever wondered what T&E actually stands for, we'll explain not only what it is, but also why the term is important in the business world, and how paying attention to your T&E spend can save your business time, hassle, and money.

---

[21] System for Award Management (SAM), accessed April 13, 2020, https://www.sam.gov/SAM/.

Two-Factor Authentication   Two-factor authentication is based on "something you have plus something you know." It requires processing something that is unique to the individual and a PIN (personal identification number) that ensures that the individual is indeed who they say they are. Time-dependent random number generators and cryptographic techniques are examples of such an authentication technique.

Two-Way Match   An invoice is received from a supplier for payment of goods or services ordered through a purchase order. Using an online invoice approval process, the invoice quantity and amount are matched to the purchase order to ensure that tolerances are met.

Unclaimed Property   Unclaimed or "abandoned" property refers to property or accounts within financial institutions or companies – in which there has been no activity generated (or contact with the owner) regarding the property for one year or a longer period. (See Escheatment)

Wayfair Decision   In the context of the Sales and Use Tax Process, Wayfair allowed states to require that sellers collect and remit sales tax based on the establishment of an "economic nexus," doing away with the previous "physical presence" test. The following states have adopted Wayfair: Colorado (notice-and-reporting only), Hawaii, Maine, Oklahoma, Tennessee, and Vermont. September 1, 2018: Mississippi. October 1, 2018: Alabama, Illinois, Indiana, Kentucky, Michigan, Minnesota, New Jersey, North Dakota, Washington, Wisconsin. November 1, 2018: North Carolina.

Work Instruction   A work instruction is a step-by-step document that depicts the actions needed to complete an activity at the transaction level and is a detailed document that may include "key stroke" information. This is a very detailed "how to" document.

Workflow Automation   A workflow consists of an orchestrated and repeatable pattern of activity, enabled by the systematic organization of resources into processes that transform materials, provide services, or process information. In accounts payable, the approval and escalation process should be automated in order to reduce invoice cost, cycle time, and the risk of fraud.

Index